THE EVOLUTION OF
INTERNATIONAL
SECURITY STUDIES

International Security Studies (ISS) has changed and diversified in many ways since 1945. This book provides the first intellectual history of the development of the subject in that period. It explains how ISS evolved from an initial concern with the strategic consequences of superpower rivalry and nuclear weapons, to its currrent diversity in which environmental, economic, human and other securities sit alongside military security, and in which approaches ranging from traditional Realist analysis to Feminism and Post-colonialism are in play. It sets out the driving forces that shaped debates in ISS, shows what makes ISS a single conversation across its diversity, and gives an authoritative account of debates on all the main topics within ISS. This is an unparalleled survey of the literature and institutions of ISS that will be an invaluable guide for all students and scholars of ISS, whether traditionalist, 'new agenda' or critical.

BARRY BUZAN is Montague Burton Professor of International Relations at the London School of Economics and Honorary Professor at the Universities of Copenhagen and Jilin. His books include: *The United States and the Great Powers: World Politics in the Twenty-first Century* (2004); *Regions and Powers: The Structure of International Security* (2003, with Ole Wæver); *The Arms Dynamic in World Politics* (1998, with Eric Herring); *Security: A New Framework for Analysis* (1998, with Wæver and Jaap de Wilde); *People, States and Fear: An Agenda for International Security Studies in the Post-Cold War Era* (1991) and *An Introduction to Strategic Studies: Military Technology and International Relations* (1987).

LENE HANSEN is an Associate Professor of International Relations in the Department of Political Science at the University of Copenhagen. She is the author of *Security as Practice: Discourse Analysis and the Bosnian War* (2006) and the co-editor of *European Integration and National Identity: The Challenge of the Nordic States* (2002, with Ole Wæver).

THE EVOLUTION OF INTERNATIONAL SECURITY STUDIES

BARRY BUZAN

Department of International Relations
London School of Economics and Political Science

LENE HANSEN

Department of Political Science
University of Copenhagen

CAMBRIDGE
UNIVERSITY PRESS

CAMBRIDGE UNIVERSITY PRESS

Cambridge, New York, Melbourne, Madrid, Cape Town, Singapore, São Paulo, Delhi

Cambridge University Press
The Edinburgh Building, Cambridge CB2 8RU, UK

Published in the United States of America by Cambridge University Press, New York

www.cambridge.org
Information on this title: www.cambridge.org/9780521694223

First published 2009

Printed in the United Kingdom at the University Press, Cambridge

A catalogue record for this publication is available from the British Library

Library of Congress Cataloguing in Publication data

Buzan, Barry.
The evolution of international security studies / Barry Buzan, Lene Hansen.
p.   cm.
Includes bibliographical references and index.
ISBN 978-0-521-87261-4
1. Security, International – Study and teaching.   2. Security, International – Research.
3. Security, International – History.   I. Hansen, Lene.   II. Title.
JZ5588.B887   2009
355′.033 – dc22   2009025609

ISBN 978-0-521-87261-4 hardback
ISBN 978-0-521-69422-3 paperback

CONTENTS

FOREWORD

There is a long as well as a short story as to why we wrote this book. The short story begins in 2005 when Lucy Robinson at SAGE asked Barry Buzan whether he would be interested in editing a four-volume reader on International Security. Barry thought it a nice idea to add Lene Hansen to the project, thereby bringing in someone with both a different perspective and a closer eye on the Poststructuralist–Feminist–Critical scene. The discussions and readings that went into selecting the articles for that reader, spanning Wolfers and Kennan from the 1940s and 1950s to recent Post-colonial and Feminist analyses of the Global War on Terrorism, led us to believe there was a book to be done on the evolution of International Security Studies (ISS) as an academic field. In the process of re-reading, we were struck by Nye and Lynn-Jones's (1988) observation that the intellectual history of ISS was yet to be written, and even more struck by another twenty years of silence on the subject. A sceptical reader might of course think that this indicates the futility, impossibility or lack of audience for such a project, but we beg to differ. We think that an intellectual history, and an account of how different perspectives play into each other, evolve and battle, is a useful thing to have. Historical context is always good, and allows ISS to enter the pantheon of related academic enterprises like Political Theory, Political Science and International Relations (IR) that do have such self-understanding. An intellectual and sociology of science history can provide those in ISS with a better sense of where they and others came from, why they might differ and about what, and which points of contestation do in fact tie the field together.

One difficulty with such a project, and a possible explanation of why ISS has not had an intellectual history, is that its sense of disciplinary identity is contested, making how to define what falls into ISS and what does not a political – and politicised – question. This issue of delineation takes us into the longer story to this book. Barry Buzan has worked for nearly forty years on security, from the heyday of traditionalist Strategic Studies over the burgeoning turns to the widening and deepening of security in the 1980s to contemporary securitisation debates. Lene Hansen came to ISS in the early 1990s, reading Walker before Waltz and Der Derian rather than Deutsch. Clearly, for someone who picked up our CVs an immediate difference in starting point and positioning in relation to traditionalist versus widening/deepening debates would spring to mind. What we had in common however was a long connection, starting at the Copenhagen Peace Research Institute (COPRI) in 1991, with the Copenhagen School – Barry as a founding figure, Lene as a boundary-testing critic. We shared intellectual links through Ole Wæver, also then at COPRI, and an interest in the concepts and ways in which different perspectives could come to understand and recognise each other. All this of course makes us part of the story that we tell, and places us more on the European side of what is mainly an Atlantic story. Although we have aimed for a full and balanced account, a version of this book written from within the US mainstream ISS community might well reflect somewhat different priorities and perspectives. And since we come from the middle and radical end of the ISS spectrum, a version written by a traditionalist or a rational-choicer would also reflect different priorities and perspectives. Self-involvement also opens up the embarrassing contradiction that what qualifies us to tell the story also threatens our detachment from it. Readers will have to judge for themselves how well (or not) we dealt with this.

Our hunch is that the duration, immensity and diversity of the ISS archive, especially when casting the inclusion net widely, which we have deliberately done, mean that coming to grips with ISS requires the memory, perspective (and stamina!) of more than one person. Our age difference has helped us not only to understand the perspectives of different generations, but also to think about how one communicates the historical context of a particular literature as well as its contemporary relevance. One aim of our project was to counteract the illusion that there is a clear 'before and after 1990' structure to ISS, with everything changing as a result of the Cold War ending and widening approaches suddenly appearing. For new entrants into ISS it is quite easy to get the impression than nothing much before 1990 matters now. We hope to show that ISS has significant coherence not just across the many approaches that now define it, but also across time. One needs a sense of the whole story in order to understand both the structure and significance of what ISS looks like now.

Our thanks to Lucy Robinson for suggesting the idea that led to this book and to John Haslam at Cambridge University Press for taking on the book project and being tolerant of its ever-lengthening word count and timetable. Thanks also to Mathias Lydholm Rasmussen, Anne Kathrine Mikkelsen Nyborg and Ian Siperco for research assistance; and to Maria-Lara Martin at the International Studies Association (ISA) Headquarters in Tucson, Arizona, for going through the files and sending us their material on the Peace Studies Section of the ISA. Many people have offered comments along the way and our appreciation goes to the audience at the ISA's annual convention in San Diego in 2006, particularly our discussant Michael C. Williams; the IR Group in the Department of Political Science, University of Copenhagen; the audience at the European Consortium for Political Research (ECPR) Standing Group on International Relations conference in Turin in 2007, particularly Francesco Ragazzi, who was the discussant; and to the three reviewers for Cambridge University Press, particularly for the suggestion that we look more closely at financing and the institutional side of ISS. Pinar Bilgin, Lene Cividanes, Lawrence Freedman, Matti Jutila, Sanne Brasch Kristensen, Jeppe Mülich, Nini Nielsen, Karen Lund Petersen, Mikkel Vedby Rasmussen, Christine Sylvester, Ole Wæver, Håkan Wiberg and Michael C. Williams did us the great favour of reading and commenting on the whole penultimate draft, and Anders Wivel did the same for particular chapters. These comments were extremely helpful to us in shaping the final manuscript. Finally, we wish to thank the Department of Political Science and the Centre for Advanced Security Theory (CAST) at the University of Copenhagen for funding most of the research assistance and multiple trips between Copenhagen and London, and the LSE for funding the rest of the research assistance.

Barry Buzan (London)
Lene Hansen (Copenhagen)
September 2008

ABBREVIATIONS

ABM	Anti-Ballistic Missile
ACDA	Arms Control and Disarmament Agency
AFK	Arbeitsgemeinschaft für Friedens- und Konfliktforschung
ARF	ASEAN Regional Forum
ASEAN	Association of Southeast Asian Nations
BMD	Ballistic Missile Defence
CAC	Council for Arms Control
CAST	Centre for Advanced Security Theory
CDSS	Centre for Defence and Strategic Studies
CEE	Central and Eastern Europe
CESS	Centre for European Security Studies
CFE	Conventional Armed Forces in Europe
CHALLENGE	Changing Landscape of European Liberty and Security
CND	Campaign for Nuclear Disarmament
CNS	Center for Nonproliferation Studies
COPRI	Copenhagen Peace Research Institute
CPREA	Canadian Peace Research and Education Association
CSIS	Center for Strategic and International Studies
CSS	Critical Security Studies
ECPR	European Consortium for Political Research
ED	Extended deterrence
END	European Nuclear Disarmament
ESRC	Economic and Social Research Council
EU	European Union
EUISS	European Union Institute for Security Studies
FRY	Former Republic of Yugoslavia
FSU	Former Soviet Union
GIPRI	Geneva International Peace Research Institute
GWoT	Global War on Terrorism
IAEA	International Atomic Energy Agency
IDSA	Institute for Defence Studies and Analyses
IDSS	Institute of Defence and Strategic Studies

IFSH	Institute for Peace Research and Security Policy at Hamburg University
IISS	International Institute for Strategic Studies
INF	Intermediate-range Nuclear Forces
IPE	International Political Economy
IPRA	International Peace Research Association
IPSHU	Institute for Peace Science Hiroshima University
IR	International Relations
ISA	International Studies Association
ISS	International Security Studies
JPR	*Journal of Peace Research*
LNW	Limited nuclear war
LSE	London School of Economics and Political Science
MAD	Mutually Assured Destruction
MIC	Military–industrial complex
MTCR	Missile Technology Control Regime
NATO	North Atlantic Treaty Organization
NGO	Non-government organisation
NNWS	Non-nuclear weapon states
NoD	Non-offensive defence
NORDSAM	Nordic Cooperation Committee for International Politics
NPT	Nuclear Non-Proliferation Treaty
NUPI	Norsk Utenrikspolitisk Institutt/Norwegian Institute of International Affairs
NWFZ	Nuclear weapon free zone
NWS	Nuclear weapon states
OSCE	Organisation for Security and Co-operation in Europe
PADRIGU	Department for Peace and Development Research, University of Gothenburg
PfP	Partnership for Peace
PRIF	Peace Research Institute Frankfurt
PRIME	Peace Research Institute in the Middle East
PRIO	International Peace Research Institute, Oslo
RAND	Research and Development (non-profit think-tank that grew out of the United States Army Air Forces)
RAWA	Revolutionary Association of the Women of Afghanistan
RMA	Revolution in Military Affairs
RSCT	Regional security complex theory
RUSI	Royal United Services Institute
SALT	Strategic Arms Limitation Talks
SDI	Strategic Defense Initiative
SIPRI	Stockholm International Peace Research Institute

SORT	Strategic Offensive Reductions Treaty
SSRC	Social Science Research Council
START	Strategic Arms Reduction Talks
TAPRI	Tampere Peace Research Institute
UN	United Nations
UNDP	United Nations Development Programme
UNEP	United Nations Environment Programme
UNESCO	United Nations Educational, Scientific and Cultural Organization
UNHCR	United Nations High Commissioner for Refugees
UNIDIR	United Nations Institute of Disarmament Research
UNPROFOR	United Nations Protection Force
USIP	United States Institute of Peace
WIIS	Women in International Security
WMD	Weapons of mass destruction

FIGURES

TABLES

Introduction

This book is about the evolution of International Security Studies (ISS), in the beginning as an independent field of study, but quite quickly absorbed as a sub-field of International Relations (IR), which was developing rapidly alongside it.[1] Like IR itself, ISS is mainly a Western subject, largely done in North America, Europe and Australia with all of the Western-centrisms that this entails. ISS is one of the main sub-fields of Western IR. Wherever IR is taught, ISS is one of its central elements. There is an antecedent literature extending back before the Second World War which can largely be characterised as war studies, military and grand strategy, and geopolitics. This includes much discussed writers such as Clausewitz, Mahan, Richardson and Haushofer, whose work still remains relevant. But we are not going to cover this literature both for reasons of space, and also because a distinctive literature about security developed after 1945 (Freedman, 1981a; Wæver and Buzan, 2007). This literature was distinctive in three ways. First, it took *security* rather than defence or war as its key concept, a conceptual shift which opened up the study of a broader set of political issues, including the importance of societal cohesion and the relationship between military and non-military threats and vulnerabilities. The ability of security to capture the conceptual centre of ISS dealing with defence, war and conflict as well as the broadness of the term was famously condensed in Wolfers's definition of security as an ambiguous symbol. In laying out the ability of security policy to subordinate all other interests to those of the nation, Wolfers stressed the rhetorical and political force that 'security' entailed despite having very little intrinsic meaning (Wolfers, 1952: 481). Second, this literature was distinct because it addressed the novel problems of both the Cold War and nuclear weapons. How to deploy, use and not use military means

---

[1] 'ISS' is not universally used as the designator for the sub-field. We use it as an umbrella label to include the work of scholars who might refer to themselves as being in 'international security', or 'security studies', or 'strategic studies', or 'peace research', or various other more specialised labels. We set out the scope of ISS in detail in chapter 1

were quite different questions in the conditions of the nuclear age, and it was from those questions that the sub-field of ISS mainly arose. Third, and related to both the total war mobilisations of Britain and the US during the Second World War, and the peculiar strategic conditions created by nuclear weapons, ISS was much more a civilian enterprise than most earlier military and strategic literatures. Strategic bombing and nuclear weapons transcended traditional military warfighting expertise in ways that required, or at least opened the door to, bringing in civilian experts ranging from physicists and economists to sociologists and psychologists. As shown during the Second World War, strategic bombing required knowledge about how best to disable the enemy's economy and infrastructure, not just how to defeat his armed forces. Nuclear deterrence quickly became the art of how to avoid fighting wars while at the same time not being militarily defeated or coerced. The centrality of the civilian element also reflects the fact that ISS has largely flourished in democratic countries, while strategic thinking in non-Western countries generally remained more firmly in the grip of the military.

Although security was a new lead concept in the post-Second World War world (Yergin, 1978; Wæver, 2006), its implications for a wider, not exclusively military–political understanding of the subject were not fully felt until quite late in the Cold War. During most of the Cold War, ISS was defined by a largely military agenda of questions surrounding nuclear weapons and a widely embedded assumption that the Soviet Union posed a profound military and ideological threat to the West. From the 1970s onwards, as the nuclear relationship between the superpowers matured, the original breadth carried by the term security began to re-emerge, opening up pressure to widen the international security agenda away from the military–political focus. Economic and environmental security became established, if controversial, parts of the agenda during the later years of the Cold War, and were joined during the 1990s by societal (or identity) security, human security, food security and others. Much of this literature stayed within the predominant national security frame of the Cold War, but some of it began to challenge the emphasis on material capabilities as well as state-centric assumptions, opening paths to studies of the importance of ideas and culture and to referent objects for security other than the state. These moves were accompanied by more critical and radical challenges to state-centrism, with the result that instead of flowing as a single river within one set of quite narrowly defined banks, ISS has broadened out into several distinct but inter-related flows of literature. In addition to the more traditionalist, military-centred Strategic Studies and

Peace Research, there is also Critical Security Studies, Feminist Security Studies, the Copenhagen School, Poststructuralism and Constructivist Security Studies.

Given that ISS has both undergone some radical changes and maintained some core continuities, and has done so quite visibly in interaction with changes in its environment, evolution is an appropriate concept for understanding its intellectual history. Our understanding of evolution is a Darwinian one that defines it as about how things adapt (or not) to the environment they inhabit, and to changes in that environment. Evolution is <u>not</u> teleological. It exposes the logic of change without either supposing any particular outcome or offering any prediction. It charts the successes, but also the failures and extinctions. In chapter 3, we set up a framework of five driving forces as a way of identifying the main environmental pressures on ISS and how it adapted to them and sometimes influenced them. A non-teleological view of evolution also leaves open the question of how to evaluate progress: evolution as a process can move towards lower levels of complexity and diversity as well as higher ones. We return to the question of progress in our summing up of ISS in chapter 9. But along the way it is <u>not</u> our aim to identify the best or only theory of international security, or to integrate all of the various literatures spawned within ISS into one 'master theory'. Rather our goal is to tell a thorough intellectual history of how the various approaches define positions within the debates about ISS.

Nye and Lynn-Jones (1988) noted twenty years ago that no intellectual history of ISS had yet been written, and this book is a belated attempt to fill that lacuna. Our longer historical perspective distinguishes our project from the current standard textbook way of presenting the sub-field of ISS. To take some recent examples, Collins (2007) is organised thematically, and most chapters focus on the substance of particular approaches or themes, while not devoting much attention to the historical context in which these arose. The book as a whole is quite aptly summed up by the first word of the title: it is *Contemporary* rather than *Historically Contextualised*. Dannreuther (2007a), Sheehan (2005) and Hough (2004) take a similar, largely post-1990, approach. Paul D. Williams (2008) is notable for taking a longer view, and like the others frames the subject through IR approaches (Realism, Liberalism, Critical Theory, etc.) along one dimension and thematic security concepts and issues along another. These textbooks are good representatives of how the field of ISS is presented, or used as a taken for granted springboard for empirical or theoretical analysis. There is no perceived need to include a section on how ISS came to have its present structure, and for new entrants ISS might almost have begun in 1990.

To approach ISS in this manner has the advantage that many different thematic and empirical areas can be covered, but it misses some of the advantages of a more historical approach. These advantages are first that an ahistorical perspective may lead to the forgetting of past knowledge which in turn makes contemporary scholars work hard to reinvent the wheel. Since ISS is a sub-field built on conceptual, normative and empirical contestation, to point to the value of past knowledge is not to say that there is one objective truth which can be uncovered. Past literatures identify a series of pros and cons of adopting a particular policy or conceptualisation of security. To take the example of George W. Bush's resurrection of anti-ballistic missile defence (Strategic Defence Initiative or SDI), there is a rich literature on the advantages and disadvantages of this policy written in the early 1980s that should be consulted, particularly before one accepts the claim by the Bush administration that such a policy entails no threatening or escalating elements (Glaser, 1984). The value of the 'past knowledge' uncovered is thus more accurately described as 'past contested knowledge'.

The second advantage of a historical perspective is that it questions commonly held assumptions about a field's development. One such myth is to tell the story of the widening approaches as caused by the ending of the Cold War. In reality there was a significant 1980s literature that laid the groundwork for the growth of widening and deepening approaches in the 1990s. The point here is not only that a historiography may correct such myths and thus give us a better understanding of what actually took place, but that it brings critical attention to the role that these myths have in the self-understanding of a discipline (Wæver, 1998). For example, the standard account of IR as having gone through three or four debates grants more legitimacy to those approaches coined as the winners and implicitly argues that the themes of each specific debate are the significant ones for understanding the substance of IR.

The third advantage of a history that 'trace[s] the political consequences of adopting a particular concept' (Hansen, 2000b: 347) is that it allows for an examination of the deeper political and normative implications of both the core concept of ISS, 'security', and three categories of concepts that are spun off from security: complementary concepts (deterrence for example), parallel concepts (like power) and oppositional concepts (such as peace). The complementary concept of containment, for example, originated in early Cold War American policies that were designed to counter what was believed to be an aggressive and uncompromising Soviet threat. Embedded in this central concept was a particular understanding of the identity of the opposing enemy, what the relationship between the American and Western Self and the Communist, Soviet East could be, and hence how security should be pursued. When 'containment' resurfaces in contemporary security discourse as a way in which terrorism should be fought, it comes with these historically constituted understandings of both enemies and the strategies to fight them. As IR-political theorists such as R. B. J. Walker (1987, 1990, 1993) and Michael C. Williams (1998, 2005, 2007) have laid out, since concepts of security are at the deeper level particular 'solutions' to a long list of important questions that concern the identity of Self and Other, boundaries (territorial and social), authority, legitimacy and sovereignty, alternative conceptualisations need to engage these political structures of meaning and to offer alternative conceptions. A historical approach can help us show how these deeper structures were formed, how they have been reproduced or challenged and why such challengers succeeded or failed.

The fourth advantage of a historical analysis is that it allows for a more dynamic conception of how a discipline, field or sub-field develops than one which organises ISS along thematic lines. Bluntly put, an account of ISS that does not have a historical dimension would not give a very good idea of why particular approaches appear on the agenda, what their relationships were to previous and contemporary approaches, and why some disappeared. The framework laid out in the following chapters is dynamic in two respects. First, it is designed to study a process of change and evolution. Second, it holds, as we will discuss in more detail below, that no single factor can explain the evolution of ISS. Neither political events nor material forces nor, for that matter, academic theories can single-handedly explain the evolution of ISS as an academic field. Epistemologically, our framework thus does not seek to make a causal claim. Indeed, we believe that the historical development of ISS proves the impossibility of explaining it in such terms, whether the explanatory variable is internal or external, material or ideational. From the point of view of those who make causality the definition of proper social science (Keohane, 1988; King et al., 1994), this is obviously a weakness of our framework, but not only is the status of causality itself challenged within IR and ISS (Kurki and Wight, 2007), it is a 'price' we are willing to pay, since a model with several interacting driving forces allows us to capture the dynamic nature of academic disciplinary evolution in a way that a monocausal framework would not. It also opens a more structural view of ISS, hopefully allowing those within it to see their own environment more clearly.

The fifth and final advantage of a historical approach is directly related to our normative view of how ISS should ideally develop at the level of sociology of science. Our normative position, to which we will return in chapter 9, 'Conclusions', is that ISS is well suited by being home to multiple perspectives. This end is served by the processes of institution-alisation which have given everybody from rational choice Neorealists to Poststructuralist Feminists places to publish and foundations to apply to (although the balance may not be an even one!). With our belief that ISS is and should be home to several perspectives, follows a normative commitment to debate and engagement not only within but between ISS approaches. Several security scholars have recently observed that ISS develops along increasingly separate tracks, on distinct European and American ones (Wæver, 1998, 2004a; Wæver and Buzan, 2007) or along the lines of Realism, Poststructuralism, Feminism and so on (Sylvester, 2007b). Assuming that this picture of ISS is correct, that the sub-field is branching out but that the branches (no longer) come together at the trunk of the tree, a historical analysis allows us to trace when particular approaches were formed and what their connection was to the central questions of the sub-field of ISS. An intellectual history facilitates the uncovering of conversations that were once there, and by bringing them back together a renewed engagement and dialogue may be generated.

For all of these reasons, this book offers something different from, but complementary to, the current crop of introductory textbooks to ISS. Our hope is that they will be read in conjunction.

Chapter 1 provides a more detailed account of the challenges involved in defining ISS. We argue in favour of including literature that self-identifies as ISS or as one of the many specific Security Studies approaches regardless of whether all other ISS perspectives agree that they should be included. We then suggest that the delineation of ISS and the substantial debates within it can be understood through four questions (referent object, location of threats, security sector and view of security politics) and that the concept of security is supported by three adjacent forms of concepts: complementary, parallel and oppositional. The last part of the chapter turns to the relationship between ISS and other academic disciplines, particularly IR. Chapter 2 looks at the central concepts at the heart of ISS: the state, government, sovereignty and authority and how they were produced historically. The chapter also introduces the importance of epistemology and the main ways in which it has influenced ISS. Part of our purpose is to describe how ISS unfolded, but we also want to understand why it evolved in the way it did, and chapter 3 looks at the five driving forces that shaped the formation and evolution of ISS. These three introductory chapters set up the framework that we use in chapters 4 to 8 to trace and explain how the subject has evolved.

Chapters 4 and 5 cover the Cold War period. Chapter 4 surveys the traditionalist perspective, looking at the 'golden age' of Strategic Studies and its decline. Chapter 5 looks at those who challenged it, whether from Peace Research and Arms Control, or from the beginnings of the widening (economic and environmental security) and deepening (Feminism, Poststructuralism) perspectives that began to emerge during the 1980s. Chapters 6 and 7 cover the period from the end of the Cold War to the terrorist attack on the US on 9/11. Again, we start with the traditional military–political perspective, and then look at the widening and deepening challenges to this, some of which move onto quite different ground from those during the Cold War. We are aware that the chronological structure of chapters 4 to 7 might reinforce the idea of a great divide between pre- and post-1990, but we hope that the continuities show through as strongly as the changes. Chapter 8 looks at the short period since 9/11 and tries to assess the impact of that benchmark event on all the strands of ISS. Chapter 9 sums up the main conclusions about the changing shape of ISS, it reconsiders the utility of the driving forces framework for explaining the evolution of ISS, and reflects on the outlook for ISS.

Since we are, among other things, providing a history of the ISS literature, our referencing will favour citing first editions rather than later ones. We certainly have not cited everything in the literature, and even so our list of references is enormous. We have tried to take on board all of the landmark writings and authors, and beyond that to give fair representations of all the significant lines of literature. When we group a set of references under a given topic this may include things that both represent and criticise a given position, school or point. We chose the Harvard system of referencing because of its economy of wordage and its placement of author information at the precise relevant points. Even without trying to include everything, in later chapters the citations sometimes become sufficiently dense that they interfere with the smooth reading of the text. Where this happens, we put the references into footnotes.

1

Defining International Security Studies

International Security Studies (ISS) grew out of debates over how to protect the state against external and internal threats after the Second World War. Security became its watchword (Wolfers, 1952; Yergin, 1978), both distinguishing ISS from earlier thinking and the disciplines of War Studies and Military History, and, as it evolved, serving as the linking concept connecting an increasingly diverse set of research programmes. Looking back on more than sixty years of academic writing on international security, the first pertinent question for an intellectual history of ISS is to define what makes up the sub-field and where the boundary zones between it and adjacent academic disciplines are located.

To delineate ISS is unfortunately not as straightforward an exercise as one might wish. The label 'international security' was not adopted from the outset, but only gradually became accepted, and there is no universally agreed definition of what ISS comprises, and hence no accepted archive of 'ISS-documents' that define our object of study. As this book will demonstrate, not only is there a large body of ISS literature, it is one whose themes, discussions and participants change across time and place. The composition of ISS has mainly been taken for granted, with the consequence that little self-reflection on what made up ISS or its boundaries has been produced. The absence of a universal definition of what makes up ISS means that ISS has at times become a site for disciplinary politics with different perspectives arguing that they should be included while others (usually different sorts of widening perspectives) should not.

The delineation of ISS is complicated by the fact that as time goes by we get a different perspective on what falls in and what does not. To paraphrase Foucault's genealogical understanding of history as always being told from the point of the present, the fact that we tell the story of ISS from a 2008 perspective means that we look at a field which has some strikingly different preoccupations, both substantive and epistemological, from those that dominated it in, say, 1972. And it would have been easier to delineate ISS had it always been explicitly centred on the concept of security. Unfortunately, this has not been the case. Indeed, after its first decade of explicit theoretical and conceptual innovation, the field's mainstream carried out its work without much conceptual reflection (Baldwin, 1997). During the 'golden age' of Strategic Studies it would have been easy to think that 'strategy' was the dominant concept, albeit strategy now dominated by civilian rather than military thinkers. Thus in 1983, Buzan (1983: 3) could point out that security was an 'underdeveloped concept' and 'seldom addressed in terms other than the policy interests of particular actors or groups, and the discussion has a heavy military emphasis'. 'Security' is, as this and the next chapter will lay out, about crucial political themes such as the state, authority, legitimacy, politics and sovereignty, but even today the majority of articles and books that fall within the discipline of ISS do not contain lengthy meta-theoretical or philosophical discussions, but speak from within an implicit position on the conceptual terrain.

Our solution to the problem of delineating ISS starts from understanding conceptual security debates as 'the product of an historical, cultural, and deeply political legacy' (M. C. Williams, 2007: 17), not as something that can be solved through references to 'empirical facts' (Baldwin, 1997: 12). This means that we take the power of inclusion and exclusion seriously. We cast our net widely and include the work of those who self-identify as participants in ISS (mainly in terms of how they title their work, who they seem to regard as their appropriate audience and, up to a point, where they publish) regardless of whether all others who self-identify with the sub-field accept them as 'members' or not. Our ambition is not to find the ISS-winner, but to provide a rich and structured account of ISS that shows how multiple perspectives connect to a set of shared discussions on security. Since our point of reference is the (contested) disciplinary history of ISS, rather than the elaboration of what we think should be the theory or concept of security, we do not follow Kolodziej (2005) in coming up with suggestions for new concepts or dimensions to be included. Nor do we offer free-standing discussions of Hobbes, Clausewitz and Thucydides or other pre-ISS Classical figures. Clearly these and other early Realist and Liberal writers have been important to the foundation and development of IR, but our concern is with the evolution of modern ISS and the use to which Classical political and military theorists have been put in the post-1945 literature, rather than with these classics in their own right.

Our specific way of delineating ISS is set out in the rest of this chapter. The next section argues that despite the surface appearance of being preoccupied with policy debates, underneath, ISS can be seen as structured by engagement with four questions: whether to privilege the state as the referent object, whether to include internal as well as external threats, whether to expand security beyond the military sector and the use of force, and whether to see security as inextricably tied to a dynamic of threats, dangers and urgency. To see ISS as structured by these four questions allows us to see how deeper theoretical and political themes are implicated in ISS, and as a consequence to point out how perspectives share common conversational ground. The third section addresses the problem that far from all ISS literature goes directly through 'security'. We suggest that ISS can be understood through 'security' itself plus three 'adjacent' concepts that support it in different ways: by being complementary and more concrete; by being more general and linking to larger literatures; and by being oppositional challenges to 'security'. The fourth section discusses the disciplinary boundary zones between ISS and other established areas of academic study, particularly IR. The fifth section lays out the Western-centric nature of ISS and discusses the ways in which this bias can be addressed by granting retrospective attention to Post-colonial criticism.

Four questions that structure ISS

There are four questions which have, either implicitly or explicitly, structured debates within ISS since the late 1940s. These questions can have different answers, but that is not to say that they are always explicitly discussed: a large part of the ISS literature simply takes particular answers/concepts as givens. The four questions are analytical lenses or tools through which to read the evolution of ISS; they are the deeper, substantial core that defines what 'international security' is about and what brings the literature together. Explicit discussions usually happen when established approaches are contested and their answers cannot be taken for granted. Viewing ISS through these questions makes it clear that there are fundamental political and normative decisions involved in defining security and that this is what makes it one of the essentially contested concepts of modern social science. Security is always a 'hyphenated concept' and always tied to a particular referent object, to internal/external locations, to one or more sectors and to a particular way of thinking about politics.

The first question is whether to privilege the state as the referent object. Security is about constituting something that needs to be secured: the nation, the state, the individual, the ethnic group, the environment or the planet itself. Whether in the form of 'national security', or later, as traditionalist 'international security', the nation/state was the analytical and normative referent object. 'International security' was not about replacing the security of the state with the security of humanity, or the individual or minorities within or across state boundaries. Securing the state was seen instrumentally as the best way of protecting other referent objects. 'National security' should thus, as many observers have pointed out, more appropriately have been labelled 'state security', yet, what the Cold War concept of 'national security' entailed was more accurately a *fusion* of the security of the state and the security of the nation: the nation supported a powerful state which in turn reciprocated by loyally protecting its society's values and interests. To what extent this was a proper way of understanding the relationship between states and their nations, between governments, citizens and populations – that is, the question of 'what or whom should be the "referent object" for security?' – has been one of the central lines of debate within ISS and will be further explored in chapter 2.

The second question is whether to include internal as well as external threats. Since security is tied into discussions about state sovereignty (whether as something to be protected or criticised), it is also about placing threats in relation to territorial boundaries. Wolfers famously described 'national security' as 'an ambiguous symbol' and he contrasted the post-Second World War political climate with the one of inter-war American economic depression, holding that the 'change from a welfare to a security interpretation of the symbol "national interest" is understandable. Today we are living under the impact of cold war and threats of *external* aggression rather than depression and social reform' (Wolfers, 1952: 482; emphasis added). 'National security' had shifted from a concern with domestic economic problems to external threats stemming from ideologically opposed, and thus presumed hostile, powers (Neocleous, 2006a). As this shift became institutionalised, the concept of 'international security' came to accompany, but not replace, 'national security', and was eventually more influential in giving the discipline its name, hence *International* rather than *National* Security Studies. This labelling concurred with the growing disciplinary status of *International* Relations (*International Security*, 1976), which was based on distinguishing international from domestic politics, of which ISS was increasingly a sub-field. The internal/external dimension was partly re-opened as the Cold War ended and the overriding concern with the external threat of the Soviet Union disappeared from American and Western security discourses. Both

IR and ISS faced mounting challenges from globalisation to blur, or even collapse completely, the inside/outside distinction.

The third question is whether to expand security beyond the military sector and the use of force. Since ISS was founded during the Cold War and the Cold War was so overwhelmingly about the military (conventional and nuclear) capabilities of foes, friends and Self, 'national security' became almost synonymous with military security. This did not mean that other capabilities were not considered, the editors of *International Security* stressed, for instance, the need to incorporate economic vigour, governmental stability, energy supplies, science and technology, food and natural resources. These were, however, to be incorporated because they impacted on 'the use, threat, and control of force', and thus on military security, not because they were to be considered security issues in their own right (*International Security*, 1976: 2). But this conception of security was not entirely uncontested. During the Cold War, Peace Researchers pointed to the necessity of granting equal priority to basic human needs and 'structural violence', and challenges to military security became an established part of ISS from the 1980s onwards as scholars called for the inclusion of environmental and economic security (Ullman, 1983; Buzan, 1983, 1984b; Mathews, 1989). Later a more general sectoral widening of security included societal, economic, environmental, health, development and gender.

The fourth question is whether to see security as inextricably tied to a dynamic of threats, dangers and urgency. 'National security' developed in a political climate where the United States, and the West more broadly, understood themselves as threatened by a hostile opponent. As in Herz's (1950) famous formulation of the security dilemma, 'security' had to do with attacks, subjection, domination and – when pushed to the extreme – annihilation. This would lead groups to acquire more capabilities, in the process rendering their opponent insecure and thus compelling both sides to engage in a 'vicious circle of security and power accumulation' (Herz, 1950: 157). Security was about the extreme and exceptional, with those situations that would not just raise inconveniences, but could wipe out one's society (Williams, 2003). During the Cold War, this seemed rather common-sensical to the mainstream of ISS: the Soviet Union constituted a clear threat, and nuclear weapons were justified as a way to deter the Soviet Union from a first strike. As the debates over the expansion of the concept of security gained ground in the 1990s, this linkage of security to urgency, and to extreme and radical defence measures, was central. Some, most prominently the Copenhagen School, argued that the concept could be expanded as long as referent objects, threats and dangers were constituted with this logic of urgency and extreme measures (Wæver, 1995; Buzan *et al.*, 1998). Critics countered that this understanding of security was itself linked to a particular Realist view of the state and international politics. In keeping with a longer critical and Liberal tradition, it was argued on normative grounds that politics could be different and that one's analytical framework should incorporate this possibility (Williams, 2003; Huysmans, 2006b: 124–144).

Security and its adjacent concepts

We have defined ISS as those approaches that self-define either with the label of ISS, or with some branch of Security Studies (Human Security, Critical Security Studies, the Copenhagen School of Security Studies, Constructivist Security Studies and so on), and held that ISS is organised around different responses to the four questions laid out above. A further way to both delineate and to get at the ways in which ISS has evolved is to understand the field as structured by a set of key concepts. Obviously, the central concept of ISS is 'security', but it is also the case that conceptually explicit discussions were few and far between after the first decade of the Cold War. Even those who challenged Strategic Studies and ISS generally did not go through the concept of security, but through the concept of peace or more concrete discussions of disarmament, arms control, peace movements and world order. The concept of security was underdeveloped and unproblematised by those who used it, and an antagonistic concept to Peace Researchers insofar as it was located on the Realist, Strategic, military side of the political and academic battles. From the mid-1980s, as the Cold War unravelled, security became increasingly explicitly addressed and it became adopted by new and former critics of Strategic Studies. *Security* approaches thus appeared which fifteen years earlier would have been unlikely to adopt this label: Critical Security Studies (with key concepts of individual security and emancipation); the Copenhagen School of Security Studies based at the Copenhagen *Peace* Research Institute; and the International Peace Research Institute, Oslo (PRIO) based journal *Bulletin of Peace Proposals* changed its name to *Security Dialogue*. This certainly did not mean that 'security' was an uncontested concept, in fact it became more contested than ever, but it showed that after the Cold War 'security' became a concept which generated – and hence could unify – debates across perspectives previously opposed.

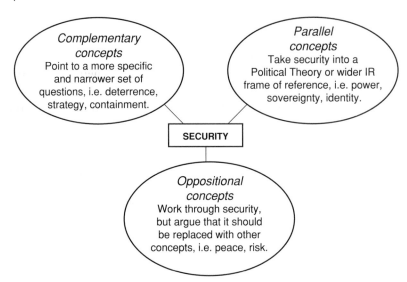

Figure 1.1.   Security and its adjacent concepts

A delineation of what falls within ISS based religiously on an explicit discussion of the concept of security would as a consequence leave out the majority of the Cold War contestants. This in turn would make it difficult to explain the resurgence of widening approaches in the 1990s, as these grew out of Cold War Peace Research, Feminism, Poststructuralism and Critical Theory. To tell the story of Cold War ISS without incorporating the criticism it generated would unduly homogenise the academic and political terrain on which ISS was situated. What we suggest is thus to see 'security' as supported by or conducted through three kinds of concepts: first, through *complementary* concepts, like 'strategy', 'deterrence', 'containment' or 'humanitarianism', which point to a more specific and narrower set of questions; second, through *parallel* concepts, like 'power', 'sovereignty' or 'identity', which take security into a broader, Political Theory or wider IR frame of reference; and third, *oppositional* concepts which work through security, but argue that it should be replaced, such as by 'peace' in Cold War Peace Research (see chapter 5) or 'risk' or 'the exception' in twenty-first-century widening debates (see chapter 8). Figure 1.1 illustrates the three kinds of adjacent concepts and their relationship to the concept of security.

The advantage of the security plus three adjacent concepts framework is that it allows us to conduct a structured conceptual analysis, particularly of those literatures that do not explicitly link to debates over the concept of security in ISS. Literatures may be 'conceptually silent' because they are adopting a taken-for-granted concept, are written in a rather straightforward empirical manner that downplays lengthy conceptual discussions, or because they come from other disciplines less reliant upon 'security' debates. Even if an approach does not explicitly discuss its conceptualisation of security, the way it mobilises complementary, parallel or oppositional concepts allows us to see the river delta of ISS perspectives as engaged in the same meta-conversation about what 'security' entails. An understanding of such conceptual points of engagement is, as we will return to in chapter 9, an important element in providing ISS with enough cohesion to make it an academic sub-field with a shared identity rather than a set of fragmented camps.

A different, but related, boundary-drawing question concerns literatures on security that are attached to prefixes not normally considered part of the ISS repertoire. Noteworthy examples include 'social security' and 'computer security'. Social security is usually considered part of discussions of wealth, income distribution and domestic justice, not 'security proper'. Computer security is a technical term used by computer scientists referring to problems in computer hard- and software, some of them accidental bugs, others as outcomes of malicious outside attackers. The standard ISS reply is that such concepts lack the drama and urgency of 'national/international' security, that they deal with domestic–individual questions in the case of social security and 'technical' rather than political–military threats in the case of computer security. In spite of a semantic similarity to (national) security, there is not a substantial, discursive resemblance.

This reply may be accurate in that these literatures do lack these characteristics and that they have historically not been considered part of ISS. But we should keep in mind that ISS is also a dynamic field that has expanded its legitimate contenders quite significantly in the past twenty years, and that what is considered to be part of it or not is not (solely) based on some static 'national/international security essence', but on how ISS evolves with its political environment. What academic and political actors manage to get accepted as part of 'international security' changes over time. Environmental security was not considered part of mainstream ISS in the early 1980s, yet it is hard to imagine it being excluded today. Such conceptual inclusion may be aided by the securitisation of hyphenated concepts, that is the constitution of something/somebody as radically threatening, as has been the case with health/disease security by prominent politicians or the media (Wæver, 1995; Buzan *et al.*, 1998; Peterson, 2002/3; Elbe, 2003, 2006; McInnes and Lee, 2006). Hyphenated securities might also make it onto the security agenda proper through conceptual analysis that explores and problematises the ways in which they are being excluded. A recent analysis by Neocleous (2006a) shows, for instance, how 'national security' was tied to domestic economic concerns during the 1930s and that this discourse mobilised the same drama and urgency as 'national security' did in the 1950s.

The disciplinary boundary of ISS

To see ISS as constituted through the questions and conceptual framework above still leaves the question of where ISS ends and other academic disciplines, particularly IR, begin. The boundary between ISS and IR is difficult to draw. In the early decades following the Second World War, the answer to this problem could have been given with some accuracy as: 'What distinguishes ISS from the general field of IR is its focus on the use of force in international relations.' In the traditionalist perspective on ISS, 'use of force' was and is primarily defined as 'state use of military force' and the threats states face are predominantly military in kind. Yet even this apparently narrow framing implies potentially quite a broad scope. It is about war and the various ways in which military power can be deployed, but also about the foundations of military power (and thus, up to a point, about economics and the socio-political structures of the state), and about the causes of conflict in international relations that result in states and other actors creating, maintaining and sometimes using military power (thus potentially bringing in not just economic, but also environmental and identity issues). This type of ISS features the general dynamics of interaction amongst rival armed forces: arms racing, arms control, the impact of technological developments and suchlike. Because of its strong state-centrism and assumptions about power struggles, it can, at the risk of some simplification, be thought of as the specialist military–technical wing of the Realist approach to IR. In the UK literature this whole understanding and approach is often labelled Strategic Studies. By the 1970s, however, the simple 'use of force' answer was becoming increasingly inaccurate. It remained true that the traditionalist position provided the foundational template, focusing on the international level and on threats that were about survival (Buzan *et al.*, 1998: 21). But as the agenda of ISS began to widen towards the end of the Cold War, and more rapidly after it, the 'use of force' answer became too narrow a description of what the field was about (at least for a large number of those participating in its debates). What increasingly distinguished ISS from IR was that it centred itself either on assumptions or on debates around and about the concept of international security.

Still there are inevitable overlaps between IR and ISS, particularly insofar as ISS has become more theoretically driven and that important IR debates simultaneously have evolved around security. As an example of the former, Waltzian Neorealism has been key to debates in the more theoretically informed parts of Realist Security Studies, particularly on how the polarity of the system impacts stability and grand strategy. There is, for instance, a rich literature on how to define polarity that is not strictly speaking about the concept of security as such, or how it may change in the light of shifting polarities, etc. (Goldgeier and McFaul, 1992; Huntington, 1993b, 1999; Waltz, 1993; Posen and Ross, 1996/7; Kupchan, 1998; Kagan, 2002). One reason this literature does not explicitly discuss the concept of security is that it takes a conventional conception of security as national security for granted.

The overlaps between IR and ISS have also multiplied in that 'security' has been selected as the arena for IR debates of a more general kind, noticeably over the status of Constructivist theory from the 1990s onwards. The programmatic statement of Conventional Constructivism in Katzenstein's *The Culture of National Security* explicitly adopted 'security' as the 'hard case' where Constructivist theories emphasising ideas, culture, norms and identity should stand trial in comparison with Neorealist and Neoliberalist approaches (Katzenstein, 1996a). Yet there was no explicit discussion of 'security' itself: what was contested were Realist explanations of state behaviour in the area of security, not whether the state should be the referent object, or whether the sector of concern should be the one of military and external threats.

Such works usually draw upon general IR literatures and debates, and there is therefore a link between telling the story of the evolution of ISS and the one of IR. Yet it should be kept in mind that our concern is with the evolution of ISS, not IR, and we will therefore not go extensively into IR literatures that have not addressed security or which have not been drawn upon explicitly by ISS. It should be stressed also that while IR is by far the main overarching discipline to ISS, it is not the only one to influence it: some of the first key thinkers on game theory, which influenced deterrence theory during the Cold War, were economists and physicists and other 'hard scientists' explicitly engaged in debates over the nuclear condition. As conceptual debates started to take off in the 1980s and flourished in the 1990s, a series of sociologists, feminist theorists, philosophers, development theorists, anthropologists and media theorists have also joined the debates in ISS. Like the classical empires of old, ISS therefore does not have clearly defined borders. Instead, it has 'frontier zones' where its debates blend into adjacent subjects, ranging from IR theory and International Political Economy (IPE), to foreign policy analysis and Political Theory. Since we cannot meaningfully cover both ISS and all of these frontier zones, we are often going to discuss the particular ISS engagements that bring in the frontier, while noting that there is a larger literature that those who wish to pursue a given theme should consult more thoroughly. We mention, for instance, the democratic peace literature in chapter 6, but do not have the space to go into all of its detailed arguments. Also, like the classical empires, these frontier zones can change, becoming more, or less, active as fashions and imperatives change. We try to show these movements in our analysis of the ISS literature in chapters 4 to 8.

Even taking a broad view of what counts as ISS has not enabled us to avoid all the difficult decisions about inclusion and exclusion. This book is much longer than we or Cambridge University Press originally thought it would be, and space constraints have been a real issue. In seeking to identify the core of the subject, and to reflect the uniqueness of its civilian strategy character, we have favoured conceptual issues over operational ones. This means that we have largely excluded the large literature on intelligence, which comes up mainly in the context of imperfect information and strategy.[1] We cover some aspects of military operations, but have not included the enormous literatures to be found in the many journals that are closely linked to the armed services, and which reflect professional military discourses. Turning to the boundary between ISS and Peace Research, we have included the literature dealing with substantial issues and conceptual debates on 'peace' that either mirrors debates in ISS or directly challenges ISS perspectives, but not covered more distinct Peace Research concerns such as peace education or the substantial literature on the practical side of conflict resolution, including conflict mediation, dispute settlement and suchlike (Bercovitch *et al.*, 2008; Sandole *et al.*, 2008). Some will no doubt think these exclusions a mistake, and they may be right. Our judgement has been that with a few exceptions, these literatures exist in their own worlds, and have played only a

1 On intelligence, see, inter alia, *Intelligence and National Security, The Journal of Intelligence History*, ISA Intelligence Studies Section (http://iss.loyola.edu/index.html – accessed 27 August 2008) and Johnson (2007).

marginal part in what we see as the great conversation of ISS. If we are wrong about this, then there is an opening for someone else to write that book.

The Western-centrism conundrum

Our focus on the evolution of ISS also implies that our analysis to some extent reflects the strengths, weaknesses and blind-spots of the discipline itself. Although ISS has evolved through engagement with particular policy events, it has not treated all events as equally important. The majority of traditional Cold War Strategic Studies was for example overwhelmingly concerned with bipolarity and nuclear deterrence, while Third World security issues were addressed almost exclusively only to the extent that they impacted on superpower relations. Questions that concerned local and internal wars, not to mention non-military security issues, simply did not register with the mainstream of the field (Barkawi and Laffey, 2006). Moreover, ISS is by birth an Anglo–American discipline which has been based on a Western conception of the state. This conception has arguably limited empirical and political relevance for major parts of the non-Western world, where the drawing of colonial boundaries irrespective of local communities and allegiances has produced a radically different set of political, economic and cultural structures (Ayoob, 1984; Krause, 1996; Bilgin, 2008).

This history of Anglo-centric (and militaristic and patriarchal) bias leaves us in a bit of a conundrum. On the one hand, it is our ambition to analyse the evolution of ISS as it has taken place, not as we wish that it should have gone. Chapter 4 on Strategic Studies during the Cold War is, for instance, concerned predominantly with the logics of nuclear deterrence under a system of bipolarity, which implies that certain events, like the Vietnam War, are played down precisely because that was the case in ISS. On the other hand, it is clearly unsatisfactory merely to register this bias without subjecting it to critical scrutiny, and we do seek to address this bias in two ways. First, we grant critical, including Post-colonial, approaches more space than they have held quantitatively. The analysis of ISS during the Cold War in chapters 4 and 5 includes, for instance, a rather substantial account of Feminism and Poststructuralism, which, relatively speaking, generated many fewer writings than did conventional military Strategic Studies at the time. Some sense of quantitative measure is significant in that it registers how the dominant parts of ISS approached security, but a qualitative measure that registers key articles, new challengers and contestation is equally significant in that it shows the way in which the field moves and changes. This implies also that more attention is devoted to the – often critical – texts that make up ISS's canon. These texts are usually more theoretical than the average one, hence our focus on significant conceptual articles and books that define or coin a particular hyphenated security concept such as Wolfers (1952) on 'national security', Herz (1950), Jervis (1978) and Booth and Wheeler (2008) on the 'security dilemma', the Copenhagen School on 'societal security' (Wæver et al., 1993) and 'securitisation' (Wæver, 1995; Buzan et al., 1998) and Deutsch et al. (1957) on 'security communities'. It also implies that there is an emphasis on those periods where approaches and concepts were formed and contested, usually when there was no established consensus on what was 'normal science' (Kuhn, 1962) and the security concept. Second, the biases and centrisms of ISS are also acknowledged through the signposting of later critiques. Thus the Western-centric notion of the state which underpins Strategic Studies is, for instance, noted in chapter 4 and discussed in chapter 5 and even more thoroughly in chapter 7.

The next chapter continues this discussion of the basic questions at the heart of ISS by turning to the historical developments that have produced the field's understanding of the state, government and politics.

2

The key questions in International Security Studies: the state, politics and epistemology

The beginning of chapter 1 briefly laid out four central questions that have been at the centre of ISS: Whose security should be protected and studied? Should the military be considered the primary sector of security? Should security be concerned exclusively with external threats or also with domestic ones? And, is the only form of security politics one of threats, dangers and emergency? This chapter will examine these questions in further detail and add a fifth: What epistemologies and methodologies should be brought to the study of security?

The majority of writings in ISS do not go to great lengths to discuss their analytical, philosophical, normative and epistemological assumptions, but it is nevertheless important to have a good understanding of these issues. Specific approaches to security always presume answers to these questions, even if they are not explicitly argued. These answers set crucial boundaries not only for how security is defined, but also for what kind of research projects and analyses are carried out. The dominant concept of security in ISS has been the one of 'national'/'international' security, it has been the concept of Realist Strategic Studies and it has been the concept that critical, widening perspectives have had to struggle with. This concept of security defines the state as the referent object, the use of force as the central concern, external threats as the primary ones, the politics of security as engagement with radical dangers and the adoption of emergency measures, and it studies security through positivist, rationalist epistemologies. But where does this concept come from? This chapter is devoted to an account of the historical processes and traditions of political thought that have been significant for producing this concept of security. Having a sense of these processes is important not only as a nice historical backdrop to the concrete perspectives and debates laid out in chapters 4–8, but because these perspectives provide particular resolutions to Classical political and normative problems.

The tendency within ISS to construct its choices in dichotomous terms means that security approaches have tended either to make the state or the individual the referent object; to construct security as either military or non-military; to draw a rigid line between external and internal security problems; and to see international – and national – politics as either inherently conflictual or as susceptible to non-violence and emancipation. Contemporary debates usually relate to these Classical stances and there is undoubtedly a Classical response to 'new' positions. This chapter shows, however, that some of these dichotomies have deeper historical ties and therefore should be seen as connected rather than opposed: there is a link between individual conceptions of security and collective ones; there is a connection between external and internal threats; and an understanding of security politics as a rational account of material capabilities exists in tandem with one based on the need to make decisions in an 'irrational' environment.

This chapter starts with a more thorough account of the role of the state in ISS with a particular view to how the sovereign state was formulated in the attempt to provide security domestically and abroad. This understanding of the state still stands at the heart of debates over the referent object in ISS. The second section examines the impact of the French Revolution on questions of societal cohesion and the understanding of the relationship between internal and external as well as military and non-military threats. The third section lays out the constitution of the state and the way in which it presupposes a particular form of politics. The fourth section presents the major epistemological approaches in ISS. The fifth section provides a brief overview of the most frequently mentioned approaches to ISS and plots their responses to the five questions that guide security.

From medieval to sovereign states

It is impossible to understand the way in which debates in ISS have evolved without having a good sense of its key referent object: the state. This is not because there is agreement on what 'state security' implies, but because all debates on what security can be and who it should be for evolve around the status of the state.

The concept of national security as it took form after the Second World War draws upon a conception of the state that reaches back hundreds of years. As R. B. J. Walker and other political theorists have laid out, there were two historical transformations that crucially impacted the formation of the modern state. The first transformation was from a medieval to a modern territorial state system, the second from a monarchical form of government to a national, popular one. The medieval world was organised through overlapping authorities rather than by a sovereign state, which meant that it was governed by two sets of authorities: churches (religious) and empires (political). In contrast to the modern state, which has supreme sovereignty over its territory, medieval authorities had to negotiate – and fight over – their claims to how a particular territory should be run. Overlapping authority was not only a feature of the relations between religious and political powers, but also of how political relations were organised. For large parts of the time, medieval Europe was governed by empires, and the centre of the empire was often too far away to project its authority effectively, at least compared to the modern state. There were multiple levels of political organisation stretching from the centre down to the village, and both authority and allegiances were less clear-cut as regional and local levels of governance supported, but also occasionally fought, higher powers. These overlapping, complex forms of organising territory meant that states or duchies could be part of a larger state or empire, giving some authority to the emperor or leader of the strongest state while still deciding over other issues.

In terms of political identity the medieval system was characterised by what Walker (1990: 10) calls the principle of hierarchical subordination: 'an understanding of the world as a continuum from low to high, from the many to the few, from God's creatures to God, from the temporal to the eternal'. All individuals were located at particular levels of society: at the top stood God, and under God, the Pope and the Emperor. The Church owned property and was thus a major economic and political player in its own right, but it also functioned to provide the Emperor with religious legitimacy: if God was at the top of the hierarchy of identities, and the Pope right under him, it was crucial for political authorities to get the Pope's blessing.

The transformation from the medieval to the modern system was significant in that it reorganised both the key principle of governance (from overlapping authority to territorial sovereignty) and the way in which political identity was understood. A central component in this transformation was the formation of the sovereign territorial state, where the interlocking levels of local, regional and empirical authorities gave way to one sovereign centre and the territorial boundary became the significant dividing line. This transformation was one where political authorities gained ground compared to the religious ones. It meant that the state became more secular and that this secularity was played out in interstate relations as well as domestically. The rise of the sovereign state was also connected to the emergence of private property (Ruggie, 1983, 1993). In the interstate arena, the birth of the territorial secular state was closely linked to the religious wars that haunted Europe in the wake of the Reformation. The Peace of Westphalia which concluded the Thirty Years' War in 1648 is dated as the founding moment when states decided no longer to interfere in each other's religious choices. One should note, however, that Westphalia was the beginning of a long historical process that through twists and turns moved towards the sovereign territorial state, not a complete break from one day to the next (Osiander, 2001).

As the international system evolved, the principle of non-interference in domestic affairs retained its central status and was seen as the precondition for creating international stability and order. Even if conflicts and wars could not be fully prevented, they could be minimised. Moving into the latter half of the twentieth century, the principle of non-interference was no longer tied to religious differences as in the mid seventeenth century, but to ideological ones, most crucially the one between the capitalist West and the communist East. By this time, domestically, the secular state principle meant that individuals were given the right to practise their (state sanctioned) religion, yet this was a private matter taking place in the private sphere or in churches. Religion was not to be directly involved in the governance of the state. What this implied, argues Michael C. Williams (1998), was not only a shift in which institutions governed society, but also in how politics was understood. Religious conflicts were seen as faith-driven and based on emotional claims to conviction and conscience. These were by their very nature based in immaterial entities and defied logical reasoning and there was therefore no way in which conflict between opposing religious positions could be solved. The clue to early modern Liberal thinkers was therefore to separate private conviction from public deliberations and to argue that the latter should be based on material, observable factors and hence on rational and objective reasoning.

The creation of peaceful relations domestically was also expressed through Hobbes's famous understanding of the sovereign state as the Leviathan providing the solution to the problem of individual security. The individual, argued Hobbes, confronted the problem of the state of nature: in the state of nature there was no authority to secure survival and individuals lived in constant fear of other individuals seeking to steal their possessions. Individuals had to sleep to survive, but sleep also made them supremely vulnerable, hence the need for a sovereign institution that would guarantee security. The 'contract' between the individual and the state is one where the individual grants the state the right to protect – and define – individual security in exchange for an acknowledgement of its sovereign authority. To Hobbes, argues Walker (1997: 67), the fear of the state of nature was so strong that 'whatever the sovereign does cannot be as bad as the condition of unrestrained competition'. But many others, including central Liberal thinkers such as John Locke, 'have been deeply skeptical of this judgement, and a large proportion of contemporary debate about security continues to oscillate around it' (Walker, 1997: 67). Conceptions of individual and collective/state security are thus inextricably linked: state security implies a particular resolution to the problem of individual security, and individual security must, since the individual is always located in relation to other individuals, assume a collective authority. Security is thus 'a condition both of individuals and of states' and 'a condition, or an objective, that constituted a *relationship* between individuals and states or societies' (Rothschild, 1995: 61). Since much of the widening debate in ISS has evolved around dichotomously opposed individual concepts of security on the one hand and collective-state defined concepts on the other, it is worthwhile keeping in mind that there is no concept that does not, implicitly if not explicitly, comprise the other.

Reading these early modern debates on the individual, the state and interstate relations through the lenses of twenty-first-century debates in ISS, one should note that there is often a move between different levels of analysis. Hobbes's understanding of the Leviathan as the solution to the state of nature was an abstract, speculative thought experiment that attempted to work through different solutions to questions of authority and insecurity. Those challenging the privileged role accorded the state by Hobbes and by Realists in ISS have usually done so on one of two empirical grounds. One line of argument goes that many real existing states are too weak or too failed to be able to provide 'their' individuals with the promised security: think of Somalia, Afghanistan, Haiti or the Democratic Republic of Congo. The other line goes that states, mainly but not only undemocratic ones, often threaten their own citizens not only by making arbitrary, harmful decisions (like going to war or allowing pollution), but also directly by prosecuting them, detaining them or murdering them: think of Burma (Myanmar), Stalin's Soviet Union, Mugabe's Zimbabwe or almost any other dictatorship. From the point of view of these critiques, to grant the state the Hobbesian, Realist privilege is not only to overlook these empirical deficiencies in how concrete states fail to provide security, but it is, perhaps even worse, to put it in a position where it is immune to criticism and does not have to justify itself. The Hobbesian response is to acknowledge that most states are far from ideal providers of security, but that the alternative to the state is far worse, an argument that shifts the empirical assessment of the state back to the speculative, abstract realm of the state of nature. What is at stake in security debates is thus often that empirical arguments and abstract ones challenge each other and this stacks the arguments in such a way that it is hard to find a resolution or even a common ground from which to debate. It also means, as Walker (1997) has pointed out, that those approaches challenging the state need to come up with alternative abstract answers to the problem of political identity and who is going to provide security in the absence of the sovereign state.

The French Revolution and domestic cohesion

The second historical transformation that is crucial to understanding the conception of the state in ISS is the birth of modern nationalism with the French and American revolutions. The transition from the medieval to the early modern state heralded a significant beginning of the dis- mantling of a hierarchy of identities, but early modern territorial states were still governed by largely non-democratic rulers. The French and American revolutions were thus a major shift in that the beheading of the monarch, either concretely or symbolically, and the introduction of popular sovereignty, accelerated the disintegration of hierarchies between different categories of people inside the state. Nationalism as a modern ideology heightened the emphasis not just on equality within the state, but also on commonality, such that citizens would see themselves as bound by a deeper sense of identity, community and belonging. The nation became in Benedict Anderson's words an 'imagined community', 'a deep, horizon- tal comradeship' (Anderson, 1991: 7) whose members shared a common social, cultural and political identity. This creation of a common historic identity worked to stabilise further the distinction between the national and the international domain. Inside the state, one had similarity, soli- darity and progress, whereas the international domain was destined to be ruled by relations of alienation, domination and conflict (Wight, 1966; Walker, 1993). Nationalism also introduced new possibilities for social mobility, particular as it was coupled to a burgeoning capitalist, indus- trial society (Gellner, 1983). Individuals were not, as in early modernity, confined by birth to a particular location within societal structures, but could rise beyond the class into which they were born through cunning and hard work.

The fusion of nationalism with the sovereign territorial state had several implications for how security was conceptualised and thus how debates have evolved within ISS. Nationalism was connected to popular sovereignty and eventually democracy, and therefore to the idea that the legitimacy of the sovereign state was based not on divine or monarchical inherent rights, but on the government's ability to rule according to the values, interests and identity of the people. This meant that the simple Hobbesian solution to the problem of security was thrown into question: the argument that the governors should not be questioned because the alternative was the state of nature, was no longer sufficient. If the government did not act according to the interest of its people it should be toppled.

From this followed an important shift in how the relationship between the state and citizens was approached. Put simply, the territorial state was concerned with threats to its territorial security and the ruler of the state with contenders to the throne. Military capabilities and the use of force were central in keeping external enemies at bay – or in conquering new territory – and in defeating domestic threats. The introduction of nationalism and popular rule changes this by making the domestic component of state security not only a matter of force and control but one of legitimacy and societal cohesion. The extent to which society was homogenous and supportive of 'its' government became a central security concern for rulers on two grounds: first, because it impacted the security of their own positions; second because it impacted the security of the state domestically, most crucially in that the absence of cohesion might lead secessionist parts of the state to seek independence or, as in the American Civil War, cause violent ideological conflict. Torn societies would also be more susceptible to fifth-column activities of enemy states. This concern with societal cohesion runs through Classical Realist writings such as those of Kennan (1947: 581), who warned that 'exhibitions of indecision, disunity and internal disintegration within this country have an exhilarating effect on the whole Communist movement', to Huntington's post-Cold War fear of immigration, decaying family values and the 'internal rot' of American society (Huntington, 1996: 303–305). The emphasis on social cohesion also implied a potential broadening of the concept of security beyond the military. Since defence was not only a matter of defending the territorial border, but also of securing domestic consensus, the internal threats a society might face could, if severe enough, be considered security problems.

The shift to a concern with societal cohesion also implied a change in how territory was considered. The Peace of Westphalia had sought to limit the number of wars through its codification of the principle of non-interference. This, however, did not mean that states did not go to war in the attempt to conquer or defend territories, 'merely' that these wars were not fought on the basis of religious beliefs. Territories were valued for their geopolitical and strategic importance and the material, economic capabilities they generated, while the identities and allegiances of the people inhabiting those territories were given little concern. From the perspective of people of conquered territories this had the positive effect that rulers, especially in large imperial states, often did not interfere much in local cultural and political relations. The advent of nationalism changed this. With its claim that nations had particular identities and that they should rule the territories on which they lived, nationalism sacralised territory (Mayall, 1990). As nationalist movements worked to install a common identity amongst the members of 'their' nations, territories could no longer be shifted around with no concerns for the status of the people and nations who lived there. This made territorial acquisitions less attractive as a hostile population would resist the 'occupier', but it also provided justifications for the political centre to nationalise, coercively if necessary, those on its territory. Although nationalism claimed that each nation had its unique essence, there was far from agreement on which nations were the right ones, who should be ruling whom and who indeed had the right to be in a particular territory. This became particularly outspoken in the social Darwinist beliefs of the nineteenth century, in which more powerful nations gave themselves the right to subjugate – through force or 'civilising colonialism' – less 'advanced' peoples.

For the majority of Cold War ISS, the focus was clearly on external threats, as shown by the *International* in International Security Studies, but this closer scrutiny of the roots of the state in ISS reveals this as somewhat misleading. Realists have privileged the security of the state and have understood security largely through the use of (military) force, but they have also paid attention to a series of other issues and capabilities, including domestic cohesion, that may impact the state's ability to project military force. The reason why the majority of Cold War ISS, at least in the form of Strategic Studies, focused on the external dimension of security was because domestic cohesion and the values to be protected were largely taken for granted, at least in the Western world. There were, however, also traditionalists such as Kennan pointing to the need to shore up internal weaknesses and dissent in the face of the Soviet threat and there was a good deal of concern in the US in the wake of the Second World War about the domestic cohesion of Western European countries with strong communist parties. Resources were put into keeping the Left out of power in Italy, and Franco was tolerated in Spain. The reason why the internal dimension of security was not emphasised by mainstream approaches to ISS during the Cold War had therefore more to do with the empirical, political context (one overwhelming, nuclear opponent overshadowing all other concerns) than with an inherent trait within the concept of national security. As the Cold War ended and ethnic conflict and civil wars came to the fore, so did questions of domestic stability and cohesion (Posen, 1993; Van Evera, 1994; Kaufmann, 1996). Many widening approaches also spoke directly to the question of societal cohesion, as in the Copenhagen School's concept of societal security (Wæver et al., 1993; Buzan et al., 1998).

Nationalism was also significant in that it opened up several understandings of international security. It claimed in its classical revolutionary form that all men (and later women) were equal as citizens, and that each individual had a set of universal rights. If the state was organised in accordance with these rights and the ideals of democracy, then there would be a move towards a better society within states. The Realist reading held, however, that while progress – economically, politically and culturally – was possible within states, abstaining from setting a common normative/religious standard that the Peace of Westphalia entailed made it impossible internationally (Walker, 1990). In this ideal-type Realist understanding of the international, no durable 'international security' is possible, only temporary accommodations within an essentially conflictual international system. There is no normative or analytical conception of the need to protect the security of other states (unless this improves the security of one's own) or the security of individuals or groups located within other states (again, unless this can be used to improve one's own strategic position).

But this Realist conception of state sovereignty and national security has not been uncontested. Looking at the claims to universal rights that the French and American revolutions entailed, the universal–particular tension can be argued in a way that emphasises the commonality between all human beings, not only the ones with whom one shares a nation. This implies the possibility of a referent object other than the state for one's own nation, to the extent that nation and state are not aligned, but also of 'individual security' and 'group/societal security', where others are made insecure by their own states. This understanding of the universality of individual rights also allows for a reading of the international as less conflictual than in Realism. This Idealist tradition of thought, which continues through Peace Research up to present Critical Security Studies, argues that if individuals are granted the possibilities of security, freedom and self-expression, then that will lead to the absence of violent conflict, not only within, but also between communities: 'global' or 'world' security is thus deemed possible. In this respect, we have a normative commitment that reaches beyond one's own state or fellow citizens and the beginning of the debates over the referent object of security: whether the international should be approached as a question of order or whether it is possible to have an international concept of justice (Bull, 1977).

The conception of politics in ISS

The Peace of Westphalia was significant for how it sought to take religious emotion out of politics, both between and within states. As Williams (1998: 215) has argued, there was a Liberal, rationalist philosophy at work which held that conflicts were more easily handled if understood in material rather than ideational (religious) terms. 'Defining threats in *material* terms (like all other phenomena) was held to allow a reasoned discourse surrounding them. To place the discourse of war and peace within the bounds of *physical* threat and the capacity for it was a *pacifying* move' (Williams, 1998: 215; see also Toulmin, 1990). Tracing this up to contemporary debates on security shows that the inclination of traditional ISS approaches to adopt positivist epistemologies and methodologies, rooted in material and empirically verifiable factors, has longer and thoroughly political, normative roots (Deudney, 2007). It implies that the assumptions about whether the state is a rational actor *and* the epistemologies that should be adopted in the study of security are linked to one another.

Clearly, the question of whether the state is a rational actor or not has major consequences for security theories: since 'international security' is at the most general level about the threats states (or other political entities) face and the responses they can and should adopt to defend themselves, it makes a huge difference what kind of actors those states are. If states are rational, it is possible to predict their behaviour – and thus define appropriate security policies – to a much greater extent than if they are not. However, exactly what it means to be 'rational' is itself a contested issue in ISS. Critics argue that to presume a rational actor is to claim that the state is and should be acting according to Realist principles. These, however, are neither objective, nor analytically or politically neutral. Theories of security are trying to explain the behaviour of states, while they themselves may have an impact on what they seek to explain. At its most basic, many Classical Realists see their analysis as a disposition to understand politics in the terms in which political actors understand themselves, and this points towards a mainly historical and empirical form of analysis. But in the period since the Second World War, IR Realism, particularly in America, took on increasingly theoretical forms, first in the supposedly timeless principles of power politics set out by Carr and Morgenthau, and later in the more formalised Neorealism of Waltz. This development paralleled that of ISS, and to the extent that ISS is, as we characterised it above, 'the specialist military–technical wing of the Realist approach to IR', it was these theoretical forms to which ISS mainly related. In its theoretical forms, Realism imposes assumptions on reality and, to the extent that it is influential, may therefore create the reality it assumes.

Rationality assumptions are intertwined with levels of analysis decisions. Structural theories, most prominently Neorealism, assume a general conception of the state that applies throughout the international system. This does not mean that each and every state will always behave rationally, but that those who do not will be punished by the structure, and will eventually either fall by the wayside or learn how to behave. Structural theories differ from those explanations that can be found at the level of foreign policy-making or other domestic-factor issues. Here, there is much greater room for asking whether states are rational or not. An important Cold War deterrence debate evolved, for example, around whether the rationality assumption held up. Could the Communist, or indeed the American, leadership be presumed to act 'rationally' in the face of nuclear escalation or would they follow a different logic or no decipherable logic at all? The problem was that deterrence logic required a certain modicum of rationality and predictability, but that there was no sure way of knowing whether such logic existed beforehand, or would continue to exist under the extreme conditions of nuclear war. The question of rationality has arisen again after 9/11, as we shall see in chapter 8.

Yet, while rational assumptions are central to many mainstream ISS theories, there is simultaneously a tension between them and the other side of 'national security' logic which is concerned with the drama, urgency and exception in security. The latter tradition has more recently been identified with Carl Schmitt, but it resonates with some of the harder elements of Realism as well. The central elements of this tradition are, argue Williams (2003) and Huysmans (2006b: 124–144), that security is about making exceptional decisions, it is about that point of danger where the distinction between Self and Other is made absolutely clear. These decisions may be influenced by material capabilities – as laid out in the account of the move to a rational security politics – but they are not rational in the sense that those who make decisions have complete information, nor are decision-makers able to fully predict what the consequences of actions and non-actions will be. This underscores the decisionist element in security politics, and the understanding of the political as a field into which policy-makers – and others – must act forcefully even under stress and without perfect information.

Epistemology and security debates

The historical processes that have underpinned the constitution of the modern concept of security have, as laid out above, also had consequences for how security should be studied. Going all the way back to Westphalia, the attempt to make security a material and rational field of deliberation was one that connected the attempt to pacify interstate relations and how knowledge was defined. There is, in other words, as argued by Williams (1998), a clear connection between the concept of security and epistemology.

Epistemology concerns the principles and guidelines for how knowledge can be acquired, and thus, in the context of ISS, the question of how one should study security. ISS was not during the Cold War much concerned with epistemological issues, although there were divisions spilling over from 'traditionalist' vs. 'behaviouralist' debates about IR theory. This, however, changed to some extent in the late 1980s and 1990s as wider debates on epistemology within the social sciences flowed first into IR and from there into ISS. Since epistemology is both a part of the Classical foundation of security and of the widening debates of the past twenty years, it is useful to have some idea of how it has been discussed.

The first epistemological distinction central to ISS is the one between objective, subjective and discursive conceptions of security. The definition of objective and subjective security was laid out by one of the early classic texts of ISS, 'National Security as an Ambiguous Symbol', by Wolfers (1952). Wolfers (1952: 485) argued that 'security, in an objective sense, measures the absence of threats to acquired values, in a subjective sense, the absence of fear that such values will be attacked'. It was, continued Wolfers, never possible to measure security 'objectively' in that subjective evaluations played an inevitable part in states' assessments. Yet, '[w]ith hindsight it is sometimes possible to tell exactly how far they deviated from a rational reaction to the actual or objective state of danger existing at the time' (Wolfers, 1952: 485). Wolfers's formulation illustrates well the tension between an objective conception of security (the absence/presence of concrete threats) and a subjective one (the feeling of being threatened or not). This tension has run through ISS during the Cold War and after, where Strategic Studies focused largely on assessing supposedly objective security threats. Objective conceptions of security usually, but not always, define security in material terms: the probability of states posing a threat or being able to deter enemies is based on their material capabilities.

Subjective approaches to security emphasise the importance of history and norms, of the psychologies of fear and (mis)perceptions, and of the relational contexts (friends, rivals, neutrals, enemies) within which threats are framed. States, like people, can reside anywhere on a spectrum from paranoid (seeing threats where there are none), through rational (assessing threats correctly), to complacent (not seeing, or not caring about, actual threats). These approaches argue that at a minimum the traditional focus on material military capabilities should be supplemented with non-material factors such as the culture of the armed forces, the level of national cohesion or the norms about the legitimate use of, for instance, chemical weapons or assassinations (Johnston, 1995; Kier, 1995; W. Thomas, 2000; Tannenwald, 2005). These studies argue that both material and ideational factors impact the actual (military) resources that states have at their disposal. More broadly, the Liberal security dilemma occurs because states misperceive each other's intentions: each state is merely striving to be defensively secure, but in doing so others falsely perceive it as being threatening. To move, as did Walt, from a balance of power to a balance of threat is itself to acknowledge the importance of intersubjective processes (Walt, 1987). Yet, while a significant number of studies in ISS have integrated subjective conceptions of security, primarily through acknowledging perceptions (Jervis, 1976), it is worth noting that this conception is still tied to the objective one. The subjective understanding of security can be a more or less accurate reflection of objective security as measured by material capabilities or objective threats. Subjective approaches do not, in other words, dispense with an objective definition of security, but contrast it with the 'filter' of the subjective.

Discursive approaches, in contrast, argue that security cannot be defined in objective terms, and hence both the objective and subjective conceptions are misleading. Security is, argues the Copenhagen School, a speech act and 'by saying "security," a state representative declares an emergency condition, thus claiming a right to use whatever means

Table 2.1. *Epistemological distinctions*

Objective conceptions	Subjective conceptions	Discursive conceptions
- The absence/presence of concrete threats - Usually defines security in relative material terms	- The feeling of being threatened or not - Emphasises social context, history and the psychologies of fear and (mis)perceptions - Maintains an objective reference	- Security cannot be defined in objective terms - Security is a speech act - Focuses on the intersubjective process through which 'threats' manifest themselves as security problems on the political agenda

are necessary to block a threatening development' (Buzan *et al.*, 1998: 21; see also Wæver, 1995). What is central to security analysis is thus understanding the process through which particular 'threats' manifest themselves as security problems on the political agenda. 'Threats' in that sense are 'objective' when they are accepted by significant political actors, not because they have an inherent threatening status. Security is, in short, a self-referential practice (Buzan *et al.*, 1998: 24). This does not imply that anything can become 'security', first, because not all political issues can be given the priority of 'security importance' at the same time, and second, because the discursive construction of 'security threats' will be influenced by a state's history, its geographical and structural position, and the (discursive) reactions it generates from others, internationally and domestically. For security speech acts to be successful, they also need to convince their relevant audiences.

The objective, subjective and discursive conceptions are summed up in Table 2.1, and they concern the status that security has, how it can be identified and studied. Another key epistemological distinction addresses the principles that should be adopted for analysing security. Here, as in IR in general, the major distinction runs between scientific and positivist approaches on the one hand, and philosophical, sociological and constitutive ones on the other. Substantially, the debate between the two approaches concerns the extent to which social science should mirror the hard sciences, that is should seek to establish causal theories of (state) behaviour. Causal theories require that variables are identified and analytically and temporally separated, so that if X causes Y, then Y has to happen if X occurs, and if X does not happen then Y must not occur either (King *et al.*, 1994). Since IR and ISS are not like a laboratory, they can only approximate the positivist research programmes of Chemistry or Physics, yet, argue positivists, one should strive to concord with positivist principles to the greatest extent possible. Post-positivists, on the other hand, insist that many of the problems with which the social sciences engage, including the one of security, are better dealt with through the use of non-positivist theories. The process through which threats are identified and given meaning is, for instance, better understood through an analysis of identity building and institutional transformation that does not lend itself to causality or quantification.

Most Realist and Liberalist approaches have followed the positivist route, combining in what Keohane coined in 1988 as 'rationalism', while Critical Constructivists, Poststructuralists and most Feminists have opted for a post-positivist, 'reflectivist' approach (Keohane, 1988). But as with the objective, subjective and discursive conceptions, one should be aware that there are many who fall outside these neatly arranged camps. Large parts of ISS during the Cold War were more concerned with the empirical evolution of the arms race and the superpower relationship than with establishing fully fledged theories. Classical Realists and Liberals were writing before the turn to positivism gained force, and one does not find causal research programmes in the seminal articles by Kennan (1947), Herz (1950) or Wolfers (1952). Yet although consciousness of epistemology is a fairly recent arrival in ISS, its presence and consequences have been influential from the beginning.

Mapping concepts of security

The first two chapters have already mentioned the labels of a number of approaches to ISS. Since we will be making much use of these labels in what follows, we conclude this chapter by linking these and their concepts of security to the discussions above. Readers might find it useful to have both a glossary of terms, and a quick guide to the similarities and differences of the various approaches. We also indicate the geographical focus of each approach, a theme we develop as we unfold the evolution of ISS in chapters 4 to 8.

- *Conventional Constructivism* – presents a counterpoint to materialist analyses by highlighting the importance of ideational factors, that is culture, beliefs, norms, ideas and identity. Usually centred on analysing state behaviour, includes positivist as well as post-positivist epistemologies and is primarily located within the US.

- *Critical Constructivism* – looks to other collectivities than the state, yet mostly concerned with military security. Adopts narrative and sociological post-positivist methodologies. Its origins are predominantly in the US, but it has since the late 1990s gained a strong standing in Europe.
- *The Copenhagen School* – partly about widening the threats and referent objects, especially societal/identity security, partly about paying more attention to the regional level, but mainly about focusing on securitisation (the social processes by which groups of people construct something as a threat), thus offering a Constructivist counterpoint to the materialist threat analysis of traditional Strategic Studies. Particularly strong in Scandinavia and Britain, and influential in most of Europe.
- *Critical Security Studies* – similar to Peace Research in its normative aims, especially regarding the emphasis on human security over state security, but using mainly post-positivist methodology. A branch of Critical Theory in IR generally, with emancipation as a key concept. Particularly strong in Britain.
- *Feminist Security Studies* – covers a variety of approaches ranging from Peace Research to Poststructuralism. Holds that women support the security policies of states through military as well as non-military functions, and that they face a series of gender-specific security problems that are never acknowledged within a state-centric conception of security. Points to the role that hegemonic masculinity plays in sustaining militaristic security policies. Originated in the mid-1980s in the US and Britain and has grown to have a global presence.
- *Human Security* – closely related to Peace Research and Critical Security Studies. Dedicated to the view that human beings should be the primary referent object of security, and therefore that ISS should include issues of poverty, underdevelopment, hunger and other assaults on human integrity and potential. Seeks to merge the agendas of ISS and Development Studies. Human Security has academic presence across the West and Japan and has been embraced by the United Nations (UN), the European Union (EU), and Canadian, Norwegian and Japanese governments.
- *Peace Research* – the Classical normative counterpoint to Strategic Studies, looking to reduce or eliminate the use of force in international relations, to highlight and critique the dangers in the (especially nuclear) strategic debate, and to give standing to individual security alongside, or sometimes against, state (national) security. Overlaps with Strategic Studies in its interest in arms control and disarmament, and arms racing,

and in some branches also in the use of quantitative and game-theoretic methods. Peace Research became quite strongly institutionalised in the Scandinavian countries, Germany and Japan, and to a lesser extent in Britain and, with different theoretical orientations, the US.

- *Post-colonial Security Studies* – points to the Western-centrism of ISS and argues that the study of the non-Western world requires security theories that incorporate colonial history as well as the attention to the specific state formations in the Third World. As the First and Third World are connected, Post-colonial Security Studies argues that it provides insight into the dynamics of both the First and the Third Worlds. Usually critical of state-centrism and has been developed by Western as well as non-Western scholars.

- *Poststructuralist Security Studies* – adopts the concept of discourse rather than ideas, argues that state sovereignty and security are products of political practices. Critical of how state-centrism constrains the possibilities for other referent objects of security, but refuses the traditional Peace Research turn to individual security. Began in North America in the mid-1980s, but from the early 1990s stronger in Europe.

- *Strategic Studies* – the Classical, traditionalist literature that defines the subject in political–military terms and focuses on military dynamics. This includes its own sub-literatures, such as those on war, nuclear proliferation, deterrence theory, arms racing, arms control, etc. Strongly materialist in approach with a tendency to take a state-centric normative position as given rather than as a subject of discussion. Generally strong across the West, but particularly in the US and Britain, and with a separate tradition in France.

- *(Neo)Realism* – Realist approaches generally have strong links to Strategic Studies in that they underpin its essentially state-centric, materialist, power-political and conflictual (and thus 'objective') assumptions about the nature of international relations. Neorealist concepts, most notably polarity (Waltz, 1979), played a big role in thinking about nuclear deterrence, arms control and arms racing. Mainstream in the US, influential, but much more contested, in Europe.

Table 2.2. maps the way in which the ISS approaches above answer the five questions laid out in this chapter.

Table 2.2. *ISS perspectives in relation to the five questions*

ISS perspective	Referent object	Internal/external	Sectors	Views of security politics	Epistemology
Strategic Studies	The state	Primarily external	Military (use of force)	Realist	Positivist (from quite empirical to formal modelling)
Neo(realism)	The state	Primarily external	Military–political	Realist	Rationalist
Poststructuralist Security Studies	Collective–individual	Both (constitution of boundaries)	All	Change of Realism possible, but not utopian/Idealist	Deconstructivist and discursive
Post-colonial Security Studies	States and collectivities	Both	All	Change of Western dominance possible, but difficult to accomplish	Critical Theory, deconstructivist, historical sociology
Peace Research	State, societies, individuals	Both	All (negative: predominantly military)	Transformation possible	Positivist (from quantitative to Marxist materialists)
Human Security	The individual	Primarily internal	All	Transformative	Mostly highly empirical or soft-constructivist
Feminist Security Studies	Individual, women	Both	All	Mostly transformative	From quantitative to Poststructuralist
Critical Security Studies	Individual	Both	All	Transformative (emancipation)	Critical Theory (hermeneutics)
The Copenhagen School	Collectivities and the environment	Both	All	Neutral	Speech act analysis
Conventional Constructivism	The state	External	Military	Transformation possible	Soft-positivist
Critical Constructivism	Collectivities	Mostly external	Military	Transformation possible	Narrative and sociological

3

The driving forces behind the evolution of International Security Studies

In chapters 1 and 2 we have sketched out what post-1945 ISS looks like as a sub-field of IR, and surveyed the key debates and approaches that have determined the shape and content of the subject. We have addressed our central theme of evolution by identifying a branching out from narrow, largely state-centric and military–political conceptions of the subject to a much more diverse set of understandings which are often in contestation with each other. In this chapter we look separately at the driving forces behind the evolution of ISS. Why was it that different conceptions of the scope, referent objects and epistemological understandings of ISS emerged when they did? Why, indeed, did ISS coalesce as a distinct subject and why did it thereafter evolve as it did? Why has there been so much change and turbulence within this sub-field when its Realist underpinnings, with their emphasis on the permanence of the military threat in world politics suggests that there should be a lot of continuity?

As we will show in later chapters, there are some significant continuities in the ISS literature, but there are also many substantial changes. Sometimes the priority of a topic declines (as with arms control and deterrence towards the end of the 1980s), and sometimes the direction changes when wholly new topics become part of ongoing debates (as with economic, environmental, societal and human security). Sometimes the content or emphasis of ISS changes *en bloc*, but sometimes it evolves in different ways in different places. This chapter discusses what explains the birth and the evolution of ISS, both its continuities and its transformations. We suggest that five forces are particularly central to this process: great power politics, technology, key events, the internal dynamics of academic debates, and institutionalisation. These five work as drivers in two different senses. Most obviously they drive ISS in the sense of shaping what it is that people choose to write about under the ISS heading, what subjects and issues they define as the main security problems of the day. Less obvious, but equally important, is that they shape <u>how</u> people write about these topics. They help to shape which ontologies, epistemologies and methods carry legitimacy, and what the societal, political and academic roles of security scholars should be. Since we present our account as a historical narrative, these two senses will be in play throughout.

The first section below presents the Kuhnian sociology of science framework which supports this type of approach. The section also describes the methodology behind the five forces framework as a combination of an empirical inductive reading of the ISS literature and a deductive analysis of the existing literature on the sociology of science and IR. The second section moves from this general framework to the key discussion in the still sparse literature on the sociology of IR, a discussion which concerns the relative merits of internal and external explanations. Having made the call for including both, section three argues how the internal and the external may be further specified. The final section of the chapter consists of a more detailed overview of the five driving forces as general analytical categories, in preparation for using them as the lenses through which to observe empirically the evolution of ISS in chapters 4 to 8.

A post-Kuhnian sociology of science

There has been no previous comprehensive analysis of the evolution of ISS that comprises the period from the mid-1940s to the new post-9/11 millennium and which covers the whole gambit of ISS from traditional Strategic Studies to Poststructuralist and Feminist approaches. Hence it is not surprising that there is no readily available sociology of science model especially fitted for ISS that we could draw upon. The five driving forces framework that we eventually decided upon was built through a combination of two different methods. Along one track we operated empirically, deriving the forces pragmatically from our reading of the literature of ISS across six decades and spanning a large array of perspectives. In that respect they can be seen as inductively generated from the ISS literature itself. These five forces were the ones, we concluded after having tried and rejected other potential candidates, which could most adequately account for the major conceptual movements, for continuities as well as transformations. What we present is thus the best outcome of a series of possible forces and models.

We also operated more deductively along the second methodological track, bringing to our reading both our knowledge of what have been the key themes and explanatory factors in IR and ISS as well as what is generally pointed to in the sociology of science literature. From that more general perspective one would expect any social structure to be shaped by the disposition of material power (great powers), by knowledge (technology), by events (history and the shadows it throws into the future), by the prevailing social constructions (academic debates), and by wealth and organisational dynamics (institutionalisation). We use the five driving forces to highlight key themes that explain how and why ISS evolved as it did. When taking a broad view of ISS, all of them are always in play, yet, as one zooms in on particular periods and approaches, some may be more significant than others. The five different forces concern very different aspects of the social structure that impacts ISS, and the forces are as a consequence neither easily empirically separable nor mutually exclusive categories. The forces interact in important and complex ways, sometimes reinforcing existing approaches, sometimes accelerating the number and strength of newcomers. As a theoretical framework, the five driving forces thus have a heuristic explanatory quality that allows us to produce a structured, yet historically and empirically sensitive analysis. But it is not a framework that seeks to make causal explanations where the impact of one force is tested against that of the others. It might have been possible to build a theoretical framework that identified more or different driving forces, yet the combination of the inductive and deductive strategies seemed to provide us with a reasonably strong epistemological footing. Ultimately, however, the 'proof' of non-causal frameworks is in their ability to generate depth as well as overview, and in that respect the utility of the driving forces framework lies in the substantial account they allow us to produce in the chapters ahead.

If we think of the sociology of science task that was in front of us, it may be conceived of as a three-layered pyramid with the sociology of ISS and our five forces framework at the top and two layers supporting it. Figure 3.1 provides a graphic presentation of these three sociology of science layers that make up the approach that we take in this book.

At the bottom of the pyramid, we have our general history and sociology of science built largely on a Kuhnian perspective. At the second level is the sociology of science literature in Political Science and IR which has centred on the question of whether external events or academic debates better explain the evolution of these disciplines. We argue in favour of incorporating both internal and external factors in our model, and that the birth and identity of ISS provides a stronger link to external events and political pressures than may be the case in Political Science as a whole.

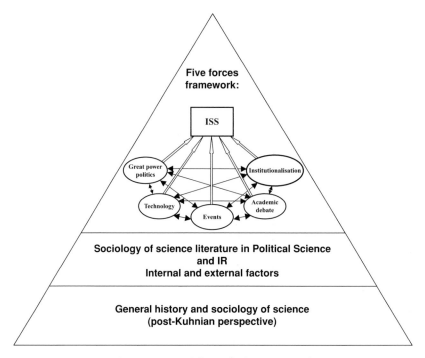

Figure 3.1. Sociology of science approach

At the top layer of the model we define the five forces and the interplay among them.

Beginning with the bottom level of the pyramid, the general sociology of science provides a broad idea of how academic disciplines – and fields and sub-fields – evolve. Kuhn's (1962) starting point was the observation that scientific discovery failed to follow the model predicted – and recommended – by Classical positivists. Positivism's model of scientific development claimed that knowledge production is (and should be) a cumulative process where researchers gradually come closer to the truth. Theories are developed and hypotheses are tested against a series of measurable observations. Yet, as Kuhn convincingly showed, scientists were quite reluctant to give up or fundamentally revise their paradigms even when key assumptions were falsified and fundamental assumptions seemed hard to justify. Kuhn argued that instead of seeing science as cumulative, one should consider it as undergoing different stages. Scientific disciplines start as pre-paradigmatic forms which develop into

paradigms based on a shared understanding of general laws, metaphysi-
cal assumptions of how 'reality' is structured, epistemological beliefs in
what constitutes good science, and respectable works and procedures.
The work that goes on inside a paradigm never fundamentally questions
key assumptions, research focus, epistemologies or world view; it is what
Kuhn described as 'normal science'. Scientific revolutions – rather than
discoveries within existing paradigms – thus come when new paradigms
are launched in opposition to older ones, usually by a new generation of
scholars whose personal and professional investment is less than in the
case of more senior ones, or by researchers coming to a discipline from
a different field, hence also with less investment in a given paradigm. A
central point is that new and old paradigms differ on such fundamental
points that they are held to be *incommensurable*: there is no way of testing
one's way out of disagreement since what is at stake is the entire framing
of the research topic, the question of what should be studied/tested and
how to interpret the results (Schmidt, 1998: 6–7). The important point
for ISS from a sociology of science perspective is that it may be difficult to
pin down exactly when paradigms are incommensurable. As Wæver notes
(1998: 716), having a debate – which may range from polite and constructive dialogue to war – itself indicates a certain modicum of cohesion and
'expresses a less than totally fragmented discipline'.

The key sociological point for our present exercise is that if knowledge
does not progress solely as a result of scientific evidence, then it is necessary
to try to take into account the other forces that play into the evolution of
any field of study. Kuhn made room for 'progress' within paradigms, but
stressed that what constituted scientific advances could only be judged by
a paradigm's own standards, not by extra-paradigmatic ones. But if there
is no given scientific standard that theories should strive to maintain, how
is it possible to make judgements about the relative merits of competing
paradigms? This question points to a key feature of academic debates as a
driving force: that in the absence of absolute, objective standards scholars
will try to establish their own ones as hegemonic. Academics, politicians,
the media and a number of other societal actors make constant claims
about which role science should play in society based on a set of deeper
political and normative judgements, and influenced by the issues, ideas
and power structures around them. ISS is a highly politicised subject
in which questions about both what should be studied and the role of
scholars vis-à-vis the security apparatus of the state have been an ongoing
source of tension and debate. To understand its evolution we need to take
on board not just the peculiar dynamics of academic debates, but also the

variety of material and ideational ways in which ISS has interacted with the wider world.

Internal versus external factors

Academic perspectives are, argued Kuhn, quite resistant in the face of 'facts' that may challenge their basic assumptions and predictions. Theories are 'filters' through which particular facts and events are granted more significance than others, and 'facts' are understood and analysed in accordance with a paradigm's basic conceptions and assumptions. Traditional security scholars would, for instance, agree that the number of deaths due to HIV/AIDS is documented, that it is very high in parts of Africa and that this strains societal and economic relations in those countries heavily affected. They would, however, not agree that this constitutes a security problem, unless military security is directly at stake (Elbe, 2003). Widening approaches may argue by contrast that HIV/AIDS constitutes a threat to societal security, that global and regional actors have successfully securitised HIV/AIDS, or that the security problems of women and children should be granted particular attention (Elbe, 2006). What is at stake in the security debates over HIV/AIDS is thus not simply the death rate as an external event, nor the material consequences thereof, but the interpretation of these facts.

A Kuhnian understanding implies at the more concrete level that we cannot expect to explain the evolution of academic disciplines as a causal process through which observed facts seamlessly propel change. Exactly how to adjudicate between internal explanations that focus on the debates within an academic field and external explanations that point to events and political developments has been a key theme in the (still sparse) literature on the evolution of IR. Schmidt (1998: 32–33) argues that 'It is a common belief that external events in the realm of international politics have more fundamentally than any other set of factors shaped the development of the field'. Taking issue with this approach, he (1998: 36) holds that 'Developments in the field of international relations have been informed more by disciplinary trends in political science and by the character of the American university than by external events taking place in international politics' (p. 38; see also Wæver, 1998: 692; Jørgensen, 2000: 10). Some events do not generate responses at all (which one would expect were there a causal relation), and events that are responded to generate multiple interpretations. Based on the political theorist Gunnell's (1993) internal approach to the evolution of the sub-discipline of Political Theory,

Schmidt (1998: 37) makes the case for a critical internal discursive history approach whose aim is 'to reconstruct as accurately as possible the history of the conversation that has been constitutive of academic international relations'.

On the whole, while we acknowledge the need to draw attention to the importance of internal dynamics in the evolution of IR and ISS, we also find the sharp dichotomy between internal and external explanations problematic for four reasons (Breitenbauch and Wivel, 2004: 416–417). First, it overdraws the extent to which external explanations are actually accepted wholeheartedly within ISS. It is hard to believe that not even the strongest empirical policy analyst or the hardest rationalist (who presumably are those advocating external explanations) would agree that theories are analytical lenses that prevent events from having a seamless or direct causal impact on disciplinary developments. Each theory might very well claim that it explains or understands the particular event better than competing theories, but that is a different claim from arguing that events causally impact the evolution of ISS as a whole.

Second, presuming that we were to adjudicate between internal and external explanations, it would be difficult if not impossible to imagine a research design that would allow for a testing of the explanatory status of the two. How does one, for instance, compare the impact of the end of the Cold War with the influence asserted by disciplinary trends? The latter are obviously crucial for how the end of the Cold War is interpreted and explained, but without this event itself there would not be this major new question on the research agenda for theories to dissect and compete over. Events may also be slightly less spectacular, but provide the ground on which more detailed internally driven debates play themselves out, as was the case of nuclear technology and Cold War deterrence theory. How would we, for instance, separate the impact of nuclear bipolarity from the import of game theory into ISS? Rather than embark on an arduous attempt to design a test, we are better suited by acknowledging that it is the interplay between internal and external factors that drives ISS.

Third, the inclusion of external explanations in our framework is supported by the general analytical claim that it is through external inputs of different kinds that academic disciplines debate and change. To rely exclusively on internal explanations would create an image of ISS – and science – as socially and politically isolated (and self-absorbed). Not only does this fit poorly, as chapters 4 to 8 will lay out, with how ISS evolved, it would produce a model which would have severe difficulties explaining change. If no inputs are made into the research process, how is it that both the balance between and the content of different ISS approaches changed over the past sixty years?

Fourth, the debate over internal and external explanations may also benefit from considering how the discipline, field or sub-field in question is situated in relation to politics and policy-making institutions. This relationship refers to the story of a discipline's founding and to how its institutional location and purpose has been debated. Academic disciplines have to different extents linked themselves explicitly to crucial external factors, including current events and political institutions. Think, for example, of the difference between the disciplines of Comparative Literature, Political Science and Physics. Since Political Science is to a much higher degree defined by a link to contemporary political events, it is also quite reasonable to expect its development to be more influenced by this factor than the other two disciplines would be. Even within the discipline of Political Science, ISS is remarkable by being founded in response to a set of (what was perceived as) very urgent 'real world/external' issues linked to the growing threat posed by the Soviet Union, particularly as it became a nuclear power. ISS definitely had a scientific ambition at its core, and as Wæver (Wæver and Buzan, 2007) has laid out, an optimism about the usefulness of science and the possibility of finding rational solutions to societal problems. Yet it was also simultaneously a discipline that aimed at delivering policy relevant knowledge. This dual ambition meant that ISS was not exclusively driven by the process of internal scientific discovery, but also by its engagement in the world of policy and by the influence of the policy world upon it. ISS has ever since been (d)riven by this intertwining of epistemological choices and a perceived obligation to speak to major political decisions (Williams, 1998). Nowhere is this more clearly illustrated than in the 'inner–outer' system in the US in which it is common for ISS writers (not all of them American) to spend part of their career in academia or think-tanks, and part of it in government. It is hard to imagine that, for better or worse, this cycle does not influence what people choose to write about and how they do so, even if not always in any predictable fashion. Comparing ISS to the field of Political Theory, for example, it may well be that the latter is explained to a higher degree by internal factors, precisely because it has not been constituted around an equally strong link with the policy world and hence does not have a similarly strong sense of external responsiveness (Gunnell, 1993).

Our conclusion at the second layer of the sociology of science is that we need a model that draws our attention to the interplay between internal and external factors, that makes their exact significance and the way in which they play into each other an empirically open question, and which furthermore provides us with a more fine-grained set of analytical tools than 'internal' and 'external'. External factors are usually discussed as one broad category where 'events' are presumably the most significant, but other external factors include great power politics and the evolution in key technologies. The resources and political agendas of foundations and think-tanks may be both an internal (to the extent that these institutions are part of ISS) and an external influence (to the extent that they grant money to ISS). We will discuss which specific driving forces to include in the next section and lay out the interplay between them.

The theoretical status of the driving forces framework

Moving now to the question of how a concrete analytical framework should be designed, we start from the assumption that it is the interplay between a set of internal and external forces that explains the evolution of ISS. We cannot think of a way of meaningfully testing the influence of each force and our proposed five forces framework is thus a 'theory' in the European sense, where the term is used for something that organises a field systematically, structures questions and establishes a coherent and rigorous set of inter-related concepts and categories, but not in the dominant American positivist sense of the term (which requires cause–effect propositions). Our dual methodology of working simultaneously from the sociology of science literature, particularly in IR, and from an inductive reading of the ISS debates themselves brought us to a framework of five forces: great power politics, technology, key events, the internal dynamics of academic debates, and institutionalisation. Several of these factors comprise both internal and external aspects, which reinforces our commitment to focus on their interplay.

Looking to the existing sociology of science literature in IR – thereby applying a more deductive methodology – those who have provided more detailed frameworks have done so with the purpose of explaining particular national approaches or, more generally, the divide between European or Continental approaches on the one hand and the American one on the other (Wæver, 1998; Jørgensen, 2000; Breitenbauch and Wivel, 2004; Wæver, 2007; Wæver and Buzan, 2007). Since what is to be explained are national (or regional) variations, there is – as in most foreign policy analysis – a logical move to emphasise explanations located at the national/regional level. The most controversial aspect of our framework may thus be that we do not include a domestic societal variable. This decision was based on the fact that our main research question was to trace and offer an explanation of the evolution of ISS as a general sub-field of IR, but that we would not attempt to cover national variations in any great detail. But since ISS was founded in the US and most of the conventional Cold War literature was driven by a US great power politics agenda, we do pay attention to specific American societal factors through the driving force of great power politics. It is true that part of the story of ISS is the evolution of distinct European and American approaches, but this is a difference that we can explain through the five driving forces without elevating societal factors to the status of a distinct driving force. Europe and the US have been situated differently in terms of great power capabilities and politics. Both during the Cold War and after, the US has had technological capabilities that Europe did not and it has been able to shoulder the costs of technological innovation in a manner that Europe could or would not afford. There were, furthermore, significant events that impacted the US and Europe differently (Vietnam, German unifi-cation and 9/11 to mention just a few), and there are different academic traditions, particularly in terms of epistemology, in the two parts of the West that again are linked to processes of institutionalisation. The five forces and particularly their interplay can in short explain the Europe/US difference especially as 'events', 'great power politics' and 'internal aca-demic debates' open up space for incorporating societal and political differences.

Although we hold that all five forces are significant for understanding the evolution of ISS, and that they are distinct in that they each constitute different lenses or forms of explanation, it is also the case that they are derived deductively from six decades of ISS literature and that not all forces may therefore be equally significant at all times. The advent of Poststructuralism in the mid-1980s was, for example, clearly connected to the general influence of Postmodern and Poststructuralist philosophy first on the humanities and later on the social sciences. Here, the driving force 'the internal dynamics of academic debate' was clearly a strong influence. Human Security, by contrast, was not linked as much to internal academic debate, but made it from the field of policy into academe (see chapter 7).

To theorise the five forces as interplaying rather than as distinct and free-standing variables implies that we may identify a transformation that starts with one, or more, force(s) which then has implications for, or at least raises questions concerning, the others. The complicated interplay between the forces implies that there is not a simple domino effect between the forces, that a change (or a continuity) that we identify in force A will automatically lead to changes in B, C, D and E. We can say that major events, like 9/11 and the end of the Cold War, apply pressure on the other forces, but exactly how different approaches to ISS then negotiate these is an empirically open question.

A good question is perhaps how the five forces relate to the ISS perspectives we examine in the chapters ahead. Is it that there are some driving forces that 'belong' to particular ISS perspectives, that great power politics for instance is a Strategic Studies force, while institutionalisation is a Constructivist one? This may seem tempting at first, but it is important to distinguish between the theoretical claims and concepts of ISS perspectives on the one hand, and how they (might) answer questions of security on the other. It would, for instance, be quite difficult to think of an ISS approach that would not accord some importance to great power politics, but approaches differ significantly in their analytical, political and normative analysis thereof. All approaches are going to point to their ability to analyse key events, but they may disagree dramatically on which events are more important, wherein their importance lies and how they should be responded to.

Analytically the forces are both a way of organising our discussion and a framework that explains the evolution of ISS, i.e. the continuity and transitions in the concept of security, the major political and empirical questions on the agenda, and the epistemology through which security is studied. This means that chapters 4 to 8, which document and analyse the evolution of ISS, are not all structured in the same way. The driving forces are used as an analytical framework in all five chapters, but with four variations.

First, 'events' has a special status in that it functions as a way of arranging the chapters into three chronological groups: chapters 4 and 5 are about the Cold War, chapters 6 and 7 are about the post-Cold War and pre-9/11, and chapter 8 is about the impact of these attacks and the subsequent 'War on Terror'. This, however, does not mean that everything changes in 1989 or 2001, but rather that these events pose a series of significant questions for ISS.

Second, there is also a division of labour logic at work that follows from the way in which the two major events in ISS have been used to structure the chapters: since chapter 5 (Cold War Challengers) is to a large extent a critical counter chapter to chapter 4 (Cold War Strategic Studies), many of the descriptions of the major events and technology need not be introduced again in chapter 5.

Third, it is, of course, not everything that fits nicely into a chronological structure, in that approaches that were first laid out during the Cold War were in most cases also important later on. Feminism and Poststructuralism were, for example, introduced into ISS in the mid–late 1980s and they are therefore dealt with at length in chapter 5. Chapter 7 will build on this presentation and ask how the end of the Cold War and the general evolution of the field of ISS impacted on these approaches. Those approaches that were genuine newcomers to the widening debate in the 1990s are thus dealt with more extensively in this chapter. These divisions of labour mean that there is a quantitative difference that one should notice (Conventional and Critical Constructivism get more pages than Poststructuralism in chapter 7), but that this does not by itself amount to a qualitative difference or to a qualitative or normative preference on our part.

Fourth, each chapter has one or more disciplinary and conceptual stories to tell or plots to unfold, and the driving forces help tell those stories (see chapter 1). But because the plots are different, the way in which the driving forces help organise the chapters also differs.

The five driving forces as general analytical categories

Great power politics

Perhaps the most obvious driver of the ISS literature has been the major movements (and non-movements) in the distribution of power among the leading states. The crystallisation of bipolarity during the late 1940s, with its peculiarly intense and militarised superpower US–Soviet rivalry, set the dominant framing of ISS for the next forty years. Within that framing, and necessary to it, was an important non-event: namely that both Western Europe collectively and Japan remained as mostly civilian powers closely associated with the US, and did not seek to reassert traditional great power military capability. This action stabilised bipolarity and extended its run. As a consequence, security analysis during the Cold War was almost synonymous with studying US–Soviet relations and a bipolar system with enmity between two superpowers whose direct and covert influence stretched around the globe. Other phenomena appeared on the research agenda, for instance the question of Third World security (Bull, 1976), but these were seen as structured (if not determined) by bipolarity.

The importance of great power politics is also evident from the debate over which polarity replaced bipolarity after the end of the Cold War, with suggestions ranging from uni- to multipolarity (Waltz, 1993; Kupchan, 1998; Huntington, 1999). Until the end of the 1980s, superpower relations had been frozen at only slightly fluctuating levels of enmity and engagement, but with the dissolution of the Soviet Union came not only a reconsideration of the polarity of the international system, but also of the relations between the great powers. Was the US going to face enemies or would its deployment of 'soft power' or 'co-optive power' stabilise the system (Nye, 1990)? And what level of resources was the US prepared to devote to security problems outside its own immediate sphere of interest (Posen and Ross, 1996/7)?

The rise of China has also been a perennial great power issue since the victory of the Chinese Communist Party in 1949, but moved more centre-stage as the only obvious 'peer competitor' to the US from the early to mid 1990s, when the demise of the Soviet Union and the economic eclipse of Japan made it more obvious. The huge expansion in China's economy, and its half-friendly, half-rivalry relationship with the West, make its status a key theme in discussions of international security, and one whose importance is almost certain to rise during the early decades of this century. The attacks on 9/11 led US policy-makers and many security analysts to define a new era. Whether the 'Global War on Terrorism' will ultimately boost or weaken the relative power of the US and exacerbate or ameliorate patterns of amity and enmity remains to be seen, but great power politics is still a key question on the agenda.

To point to great power politics as a driving force is also to note that ISS began as an American discipline, focused on American security and written by Americans (although some had emigrated from Europe to the US before or during the Second World War) (Kolodziej, 1992: 434). European approaches might have gained more ground after the end of the Cold War, but as Ayoob (1984) and Krause (1996) point out, it is still the Western model of the state which forms the core of ISS. The US-centrism that has infused the birth of ISS and its development during the Cold War means that the particularities of the US as a state and society have been, and remain still, one of the central driving forces of ISS; hence there is an analytical incorporation of a domestic societal variable under the driving force of great power politics.

US dominance was large during the Cold War, but from the 1990s onwards, with the US as the sole superpower, the particularities and peculiarities of the US became even more influential. It is not that the US is unique in having its own peculiarities: all countries do. It is that the dominant position of the US makes its peculiarities matter much more than those of less powerful states. This is a massively complicated and controversial topic which pushes enquiry towards the large literature on American exceptionalism (Buzan, 2004a: 153–182).

A distinctive feature of the US is that its geography and history have insulated it from the rigours of war and the balance of power to a much greater extent than is true for most of the countries of Eurasia. Isolationism has been an option for the US in a way that it was not for other powers, and the US has strong traditions against military entanglements and engagements abroad. It also has as its norm a higher standard of national security: a desire to be absolutely secure against outside threats as it largely was for much of its history. The Soviet threat was sufficiently global, and sufficiently challenging to the much cherished American idea that their country was the model for the future of humankind, to draw the US out of isolationism. But even though the US accepted a long-term global commitment against a broad-spectrum challenger, it still did not abandon its high standard for national security (Campbell, 1992). One can read this into both the frenzied US reaction to Sputnik (see chapter 4), and, up to a point, into the obsession with working out the last detail of deterrence logic in order to ensure that the US would not be caught at a disadvantage. Even clearer is its impact on the Anti-Ballistic Missile/Ballistic Missile Defence (ABM/BMD) project, where the promise was precisely of invulnerability to attack. The allure of that goal made ABM/BMD a central feature of US strategic thinking and policy, despite the fact that the technology has never come close to delivering the promise, and that many experts argue that it never will. It is also visible in the decision to retain unprecedentedly high relative levels of military expenditure after the end of the Cold War, though there one might want also to look at bureaucratic and domestic political factors. The high expectation of security can additionally be seen in the US response to 9/11. The shock of vulnerability ran deep in the US, in ways that it has been difficult for societies with less stringent expectations of security to understand or empathise with.

Summing up this discussion, the driving force of great power politics comprises: the distribution of power among the leading states (the polarity of the international system); the patterns of amity and enmity among the great powers; the degree of involvement and interventionism by the great powers; and their particular societal dispositions towards levels of security. These elements are to some extent related, at least according to a Realist logic. In a bipolar system, for instance, there would tend to be stronger patterns of enmity than in a multipolar one, and a bipolar system would also presuppose that its two superpowers were driven to a high degree of interventionism. One may indeed argue that a great power has to show at least the traces of a desire to be involved in global politics (Buzan and Wæver, 2003: 35). Yet while these four elements may be related they are also distinct: the bipolar structure witnessed both periods of détente and 'colder Cold Wars' where the level of amity/enmity fluctuated, and US–EU relations have done so as well over the last two decades of unipolarity combined with a European great power. And, the interventionism of the US receded after the Gulf War of 1990–91 and Somalia only to return in full with the 'intervention' in Kosovo, all under the same polarity structure. From the US concern with enemies also arises the question of whether or not the US in particular, and great powers in general, need enemies or threats in order to define themselves and ease the problems of domestic governance. As one moves into the study of enmity one may also ask more specific questions about how 'enmity identity' is constructed: is it an entire nation/civilisation or culture which is seen as radically opposed to 'Us' or is it because that country is run by a corrupt, power-mongering elite? Is enmity connected to a barbaric identity that cannot be transformed, or is it based simply on states being self-sufficient, rational actors within an anarchical structure (Hansen, 2006)?

The technological imperative

Almost equally obvious as a driver of ISS is the continuous unfolding of new technologies and the need to assess their impact on the threats, vulnerabilities and the (in)stabilities of strategic relationships. The arrival during the mid-1940s of the atom bomb was pretty much the foundational event for Strategic Studies and the impact of nuclear – and nuclear related – technology during the Cold War can hardly be exaggerated. Nuclear weapons provided a huge surplus capacity of destructive power for the first time in military history. Long-range ballistic missiles speeded up delivery times and were capable of carrying nuclear warheads, a technological development that liberated nuclear weapons from vulnerable bomber delivery systems, and greatly increased the capacity to make a first strike against opponents. Whereas nuclear warheads and intercontinental missiles were real developments feeding huge quantities of ISS literature, the enormous and ongoing literature on ABM/BMD reveals that even potential technology developments could have major impacts on both strategic relations and ISS.

Technology need not be exclusively military in kind to make an impact on ISS. The history of military and civilian technologies is often one of interplay and 'dual-use'. The Internet, for instance, was originally developed as a military technology, as a distributed network transmitting information under a nuclear attack. Nuclear technology, to take another example, has a military as well as a civil side (energy and medicine) that can be difficult to differentiate, a fact which also complicates the assessment of nuclear proliferation. The same dilemma is applicable to biological and chemical weapons or to the communications technologies applied in both civilian consumer electronics and battlefield management.

If the concept of security is expanded beyond the military sector, the list of technological factors that can drive security debates grows as well. If HIV/AIDS is seen as a threat to regional security in parts of Africa and Asia, the retroviral technology for treating those infected is key to the spread and consequences of the disease (Elbe, 2006). Or, if the environment is threatened by the effects of industrialisation, then the technologies implicated in these threats and their solution become central. The attacks on 9/11 and the 'Global War on Terrorism' show that technology and the identification of threats and enemies are intimately linked and that the list of technologies central to ISS changes over time.

The question of how technology impacts economic, political, military and cultural developments has been a topic of great debate in the social sciences and to speak about technology as a driving factor thus raises the spectre of technological determinism (Levy, 1984; Paarlberg, 2004). Yet while technology is undoubtedly a main driver in the development of ISS, it is by no means a determining one: first, because technology is itself influenced by the other driving forces; and second, because there are human agents (civilian and military, commercial and public) who make decisions about which technology to develop. The evolution of nuclear technology during the Cold War was, for example, hugely impacted by the bipolar confrontation between the US and the Soviet Union. Once in the world, technology creates pressures of its own, which again impacts the political process, but this is a complex process of feedback between technology and the other driving forces and human decisions, not one of determinism.

Events

As the discussion above has already indicated, it is impossible to imagine the birth and the evolution of ISS without the impact of key events, but it is equally important that this impact is theorised in a way that does not claim events as a causal force that simply exerts its power on a pliable academic community. Hence we theorise events in a Constructivist manner and emphasise the interplay between events and the other driving forces. Events come in various forms, and they can change not only relationships among the powers, but the academic paradigms used to understand those relationships. The most dramatic are specific crises that not only become objects of study in their own right, but which change existing understandings, relationships and practices in the wider strategic domain. Two examples of this type are the Cuba Missile Crisis in 1962 (Snyder, 1978; Weldes, 1996) and the terrorist attacks on the US on 9/11 (Barkawi, 2004; Der Derian, 2005).

Other events take the form of steady processes unfolding over time that change the knowledge, understanding and consciousness that support existing practices. A good example of this is the rise of environmental concerns and the move of the environment from a background variable to a foreground one (Ullman, 1983; Deudney, 1990). There was no specific crisis that put environmental issues into the forefront, but rather a steady drip of new information, new understandings and a rising public consciousness that grew sufficiently wide and deep to open a place for environmental security in policy debates and the ISS literature. The identification of key events might often seem common-sensical: it is not hard to see the impact of the Soviet Union gaining nuclear weapons, its dissolution in 1991, or the attacks on 9/11. Yet in analytical terms one should note that events are in fact politically and intersubjectively constituted. It is the acknowledgement (or not) by politicians, institutions, the media and the public that something is of such importance that it should be responded to, possibly even with military means, that makes it an 'event' (Hansen, 2006). Herein lies much controversy over why events that kill or maim huge numbers of people in the Third World (hunger, disease, civil war) often fail to get constructed as security events in the West.

We divide events into three categories. *Constitutive events* are those singled out by a theory as major occurrences which have given rise to the theory in question or which are seen as reinforcing the basic tenets of the theory either because they confirm central analytical assumptions or because they can be explained by the theory. A particular kind of constitutive event is what Parmar (2005) has called *catalysing events*: events that politicians or academics have been waiting for in the belief that these would 'permit their relatively unpopular ideas and schemes for a radical foreign policy shift to gain an attentive public hearing' (Parmar, 2005: 2). Catalysing events may be identified methodologically prior to an event if they are constituted as such in discourse. After the catalysing event has taken place, we may trace how it is constituted in support of the shift in question. One of the examples provided by Parmar is the Japanese attack on Pearl Harbor in 1941 which was the 'shock' that men in the US State Department felt that the isolationist public needed to enter the Second World War (Parmar, 2005: 17). As Parmar notes (2005: 8), to take advantage of catalysing events 'requires planning, organization, publicity and political positioning', which is to say that events do not become catalysing – or indeed key events at all – without the support of other driving forces.

Significant critical events are those that appear to challenge key aspects of the theory in question. Significant critical events are put on the agenda due to pressure from the media, policy initiatives or other, competing theories and they may lead the theory in question to expand its research agenda in response to these 'new questions and themes'. Or it may lead the theory to offer elaborate justifications as to why it is able to account for these alleged 'critical' events. Or it may cause the theory to offer minor adjustments to its basic assumptions and hypotheses. A good example of a significant critical event is the upsurge in so-called ethnic intra-state wars as these were taken on board by Neorealist scholars during the first half of the 1990s (Posen, 1993; Van Evera 1994; Kaufmann, 1996). The third category of events are *deferred critical events*, that is events that are constituted as significant by other political, media or academic actors, but which the theory either chooses to ignore, or to categorise as not falling within the scope of proper ISS. As an illustration of deferred critical events we may point to issues such as wartime rape, honour killings and sex-trafficking, which in spite of being granted significant media and policy attention have not led most security scholars to incorporate gender issues (Tickner, 1997, 2005; Hansen, 2000a).

Because different perspectives will constitute events differently, there is not a simple one-to-one relationship between 'the real world' and ISS. What register as events and facts are also implicated in the very conceptualisation of security within a particular approach. Since what we are tracing is the evolution of ISS and not the real world, the events that we are going to identify are also those that have been granted ISS significance. Our accounts of key events in chapters 4 to 8 are thus through the lens of what has been analysed and debated, not a balanced account of what happened in the world as such. That said, we should also understand ISS as a sub-field that is itself struggling with other sub-fields and disciplines for funding, prestige and the claim to 'policy relevance'. This means that

ISS cannot neglect entirely what other fields and actors, not least policy-makers, constitute as key events.

The internal dynamics of academic debates

A positivist model of how academic knowledge is created would, as noted above, predict that ISS has evolved progressively in response to key events, new technologies and great power politics. Hypotheses would be derived, falsified or verified, and theories revised, expanded or abandoned in response. The actual development of ISS is, however, much more con-flictual due to the absence of consensus on what scientific model should be adopted and the inherently political nature at the heart of the field. IR literature, including ISS, is much affected by current affairs, but it is also affected by changes in theoretical and epistemological fashion which may or may not have any immediate link to what is going on in the real world. Looking more systematically at the internal dynamics of academic debates, there are four dimensions within this driving force that are of significance for the evolution of ISS.

First, what drives the social sciences, including ISS, is to a large extent debates on epistemology, methodology and the choice of research focus. As shown in chapter 2, the call for objective measures and rational science has been part of ISS since the early 1950s, and discussions of epistemol-ogy and methodology have been central ever since, particularly from the late 1980s onwards. A distinctive and recurring feature of ISS debates is the dichotomy that obtains between the hard positivist understanding of theory which dominates in the US, and the softer reflectivist under-standings of theory found more widely in Europe (Wæver, 1998). This reflects a deeper divide in the whole approach to what 'theory' means in IR, as was laid out in chapter 2. US social science is particularly receptive to rationalist, economistic approaches to its subject, a feature again on display from the early years of deterrence theory and onwards whereas critical, predominantly European, approaches have emphasised interpre-tative and hermeneutic forms of analysis. Once in place, academic debates have a quite considerable life of their own. One could be cynical about this, and point to careerist motivations for doing various kinds of writ-ing, and distortions of priority created by both state and private funders, but the core fact is that academics thrive on argument, and most schol-ars believe that competition between different interpretations of things is essential to the pursuit of understanding. In the social sciences, com-peting interpretations of problems can be primarily normative, such as those between Strategic Studies on the one hand and Peace Research and Critical Security Studies (CSS) and Human Security on the other. Or they can be primarily analytical, as in the debate about whether deterrence is easy or difficult. Mixtures are also there, as in the ABM/BMD debates.

Second, academic debates in ISS are influenced by developments in other academic fields. ISS has relied upon significant imports from other disciplines, and not just on Mathematics and Economics which delivered most of the first generation of nuclear strategists. These imports include: game theory (Jervis, 1978); Cognitive Psychology (Snyder, 1978); Linguistics (Cohn, 1987; Wæver, 1995; Fierke, 1996); social theory (Dalby, 1988; Price, 1995; Wyn Jones, 1995; Krause, 1996; Hansen, 2000a; Bigo, 2002; Der Derian, 2005); Political Theory (Walker, 1990; Williams, 1998); Development and Post-colonial Studies (Ayoob, 1984; Krause, 1996; Thomas, 2001; Barkawi, 2004); and Feminist Theory (Cohn, 1987; Grant, 1992; Tickner, 2004; Hansen, 2006). The impact of these disciplines and their debates have been felt in ISS both in terms of how security should be conceptualised/what should fall under the rubric of ISS, and in terms of how it should be analysed. This, however, has not been all a one-way street: during its golden age ISS also exported to other disciplines significant advances in game theory and systems analysis.

The close relationship between ISS and IR and Political Science, and periodically to other disciplines as well, imply, as noted in chapter 1, that there is a 'frontier zone' between ISS and these adjacent fields or disciplines. The existence of frontier zones also indicates that there are different kinds of relationships between ISS and the other fields/disciplines. Most crucially there is an important difference between those ISS approaches that came out of general IR to pick ISS as a particular (difficult) case, such as Constructivism, and those, like Critical Theorists, Feminists or Post-structuralists, who chose security, not because of its epistemological or methodological status, but because this was considered a hugely important political question to engage. During the Cold War, ISS had close links to (Neo)realism, a link fortified by the division of labour between ISS and IPE, which emerged as the other great sub-field of IR in the 1970s. IPE partly defined itself against ISS, the two sub-fields carving up the terrain of IR so that IPE claimed the cooperative, joint-gains side of the subject, with ISS claiming the conflictual, relative gains one.

Third, a particular feature of academic debates in ISS which reflects its political and politicised nature concerns the political and normative status of security scholars. ISS is constituted as an academic field, which means that it gains its legitimacy from being a particular form of knowledge however broadly conceived. But it is also a field which has been formed around a set of perceived urgent policy questions and the boundary between the academic and the political, the scholar and the advisor, has thus always been a tenuous and debated one. Academics may choose to act politically, either directly as advisors or as public intellectuals who engage in debate in the attempt to influence policy decisions. The advisory role blurs in most cases the lines between scientific authority and policy advocate, while the identity of the public intellectual is built upon a particular epistemic authority that sets him or her aside from 'the average citizen'. As an illustration, many universities have a policy for how staff should be listed when making media appearances: when speaking on matters of security one gives one's university affiliation, when writing about the joys of gardening one does not. Security scholars may speak about politics, as did prominent Realists in the lead-up to the war against Iraq in 2003 (Mearsheimer and Walt, 2003), but they also need to be careful to make sure that they do not compromise their academic authority and become viewed as 'merely' politicising. Exactly where the boundary between the academic and the political is drawn can, however, be difficult to tell; it is contextually constituted and may differ from country to country and perhaps even from university to university. The combination of the high politics nature of 'security' and the absence of any objective definitions of the 'good security analyst' means that ISS has witnessed heated discussions of the drawing of the academic–advisory boundary both within and across approaches.

Fourth, ISS is also impacted by the 'meta-view' that scholars hold about how the field should evolve. This goes back to the Kuhnian discussion of academic paradigms and commensurability above and underlines that there are different views on whether ISS is – or should be – a field made up by only one approach or whether it thrives on debate across different approaches. If ISS is made up of different perspectives, are these incommensurable or is there, in spite of the different views of referent objects, threats and politics, a substantial and thematic core that ties the field together, thus constituting a 'meta-commensurability'? Do security scholars have a responsibility to engage across paradigms, or may they just as well try to either exile or ignore opponents? Different scholars have responded differently to these questions and their responses have important consequences for how ISS evolves as a field, both for its diversity and for its culture of scholarly communication and engagement. We address this explicitly in chapter 9, where we discuss whether ISS has become a delta connecting a variety of approaches or whether it has retreated into a series of inward-looking camps.

Institutionalisation

To identify institutionalisation as a driving force is to further highlight that academic debates do not unfold in an economic and structural vacuum. Simply put, for there to be an academic discipline (Political Science), or a field (IR), or a sub-field (ISS), there has to be a set of supporting institutional structures and identities. Academic disciplines and fields are not objective representations of reality, but rather particular ways of looking at, and generating knowledge about, the world (Foucault, 1969, 1970). As a consequence, it is essential for there being a field of study that there is an academic community that self-identifies as, for instance, security scholars or IR theorists. The institutionalisation of any subject involves not only the allocation of resources and the embedding of a certain process of reproduction, but also brings with it the bureaucratic dynamics of organisations. Since organisations, once established, are often hard to kill, institutionalisation also creates a type of inertia (which could be seen as momentum) carrying the past into the future. The institutionalisation of ISS through generations of hiring practices might easily breed a certain conservatism as far as broadening the concept of security is concerned. Institutionalised conceptions might also 'slow down' the impact of key events, as when Neorealism managed to reinvent itself after its failure to predict the end of the Cold War. But other aspects of institutionalisation, for instance a change in funding programmes, may also speed up the effect of other forces.

Surprisingly little has been written about this in relation to IR and ISS so we need to explain it at greater length than for the other driving forces. Simply put, institutionalisation may be seen as comprising four overlapping elements: organisational structures, funding, the dissemination of knowledge, and research networks. These are summed up in Table 3.1 and will be laid out in more detail below.

First, institutionalisation identifies the way in which ISS is conducted within – and hence supported by – a set of organisational structures. Organisations range from the academic ones of universities through

Table 3.1. *The driving force of institutionalisation*

| Organisational structures | Funding | INSTITUTIONALISATION | |
		Dissemination of knowledge	Research networks
Academic Universities - Undergraduate and graduate programmes/ degrees - Departments and positions in Security Studies *Academic/policy* Research centres *Policy/advocacy* Think-tanks	- Governments - Foundations - Universities - Think-tanks	*Academic* - Publications (books, journals, etc.) - Conferences *Public* - Expert appearances - Public intellectual	- Conferences - Digital networks - Visiting positions - Placement of PhDs

research centres to think-tanks with a more explicitly political agenda. Policy research may be carried out by all organisations, but tends to play a stronger role in think-tanks and research centres. Beginning with academic institutions, ISS is concretely influenced by the way in which departments educate, grant degrees, conduct research and fill positions on a given subject. The very fact that courses on Strategic Studies were taught from the late 1960s onwards institutionalised ISS within academe as well as in the policy world. Tenured professors make decisions on what future students learn and they decide which graduate students are accepted and on what topics. Successful graduate programmes are characterised by the ability of graduating PhDs to find jobs at respectable universities and policy institutes, and hiring policies at universities are thus extremely central to institution building (Betts, 1997).

In contrast to academic institutions which are presumed to be adopting an objective, analytical stance, think-tanks – and the foundations supporting them – are often mapped according to political–ideological categories: the American Enterprise Institute, the Heritage Foundation and the Hoover Institution are considered Conservative; the Center for Strategic and International Studies is centre-right; the Council on Foreign Relations and RAND are centrist; the Brookings Institution and the

Carnegie Endowment for International Peace are centre-left. Turning to foundations, the Ford Foundation, John D. and Catherine T. MacArthur Foundation, Pew Charitable Trusts and the Rockefeller Foundation are defined as Liberal, whereas some of the major Conservative ones include John M. Olin Foundation (closed by 2005), Sarah Scaife Foundation, Earhart Foundation and Lynde and Harry Bradley Foundation (McGann, 2007: 25, 63). These categorisations provide some indication of what work is going to be carried out or supported by the think-tank or foundation in question. Yet we should also be cautious about making rigid connections between think-tank labels and the kind of ISS research which is being supported or the policy stance adopted. Foundations and think-tanks differ in how explicit and narrowly their political agenda is defined, and they differ in how they balance or mix the scholar/advisor constellation discussed above. A particular ideological agenda may not exclude supporting works that come to quite different readings of global security politics, and hence the (Western/American) policies to be pursued. The John M. Olin Foundation, for instance, sponsored both Fukuyama's 'End of History' and Huntington's 'Clash of Civilizations' projects, which shows that institutions may also see themselves as thriving on debate (within particular parameters) (Wooster, 2006).

To point to the influence of think-tanks, one of the most politicised issues concerning institutionalisation, indicates that the boundaries around ISS can sometimes be difficult to draw. The analytical and methodological criteria we apply when distinguishing between ISS scholarship and 'pure' policy advocacy is thus an open one based on how it is viewed by others in the field. Work conducted in think-tanks may sometimes be part of ISS, as in the case of RAND scholars' path-breaking contributions to game theory and deterrence thinking, while in other cases it is perceived as so ideological that it is not a part of ISS as such. That this boundary is sometimes hard to draw is illustrated by the debate over US Neo-Conservatives and their impact on the Bush administration. As pointed out by Williams (2005: 308), Neo-Conservatives do not publish in academic journals nor do they engage in academic theoretical debate inside IR or ISS. They prefer magazines and newspapers and concrete issues, and often adopt a 'polemical language that sits uncomfortably with the culture of scholarly discourse'. Yet, argues Williams, the impact of this movement on the Bush administration and the deeper resonance between Neo-Conservative discourse and key Political Theory themes justifies a consideration of Neo-Conservatism as IR theory. This grey zone between policy and academe is on the one hand an analytical and methodological challenge – it's always easier if the material at hand falls neatly into distinct boxes – but it is also on the other hand an indication of the fact that ISS is a field that has been constituted by an ambiguous juggling of the objective detachment of the analytical observer and the passionate ideological commitment of the concerned citizen.

The discussions of the significance of think-tanks and foundations often concern their ability to influence either the policy world or the academic world of ISS. The question of political influence also comes to the fore in discussions of the links between ISS and governmental institutions. To the extent that universities and other research institutions are publicly funded they are of course dependent on governments – and parliamentary support more broadly – granting priority to higher education. Depending on the political system in question, public funding may be more or less explicitly targeted and come with particular restrictions. Much security analysis adopts an implicit view of scholar–state cooperation as either unproblematic or as desirable: since ISS should be 'policy relevant', working for the state as a consultant or periodic employee is uncontroversial. Yet, there is also a body of work that takes a much more critical view of such collaborations. Criticism may be raised in the context of particular policies, as in the debates over the US and the Vietnam War, or who 'lost' China, or policies that break with essential civil liberties and human rights. Criticism may also be raised not only against particular policies, but towards collaboration with the state in general (Oren, 2003). This view of the state ties in with state-critical approaches more broadly, particularly Poststructuralism, parts of Peace Research, and Critical Security Studies (see chapters 5 and 7).

Second, the level and kind of funding provided by governments and foundations is obviously important – without economic support it is hard to envision how organisations could work. In countries characterised by high levels of public spending on education and research it might make a significant difference that resources are invested not only in university education and research, but in research centres such as the Copenhagen Peace Research Institute (COPRI), home of the Copenhagen School (Huysmans, 1998a), the Stockholm International Peace Research Institute (SIPRI), PRIO and the Norsk Utenrikspolitisk Institutt (NUPI). Foundations have significant discretion to target their financial support towards particular programmes, and to foster or inhibit new directions. The growth in widening approaches in the 1990s was, for instance, aided by a series of American foundations (Nye and Lynn-Jones, 1988: 21; Kolodziej, 1992: 437). Funding patterns also impact ISS more indirectly through the way in which universities make internal allocation between academic departments, and within departments between different subjects. Successful degree programmes in turn provide economic input as students bring tuition fees to universities.

Third, a crucial element in the institutionalisation of academic disciplines is the formation and dissemination of its research. Academic publication works both as a way of disseminating knowledge to students through curricula and textbooks, and as a way of gaining individual and institutional academic prestige through top journals – seen by Wæver as the 'crucial institution of modern sciences' – and book publishers (Wæver, 1998: 697). Although scholars rarely make much money on their publications, to publish is a commodity that is valued within the reward system of academe in that prominent publications often generate support for the researcher's institution and hence provides the researcher in question with bargaining power when jobs and promotions come up. As a consequence, such things as the reviewing procedures adopted by top journals are significant for the degree and form of gate-keeping that may be taking place, and hence what becomes considered, and institutionalised, as legitimate research.

Another crucial component in the dissemination of academic research is conferences where researchers meet, network and test their arguments prior to official publication. While academic publications may form the backbone of a discipline's intellectual institutionalisation, the wider public dissemination might be significant as well in that this demonstrates the broader societal value of a body of research – and hence why it should be supported financially. Security scholars thus often function as public intellectuals and experts by writing op-eds and essays for a non-specialist audience and by being interviewed for print and electronic media.

Institutionalisation is not only about the impact of material resources on the waxing and waning of academic disciplines – and the sub-fields and particular approaches within them – it is also about ideational, symbolic and normative factors. Quoting institutional sociologist Richard Scott, Williams has pointed to institutionalisation as 'the process by which a given set of units and a pattern of activities come to be normatively and cognitively held in place, and practically taken for granted as lawful (whether as a matter of formal law, custom or knowledge)' (Williams, 1997: 289). Institutionalisation points to what is considered legitimate, both as an academic discipline or field and as a form of knowledge, and it relies upon and (re)produces structures of knowledge, trust and symbolic power (Williams, 1997). Here the fourth element of institutionalisation, the building of research networks and the legitimation of particular forms of research that happens within them, is hugely significant. Research networks are built through professional associations, meetings at conferences, the exchange of faculty and students through visiting programmes, the placement of graduating PhDs by senior professors, and through daily communication about research projects. To give just a brief indication of how this has changed over the six decades since ISS began, consider how email and cheap airfares have revolutionised the way in which researchers can meet and stay in touch. Although difficult to theorise, and certainly to quantify, personal sympathies and animosities may also be highly important for the way in which research communities evolve.

Summarising the brief overview of institutionalisation above, we will work with this driving force analytically and methodologically in three ways. First, we are relying upon existing accounts of different aspects of institutionalisation which are relatively empirical and historical. These accounts are usually not particularly critical of the subject under investigation, although they do not necessarily praise it either. Second, where necessary we have conducted preliminary primary research to fill in some of the gaps in the existing literature, for instance in getting an overview of the financial flows of think-tanks and foundations. Third, we deal with critiques of institutionalisation as part of ISS debates. There is, as a consequence, a division of labour between chapters 4 and 5, where the former tells a fairly straightforward story of how Strategic Studies became institutionalised and institutionally supported during the Cold War. Chapter 5 then covers both the institutionalisation of Peace Research and other alternative approaches to security that emerged in the 1980s and the critical analyses made of the institutionalisation processes covered in chapter 4. Chapters 6 to 8 follow a similar strategy of examining both the institutionalisation of the approaches covered and the latter's critical account of institutionalisation itself.

4

Strategic Studies, deterrence and the Cold War

This chapter focuses on the Cold War and the military, political, technological and strategic aspects of the superpower rivalry as theorised by the Strategic Studies core of ISS. The central theme of that story is how nuclear weapons influenced, and were influenced by, the rivalry between the US and the Soviet Union.

The distinct field of study we are calling ISS did not crystallise out until the mid-to-late 1940s, and neither the field nor the concept of security were fully formed and accepted from day one. What emerged in the US, and to a lesser extent Europe, during the 1940s and 1950s was a category of work at the intersection of military expertise and university based social science, aimed at addressing the policy problems arising from nuclear weapons and the broad-spectrum challenge posed to the West by the Soviet Union. These problems were seen as urgent. Because of their crucial contributions during the Second World War, civilian experts, mainly physicists and social scientists, could now specialise in military issues under the heading of security, which unlike 'war' or 'defence' nicely bridged the military and non-military aspects of the subject. As well as having relevant technical expertise not possessed by the military, a large and influential civilian cohort helped to address specifically American concerns about the dangers of society becoming militarised by a long-term struggle (Lasswell, 1941, 1950; Huntington, 1957; Deudney, 1995, 2007: 161 ff.). One of the reasons why this was a uniquely American moment was that this period was when the US left behind its traditional foreign policy of political isolationism and entered into long-term struggles and commitments as the central player in the global balance of power.

This momentous transition explains why the development of ISS was encouraged by US government funding for 'strategic' research. Not only was permanent global strategic engagement a new game for the US in a way that it was not for other countries, but nuclear weapons opened a new game for everyone. As succinctly put by Betts (1997: 14), 'Nuclear war spurred theorizing because it was inherently more theoretical than empirical: none had ever occurred'. As it began to be clear that the Cold War could become a drawn-out, all-encompassing and existential struggle, the idea took hold that one needed a form of integrated understanding, where different forms of knowledge could be combined. This was a major part of the reasoning behind the US National Security Act of 1947 (in addition to closer coordination of the services plus intelligence reform). When the US moved towards institutionalising an unprecedented level of military mobilisation, this could not be done purely in terms of 'war' or 'defence' without the spectre of the garrison state (Lasswell, 1941) threatening the values of American liberalism. This is a central part of the explanation for the rise of the term 'security' to cover mobilisation in more inclusive and 'civilian' terms (Wæver 2004b, 2006), and it conditioned a particular space for civilian expertise in a military-centred universe. This nexus of peculiarly American concerns explains a lot about the origins of ISS.

The first decade after the Second World War is described by David A. Baldwin (1995: 121–122) as 'the most creative and exciting period in the entire history of security studies', perhaps because 'no single research question dominated the field', hence there was a broader consideration of non-military techniques of statecraft and of domestic affairs than later became the norm. As the Cold War went on and Security Studies went through its so-called golden age between 1955 and 1965, these conceptual discussions receded and the sub-field became almost exclusively devoted to the study of nuclear weapons and bipolar rivalry. One of the central plotlines of this chapter is how the Strategic Studies understanding of the state, dangers and insecurities became institutionalised to such an extent that the majority of Strategic Studies literature felt no need to explicitly discuss its conceptualisation of security.

This did not, however, mean that there were no debates within ISS and the four questions laid out in chapter 2 resurfaced in discussions of the rationality of states in general, and the Soviet Union in particular, and hence over the way in which security politics should be understood. There was also a recurring concern with the significance of societal cohesion, in the West as well as the Soviet Union. While there was general agreement that the latter was the enemy of the US and the so-called Free World, there were rich discussions of the interplay between technology and amity/enmity which had an impact both on how Cold War contestations of Strategic Studies were made and on post-Cold War debates on the role of the state and military technology. ISS was simultaneously productive, influential and fashionable. With its core centred around game theory and nuclear deterrence, it had the appearance of being method-ologically coherent, and because of the explicit link to public policy it was also generously funded. This 'golden age' was the formative period of the new sub-field, and therefore defined the position from which subsequent studies of the subject had to proceed.

The main goal of this chapter is to show in more detail how the five driving forces can explain both the initial demand for ISS, its first concep-tually driven decade and its continued evolution through the golden age of Strategic Studies and into the later parts of the Cold War. The detailed story of how nuclear strategy evolved during its first four decades has been told by Freedman (1981a), and it is not our intention to repeat that effort here. Instead, we want to locate the main themes of that literature within a broad brush story of the historical background to the literature of ISS. But the Cold War period is not just interesting as history. It estab-lished the meaning of what 'international security' is about, and did so with sufficient depth that this still serves as the centre of gravity around which the many subsequent widening and deepening debates within ISS revolve.

Great power politics: the Cold War and bipolarity

The Cold War emerged during the mid-to-late 1940s as the new power structure created by the outcome of the Second World War settled into place. Its two big defining features came into play almost simultaneously: nuclear weapons and a rivalry between the US and the Soviet Union. This rivalry was made exceptionally intense not only because they were the big winners of the 1939–45 war, overawing all of the other erstwhile great powers, but also because they were the champions of mutually exclu-sive ideologies (democratic capitalism, totalitarian communism) each of which claimed to own the future of humankind. This rivalry, and the fact that the US and the Soviet Union quickly became by far the largest holders of nuclear weapons, was captured in the concepts of *superpower* and *bipolarity*. One enduring question of both the Strategic Studies and IR theory debates was whether the simple fact of bipolarity, or the exis-tence of nuclear weapons, did more to explain the character of the Cold War (Waltz, 1964; Goldgeier and McFaul, 1992: 469, 490). Was bipolarity stable simply because a two-party, zero-sum game eliminated much of the uncertainty and possibility of miscalculation from superpower relations, as Waltz (1979) so famously maintained? Or was bipolarity intrinsically unstable, as suggested by Classical bipolarities: wars to the death between

Athens and Sparta, and Rome and Carthage? If bipolarity was unstable, then only the fear of national obliteration posed by nuclear weapons stopped it from spiralling into war.

There was some challenge to the bipolar framing from China after Mao's break with Moscow in the late 1950s, with some thinking of China as a third power, at least in Asia, because of its willingness to challenge both superpowers (Hinton, 1975; Segal, 1982). Yet the bipolar framework held firm throughout the more than four decades of the Cold War. Japan and Western Europe were closely allied with the US and accepted its military dominance and leadership. Even when they surpassed the Soviet Union economically, both remained politically weak, and the US remained very much the dominant partner in both the North Atlantic Treaty Organization (NATO) and the bilateral alliance with Japan. With the brief exception of the 'Japan as number 1' flourish in the late 1980s, neither sought to, nor was thought able to, challenge bipolarity. The huge superpower military establishments and arsenals of nuclear weapons sustained it even after the economic challenge from the Soviet Union (which seemed formidable in the 1950s and 1960s) had faded into palpable backwardness and decline. This meant that right to the end of the Cold War, bipolarity stood as the general framing for nearly all strategic theorising. Whether it was about deterrence, arms racing, arms control or alliances, the underpinning assumption of Cold War Strategic Studies was bipolarity (Buzan, 1987a: 173–177). This assumption is extraordinarily prominent in deterrence theory, and goes some way to explaining the attractions of game theory, especially 'chicken' and 'the prisoner's dilemma' (Snyder, 1971). These two games depend on two-player assumptions (without which they quickly get too complicated) and thus mirror bipolarity. Bipolarity also explains US and Soviet sensitivity to nuclear proliferation, which more than anything else could threaten their status and privileges as the only members of 'the big two' club.

The bipolar framing of the Cold War manifested itself in the geostrategic policy of containment. The rivalry between the US and the Soviet Union developed from the ceasefire lines of the Second World War, and quickly settled into a US attempt to ring the Soviet bloc with allies (NATO, Japan, Iran, Pakistan, South Korea, Thailand, Taiwan, etc.) to prevent further expansion of the communist world. The Soviet response was to try to breach, or jump over, these containment barriers. This strongly territorial formation explains the significance of crises in Berlin, Korea, Cuba, the Middle East and Vietnam, all of which were seen as crucial to maintaining or breaching the lines of containment. Once China emerged as a power opposed to both the US and the Soviet Union, a secondary game of containment opened up with the Soviet Union trying to contain China by making alliances with India and Vietnam. The communist victory in China was initially seen in the West as a big victory for Moscow, but by the mid-1970s China could be seen in Washington as part of the containment of the Soviet Union.

Two of the other analytical components of great power politics laid out in chapter 3 are the patterns of amity and enmity among the great powers and their degree of involvement and interventionism. In Cold War ISS these two components were deeply intertwined in that the Soviet Union was viewed as a hostile enemy Other whose communist ideology professed the downfall of capitalist societies and the subsequent spread of communism to the whole planet. In the West, and especially in the US, a characterisation of the Soviet Union as a ruthless and implacable opponent requiring long-term containment and vigorous ideological challenge quickly became sedimented as the foundation of US policy. Part of this rivalry was the necessity to prove false the Marxist projection of capitalism as exploitative, polarising and doomed to terminal crisis. The broad-spectrum nature of the challenge from the Soviet Union was a key reason for the shift to policies based around the concept of *national security* (Smoke, 1975; Yergin, 1978; Neocleous, 2006a), which itself became an ongoing subject of debate in the literature (Wolfers, 1952; Buzan, 1983). Kennan's (1947) powerful 'X' article was instrumental in setting this path, and his image of the Soviet Union remained deeply influential through to the end of the Cold War. Although constituting its foreign policy and intentions in radically different terms, the US shared the Soviet Union's interventionist – and messianic – stance, in that it, too, believed in the eventual downfall of the opponent's political and economic system and the rise of a global order based on its own model. As in communist ideology, this stance was grounded in an economic analysis combined with an unquestioned normative certainty about the virtues of one's own societal mode of organisation.

Yet if there was general consensus that the Soviet Union was radically opposed to the West, and the US in particular, there were still crucial differences as to how Soviet Otherness and enmity was constituted. These differences grew out of more general assumptions about the state and the international system and thus also pointed to different ways in which nuclear bipolarity could be managed. The first line of discussion was over how to define Soviet intentions. Kennan famously held in this 'X-article' in 1947 that the Soviet leadership was inextricably tied to an ideology of communist superiority and capitalist downfall. Hence one should take no expressions of trust and accommodation at face value but view them as tactics in the battle for long-term domination. Soviet officials were like 'toy automobiles' unable to break from the party line and 'unamenable to argument or reason which comes to them from outside sources' (Kennan, 1947: 574). Kennan's remedy was an unwavering containment of the Soviet Union 'at every point where they show signs of encroaching upon the interests of a peaceful and stable world' (Kennan, 1947: 581). Others argued that the Soviet Union took a much less aggressive stance. The founding father of Neorealist theory, Waltz held, for example, that the Soviet Union had 'assumed a posture of passive deterrence vis-à-vis her major adversary, whom she quite sensibly does not want to fight' (Waltz, 1964: 885). Waltz came to a different view of the Soviet Union, not because he held a more amiable view of Soviet ideology and its leaders, but because in his theory, bipolarity exerted a disciplining effect on the leaders of great power states that 'will strongly encourage them to act in ways better than their characters might otherwise lead one to expect' (Waltz, 1964: 907). Two further assumptions underlay Waltz's structural analysis. First was that international polarity held a stronger explanatory power than unit-level factors like ideology or the composition of a state's leadership. Second was the view that the Soviet Union was fundamentally a rational actor capable of understanding that managing nuclear bipolarity rather than embarking on an expansionist military policy would be in its own best interest.

In the later period of the Cold War, the debate over rationality was influenced by a growing concern with the extent to which the Soviet Union was in several important respects a different type of actor from the US, with different concerns and understandings (Kolcowicz, 1971; Ermarth, 1978; Snow, 1979; Gray, 1980; Holloway, 1980; Erickson, 1982; Hanson, 1982/3). Was the Soviet Union ruthless, expansionary and driven by revolutionary fervour, or was it essentially defensive and moved by feelings of inferiority to the West? What difference did Russian military culture and tradition make, and did the Soviets understand concepts such as deterrence in the same way as Western theorists and policy-makers did? Did the Russian language, indeed, have a word for deterrence? Could the Soviets be trusted to pursue apparent joint interests in survival and accident avoidance, or was the Kremlin not to be trusted to keep agreements, and to be assumed as always seeking strategic advantage under the guise of arms control? Did they calculate 'unacceptable damage' in the same way as Americans did, or was the Soviet Union, and even more so Mao's China, a hard and ruthless player, prepared to accept huge casualties, while the US was relatively soft and easy to threaten?

Waltzian Neorealism was built on the assumption that states, including the Soviet Union, were rational actors, and other scholars such as Jervis held that Soviet military doctrine was not that dissimilar to that of American military officials, that their 'ideas are not particularly Russian or particularly Marxist but simply those one would expect from people charged with protecting society and winning wars' (Jervis, 1979/80: 630). The Russians understood 'very well the potency of the American threat to destroy their society'; the difference between the two countries resided rather in the different distributions of power between civilian and military leadership (Jervis, 1979/80: 630). Others agreed with Kennan that more fundamental differences between the East and West were to be found. According to Colin S. Gray (1980: 139), there were 'no functional Soviet equivalents to the Western theories of deterrence, limited war, and arms control, just as the key Western concepts spawned by those theories – stability, escalation control, bargaining, sufficiency/adequacy, and the rest – appear to play no identifiable role in guiding Soviet military planning'. Those who emphasised Soviet difference fell into two broad camps: there were those who, like Kennan, linked Soviet enmity to the communist ideology of its leadership, while arguing that the Russian people were inadequately represented by this ideology and would eventually topple 'their' leaders. Others like Gray claimed that what explained the adoption of this ideology was 'a Russian national political character marked by cunning, brutality, and submissiveness' and that Soviet strategic culture was thus 'at root, Russian rather than Marxist-Leninist' (Gray, 1980: 142). Although couched in more concrete, empirical terms, these discussions foreshadowed later ISS debates over the significance of cultural factors versus material capabilities, and of the importance of societal cohesion and 'national identity fit' between governors and governed.

There was no easy way of settling such questions: Western access to the Soviet Union and China was severely restricted and estimates of their intentions were thus deduced from a combination of these countries' observed behaviour, and assumptions about ideology, national identity and structure of government. The tricky thing was that behaviour often lent itself to multiple interpretations depending on which deeper assumptions about actor rationality and the specific views of the enemy Other ISS analysts held. Underneath these debates was also a more fundamental analytical difference between Neorealist explanations located at the level of the international structure where actor rationality was a basic ontological assumption, and unit-level explanations that allowed for a greater range of 'irrational' behaviours where 'rationality' itself was contextualised and changing over time and space. Game theory, which constituted an important part of ISS – particularly since the absence of nuclear exchanges between the superpowers created an analytical space for the modelling of hypothetical encounters – can be seen as taking up a middle ground. Most games allowed for multiple (initial) forms of state rationality (cooperative, deceiving, secretive, distrustful, etc.), but also often positioned the ability of states to recognise the virtues of cooperative behaviour if games were played repeatedly, hence becoming more 'rational' (Jervis, 1978). As a consequence, at the core of ISS were diverging empirical as well as normative views of how the patterns of amity and enmity could evolve, leaving the dispute about them as part of what differentiated hardliners, moderates and pursuers of peace (more on this in chapter 5). One should note that ISS deterrence logic, the difference between particular approaches above notwithstanding, always entailed a fundamental ambiguity. A minimum of common understanding and rationality between the two great powers had on the one hand to be assumed for deterrence to work. If the Soviet Union was flat out unpredictable and insane it would not make much difference which strategies the West adopted and it might well be the safest thing to do to initiate a preventive attack. On the other hand, deterrence logic always retained an element of uncertainty at its core: even if the Soviets were presumably sufficiently rational not to attack out of the blue, how could one know for sure? The advent, spread and development of nuclear weaponry made the answers to these questions of the utmost importance.

The technological imperative: the nuclear revolution in military affairs

The development of Cold War Strategic Studies took place in a context in which the bipolar power political framework of the Cold War became broadly stable, but the technology surrounding nuclear weapons was highly dynamic. Nuclear weapons technology (meaning not just the warheads themselves, but also their delivery systems) underwent very rapid and dramatic development throughout the Cold War, and indeed beyond, generating an ongoing strategic imperative that lay at the heart of the problematique of ISS. Discussion of the evolutions of military technology and their strategic consequences became the principal concern of the literature (Brodie, 1976; Snow, 1979; Martin, 1980; Luttwak,

1980a; Buzan, 1987a). During these decades, nuclear weapons and many of their associated systems were in the middle stage of the classic 'S-curve' of technological development where improvements are rapid before the technology matures and its performances level out. To get a sense of this 'S-curve' think of the long and very slow development of aircraft during the nineteenth century, the extremely rapid developments in range, speed, size, altitude and reliability from the Wright brothers' flight in 1903 to Concorde and the SR-71 in the 1970s, and the levelling out thereafter.

Explosive power multiplied many times. Accuracies of delivery shrank from several kilometres to a few metres. Unstoppable ballistic missiles replaced vulnerable bombers as the principal carrier of nuclear weapons, in the process reducing potential delivery times from many hours to thirty minutes or less. The power-to-weight ratios of warheads improved hugely, meaning first that smaller rockets could carry the same payloads, and later that one rocket could carry many warheads. Smaller, lighter warheads meant that nuclear weapons could be mounted onto tactical missiles and even put into artillery shells. Missiles became not only more accurate, but more reliable, and with solid instead of liquid fuel having response times of seconds rather than hours. All of these developments enabled missiles to be sent to sea in submarines, making them very difficult to detect, and potentially shortening the warning time between launch and arrival to a few minutes. Rocket, radar and guidance technology improved to the point where it became technically possible, and in the US context politically necessary, to think about developing ABM systems. All of this was neatly summed up by Brown's (1977: 153) observation that:

> For thousands of years before [1945] firepower had been so scarce a resource that the supreme test of generalship lay in conserving it for application at the crucial time and place. Suddenly it promised to become so abundant that it would be madness ever to release more than the tiniest fraction of the total quantity available.

By the late 1970s the superpowers had accumulated many tens of thousands of nuclear warheads, so the point about the 'tiniest fraction' was not merely rhetorical.

As noted above, bipolarity conditioned the whole argument about nuclear deterrence, but this general truth was moderated by the specific nature of the military balance between the US and the Soviet Union, which varied over time. Until the mid-1950s, the US had a monopoly first of nuclear weapons, and then of long-range bombers with which to deliver them. Deterrence was easy for the US under these conditions, with the Soviets having only their conventional military superiority and nuclear threats in Europe to offer a counter-threat. The launching of Sputnik in 1957 changed all this, by demonstrating that the Soviet Union had mastered (if not yet deployed) rocket technologies that would enable them to strike the US quickly and unstoppably, and also threaten the then largely bomber-based US nuclear forces. From the late 1950s onwards, and as anticipated by the early writers on the nuclear age, the game was increasingly one of mutual nuclear deterrence with the Soviet Union moving steadily towards a general nuclear parity with the US. This process was not smooth. Large uncertainties were introduced not just by technological developments, but also by misinformation about who had deployed what: the bomber and missile 'gaps' of the mid and late 1950s, in which Soviet secrecy and American domestic politics combined to produce huge US overreactions to non-existent Soviet 'leads'. During the 1950s and 1960s the basic rules and dynamics of mutual nuclear deterrence were worked out in detail (Kissinger, 1957; Wohlstetter, 1959; Kahn, 1960, 1962; Schelling, 1960), though many had been anticipated by earlier writers responding to the first arrival of nuclear weapons (Brodie, 1946, 1949; Blackett, 1948). Whether these theoretically elegant rules of the game would actually work during a real crisis was an ongoing question. Could decision-makers stay rational in a crisis (Green, 1966; Allison, 1971; Jervis, 1976)? Would the armed forces actually follow the official policy, or would their implementation of orders in effect create escalation? During the 1970s the US more or less accepted nuclear parity with the Soviet Union as the basis for arms control negotiations, though this position was rolled back during the increased tension of the so-called 'Second Cold War' from the late 1970s to the mid-1980s, when the Reagan administration pursued defences against ballistic missiles and other aspects of warfighting strategy as a way of reasserting US superiority.

Technological developments locked the superpowers into a fierce arms race with both quantitative (how many missiles/warheads?) and also qualitative (how accurate, how quickly delivered, how well protected against pre-emptive attacks?) dimensions (Wohlstetter, 1974). They also generated an accompanying space race, in which the two superpowers competed to be first to master orbital, then manned orbital and interplanetary probes, and finally moon-landing technologies. Arms racing not surprisingly became another staple topic in the literature (Huntington, 1958;

Gray, 1971, 1974; Bellany, 1975; Rattinger, 1976; Hollist, 1977; Russett, 1983: Levine and Carlton, 1986; Buzan, 1987a: 69–131), giving yet more weight to what seemed to be the material driving forces defining the strategic agenda. There were obvious comparisons to be made between earlier arms races, such as the famous naval rivalry between Britain and Germany before 1914, and the nuclear race between the superpowers. Both reflected the continuous pressure of rapid technological development on military options that had been a feature of international relations since the industrial revolution (Buzan, 1987a). Like earlier industrial arms races, the superpower one was driven not just by action–reaction between rivals, and more or less autonomous improvements in technology, but also by the lobbying power of arms industries and military establishments. Eisenhower's warning about the influence of a 'military–industrial complex' (MIC) in American life unfolded into a whole literature on how domestic politics influenced what sorts and amounts of weapons the superpowers acquired (Kurth, 1973; Rosen, 1973; Allison and Morris, 1975; Freedman, 1981a: ch. 22; Evangelista, 1984, 1988; Buzan, 1987a: 94–113; McNaugher, 1987).

An interesting theme in the literature on the MIC was that while the US had an MIC, and so faced the problem of domestic industrial and military interests taking advantage of the Cold War to further their own goals, the Soviet Union virtually was an MIC, with a large part of its economy devoted to the production of military power. That the US was a capitalist democracy mattered, and played importantly into the general American enthusiasm for – and belief in – technological and scientific solutions (Wæver and Buzan, 2007: 386). On the one hand, one might think that capitalist political economies, with their general preference for capital over labour, would naturally lean towards high technology solutions to military challenges. The logic of capitalism points to capital intensive solutions regardless of whether the problem is production or destruction, a leaning reinforced by a democracy's natural desire to minimise risks to its citizen/soldiers. On the other hand, the very awareness of the MIC in the US reflected a keen and sustained interest in the economics of defence. Despite the 'gold-plated' reputation of US military procurement, the strategic debates were not just driven by new developments in technology and calculations of Soviet military capability. Discussions about possible new technologies were also much concerned with cost-effectiveness, and calculations about how to achieve desired military goals in the most economic fashion (Kapstein, 1992). And while the US was not close to the Soviet model of being an MIC, it is clear that the large and sustained US military expenditure served Keynesian purposes (i.e. the state channelling large sums of public money into the economy) for the US economy that it would have been ideologically difficult for US governments to do without making themselves vulnerable to charges of socialism or big-government. In other words, military spending in the US played the same role that government spending on industrial policy played in most other Western states. Unlike in Europe, where there was no ideological barrier to Keynesian state spending, this element of military Keynesianism in the US eased the politics of military budgets (Russett, 1983).

But regardless of whether the development and acquisition of new military technology was driven domestically or by arms racing, the fear was that failure to keep up would make one's nuclear forces vulnerable to first strike by the enemy. Any such development would neutralise the effects of mutual deterrence by fear of retaliation on which both sides relied. For example, if one's missiles were liquid-fuelled, and took an hour to launch, but one's opponent could launch a surprise attack which would give only thirty minutes' warning, then the opponent had powerful incentives to strike first. From this foundational insecurity arose a huge and elaborate body of theory and argument about incentives to attack (or not) under various conditions of nuclear balance, and the need to create a 'secure second strike' force able to retaliate even after a major first strike (Wohlstetter, 1959; Rosecrance, 1975; Howard, 1979; Jervis, 1979, 1979/80; Art, 1980; Gray, 1980; Lodal, 1980; Weltman, 1981/2; George, 1984; Allison *et al.*, 1985). Formal theoretic ways of thinking were called in to help in understanding the 'game' of deterrence and bipolar superpower rivalry (Snyder, 1971; Jervis, 1978).

Much of this literature was heavily dependent on the assumptions of rationality laid out above (Steinbruner, 1976; Snyder, 1978) to work out the great chains of if–then propositions that characterised deterrence theory: if A attacks B in a given way, what is B's best response, and what would A then do in reply, and then . . . and then . . . The foundational insecurity here was that of being disarmed by one's opponent in a first strike (a so-called 'counterforce' strike). This fear was real in the early phases of the Cold War when nuclear arsenals were relatively small, slow to launch and not well protected. It diminished from the later 1960s as nuclear arsenals got larger and much harder to attack (particularly when missiles were put into submarines), giving an effective secure second strike. But it was replaced by another, more subtle, fear known as the *ex ante ex post* dilemma (Rosecrance, 1975: 11–12; Steinbruner, 1976: 231–234). This envisaged a counterforce attack by one side (B) against the other (A) in which A loses more of its nuclear weapons than B uses in its first strike. Such an outcome was plausible if the attacker used the multiple warhead missiles that became widely available during the 1970s. If B attacked with ten missiles each with ten warheads, it might eliminate up to 100 of A's missiles. The dilemma is about what A would then do. It is not completely disarmed, and could either retaliate by striking B's missile silos or B's cities. Attacking B's silos would be potentially wasteful of A's remaining missiles because it is unclear which ones are empty and which ones are still holding missiles. The chances of eliminating B's ability to retaliate would thus be slim. Alternatively, escalating by attacking B's cities would mean effectively committing suicide, because B would then be able to use its remaining missiles to retaliate and destroy A's cities. Would rationality suggest that A should not retaliate in the first place, thereby having to accept the attack without making any retaliation? To do that might indeed be rational, but the possibility of it undermined the whole structure of deterrence by seeming to give incentives for aggressors to make counterforce first strikes. Getting these great chains of reasoning right was seen as crucial to developing the best military options that would deter the enemy from attacking in the first place.

The seeming impossibility of working out plausible rational responses across the entire range of complexities thrown up by nuclear war scenarios, led to an increasing acceptance that the effectiveness of deterrence lay in the possibility, or even likelihood, of irrational behaviour. Not many continued to believe that the rationality assumption would hold once nuclear exchanges, even limited ones, began. The 'threat that leaves something to chance' (Schelling, 1960: ch. 8) was a theoretically sophisticated answer to the otherwise unsolvable *ex ante ex post* policy dilemma. Potential attackers would be deterred precisely by the fear of an irrational response, whether on the individual level (anger, revenge), or the bureaucratic one (breakdown in command and control). But if deterrence depended on irrationality, then much of the incentive for elaborate theoretical scenario spinning, and thus for Strategic Studies itself, went out the window.

The whole edifice of deterrence theory was also continuously under pressure from new developments in technology that might make one more, or less, vulnerable to attack, and often the arguments were about which types of technology to pursue (or not) in order to improve one's position. Much ink was spilled among other technological choices over the costs and benefits of putting multiple warheads on missiles; of pursuing high levels of accuracy with so-called precision-guided munitions; of developing supersonic bombers; of developing neutron bombs (designed to produce a lot of radiation and little blast, so killing people but not destroying property); of deploying cruise missiles; and of building elaborate protected hiding places for land-based intercontinental ballistic missiles.

One of the fiercest, and still ongoing, debates of this sort was about ABM, aka BMD, systems, under argument since the late 1960s (Stone, 1968; Brodie, 1978; Lodal, 1980; Independent Commission on Disarmament and Security Issues, 1982; Glaser, 1984, 1985; Hoffman, 1985), and still today (Glaser and Fetter, 2001; Powell, 2003; Karp, 2004). Part of the argument was about whether it could be done or not with existing or likely technology, and involved everything from particle beams mounted on orbiting satellites to super-fast interceptor rockets and elaborate radars. But the more interesting theoretical part was about what impact deployment of an effective, or even partly effective, BMD would have on strategic nuclear stability. The immediate allure was that BMD offered an escape from the whole logic of deterrence, and especially from having one's population held hostage under the grim, but supposedly stabilising, logic of the Cold War's most notorious acronym, MAD (Mutually Assured Destruction). It could thus be posed as a return to national defence by blocking an attack. One obvious problem was that this defensive measure would give its first possessor a free hand to launch an offensive first strike against its rival without fear of retaliation. Another was that, unit for unit, BMD was always going to be much more expensive to deploy than offensive missiles because shooting down missiles was intrinsically and massively more difficult than simply firing them from one place to another. Moves towards BMD thus threatened to trigger an unending arms race in which BMD deployments would be countered by the addition of enough offensive missiles equipped with penetration aids to swamp the system. In the event, and mainly because mastering the technology looked like a fabulously expensive venture of very uncertain outcome, the two superpowers deferred this issue in the ABM Treaty of 1972, which restricted deployment but not research. Ronald Reagan's SDI in the early 1980s, designed partly as an attempted escape from MAD, and partly to roll back the strategic parity that the US had accorded the Soviet Union during the 1970s, put BMD back onto the US agenda, where it has remained ever since. With its promise of escape from MAD, BMD proved particularly attractive in US domestic politics, helped there by its appeal to enthusiasm for technological fixes, and its amenability to being staged as defensive (the protests of strategists about its destabilising consequences notwithstanding).

In addition to the pressures from rapidly evolving technologies, there was an ongoing fundamental disagreement about the basic nature of nuclear deterrence itself, and whether it was easy or difficult to achieve (Jervis, 1979/80; Gray, 1980; Lodal, 1980; Buzan, 1987a: 173–196). In part this overlapped with the technology debates, but apart from assuming the existence of deliverable nuclear weapons it was not heavily dependent on their details. Some thought that nuclear weapons made deterrence easy, because any even half-rational actor would be given extremely serious pause by the prospect of obliteration. In other words, possession of a nuclear arsenal sufficient for 'assured destruction' would basically suffice, leading to a so-called 'minimum deterrence' strategy. Others, taking a maximum deterrence approach, calculated that a ruthless rational actor (as Kennan had postulated the Soviet Union to be) would require not only a threat of high damage, but also a near certain probability that such a retaliation would be delivered, before deterrence could be effective. Because of the *ex ante ex post* dilemma outlined above, providing a high certainty of retaliation under conditions of mutual deterrence was difficult. Logic might dictate that retaliating after being struck was an irrational act, thus opening the opportunity for the ruthless aggressor to think about attacking in the first place.

Minimum deterrence offered a kind of stability in easy parity, and also economy, but at the risk of vulnerability to utterly ruthless opponents prepared to gamble in the face of huge threats to their own survival. Its logic also provided incentives for so-called 'horizontal' nuclear proliferation (the spread of nuclear weapons to states not previously possessing them), making it seem fairly straightforward for lesser powers to acquire a great equaliser (Waltz, 1981). Bipolarity defined a nuclear club of two, and associated nuclear weapons with superpower status. Britain, France and China had, by the early 1960s, joined the nuclear club, obliging the two superpowers to assert their difference by acquiring much bigger nuclear arsenals than the new arrivals. One of the few things the US and the Soviet Union agreed on was that they did not want additional nuclear powers. This concern was initially focused on other industrialised states, particularly Germany and Japan, but during the 1970s shifted more to Third World states such as Argentina, Brazil and India, and also to Israel and the Middle East, and South Africa. Any horizontal proliferation not only questioned the superpowers' status, and complicated their options for military interventions, but also raised the risk of nuclear war, whether intentional or accidental. In what became the leading example of superpower cooperation during the Cold War, the US and the Soviet Union led the way in promoting a nuclear non-proliferation regime which tried to promote the spread of civil nuclear technology while blocking the acquisition of military nuclear capabilities by other states. Although mainly subordinate to the agenda driven by expanding and evolving superpower nuclear arsenals, horizontal nuclear (non-)proliferation became a large and elaborate subject in its own right within the Cold War ISS literature, which we will look at in chapter 5.

In contrast to minimum deterrence, maximum deterrence thinking offered higher entrance costs to would-be nuclear weapon states, and an expensive, open-ended arms race to existing nuclear weapon states. The supposed gain was to close loopholes against extreme aggressors who might take risks along the lines of the *ex ante ex post* dilemma, or try to find other ways around the military paralysis of nuclear deterrence by, for example, making small, swift, military attacks. Dealing with this contingency generated demands for huge and elaborate forces capable of responding to aggression at any level, and of maintaining 'escalation dominance' throughout a complicated and possibly extended spectrum of conventional and nuclear warfighting. Maximum deterrence thinking rested on the assumption of a highly aggressive, risk-taking and opportunistic opponent. Given the experiences of the Second World War (the successful surprise attacks by Japan on the US and by Germany on the Soviet Union), this assumption was not historically unreasonable, and was supported by the understanding of the Soviet Union in the US embedded by Kennan. Maximum deterrence thinking was pushed along by three factors: a certainty-seeking understanding of the logic of bipolar deterrence plus a high threat perception of the Soviet Union; successful lobbying within the US by the MIC (Kurth, 1973); and the problem of extended deterrence that arose when the US guarantees to protect Europe had to be implemented in the face of a growing Soviet ability to strike the US with nuclear weapons.

Extended deterrence (ED) links the technological driver to the great power politics theme discussed above. Mutual nuclear deterrence exclusively between the US and the Soviet Union was a fairly straightforward proposition, albeit with some pretty complicated ramifications. But during the period when it had a nuclear monopoly, the US took on an obligation to defend Western Europe from the Soviet Union (embodied in the 1949 NATO alliance). Extending the US nuclear umbrella was uncomplicated when the US nuclear monopoly made deterrence easy, even in the face of much superior Soviet conventional military strength in Europe. But it became fiendishly difficult when the Soviets also acquired the capability to threaten the US with nuclear weapons. How could the European allies believe that the US would retaliate against the Soviet Union for, say, an attack on West Germany, when the consequence could be Soviet retaliation against American cities? This question and its many variants haunted Western strategic thinking from Sputnik onwards (Beaufre, 1965; Rosecrance, 1975; Snyder, 1978; Jervis, 1979/80; Gray, 1980; Martin 1980; Cordesman, 1982; George, 1984; Huth and Russett, 1984; Allison *et al.*, 1985; Huth, 1988). It was also central to the literature on NATO and its recurrent discontents over especially nuclear strategy, which was another major theme in the ISS literature (Luttwak, 1980a; Bertram, 1981/2; Freedman, 1981/2; Hoffmann, 1981/2; Treverton, 1983; Duffield, 1991; Zagare and Kilgour, 1995).

The questions arising from ED were addressed, though not settled, in various ways. Uncertainty over the US nuclear guarantee provided incentives for the European powers to acquire their own nuclear deterrents (which Britain had already done, and France proceeded to do), and made for a kind of permanent crisis in NATO about the credibility of its deterrent posture and the division of labour between the US and its European allies. Mainly it pushed the US into taking various measures to strengthen its commitment (by basing its own troops in Europe in substantial numbers), and to increase the risks to the Soviet Union of 'salami tactics' (taking one slice at a time and so staying below the threshold at which nuclear weapons would be used) by such measures as integrating so-called 'tactical' nuclear weapons ('tactical' being mainly defined by short or intermediate, rather than intercontinental range) into NATO's forward deployments. 'Flexible response', as this doctrine came to be known, led inexorably towards the logic of maximum deterrence by trying to find force deployments able to meet all of the possible types and levels of Soviet threat to Europe. Since NATO never managed to match Soviet conventional strength in Europe, the commitment to extended deterrence fed the nuclear logic that strengthened maximum deterrence thinking and policy in the US. Europe was always the main issue in extended deterrence, but the problem affected US relations with other allies such as South Korea and Japan, which were also under its nuclear umbrella.

Extended deterrence and flexible response spurred another concern intrinsic to the whole logic of maximum deterrence, and also linked to rival superpower interventions in crises and conflicts in the Third World: escalation and how to control it (Ball, 1981; Clark, 1982; George, 1984; Allison *et al.*, 1985). The practice of extended deterrence inevitably led to scenarios about low-level warfighting in response to local aggression, and how to respond if the opponent raised the ante by moving to higher levels of force, especially to the use of 'tactical' nuclear weapons (Davis, 1975/6). Maximum deterrence required meeting threats at every level, but this ran into difficulties when tactical nuclear weapons were embedded in forward-based units. Should one use such weapons early, or take the risk of losing them to the attacker? If nuclear exchanges began, could escalation be controlled or, once started, would it become uncontrollable, meaning that even a small nuclear use carried a big risk of ending up with all-out nuclear war between the superpowers? These escalation questions were as much a problem in relation to crises arising in the Third World (more on these below) as they were for the defence of Europe. Maximum deterrence logic required that rationality prevail, and that limited nuclear war be containable, but there were as noted above real doubts about whether such cool-headedness and fine tuning would be possible once command and control systems came under the intense and unpredictable pressures of actual nuclear warfighting. Maximum deterrence logic and ED thus pushed deterrence theory into fantastic complications. The great chains of if–then propositions became so long, and rested on so many questionable assumptions about both technological performance and human rationality, particularly under stress (Snyder, 1978), that the credibility of the theory itself came into question.

Although most of Strategic Studies was concerned with working out the novelties of nuclear-age military relations, there was also work that covered enduring fundamentals of the military agenda in any period: the utility of force/war (Howard, 1964; Knorr, 1966; Hoffmann, 1973; Martin, 1973; Keohane and Nye, 1977: 27–29; Art, 1980; Mueller, 1989), and the question of whether offensive or defensive strategies were the most appropriate in the technological conditions of the day, and what the consequences of pursuing either would be (Quester, 1977; Jervis, 1978; Levy, 1984; Van Evera, 1984). Looking beyond nuclear questions, there were virtually no considerations related to the specifically technological demands produced by conventional wars in the Third World.

The pressure of current affairs and 'events'

Bipolarity and nuclear weapons certainly set the main framing for the evolution of ISS during its first four decades, but they were not the only driving forces in play. Looking first to the constitutive events that impacted Strategic Studies, the end of the Second World War and the rise of the Soviet Union and the US as antagonistic superpowers was, of course, the foundational event that the discipline set out to both explain and advise policy-makers about. As the Cold War unfolded, a mixture of constitutive and significant critical events worked to reinforce this view of the Soviet Union while also expanding the scope of ISS. The events that made a significant impact on the evolution of ISS were: Berlin (the Soviet blockade of West Berlin in 1948–49, and the building of the Berlin Wall in 1961), the Korean War (1950–53), the Cuba Missile Crisis (1962), the Middle Eastern oil crisis (1973) and the Vietnam War (1964–75). One might add the Suez Crisis (1956) generated by Egyptian President Nasser's nationalisation of the Suez Canal, which pitched long-term allies Britain and the US against each other and confirmed bipolarity and the inability of the European powers to operate independently from the US. It also inaugurated US engagement in the Middle East, but it did not have a major impact on the ISS literature as such. The launching of Sputnik (1957) and other key technological innovations have been covered under technology.

The crises in Berlin and Korea served mainly as constitutive events that confirmed in the West the expansionist view of the Soviet Union (and China) and the need for containment. The war in Korea inaugurated a major rearmament in the US and up to a point Europe. It consolidated the idea in the West of a 'communist bloc', and provided a real example of the extended deterrence and containment problems that NATO faced in Europe. US possession of nuclear weapons deterred neither the North from invading the South, nor the Chinese from intervening against the US counter-invasion of the North. Containment clearly had to involve both conventional and nuclear capabilities.

The crisis caused by the Soviet emplacement of nuclear-armed missiles in Cuba in 1962 brought the world closer to nuclear war than it has been before or since. It was consequently the biggest 'event' for the evolution of ISS during the Cold War. Not only did the crisis generate a substantial literature of its own that continued long after the ending of the Cold War, it also provided lessons that impacted on the ISS debates in several different ways, thus making it both a constitutive and a significant critical event that expanded the topics on the agenda of ISS (Horelick, 1964; Abel, 1966; Kennedy, 1969; Allison, 1971; Din-erstein, 1976; Snyder, 1978; Lebow, 1983/4; Landi et al., 1984; Tracht-enberg, 1985; Garthoff, 1988; Allyn et al., 1989/90; Scott and Smith, 1994; Weldes, 1996; Bernstein, 2000; Pressman, 2001). Most obviously, the Cuba Missile Crisis generated an interest in crisis management as a key area of concern within ISS. It underlined the dangers of escalation in an action–reaction process and exposed the need for reliable means of communication between Washington and Moscow. This need was quickly met by the installation of a 'hot line'. The crisis provided a neat template for looking at the reality of how decisions get made, and questioning the rationality assumptions central to deterrence theory (Allison, 1971; Janis, 1972; Jervis, 1976). Knowledge of the various military response options considered by the US, and the effectiveness of the naval 'quarantine' of Cuba by the US, fed into and validated the utility of 'flexible response' then being discussed by NATO, but the underlying concern was understanding the actual and potential production of irrationality in foreign policy-making, especially in the US. It could be argued that the experience of staring into the nuclear abyss for days on end sensitised both policy-makers and the ISS community, not to mention the peace researchers and activists, to the need for management of the nuclear arms race. Cuba demonstrated the common interest of the two superpowers in survival, and so paved the way for the rising interest in arms control and détente that began during the 1960s.

Like the Cuba crisis, the Middle East crisis of 1973 again underlined the problem of unwanted escalation, though this time not in a direct confrontation between the superpowers, but as a consequence of both being drawn into regional conflicts on behalf of their allies. By the early 1970s, nuclear forces on both sides were much larger than a decade earlier, much more based on missiles, and with much more sophisticated warning systems and shorter response times. As both superpowers got involved in the conflict between Israel and its neighbours, the interlocking of their alert systems signalled a new form of escalation problem in which automated systems and protocols could ratchet up levels of alert as each side reacted to the other. The intense time pressures within the logic and technology of nuclear deterrence seemed to necessitate such automation, but doing so then created a danger of unwanted escalation all the way to war.

The ability of events to found, expand and reorient a field of research is often only fully detectable in hindsight. In retrospect, perhaps the main impact of the 1973 Middle East crisis was, especially in the US, to put economic security and international terrorism onto the ISS agenda (Nye, 1974; Knorr and Trager, 1977) as well as introduce 'interdependence' and International Political Economy into IR, and up to a point ISS, agendas (Keohane and Nye, 1977; Gilpin, 1981). The use of the 'oil weapon' by the Arab states forced the US to notice that Western prosperity and US hegemony depended on the availability of cheap oil, much of it from the Third World (IISS, 1975a, 1975b; Maull, 1975; Odell, 1975; Krapels, 1977). More broadly, this triggered awareness that denial of access to other strategic resources by cartels seeking political leverage could, and in some views should, be seen as a strategic threat (Connelly and Perlman, 1975; Foley and Nassim, 1976). Less visible at the time was the fact that this crisis drew the US much more deeply into the Middle East on the side of Israel, thus creating a set of acutely contradictory objectives (support for Israel and maintenance of stable relations with the oil-producing states) which would increasingly entrap US foreign policy over the subsequent decades. The ongoing crisis between Israel on the one hand, and the Palestinians in particular, and the Arab states generally, on the other, bred terrorism, and how to respond to it, as a new subject within ISS (Dugard, 1974; Bell, 1975; Fromkin, 1975; Stern, 1975/6; Clutterbuck, 1976; Pierre, 1976; Wohlstetter, 1976; Hopple, 1982; Wilkinson, 1986; Wilkinson and Stewart, 1987). Because this literature was mainly focused on the relatively localised terrorism stemming from the Arab–Israel conflict, it was largely marginal to the central strategic preoccupations of Cold War Strategic Studies.

The most significant candidate for the category of deferred critical events was substantial intra-Third World events such as the Iran–Iraq War during the 1980s. Third World security was largely discussed as part of the superpowers' global rivalry, and this perhaps explains the relative lack of concern about Western support for anti-communist military dictatorships. Only a few ISS writers, to be further discussed in chapter 5, pointed to the security concerns of Third World states in their own right (Girling, 1980; Kolodziej and Harkavy, 1982; Ayoob, 1984; Thomas, 1987; Azar and Moon, 1988). Many relatively minor superpower engagements in Africa, Central America or elsewhere just became small parts of the general literature without making much impact on its main lines of thought (e.g. IISS, 1981). In a general sense, this literature might be seen as a response to decolonisation as a broad 'event', but without the ability to fundamentally change the basic scope or analytical assumptions which characterised Cold War ISS.

The war in Vietnam constituted a particularly critical case, but for an event of such scale and political controversy it made surprisingly little impact on the ISS literature, thus making it the strongest single incident of a deferred critical event. There were rather few articles in IR or Strategic Studies journals (Fishel, 1966; Hunter and Windsor, 1968; Thompson, 1969; Goodman, 1972), and the IISS did not devote even one *Adelphi Paper* to it. In the Cold War context, the Vietnam War was primarily about US containment policy and the 'domino theory' fear that allowing a breach anywhere in the US wall around the communist world would result in a cascade of conversions to communism in the Third World. Along with events in Africa and Central America, it gave rise to a sub-literature on guerrilla war and counterinsurgency (Johnson, 1968a, 1968b; Soderlund, 1970), and cruelly exposed the difficulties for the US in fighting limited wars in the periphery as part of containment (Mack, 1975). It also highlighted the limits of the abstract strategic theory then at its height in relation to deterrence, but seemingly useless in a war where body counts and battles won seemed to bear no direct relationship to the politics of victory and defeat (Gray, 1982b: 90). Perhaps most importantly, the defeat suffered by the US in the Vietnam War generated a sustained doubt in the US about the utility of force in general, and US ability to fight limited wars in the Third World in particular – the so-called 'Vietnam syndrome' (Herring, 1991/2). In the postmortem literature on what went wrong two key lessons crystallised: technological preponderance did not win wars, and domestic cohesion was essential, both to the enemy's ability to suffer high levels of casualties and for the ability of Western media to sway the support of the public (Cooper, 1970; Kalb and Abel, 1971; Ravenal, 1974, 1974/5; Grinter, 1975; Fromkin and Chace, 1984/5).

In the main, superpower concerns dominated, and the discussion of the Third World within ISS was therefore mainly tied into its consequences for the central balance. The literature focused on five possible effects: containment (how would instabilities and conflict in the Third World affect the structure of superpower spheres of influence?), extended deterrence (could Third World allies be supported by superpowers extending their nuclear umbrella to them?), escalation (was there a danger that the central stability of deterrence could be upset by the superpowers being drawn into Third World conflicts between their clients and allies?), nuclear proliferation (see above and chapter 5) and economic security (could Third World supplier cartels disrupt the Western economy by raising prices or restricting supply?). Consideration of deterrence logics outside the superpower framework was rare (Rosen, 1977; Waltz, 1981).

The internal dynamics of academic debates

In a broad brush perspective, the internal academic dynamic of Strategic Studies across the duration of the Cold War can almost be seen as following the same 'S-curve' described for technology earlier in this chapter. It had a slow start, a dramatic period of development and then a levelling off. Stimulated by nuclear weapons and the Cold War, it begins to gather strength during the 1940s and 1950s, reaching a kind of peak in the 1950s and 1960s golden age with a string of classic books centred around nuclear deterrence (Brodie, 1946, 1959; Kissinger, 1957; Osgood, 1957; Kahn, 1960, 1962; Rapoport, 1960, 1964; Schelling, 1960, 1966; Snyder, 1961; Singer, 1962; Green, 1966; Morgan, 1977). There were inputs from many disciplines and a real sense of excitement driven by the intrinsic intellectual interest of the problem, the sense of fear and urgency about what choices to make in practice, and the high public profile and generous resourcing of nuclear strategy.

But by the 1970s, the main breakthrough work had been done, and some of the enthusiasm was waning as both the superpower relationship and Strategic Studies itself became more routine and institutionalised. The theoretical debates about deterrence were beginning to sink under the weight of their own logical complexity (Freedman, 1991). The nuclear balance had reached a kind of stalemate which seemed fairly stable, and about which there did not seem all that much more new to say except for responses to technological developments, most notably in defences against ballistic missiles. Mainstream Strategic Studies literature succumbed to hectic empiricism, in which the main job of analysts was to keep up with ever-changing technologies and political developments. On a deeper level, some academics and some policy-makers drifted towards a kind of exhausted acceptance of existential or general deterrence, where the main effect came not from ever more elaborate and less credible preparations to meet every contingency, but from the simple existence of nuclear weapons and fear of them being used (Waltz, 1981; Morgan, 1983; Freedman, 1988).

As noted above, one of the distinctive features of Strategic Studies (and ISS more broadly) was and is the involvement of civilians in strategic thinking, an involvement which produced a number of distinctive outputs. Systems analysis, for example, which was a method for solving problems of force structure and resource allocation, was based on economic theory as well as on operations research developed by natural scientists, engineers and economists during the Second World War (Smoke, 1975: 290–293). Several pioneering RAND studies were implemented into policy, notably the famous 'air bases' study by Wohlstetter, a mathematician, and his associates (1954). Some of the leading representatives of this way of thinking entered the Kennedy administration labelled as McNamara's 'whiz kids' (Kaplan 1983; Brodie 1965). From there, this method and related RAND techniques like the 'Planning-Programming-Budgeting-System' 'spread through most of the federal government' (Smoke, 1975: 292).

This unfolding of Strategic Studies meshed with both the problem-solving disposition of American social science generally, and its preference for values of 'objective' science (quantification and hard theory) as opposed to the traditionalism (history) and normative approaches (academic and activist) that were the main approaches in Europe. Wæver (Wæver and Buzan, 2007: 388; see also Smoke, 1975) argues that:

> Under a Cold War situation with a booming US economy, a mood of technological optimism and a willingness to support social science as part of the solution to social challenges (including not only the Cold War struggle but social problems of all kinds), the reward was high for new approaches that seemed to move IR in the direction of the use of scientific methods and tools ranging from coding of events data allowing for computerized data processing through cybernetic models and experimental psychology to game theory. Deterrence theory became a success story in this context for two reasons. On the one hand, it produced a seemingly productive ('progressive') research programme where theoretical work produced ever new and more complex problems which could in turn be dealt with by new theoretical moves. On the other hand, all this seemed highly useful because the theories actually produced their own reality of abstractions, the world of 'secure second strike capability', 'extended deterrence' and 'escalation dominance'.

There was a noteworthy synergy between the commitment of Strategic Studies to 'scientific' methods (positivism, quantification, game theory) and the parallel enthusiasm in much of American Political Science and IR for 'behaviouralism' which sought not just to bring the epistemology and methods of the natural sciences into the social ones, but to judge what counted as knowledge by those standards. Here golden age Strategic Studies with its system theories, game theory and quantification was in the vanguard, showing the rest of IR what could (and should) be done. The steady absorption of Strategic Studies into the expanding and consolidating field of IR was facilitated by this synergy.

Moving from the golden age to the full forty-five years of Cold War Strategic Studies, the general commitment to 'scientific' methods and positivist, rationalist forms of scholarship comprised quite a diverse set of analytical and methodological approaches. Waltzian structural Neorealism drew explicitly on micro-economics, with its rational actor assumptions taken from the level of the individual human being or firm, and applied these to states. Structural Realism as well as Strategic Studies more broadly lent itself to quantitative studies of large data-sets, a methodology aided by the introduction of computers in the 1950s and 1960s, as well as to comparative case-studies which became the norm in the influential journal *International Security* published from 1976. Game theory constituted yet another form of scientific scholarship based not on the correlates deduced from data-sets or historical case-studies, but on the running through of different scenarios and mathematical equations built around different actor assumptions and the prospects for conflict or cooperation. The fact that no nuclear exchanges took place, and hence did not generate quantifiable data, made game theory particularly suited for the development of deterrence theory. As game theory evolved during the 1950s and 1960s it was also greatly aided – and in fact spurred – by the construction of computers powerful enough to run games through a large number of cycles (Edwards, 1996). One should note, though, that a large part of what was written on international security did not evoke high theory or complicated deductive or quantitative techniques but came in the form of rather straightforward empiricist scholarship with contemporary history and policy problem-solving as the principal framings.

The passions for 'scientific' method were mainly, though as we shall show in the next chapter not exclusively, American. In Europe, though again not exclusively, there was more support for historical and normative approaches. This epistemological clash was represented by the famous exchange between Hedley Bull (1966), who defended 'traditional' methods and was sceptical about scientific ones, and Morton Kaplan (1966) who defended the behavioural move. In the event, however, it was normative differences that were the most prominent dividing feature of the discourse about nuclear weapons and, as with the methodological divide, this largely resulted in the formation of two sides shouting past each other (the opposition to Strategic Studies is surveyed in the next chapter). In general the two sides stuck to their positions, though in the self-reflections on the state of the field (Bull, 1968; Gray, 1977, 1982a, 1982b; Booth, 1979; Howard, 1979; Freedman, 1984b) that were a staple of the Strategic Studies literature, there was some attempt to address the normative critiques of Strategic Studies from Peace Research.

Although dominated by American scholars, Strategic Studies was by no means an exclusively US field. Some innovative thinking was done in Europe, perhaps most notably Hedley Bull's (1961) path-breaking work on arms control. British and French military thinkers made some impact on both deterrence theory generally, and on the more self-interested topics involving the endless debates about NATO and how to make extended deterrence work (Liddell Hart, 1946; Blackett, 1948, 1956; Gallois, 1961; Beaufre, 1965), as did some strategic analysts (Noel-Baker, 1958; Aron, 1965; Hassner, 1968; Howard, 1973, 1976, 1979, 1981; Pierre, 1973; Freedman, 1981a, 1981b, 1981/2, 1988; Joffe, 1981). But regardless of which side of the Atlantic they were on, most of those involved in Strategic Studies followed the 'S-curve' described above and faced the same crisis of relevance when the Cold War ended.

Institutionalisation

The story of how a new field, ISS, arose and became established is not 'only' one of great power politics, technology, events and academic debates. It is also crucially a story of how the field became institutionalised, how it achieved a standing and a legitimacy that allowed it to build research programmes, get funding, find outlets for the dissemination of its results and make researchers self-identify as 'security scholars'. Institutionalisation can thus be seen as a driving force that is at first produced through the successful interplay of the four others, but which also, once the process of institutionalisation gains ground, becomes a driving force in its own right. A field which is strongly institutionalised is one with good chances of succeeding in the competition for funds, policy influence and prestige. Institutionalisation may be a conservative force, but it may also be a driving force that pushes ISS in new directions.

A general idea of how this institutionalisation occurred can be gained from looking at five different aspects of it: the establishment of ISS courses and institutes within universities; the creation of specialist sections within academic associations; the development of specialist ISS journals; the founding of ISS think-tanks; and the setting up of funding programmes (by government and foundations) aimed at promoting ISS. It is not within our resources to tell this story comprehensively, particularly at the level of how concrete research networks were formed, but we can certainly demonstrate the general pattern. Here we focus mainly on the institutionalisation of Strategic Studies itself: the story is of how a new field arises and becomes established.

Prior to the formation of a field of ISS there had, of course, been a long tradition of studying war that security scholars could draw upon. The Royal United Services Institute (RUSI) was founded in 1831 on the initiative of the Duke of Wellington to study naval and military science, and its journal dates from 1857. The US Army War College is more than a century old. As already noted, the ISS that emerged as a self-conscious field after the Second World War in part built on this tradition, but as noted above was also distinctive in purpose and personnel, and carried the new label and wider orientation of international security. Broadly speaking, the development and institutionalisation of ISS proceeded in parallel with that of IR more widely as a field/discipline distinct from Political Science, History and International Law – distinct here meaning having its own academic associations, departments, degrees and journals. ISS did not start as part of IR, and some of its early key thinkers, for example Schelling, probably never thought of themselves as part of IR. But their many overlaps, synergies, shared personnel and intertwined processes of institutionalisation steadily drew them together. By the late 1960s, ISS had become one of the major sub-fields of IR without anyone really noticing this happening. It was not uncommon for major figures in IR theory, such as Bull, Jervis and Waltz, also to be active writers in ISS.

A few of the institutions in which ISS was to be pursued existed before the Second World War (e.g. the Brookings Institution think-tank founded in 1927), but most of them came into being as the subject of ISS developed, a process that is still ongoing. The US Army formed a Strategic Studies research group in the mid-1950s, which during the 1970s became the Strategic Studies Institute of the US Army War College. The International Institute for Strategic Studies (IISS) was founded in London in 1958. In universities, the Institute of War and Peace Studies at Columbia University was established in 1951, and the Department of War Studies at King's College London also in the 1950s. The Mershon Center for International Security Studies at Ohio State University was inaugurated in 1967, consolidating programmes on defence and national security that dated back to the mid-1950s, funded by a private bequest. On the government side of things, the US established an Arms Control and Disarmament Agency (ACDA) in 1961, and in 1965 the Indian Defence Ministry set up the Institute for Defence Studies and Analyses (IDSA). In its 'Survey of Strategic Studies' (1970) the IISS listed 128 places in 29 countries where research in Strategic Studies (interestingly including Peace Research) was being pursued. Most of these were in the West and Japan, with the US accounting for 20 and the UK 13, but Eastern European and some Third World countries also had significant representation.

The 1970s and 1980s continued this trend, with ever more think-tanks, university programmes and institutes coming into being. Stanford University's Arms Control and Disarmament Program was founded in 1970, and the Oxford University Strategic Studies Group in 1971. The International Security Studies section of the International Studies Association (ISA) was also set up in 1971, the Institute of Strategic Studies Islamabad in 1973, the Canadian Institute of Strategic Studies in 1976, and the Center for Peace and Security Studies, Georgetown University and the Center for Strategic Studies, Tel Aviv University, both in 1977. In Geneva, the Programme for Strategic and International Security Studies was started in 1978 as part of the Graduate Institute of International Studies. In the US, a National Defense University was formed in 1976 by the merger of earlier programmes and in 1984 this created its own research arm, the Institute for National Strategic Studies. Johns Hopkins University formalised its Strategic Studies programme in 1980 and the Committee on International Security Studies of the American Academy of Arts and Sciences began to function during the late 1980s. A benchmark for how widely and deeply ISS had become institutionalised by the late 1980s was the establishment in 1987 of Women in International Security (WIIS) based in Georgetown University and dedicated to increasing the influence of women in foreign and defence affairs. It has subsequently expanded to 1,400 members – women and men – in over thirty-five countries from academia, think-tanks, the diplomatic corps, the intelligence community, the military, government, non-governmental organisations, international organisations, the media and the private sector (http://wiis.georgetown.edu/about/ – accessed 2 January 2007).

Think-tanks and foundations also played a crucial role in supporting the birth and Cold War evolution of Strategic Studies. Some think-tanks undertook work that fell squarely within ISS itself, with RAND and the IISS being the most prominent examples. Others were significant in that they sponsored academic programmes and university centres. As noted in chapter 3, foundations and think-tanks are often listed along a Liberal–Conservative ideological spectrum, and as a rough general rule, Conservative institutions would be stronger supporters of conventional Strategic Studies, while Liberal institutions have, relatively speaking, been more generous in their funding of Peace Research, Arms Control and, from the early 1980s, programmes devoted to the rethinking of the concept of security itself. That said, some foundations bridged these divides by providing support for Strategic Studies as well as for Peace Research and Arms Control. Think-tanks and foundations differed and differ furthermore in how explicitly ideologically they conceive of themselves with, for instance, the American Enterprise Institute and the John M. Olin Foundation taking an explicitly political–normative position, while others such

as the Brookings Institution or Ford Foundation emphasise political ideology less while highlighting their contributions to academic knowledge
production.

Institutionally, foundations and think-tanks are often interwoven as
foundation grants are essential to the upkeeping and growth of think-
tanks. Looking to the key think-tanks and foundations which underwrote
traditional Cold War ISS, the question of where to draw the line between
ISS and the policy world becomes a crucial, but also a blurred, one. A
narrow definition of what falls within the ambit of the institutionalisation of ISS would look exclusively to those think-tanks and foundations
which either conducted or funded academic research, whereas a broader
definition would incorporate those institutions that more explicitly target
policy-makers in a manner that mixes academic knowledge and policy
advice/advocacy. Starting from a more narrow definition, the cases of
RAND and IISS noted above are the most prominent examples of think-
tanks with a clear academic status which impacted core elements of ISS.
RAND's contribution to game theory and deterrence thinking during the
golden age of Strategic Studies has already been noted, and although later
decades did not produce similar path-breaking theoretical contributions,
RAND continued to make a crucial input at the level of empirical security
analysis. Locating RAND on the political landscape of security institutions, its strong reliance on government contracts has led some to view
it as compliant with, and hence politically skewed towards, state policies,
while others have viewed it as less ideologically driven and pointed to
it being supported by a variety of foundations including Ford, Bill and
Melinda Gates, and the Pew Charitable Trusts (Oren, 2003). Looking
to the UK, the IISS, which was during the Cold War perhaps the pre-
mier specialist Strategic Studies think-tank, was the source of several key
periodicals in the field (*Survival, Adelphi Papers, The Military Balance,
Strategic Survey*).

Broadening the scope to cover think-tanks known for their more
explicit Conservative ideological agenda and hence often a stronger focus
on influencing policy and public debate, rather than on 'pure' ISS theory work, we find first the American Enterprise Institute, a think-tank
founded in 1943 as a promoter of free enterprise capitalism. The American
Enterprise Institute was and is a large recipient of money from Conservative foundations, including the John M. Olin Foundation, the Sarah Scaife
Foundation, the Smith Richardson Foundation, and the Lynde and Harry
Bradley Foundation (www.aei.org/ – last accessed 16 November 2007).
The importance of the American Enterprise Institute fellows has not been

so much in the key field of ISS theory, but as individuals combining the roles of academic analysts, policy advisors and public intellectuals. Some of the most prominent fellows associated with the American Enterprise Institute during the Cold War were Richard Perle, Assistant Secretary of Defense for International Security Policy under Reagan, and Irving Kristol, the founding father of the Neo-Conservative movement which rose to a prominent position with the election of George W. Bush in 2000 (Williams, 2005). The confluence of think-tanks and the policy world was further indicated by the claim that the American Enterprise Institute played a key role in developing and implementing President Reagan's contested policy in Nicaragua in the 1980s when the CIA trained the 'Contra' insurgents.

Another prominent Conservative think-tank is the Heritage Foundation, founded in 1973 by an initial grant from beer magnate Joseph Coors, defined by Abelson (1996: 49) as the archetypal advocacy think-tank (www.heritage.org/ – last accessed 16 November 2007). The Heritage Foundation has also been supported by major Conservative foundations including the Sarah Scaife and the John M. Olin foundations and like the American Enterprise Institute has been linked with the Reagan administration's support for anti-communist forces in Nicaragua, Guatemala and El Salvador. That competition between like-minded institutions is also a challenge to foundations is evidenced by the prominent Olin Foundation's decision to support the Heritage Foundation rather than the American Enterprise Institute in 1986. The Center for Strategic and International Studies (CSIS) founded in 1962 through the Conservative Sarah Scaife Foundation should be mentioned as an example of an institution first based at a university (Georgetown University's School of Foreign Service), but whose (perceived) ideological agenda led the university to cut ties in 1986. Other prominent think-tanks/policy institutes based at universities include the Conservative Hoover Institution founded in 1919 through a donation to Stanford University made by Herbert Hoover to support the Hoover War Collection. Finally, at the end of the Cold War, the United States Institute of Peace was founded in 1986 through an act signed by President Reagan.

An important think-tank operating with strong academic credentials and an explicitly political agenda is the Hudson Institute, founded in 1961 by prominent RAND strategist Herman Kahn (www.hudson.org/ – last accessed 16 November 2007). The Hudson Institute was explicitly concerned with what it saw as left-wing nuclear pessimism arguing both the necessity and feasibility of nuclear deterrence. Prior to his death in

1983, Kahn expressed support for Reagan's agenda as well as optimism regarding the strategic use of space. Until the end of the Cold War the Hudson Institute received substantial government contracts and support from major Conservative foundations.

Not all think-tanks had explicitly ideological agendas and some carried out work that fell in part within Strategic Studies, in part within more critical approaches to arms control (see chapter 5). These included the Brookings Institution, the Council on Foreign Relations which also publishes *Foreign Affairs*, the London-based Royal Institute of International Affairs – Chatham House (founded in 1920), the Woodrow Wilson International Center for Scholars, established by the American Congress in 1968, and national institutes of international affairs, such as the Finnish Institute of International Affairs (1961), the Swedish Institute for International Affairs (1938), and the Norwegian Institute of International Affairs (1959).

As this short account of how think-tanks contributed to the institutionalisation of ISS shows, telling the story of think-tanks is also telling the story of the significance of major foundations. Chapter 3 provided a list of the largest Liberal and Conservative foundations, and although we should be careful not to overdraw the distinction between the two as far as providing funding for ISS is concerned, it should be clear from the account above that Conservative foundations, most prominently the Lynde and Harry Bradley Foundation, the John M. Olin Foundation, the Sarah Scaife Foundation and the Smith Richardson Foundation played key roles in supporting think-tanks. But foundations also made grants to universities, thereby directly impacting the institutionalisation of ISS in another way. Most significant in this respect is probably the John M. Olin Foundation, founded in 1953 by John M. Olin, who turned a small family company into one of America's largest suppliers of guns, ammunition and chemicals (Wooster, 2006). John M. Olin retained tight control over the foundation, thus, when his alma mater, Cornell, 'capitulated' to student protesters in 1969, Olin stopped his contributions (which all combined had come to five million dollars). His fear that the foundation might drift from his Conservative agenda also led him to disband it by 2005. During the 1970s and 1980s the foundation had an important impact on ISS: it provided, for example, funding for the International Security Program at Yale, and the John M. Olin Institute for Strategic Studies at Harvard, which began in 1989.

Although ISS did eventually develop a whole suite of specialised publications, including a number of textbooks (Baylis *et al.*, 1975, 1987;

Russett, 1983; Buzan, 1987a), initially the academic discussions about international security took place in less specialised journals. An indication of this can be seen in a selection of key articles in the evolution of ISS (Buzan and Hansen, 2007). This shows that the debates about international security occurred not just in IR and foreign policy journals such as *World Politics, International Affairs, International Studies Quarterly* and *Foreign Affairs*, but also in Political Science journals such as the *American Political Science Review* and *Political Studies Quarterly*, and general social science and humanities journals such as *Daedalus*. Interestingly, the first specialist ISS journal appeared in Europe, *Survival* in 1958, with the main US entry *International Security* not starting until 1976. Others followed: *Terrorism/Studies in Conflict and Terrorism* (1977), *Journal of Strategic Studies* (1978), *Arms Control/Contemporary Security Policy* (1980), *Intelligence and National Security* (1986), *Terrorism and Political Violence* (1988) and *Security Studies* (1990), and these can be seen both as an expression of how prominent ISS had become and as part of a wider process of expanding numbers of IR journals generally. These more specialised journals certainly facilitated an expansion of the ISS literature, but they did not acquire anything like a monopoly position. The general IR journals remained important forums for ISS debates, including later arrivals such as the *British Journal of International Studies* (1975) (later *Review of International Studies*), the *European Journal of International Relations* (1995) and *Cooperation and Conflict* (1965).

By the end of the Cold War, Strategic Studies had put down deep institutional roots. As a student, you could take courses, and sometimes whole degrees, in it at hundreds of universities. From there, you could look to jobs in teaching, media, research, public policy, think-tanks, government and the military. Once courses and degrees and think-tanks had been institutionalised, they fed student demand for ISS, not just because they seemed interesting and relevant to major questions of the day, but because they offered good careers. In the US, ISS had become one of the big two subjects within IR, more or less dividing the field with IPE on the basis of a division of labour between the conflictual and cooperative aspect of international relations (Caporaso, 1995; Wæver and Buzan, 2007). Interestingly, as this division of labour itself became institutionalised into separate journals and associations it stunted the development of the economic security literature that came out of the Middle East oil crisis.

In sum, over the four decades of the Cold War, and not least because of its intimate connection to the public policy problems generated by the

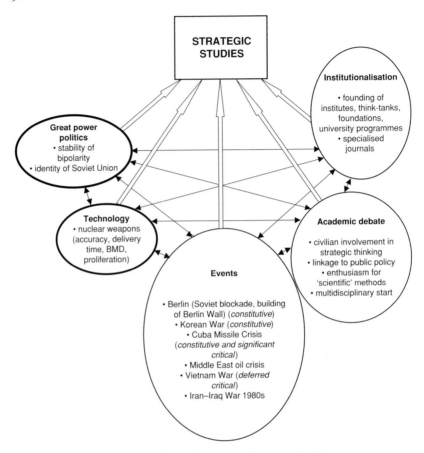

STRATEGIC STUDIES

Institutionalisation
• founding of institutes, think-tanks, foundations, university programmes
• specialised journals

Great power politics
• stability of bipolarity
• identity of Soviet Union

Technology
• nuclear weapons (accuracy, delivery time, BMD, proliferation)

Academic debate
• civilian involvement in strategic thinking
• linkage to public policy
• enthusiasm for 'scientific' methods
• multidisciplinary start

Events
• Berlin (Soviet blockade, building of Berlin Wall) (*constitutive*)
• Korean War (*constitutive*)
• Cuba Missile Crisis (*constitutive and significant critical*)
• Middle East oil crisis
• Vietnam War (*deferred critical*)
• Iran–Iraq War 1980s

Figure 4.1.   The main drivers of Strategic Studies

Cold War, Strategic Studies had acquired formidable weight and momentum. The success of its institutionalisation combined with its linkage to the military problems of the Cold War meant that when the Berlin Wall fell, Strategic Studies in particular, and ISS in general, were faced with an existential crisis. How could all this survive once its core problem was no longer there? More on this in chapters 6 and 7. In Figure 4.1 we illustrate the main driving forces that impacted the birth and evolution of Cold War Strategic Studies, their main content and interplay. Those circles with a thicker line exerted a particularly strong impact.

Conclusions

Looking to the five driving forces, the main drivers behind this foundational stage of ISS were thus unquestionably *great power politics* and *technology*. These two driving forces highlight the way in which the enemy image of the USSR became fixed in the US at an early stage, and how this played into the impact of nuclear weapons, and the rapidly evolving technology associated with them. The other three driving forces were, however, by no means unimportant. *Events* were significant first of all because it was key events in the mid and late 1940s and early 1950s which produced the very Cold War that Strategic Studies was founded upon. Throughout the Cold War there was a series of events that fortified the view of the Soviet Union as an enemy, but also expanded the agenda of ISS. The two most critical events during the Cold War that challenged the geographical and sectoral scope of Strategic Studies were wars in the Third World, most crucially the Vietnam War, and the oil crisis of the 1970s. Turning to the importance of *internal academic debates*, this is a less crucial driving force in that for most of the Cold War, mainstream ISS (Strategic Studies) had little interest in epistemological questions, though there was a de facto predominance of rational, empirical and positivist approaches, albeit often mixed in with elements of history, as with Classical Realist IR. To a large extent, this literature was driven by the policy problems facing mainly the US, and to a lesser extent those of its allies (e.g. Beaufre, 1965). Yet if the Cold War saw few of the epistemological discussions that we have become accustomed to since the 1980s, the diversity of disciplines that impacted early ISS was still significant for constituting both the scope and methodology of the field. The driving force of *institutionalisation* finally laid out the way in which Strategic Studies and ISS developed as an academic field, how it received substantial public and private funding and how think-tanks and venues for teaching and publication underpinned its birth and growth.

As the Cold War came to an end, the operation and interaction of the five driving forces began to change dramatically. Current affairs and events, which had largely made their impact within the context of the Cold War, were completely overshadowed by the cosmic central collapse of both ideological and political–military bipolarity. From the mid-1980s, as Gorbachev began to reverse the image projected by the Soviet Union, developments in great power politics became the dominant driver. The Cold War itself began to wind down, taking with it the debates about the nature of the Soviet Union, the sense of urgency that had attached to deterrence theory, containment policy and extended deterrence, and even much of the fear of nuclear weapons that had dominated ISS since the beginning of the nuclear era. There had already been some decline in the pressure from the technological driver as nuclear weapons and their delivery systems became technologically mature, levelling out at the top of the 'S-curve' from the late 1970s onwards. But as we will show in chapter 6, the winding down of the Cold War did not take away an ongoing preoccupation with new military technologies, and neither did it remove concern about nuclear weapons. As the focus on superpower arsenals receded, that on horizontal proliferation became more prominent.

As already noted, the ending of the Cold War posed a possible crisis for the extremely successful institutionalisation of Strategic Studies, which now faced hard questions about its relevance, resourcing and bureaucratic survival on anything like its 1980s scale. It also derailed the internal dynamics of academic and policy debates. The 1980s intellectual drift of Strategic Studies into an unattractive choice between an existential deterrence dependent on irrationality, and a full-spectrum deterrence dependent on a sustained rationality so complex as to make its plausibility questionable, was simply swept away. With the Cold War gone, these questions became of only theoretical interest. And since Strategic Studies had lived on its linkage to public policy questions, theoretical interest was not nearly enough to sustain engagement by the large establishment that had grown up during the Cold War. Gone also was the whole problem of managing extended deterrence that had so much defined political and intellectual tensions across the Atlantic. With the Soviet Union disappearing as a threat, Europe no longer needed US protection. The problem with NATO shifted from how to share the burdens and risks of extended deterrence to whether NATO was necessary at all, and if it was, then for what?

With the end of the Cold War, Strategic Studies faced a crisis born of the very success that its marriage to the superpower nuclear rivalry had given it. Despite this crisis, it was the Cold War development of ISS that set the template for 'international security' to which all of the contemporary and subsequent wideners and deepeners had to relate. But before we look at how ISS rose from the ashes of the ending of the Cold War, let us turn to the Cold War approaches which questioned Strategic Studies' reading of nuclear deterrence, the nature of the state, and the privilege accorded to state-centric, military security.

5

The Cold War challenge to national security

This chapter is devoted to those approaches which in various ways challenged Strategic Studies. These approaches had one thing in common – namely their criticism of Strategic Studies – but they also differed so much in their choices of key analytical and political concepts that it would be difficult to present them as one approach and to take this approach through one driving force after another. A significant challenge to Strategic Studies (although in part operating from within it and in part rooted in Peace Research) was Arms Control, which emphasised the collective risk to survival arising from the intersection of superpower rivalry and nuclear weapons.[1] The Peace Research branch of Arms Control offered a very different, more normatively and politically driven, view of nuclear deterrence than Strategic Studies. But it was still, when viewed through the lens of the four questions that structure ISS laid out in chapter 1, an approach to security that focused on security's military dimensions and on external threats. The extent to which most Arms Control Peace Researchers envisaged bipolarity as a structure that could be eased but not eradicated, was striking. Détente – the political alternative to containment and deterrence – was seen as 'rivalry with lower risks of war, not an end to rivalry' itself (Buzan et al., 1990: 9; see also Pastusiak, 1977; Schlotter, 1983).

Other parts of Peace Research took a more radical approach, analytically as well as politically, arguing that governments on both sides of the Iron Curtain held their populations – and the planet – hostages to nuclear disaster. This constituted 'humanity' or the individual as the referent object rather than the state, thereby invoking the long-standing

---

[1] Given that Arms Control had roots in both Strategic Studies and Peace Research, how to place it in these chapters posed a problem. To put it in chapter 4 would have meant splitting the discussion, while putting it in chapter 5 risks underplaying the extent to which major elements of Arms Control were outgrowths of the Strategic Studies debates. It was not a big enough topic to justify a separate chapter, yet its inclusion here is one reason this chapter is so long.

Liberal tradition of critically scrutinising the relationship between citizens and the institutions of authority and sovereignty described in chapter 2. Peace Researchers of the 1960s and 1970s did not, however, go through the concept of security in launching their critique of Strategic Studies, but through the oppositional concept of 'peace'. Peace Researchers further divided 'peace' into positive and negative peace. Negative peace was defined as the absence of war, large-scale physical violence or personal violence and opened up a research agenda on military security (Galtung, 1969: 183). Positive peace had multiple connotations. In the 1950s and 1960s, it was defined as 'the integration of human society' (*JPR*, 1964: 2), but towards the end of the 1960s, it was reformulated to include 'structural violence', which emphasised social injustice and inequality (Galtung, 1969: 168, 171, 175). Successful academic concepts often owe their popularity to their ability to encapsulate a body of existing or burgeoning research while simultaneously outlining a conceptually focused new research agenda. Structural violence fitted this formula perfectly. It provided an anchor for work on development issues, imperialism, domestic conflicts in Western as well as Third World societies, environmental resources, human rights and economic exploitation. It incorporated parts of a critical Marxist agenda while not endorsing the radical Marxist call for violent revolution. Yet, in a premonition of post-Cold War widening debates in ISS, this expansion of 'peace' beyond the absence of war/conflict was criticised, not only by Strategic Studies, but from within Peace Research itself.

Like Strategic Studies, neither Arms Control nor Peace Research explicitly foregrounded 'security', featuring instead complementary, parallel and oppositional concepts: détente, arms control, peace, structural violence, basic human needs and social justice. In 1983, Buzan (1983, 1984a) could thus describe security as 'an underdeveloped concept', but as the decade wore on, 'security' appeared as a concept bridging the fields of Strategic Studies and Peace Research. The concept of *common security*, coined by the Palme Commission in 1982 linked arms control and broader concerns for the livelihood of people across the globe and became a popular concept connecting the policy world and the critical parts of ISS. Articles which expanded the military conception of security into environmental and economic security began to appear in such prominent journals as *International Security* (Ullman, 1983) and *International Organization* (Buzan, 1984b). Finally, two new academic perspectives, Poststructuralism and Feminism, which had made an impact on the social sciences and the humanities in general, grew out of Peace Research to establish themselves as distinct approaches. This literature was much smaller quantitatively speaking than Arms Control or Strategic Studies, yet, in the light of the changes brought about by the end of the Cold War, it turned out to be significant for how ISS has evolved. Had there not been a small but growing concern with broader concepts of security in the 1980s, it is doubtful whether widening approaches in the 1990s could have capitalised to the extent that they did on the ending of the Cold War.

To handle the several strands of opposition to Strategic Studies we structure the chapter as follows. The next section assumes that the reader has the account of Strategic Studies and the manner in which the five forces drove this literature reasonably fresh in mind, and focuses on how the two driving forces of great power politics and technology drove Peace Research and Arms Control to a <u>different</u> view of deterrence and military technology. Since Peace Research to a large extent functioned as a mirror image/attacker, and thus centred largely on the same set of events as Strategic Studies, there is no particular section on this driving force.

The third section focuses on the conceptualisation of positive peace as integration, an expansion of the research agenda that implies both a challenge to the Realist understanding of international security and a more thorough concern with the importance of domestic cohesion. Looking to the driving forces, this research was partly spurred by a combination of events such as the formation of NATO and the European Economic Community, the growing density of mass media coverage, and the impact of peace movements and civil rights movements. It was also driven by internal academic factors insofar as positive Peace Research drew upon a longer Idealist–Liberal tradition that makes different assumptions about state identities. The fourth section turns to the reformulation of the concept of positive peace as structural violence, a challenge to both Strategic Studies and older Liberal Peace Research traditions driven by events which were to a large extent also linked to great power politics (decolonisation as a longer process, the oil crisis of the early 1970s, wars in the Third World, calls for a New International Economic Order, environmental degradation and the student uprisings in the late 1960s) and by internal academic debates, most significantly the popularity of Marxist and post-Marxist theories in the wake of the student protests in the late 1960s.

The fifth section is concerned with the internal dynamics of academic debate within Peace Research, and it examines first the debates over whether negative, military peace/security should be privileged, or whether positive peace should be given equal status. The analysis also examines the shifts in the relative balance between positive and negative approaches, relating it to events and academic fashions outside Peace Research itself. It presents the debates over epistemology and methodology within Peace Research which pitched behavioural, quantitative and game-theoretical approaches against broader normative, but still largely positivist, perspectives.

The sixth section is also driven by internal academic forces insofar as it examines the turn from the concept of peace to the concept of security. First comes a shorter section on *Common Security*, before two separate accounts of how Feminist Security Studies and Poststructuralism followed on from a Peace Research agenda. The seventh and final section of the chapter turns to the question of institutionalisation and provides an account of how Peace Research as a whole was brought into the institutions of academe through university education and research, journals, textbooks and associations, and how it was supported by foundations and think-tanks.

Peace Research and Arms Control

Peace Researchers questioned both the morality and the rationality of Strategic Studies (Bull, 1968; Wiberg, 1981) and the meanings of war and peace (Galtung, 1969). They worried about the seeming co-option of the academic debates (and some of the debaters) by the national security policies of the US in particular and the Western alliance as a whole. There was a monumental set of ethical questions raised by nuclear deterrence (Winters, 1986), not the least of which were the explicit leaving of one's population as hostage to the other side's nuclear weapons in policies of MAD, and the explicit willingness to plan the mass murder of the other side.

The motives and political analysis behind this opposition varied sharply and came in many mixtures: traditional pacifists opposed to all violence; nuclear pacifists opposed to the threat that such weapons posed to the survival of the human race; ideological sympathisers and fellow-travellers on the political left who saw the US as equally, or more of, a threat than the Soviet Union; strategists (working under the new topic of Arms Control) who came to think that the dangers of nuclear rivalry created a common interest in survival between the two superpowers; and people who argued that the ideological struggle of the Cold War was not the only, or in some cases even the most important, international security issue

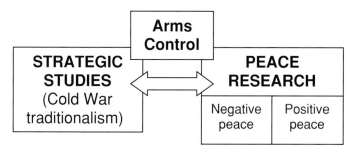

Figure 5.1.   The location of Arms Control on the terrain of ISS

facing humankind. These perspectives formed a spectrum with Strategic Studies at one end, Peace Research at the other and a range of views in the middle that we might loosely call Arms Control. Arms Control was not independent from Peace Research and Strategic Studies but overlapped with both. It was in one sense a product of golden age strategic thinking, and in another part of the reaction against such thinking. On its Strategic Studies end, Arms Control demonstrated that many strategists had normative concerns not only about the fate of their own side in the Cold War, but also about more collective aspects of morality and survival. It is not without significance that *Survival*, the journal of the London-based IISS, could equally well have been the name of a Peace Research journal. This in-between position that Arms Control had within ISS is illustrated in Figure 5.1.

Both Peace Research and Arms Control involved not only the moral, historical and political questioning of Strategic Studies, the Cold War and nuclear policy, but also hard technical critiques of deterrence theory and strategy, and of the narrowing of the international security agenda down to an obsessive concentration on the superpower military rivalry. As with early Strategic Studies, Peace Research also contained its share of natural and social scientists who brought the positivist methodological tools of their disciplines with them. Despite the fact that in retrospect this was in substance and method a single conversation, in practice, during the Cold War, Peace Research and Strategic Studies (along with Realist IR in general) were mainly staged as opposites and political enemies, with Arms Controllers suspended uncomfortably across the political gulf between them. Much of this oppositionalism was framed in the classic Realist versus Idealist mould of IR, and thus at a higher level of abstraction concerned very deep ontological assumptions about human nature and the state (Carr, 1946). Each side was secure in its own moral high ground and viewed the other as a threat to its project. Some Peace Researchers saw Strategic Studies as complicit in legitimising the prologue to nuclear extermination, while some strategists saw Peace Research as at best naive Idealism, offering prescriptions dangerously detached from reality, and at worst as a kind of fifth column for the Soviet Union. Arms Control was a fragile bridge between these positions. This spectrum was not evenly distributed in either time or space. In the early decades of the Cold War, Strategic Studies unquestionably dominated both intellectually and politically, especially in the US. As the Cold War wore on, and deterrence theory became more complicated and less convincing, room opened up for the Arms Control middle ground everywhere. Peace Research was always politically stronger in Europe and Japan than in the US, though perhaps dominant only in parts of Scandinavia and Germany (Onuf, 1975; Reid and Yanarella, 1976).

Great power politics: the Cold War and bipolarity

For Peace Research and Arms Control, as for Strategic Studies, super-power bipolarity was the foundational political and strategic fact. Just as the whole edifice of deterrence theory was largely constructed on the assumption of a two-player game, so also was much of the literature on arms control, disarmament and arms racing. Bipolarity framed both the strategic agenda and the political one. To the extent that the differences between Strategic Studies and Peace Research were political, these also were framed as being on one side or the other, or else trying to escape the bipolar construction by seeking some kind of third way where bipolarity did not equate to bottomless antagonism and a complete lack of shared interests.

Although there was widespread acceptance of the fact that the world had become bipolar, and that the US and the Soviet Union represented deeply opposed views of what humankind's political, economic and social future should look like, this did not mean that everyone thereby accepted the orthodox Western view of either what caused the Cold War or how such a 'war' needed to be fought. Dissidence was possible on political grounds, by rejecting the argument that it was Soviet aggression that was responsible for the Cold War. Some interpreted Soviet moves as basically defensive against a surrounding West that threatened the Russian revolution from a position of greater economic and military strength. In this view, the US was as much an aggressor as the Soviet Union. More moderate versions, some anticipating later Critical and Constructivist approaches, questioned whether the Cold War conflict was real, or just a construction set up for the convenience of the ruling elites in the two superpowers (Kaldor, 1990). Dissidence was also possible on military grounds, as to whether raising the dangers of nuclear war was an appropriate response to ideological and superpower bipolarity.

Within this bipolar framing, the particular position of Western Europe looms large on two grounds: its pig-in-the-middle position as the front line and principal prize of the Cold War, and the differences between its domestic politics and those in the US. Thus there was a tendency to allocate more space to the particular question of European security in moderate Peace Research and Arms Control than in US-centred Strategic Studies.

On positional grounds, the US–Europe political divide was amplified by the fact that Europe was the main front line in the Cold War and therefore at considerable risk of becoming the first, and perhaps the only, battlefield in any superpower hot war. In the orthodox framing, a dependent and under-armed Western Europe was being defended by the US against a shared threat from the Soviet Union, and this risk was therefore both unavoidable and reasonable. NATO was the political and military framework within which to handle the stresses created by an alliance that was not only unequal, but had continuously to juggle the tensions between defending Western Europe and its people on the one hand, and providing forward defence for the US on the other (De Porte, 1979; Grosser, 1980; Bull, 1982; Rogers, 1982; Windsor, 1982; Cohen, 1982/3; Lundestad, 1986; Garnham, 1988). In dissident perspective, US policy was more about the forward defence of itself, and creating strategies that ensured that if any fighting did take place, it should be as far away from the US as possible. This way of thinking was one natural response to the US and NATO shift towards limited nuclear war (LNW) strategies during the 1970s. LNW meant that the opening (and possibly only) phases of an East–West war would be fought in Europe, escalating fairly quickly to the use of 'tactical' nuclear weapons. The result would be the certain obliteration of most of Germany, Denmark, Poland and Czechoslovakia, and possibly of much of the rest of Europe as well.

The seeming inequity of risk, and the questionable sanity of a policy that involved destroying countries in defence of their freedom, opened up powerful intellectual and political opposition to both nuclear strategy and those whose work seemed to legitimise it by reducing it to a kind of economistic science of mass threat. Western Europeans generally accepted the need to deter the Soviet Union even though many of them were less inclined than Americans to accept extreme enemy images of it. They were caught in the contradiction of desiring to keep defence expenditure low, yet wanting to avoid too much dependence on and subordination to the US. Europe was the likely first victim of any nuclear war, but since it would not provide adequately for its own defence, also the most dependent on nuclear weapons to provide deterrence.

This positional factor alone would have been enough to support more dissident thinking in Western Europe than in the US, but it was complemented and reinforced by domestic political factors within Europe. European politics contained much stronger leftist parties, including communist ones, than was the case in the US, which famously lacks a strong leftist political tradition (Moravscik, 2002: 352–357). Partly because of this, Europeans were much more aware of the huge part that the Soviet Union had played in the defeat of Nazi Germany, and there was much more socialist sympathy than in the US for at least part of what the Soviet Union claimed to stand for. In the first decade of the Cold War, and much more in Europe than in the US, years of Second World War pro-Soviet propaganda had to be undone in order to make the Cold War project legitimate among the electorates. Subsequently, although majority opinion in Western Europe mainly did come around to the official framing of the Cold War, very substantial minorities (and in some places majorities) either did not accept the Soviet Union as an enemy or held more neutral positions, seeing both superpowers as equally to blame for the Cold War. There was also significant anti-militarism in many countries, some of it as part of left-wing views, some a reaction against war from the horrors of the 1914–45 experience.

The combination of these positional and political factors meant that there was a strong peace movement active in many Western European countries.[2] The first peak of this was in the 1950s and early 1960s when the Campaign for Nuclear Disarmament (CND) campaigned against nuclear weapons and the possibility that they would be used to 'defend' Europe. The second was during the late 1970s and early 1980s in the European Nuclear Disarmament (END) campaigns against the deployment of US-controlled cruise and Pershing 2 missiles in Western Europe, and up to a point also against the Cold War itself (Burke, 2004). These campaigns were a formative event for peace movements as well as peace researchers. There were close personal links between this activism and Peace Research,

---

[2] France was an exception to this rule, having no strong anti-nuclear movement (Fontanel, 1986).

and those political connections were a substantial part of what alienated Peace Research and Strategic Studies.

The technological imperative: the nuclear revolution in military affairs

Again in parallel with Strategic Studies, Peace Research and Arms Control were in large part motivated by, reacting to, and trying to influence, developments in military technology. The dominant driver was nuclear weapons and what to do about them. For orthodox strategists, the driving force of the ever-unfolding nuclear revolution was how to respond in national security terms to new capabilities that either had, or might soon, come into the hands of the enemy. For most Peace Researchers, and Arms Controllers, this problem was either paralleled, or overridden, by seeing nuclear weapons themselves as the main source of threat, and humankind as a referent object with an equal or greater claim to survival than that of states. While there was no doubt that the two superpowers posed mortal threats to each other, as their nuclear arsenals expanded to tens of thousands of warheads, some became more concerned about the threat that unleashing such arsenals would pose to human existence. For the first time humankind had attained the capacity to commit species suicide. Given the hair-trigger preparedness for war on both sides, and the complexity and fallibility of their interlocked warning and command and control systems, there was some risk that humankind would terminate itself through the potential for accident that was built into the design of MAD and the whole project of nuclear deterrence. Among other things, the 1962 Cuba Missile Crisis, a formative and critical event for Peace Research as well as Strategic Studies, had shown just how easily and quickly the superpower confrontation could be brought to the brink of nuclear war. Thus, while one side of the ISS literature pursued the problem of how to make nuclear deterrence work as a national security strategy, another side increasingly saw nuclear weapons and deterrence strategies (especially maximum ones) as posing their own distinctive threat to the survival of all human beings regardless of ideology.

It is a theme of this book that, despite its increasing diversity, ISS can be understood as a single conversation organised around a core concern with international security. Surprisingly perhaps, nowhere does this coherence become more obvious then when one looks at those Peace Research and Arms Control literatures of the Cold War that focused on military technology. Despite what was frequently strong political hostility backed up by institutional differentiation (see below), the actual agendas

of Peace Research and Strategic Studies on this topic overlapped extensively. Sometimes there were normative differences, most obviously about
whether national security or humanity was the purpose of the game, and
whether these were compatible or irreconcilable goals under Cold War
conditions. These differences were most obvious in relation to arms control and especially disarmament. But in some areas of arms control, and
much of the discussion of arms racing, deterrence theory and nuclear
non-proliferation, these normative differences often mattered little. Even
the discussions about transarmament, non-offensive defence and civilian
defence that were generated by Peace Researchers can be seen as in some
senses complementary to the Strategic Studies debates about extended
deterrence.

Disarmament has a long record as the principal plank for many kinds
of peace movement. Arguments for it ranged from moral (weapons as
bad in themselves), through economic (the opportunity costs of military expenditure in terms of schools, hospitals and other civil goods
in the industrial countries, and to development prospects in the Third
World), to pragmatic (arms racing as a cause of war, a particularly powerful argument in the wake of the First World War of 1914–18). Those
opposed to such movements saw disarmament as at best naive, and at
worst as a kind of treason designed to make the state vulnerable to its
enemies. This latter view was facilitated by the left-leaning character of
many peace movements and their leaders. To this traditional mix, nuclear
weapons added the fear that the human race might exterminate itself
and massively damage the planetary ecosphere. This fear for the survival
of humankind (or at least of Western civilisation) was not entirely new,
having been a feature of peace campaigners during the 1920s and 1930s
in relation to the threat of fleets of bombers destroying cities with poi-
son gas and high explosives. But nuclear weapons made this threat real
and undeniable, and consequently one feature of the Cold War was mass
movement campaigns such as CND and END calling for the abolition of
nuclear weapons. Mainly this demand was for multilateral nuclear disarmament of all of the nuclear weapons states, but some of those who
saw the danger of nuclear extermination as high also advocated unilateral
disarmament.

The demand for nuclear disarmament was not just a matter of public
protest movements. Especially during the late 1940s and the 1950s, disarmament talks were a formal, if ineffective, part of superpower diplomacy.
More dramatically, complete nuclear disarmament was also a formal,
if insincere, commitment by the nuclear weapon states that adhered to

the Nuclear Non-Proliferation Treaty (NPT) of 1968. They promised in article 6:

> to pursue negotiations in good faith on effective measures relating to cessation of the nuclear arms race at an early date and to nuclear disarmament, and on a Treaty on general and complete disarmament under strict and effective international control.

The failure of the nuclear weapon states to live up to their commitments under this article was a recurrent theme in the quinquennial NPT review conferences throughout the Cold War and beyond.

Although it was probably the most divisive and politicised subject in that part of the ISS agenda driven by military technology, disarmament was thus an acknowledged topic even for Strategic Studies. There was no shortage of proponents at the conjuncture of peace movements and Peace Research (Noel-Baker, 1958; Falk and Barnet, 1965; Brandt, 1980; Independent Commission on Disarmament and Security Issues, 1982; Frei and Catrina, 1983; York, 1983; IDS, 1985). Textbooks aimed at the mainstream ISS market generally had substantial discussions of disarmament (Singer, 1962; Baylis *et al.*, 1975, 1987; Buzan, 1987a), and respected IR theory writers did not hesitate to discuss it seriously (Bull, 1970; Singer, 1970; Morgenthau, 1978: 391–416).

But while disarmament remained a key issue for peace movements and some Peace Researchers, by the 1960s it was being pushed into the margins of ISS by the new concept of Arms Control. Disarmament confronted the threat posed by military technology and the arms dynamic with the seemingly simple and morally clear prescription of getting rid of them. This simplicity and clarity was the key to both its popularity among peace movements and its lack of popularity amongst strategists and IR Realists, who thought its apparent simplicity wrong and dangerous. Arms Control tried to establish a halfway house between these two extremes. It did not problematise weapons as such, but stood for a managerial approach to military technology and the arms dynamic that would aim to maximise their security utility and stability, and minimise their dangers. Arms Control could include arms reductions or even eliminations, and thus incorporate parts of the disarmament agenda, but it might also point to increases in some types of weapons thought of as stabilising. It included a range of other ideas such as freezes on deployments, force restructuring to reduce provocation and the risk of accidents, and a variety of stabilising measures such as communication between enemies, bans on certain technologies, and restrictions on testing and deployment and suchlike (Harvard Nuclear Study Group, 1983: 203–212; Committee on International Security and Arms Control, 1985). The theory, history and problems of arms control quickly became a staple of ISS textbooks (Singer, 1962; Baylis *et al.*, 1975, 1987; Buzan, 1987a).

Arms Control sought both to escape from the sterility and unreality of negotiations on disarmament, and to address some real practical problems being generated by the superpower arms race. It quickly attracted people from both the Strategic Studies and Peace Research ends of the ISS spectrum, but it was a fragile bridge between them. Some of those whose real interest was disarmament could buy into Arms Control as an intermediate stage, something that could be used to pave the way towards disarmament by building confidence and reducing tensions. But few strategists saw it this way, and to the extent that they supported Arms Control at all saw it as an end in itself, simply to help stabilise deterrence, not as a means to disarmament. Arms Control was technical and complex rather than clear and simple. It tended towards moral neutrality on military technology and was not necessarily against nuclear weapons in themselves. For this reason it had little of the intrinsic moral mobilising power of disarmament. Its only claim in this direction was its linkage to superpower détente: inasmuch as arms control became the practical expression of improved relations between the superpowers and a lowered risk of war it could establish moral currency in the public mind. Nevertheless, its constituency was mainly experts on both ends of the ISS spectrum, and as it became seen as simply permanent tinkering with the arms dynamic it was vulnerable to losing the support of those who wanted more.

Although there were precedents for arms control – most notably the 1922 Washington Naval Agreements that set ratios on naval power after the First World War – the idea of arms control as a specific strategic concept began to evolve during the late 1950s as part of golden age strategic thinking (Freedman, 1981a: 130–207). The key statement was Bull's 1961 book *The Control of the Arms Race* (see also Brennan, 1961; Schelling and Halperin, 1961; Singer, 1962), and from there both a literature and a practice burgeoned. During the 1960s the US and the Soviet Union negotiated a number of significant agreements, amongst the highlights of which were the Partial Test Ban Treaty (1963), the hot-line agreement (1963), the agreement on peaceful uses of outer space (1967), the Nuclear Non-Proliferation Treaty (1968), the Seabed Arms Control Treaty (1971), the ABM Treaty (1972), and the Biological Weapons Convention (1972). During the 1970s, arms control was mainly focused on the two long rounds of the Strategic Arms Limitation Talks (SALT I, 1969–72; SALT II, 1972–79).

By the end of the 1970s arms control, like the superpower détente with which it had become associated, was in trouble, both because of its failure to stem the growth of huge nuclear arsenals and because US–Soviet relations had moved out of détente and into a new round of distrust and heightened rivalry. SALT I produced what were generally acknowledged as substantive agreements limiting ABM deployments and offensive nuclear missiles (though whether these agreements were a good or bad thing for strategic stability was hotly contested). SALT II produced ceilings on nuclear delivery systems and warheads, but these were set so high that they simply seemed to legitimise the vast expansion of superpower nuclear arsenals that had gone on during the 1970s. Intermediate-range Nuclear Forces talks (INF), and Strategic Arms Reduction Talks (START) ran respectively from 1981 and 1982 to 1983, but got nowhere due to the tensions of the post-détente 'Second Cold War' and collapsed, more or less ending superpower arms control activity until the Cold War itself began to thaw. After a period of gloom, strategic arms control picked up again from the mid-1980s as superpower relations began to warm. In 1985, negotiations on both INF and START resumed, to be joined by talks on Conventional Armed Forces in Europe (CFE). These produced a series of agreements between 1987 and 1993 to reduce both nuclear and conventional force levels substantially, and to reconfigure them into less threatening forms. A missile technology control regime was agreed in 1987 and a chemical weapons convention in 1993. As the structures of the Cold War fell away these agreements became less about managing an arms race, and more akin to the demobilisations that followed the end of the First and Second World Wars.

The literature on arms control was mainly focused on nuclear weapons and their delivery systems, though there was also concern about chemical (Robinson, 1984), and to a lesser extent biological, weapons. Within the nuclear framing there were two core topics: arms control for the superpowers and the prevention of nuclear proliferation to states other than the five nuclear weapon states (NWS) recognised in the NPT (the US, the Soviet Union/Russia, Britain, France and China). While arms control for the superpowers was, as suggested, a controversial and often divisive topic, there was a much higher degree of consensus across the spectrum of ISS that nuclear proliferation was a bad thing.

Looking first at arms control for the superpowers, there was an advocacy literature stemming from the founding works cited above, and generally arguing the need for more and better arms control in order to stabilise the superpower arms race (Bull, 1976; Dahlitz, 1984). As the practice of arms control got under way it was not uncommon during the 1960s and 1970s for this advocacy to be linked to the maintenance of détente, a view that some thought was to prove fatal to the whole process (Blechman, 1980: 106–112). It could also, of course, be linked to the maintenance of deterrence (Calvocoressi, 1984). The bulk of the huge literature on arms control reports, analyses and makes proposals about the negotiations, implementations, problems (compliance/cheating) and side effects, and as both achievement and optimism waned during the 1970s, reflected on what went wrong (Terchek, 1970; Newhouse, 1973; Gray, 1975; Nerlich, 1975/6; Goldblat, 1978; Blechman, 1980; Luttwak, 1980b; Burt, 1981; Sharp, 1981/2; Adelman, 1984; Brown and Davis, 1984; Freedman, 1984a, 1984b; Tuchman, 1984; Schear, 1985; Steinberg, 1985; Steinbruner, 1985; Sartori, 1985/6; Schelling, 1985/6; Pieragostini, 1986; Barker, 1987; Dusch, 1987). The driving force of technology behind both the problems of and opportunities for arms control were always a conspicuous part of the literature (Gelber, 1974). The Peace Research end of the spectrum was mainly disappointed that arms control had not done much to constrain the arms race, while the Strategists were more concerned that it had not done much to constrain Soviet military power.

One interesting section of this literature was that devoted to analysis of US–Soviet differences in relation to arms control (Sienkiewicz, 1978; Legvold, 1979; Pick, 1982; Rivkin, 1987; Guertner, 1988). This concern ran parallel to that in the literature on rationality and deterrence discussed in chapter 4. But for Arms Control the concern about the difference between East and West was even more intense, because to a vastly greater extent than deterrence, arms control depended on cooperating with the Soviets, and being able to verify that agreements were being kept (Bhupendra and Barnaby, 1984; Voas, 1986). Like disarmament, it was thus acutely vulnerable to cheating, deception and problems of verification, and to differences of opinion across the ISS spectrum about whether the Soviet Union was essentially a defensive rational actor sharing an interest in stability and a degree of coexistence, or a ruthless, offensive opportunist (Singer, 1962: 15–17). Although these concerns were almost entirely framed by superpower bipolarity, China and arms control also began to attract attention before the end of the Cold War (Segal, 1985, 1987; Johnston, 1986).

The second main theme of nuclear Arms Control was about preventing the spread of nuclear weapons to non-nuclear weapon states (NNWS). This became a large and distinct literature generally framed around the term 'nuclear (non-)proliferation', and both Strategists and Peace Researchers broadly agreed that the spread of nuclear weapons was undesirable. The consonance of this position with that of the two super-powers, who were the principal promoters of non-proliferation, exposed an embarrassing hypocrisy affecting this literature. Like the superpowers, many strategists were caught favouring nuclear weapons for some or all of the existing five NWS, but opposing them for everyone else. One notable maverick in these ranks was Waltz (1981), who famously argued that because nuclear weapons were an effective deterrent to war, 'more may be better' in constraining interstate conflicts worldwide. Those on the Peace Research end were less compromised here because they generally opposed nuclear weapons for everyone. This underlying divide on motives did not, however, much disturb the dominant line in the literature that prevent-ing or at least curbing the spread of nuclear weapons was the central goal.

The Peace Research logic was mainly driven by a desire to lower the statistical probability of nuclear weapons being used. This line of thinking had close connections to nuclear disarmament, and the NPT bargain in which stopping the spread of nuclear weapons should be accompanied by efforts to eliminate those already in existence. The strategic logic for non-proliferation shared the concern with accidents and higher probabilities of use, but rested also on a desire to preserve the status of the nuclear superpowers, and to prevent third parties from triggering superpower wars by launching so-called catalytic strikes, where uncertainty as to the attacker would trigger responses against the other superpower. China, for example, when it was at odds with both superpowers during the 1960s, might have been tempted to trigger a war between them. Many strategists opposed nuclear disarmament on the grounds that because the possibility of cheating could not be removed, and the incentives for it would be high, it would be a less stable configuration than a nuclear-armed deterrence. Once the knowledge of how to make nuclear weapons was available in society, the incentive to rearm would be there, and the first to do so could have a huge advantage.

As with the literature on superpower arms control, that on non-proliferation was a mixture of advocacy, reporting on developments, and policy analysis and prescription. There was a substantial general literature covering present and likely future developments in proliferation, techno-logical and political issues, policy and progress in various countries, and the possible consequences of allowing nuclear weapons to spread (Fisher, 1971; Young, 1972: 23–81; Quester, 1973; Bull, 1975; Maddox, 1975;

Marwah and Schulz, 1975; Walker, 1975; Schelling, 1976; Kapur, 1980a; Harkavy, 1981; Poneman, 1981; de Mesquita and Riker, 1982; Dewitt, 1987; R. C. Karp, 1991). In addition, there was literature about missile proliferation (Hsieh, 1971; Karp, 1984/5, 1991; Navias, 1989; Potter and Stulberg, 1990: Dunn, 1991), about the implications of proliferation for deterrence and war (Berkowitz, 1982; de Mesquita and Riker, 1982; Kaiser, 1989) and about the possibility of nuclear terrorism (Beres, 1979). The *SIPRI Yearbooks* contained extensive annual updates on most aspects of nuclear proliferation. Because the subject touched on so many aspects of IR, from regime theory and technology, through North–South relations and area studies, to Strategic Studies and Peace Research, its literature was published in a remarkable variety of journals. It was even possible to teach whole courses on proliferation at universities, and some of the books were published with this in mind, as well as for a wider public audience (Beaton, 1966; Young, 1972).

The subject gained some of its popularity because of concerns over the technological and political links between civil and military nuclear applications. Civil nuclear power was controversial in its own right. Because there were close connections between some key aspects of the technology (especially the enrichment of uranium and the reprocessing of spent reactor fuel), this meant that there were economies of scale to be gained in pursuing both civil and military nuclear power, as all of the early nuclear weapon states, and later India, did. Civil nuclear power could not be wholly insulated from military implications, and this fact was at the heart of the controversial Faustian bargain in the NPT (Greenwood *et al.*, 1976; Camilleri, 1977, 1984; Wohlstetter *et al.*, 1979: Lovins *et al.*, 1980; Brenner, 1981: 1–93; Dorian and Spector, 1981). States that renounced nuclear weapons via the NPT won the right to have access to civil nuclear technology, and that access could be used to prepare breakout options by shortening the lead time for making nuclear weapons.

What came to be known generally as 'the non-proliferation regime' was in fact composed of many different elements, and whether these were complementary or contradictory was one theme of the debates. At the core of the regime were its two multilateral components: the NPT, and the International Atomic Energy Agency (IAEA) which was responsible for the system of safeguards (accounting, monitoring, inspection) built into the NPT (Quester, 1970; Young, 1972: 82–135; Imber, 1980; Lodgaard, 1980; Gummett, 1981; Dahlitz, 1984; Schiff, 1984; Fischer and Szasz, 1985; Nye, 1985; Simpson, 1987; Smith, 1987; Tate, 1990). Although the NPT was aimed at being universal, and except for a few holdouts such as Israel, India and Pakistan, nearly was, there were also regional nuclear weapon free zones (NWFZ), sometimes with slightly different conditions, and discussions about whether there should be more.[3] In addition to these multilateral approaches, there were also more elitist elements in the non-proliferation regime. These included supplier clubs, in which the main producers and sellers of civil nuclear technology coordinated the security conditions they would demand from purchasers, and various unilateral US policies on non-proliferation (Chari, 1978; Hildenbrand, 1978; Imai, 1978; Williams, 1978; Yager, 1980; Brenner, 1981: 93–245; Lellouche, 1981; Simpson, 1982). In addition to all of this, there were many studies of individual countries and their policies on nuclear weapons.[4] The bulk of this literature was about the nuclear programmes and policies, and technical capabilities, of the countries, and the implications of these for the non-proliferation regime.

Arms control was not the only technology-driven area in which the key themes and debates in Strategic Studies had their counterpoints in the Peace Research literature. Deterrence was another (Doran, 1973; Weede, 1983; Wallace *et al.*, 1986; Nalebuff, 1988; Tunander, 1989; Huth, 1990). So also was arms racing (Brubaker, 1973; Chatterjee, 1974; Lambelet, 1975; Krell, 1981; Diehl, 1983, 1985; Intrilligator and Brito, 1984; Leidy and Staiger, 1985; Gleditsch and Njølstad, 1990) and the evolution of military technology (Kaldor, 1982). Much of quantitative Peace Research took its inspiration from the pioneering work on arms racing of Richardson (1960a, 1960b; see also Rapoport, 1960: chs. 1–2; Bellany, 1975). Both sides shared an interest in linking arms racing and war, and in the irrational aspects of weapons accumulation due to bureaucratic politics and suchlike intervening variables. In general, the Peace Research and Arms Control

---

[3] These included the actual Latin American Nuclear Weapon Free Zone (Stinson and Cochrane, 1971; Redick, 1975, 1981) and the South Pacific one (Power, 1986; Mogami, 1988), and proposed ones in the Indian Ocean (Buzan, 1981; Vivekanandan, 1981) and the Balkans (Klick, 1987).

[4] China (Halperin, 1966; Hsieh, 1971; Segal, 1981; Tan, 1989); Britain (Pierre, 1970; Carlton, 1976; Seignious and Yates, 1984), with a theme of Britain as the possibly first ex-nuclear power (Freedman, 1981b; Dombey *et al.*, 1987); France (Mendle, 1965; Lieber, 1966; Seignious and Yates, 1984), including the curious case of the lack of anti-nuclear peace movements in France (Fontanel, 1986); Canada (Lentner, 1976); Yugoslavia (Gedza, 1976); India and Pakistan (Edwardes, 1967; Imai, 1974; Rao, 1974; Marwah, 1977, 1981; Betts, 1979a; Kapur, 1980b; Thomas, 1986; Chellaney, 1991); the Middle East (mainly Israel, Iran, Iraq) (Freedman, 1975; Rosen, 1977; Feldman, 1981; Pry, 1984; Bhatia, 1988); Africa (Cervenka and Rogers, 1978; Betts, 1979b; Mazrui, 1980; Adeniran, 1981; Ogunbadejo, 1984; Moore, 1987); and Argentina and Brazil (Rosenbaum and Cooper, 1970; Gall, 1976; Gugliamelli, 1976; Lowrance, 1976).

agendas were not much driven by international political events, a rare exception being one attempt to apply the Richardson models of arms racing to escalation in the Vietnam War (Alcock and Lowe, 1969). For the most part they marched to the drumbeat of nuclear weapons and the technological dynamics of the superpower arms race. Events within that frame, such as public health scares over fallout from nuclear testing during the 1950s, the Indian nuclear test in 1974, and the superpower deployments of intermediate range missiles in Europe in the late 1970s, also made an impact on public opinion, about which more in the next section.

Although Peace Research and Strategic Studies overlapped in many places, Peace Research did develop one distinctive response to the problems posed by technology and military strategy: non-offensive defence (NoD, aka non-provocative defence). The central idea of NoD was to overcome the security dilemma by designing mainly barrier modes of defence that could stop an invasion, but not pose any threat of counter-invasion or retaliation (Berg and Lodgaard, 1983; Dankbaar, 1984; Galtung, 1984; Boserup, 1985; Windass, 1985; Agrell, 1987; Møller, 1987; Saperstein, 1987; Dean, 1987/8). This happened during the last decade of the Cold War, when some in Peace Research were moving towards a more security-defined agenda (Wæver, 2008). This narrowing of the gap became acceptable enough for NoD occasionally to sneak into mainstream Strategic Studies (Gates, 1987) and general IR (Buzan, 1987b) journals. It extended an earlier literature on the people's war style of dispersed but very deeply prepared armed resistance to occupation (Johnson, 1973; Roberts, 1976; Fischer, 1982), and on the fringes also to unarmed, but organised, national resistance to occupation (Roberts, 1967; Boserup and Mack, 1974; Sharp, 1985). The mainstream NoD literature was an attempt to take NATO's defence problem seriously, and engage with it on military terms, without thereby threatening the Soviet Union and so perpetuating a security dilemma and a risk of nuclear war.

Positive peace, integration and societal cohesion

The military wing of Peace Research and Arms Control did not go into a detailed conceptual analysis of security, although it did rearticulate the understanding of security of Strategic Studies in important respects. Perhaps most crucially, it held that the antagonistic view of international relations, and the Soviet Union as the embodiment of the enemy state, could be transformed through negotiations, confidence-building

measures, arms reduction treaties and common institutional arrangements. In terms of the referent object and the sectors to which security
was applicable there was a similarity to Strategic Studies in that military
security was privileged as the object of analysis and states were constituted
as the key actors.

But other Peace Researchers called for expanding the scope of analysis
from the negative peace of war avoidance to the 'positive peace' study
of 'the integration of human society' and for considering all forms of
group-based conflicts, not only interstate ones (*Journal of Peace Research*,
1964: 2). This line of Peace Research focused on the linkages between
societal and state-level integration and drew upon Deutsch and his concept of security communities (Kemp, 1985: 134). Security communities
came in two forms: amalgamated ones which involved the merger of
states, and pluralistic ones which stopped short of institutional merger,
but where processes of interstate and trans-state societal integration had
led to such commonality in values and trust that war was no longer considered a viable way to resolve conflicts (Deutsch *et al.*, 1957). The case of
the North Atlantic area in the 1950s became Deutsch's primary example
of a pluralist security community, while the European Economic Community was advocated by first-generation European integration theorists
as an example of a (future) amalgamated security community. Others
examined the connections between conflict on the one hand, and com-
munication/integration on the other, as in Gleditsch's studies of airline
networks and conflicts (Gleditsch, 1967, 1977), or the transmission of
cultural values from one country to another (Sauvant, 1976; Wilson and
Al-Muhanna, 1985).

Liberal Peace Research was based on the premise that individuals and
nations could change their (mis)perceptions about each other, and that
enemy images were not always realistic. Peace Researchers should critically interrogate the accuracy of such enemy images and governments'
strategic mobilisation – or manipulation – thereof (Deutsch, 1957: 201;
Loustarinen, 1989). More benignly, governments and mass media might
be unaware of how their enemy constructions perpetuated conflicts that
could be solved. In response, Deutsch suggested the establishment of 'an
"early warning system," in regard to the mass-communication aspects
of interstate conflicts' that would detect when 'the image of a particular "enemy" country is reaching the danger point' (Deutsch, 1957: 202).
The concern with how governments and mass media produce or manip-
ulate enemy images resonated with the long-standing United Nations
Educational, Scientific and Cultural Organization (UNESCO) tradition

of seeing war as starting in people's minds. A significant body of Peace Research was thus devoted to the study of public opinion and propaganda, including how children and young people were socialised into accepting enemy images and ideas about war and peace (Deutsch, 1957: 203, footnote 4; Cooper, 1965; Becker, 1973).

A related body of literature dealt with news coverage, particularly foreign policy news. Here, the concern was with which events were selected as 'coverable' by the media, particularly with the tendency of the media to select violent events and report these in simplified and sensationalist ways (Galtung and Ruge, 1965; Östgaard, 1965; Smith, 1969). Peace Researchers called for a reversal of these tendencies and for a more balanced news coverage which would provide a space for realising the commonalities among diverse peoples and for less violent forms of conflict resolution (Östgaard, 1965: 55). Situating Peace Research's concern with news coverage on the broader terrain of ISS, this literature reads in some respects as early studies of the 'CNN-effect' that became popular in the 1990s and which argues that politicians are pressured to intervene in response to intense media coverage. Yet, it is important to notice that the goal of Liberal Peace Research was not to mobilise violent interventions by third parties, but to push the media to support non-violent forms of conflict resolution. The concern was with news criteria in and of themselves, not the actual connection between news coverage and foreign policy behaviour. Moreover, the visual ontology adopted by Peace Researchers was a fairly objectivist one. Deutsch (1957: 201) called for researchers to 'find out to what extent these images are realistic, that is, to what extent they do correspond to objective factors beyond their control', and Galtung and Ruge (1965: 64) were concerned with 'the selective and distorting factors' that came between the event itself and 'its' media representation. Perceptions of reality might be more or less in concordance with reality itself, but the two – reality and media representation – were ontologically and analytically distinct. This marks an important difference between early Peace Research and later discursive approaches that hold that 'reality' is formed through structures of (media) representation and that one should study how representational structures establish and legitimise particular foreign and security policies rather than compare reality to news coverage.

The explicit concern with the process of enemy formation rested on the deeper assumption that states need not perceive each other through a Realist optic (as described in chapter 2), but could engage through cooperation. Liberal Deutschian Peace Research also opened up another critical front in the debates between Strategic Studies and Peace Research

Table 5.1. *Peace Research on societal cohesion*

Institutional focus policy area	Extra-parliamentarian	Parliamentarian
Foreign policy	Peace movements	Public opinion – e.g. gender gap (democratic peace)
Domestic policy	Civil rights/African American movements	*Domestic election studies (not key concern of PR)*

in that it foregrounded the relationship between governments and populations and the question of societal, domestic cohesion, identified as a key element in security debate in chapters 1 and 2. Realist writers such as Kennan were also concerned with domestic cohesion, but as seen from the vantage point of the state: How could the government drive a wedge between the governments and populations of enemy states like the Soviet Union, and how could they prevent forces of dissociation domestically?

This Liberal Peace Research literature was structured along two dimensions: first, whether it was concerned with foreign policy or domestic (social, class, racial, ethnic or religious) issues; second, whether it was focused on extra-parliamentary forces or on parliamentary forms of influence. Combining these two dimensions, we get the four options shown in Table 5.1.

Beginning with the extra-parliamentary combinations, this category problematised political leaderships' claims to represent society. The existence of social movements questioned the basic premise of modern democratic society, namely that those elected provide legitimate and adequate political solutions. The best example of this form of societal division was the anti-nuclear peace movements which were formed from the late 1950s with the so-called Easter marches first taking place in Britain in 1958. In a few years, marches spread to most of Western Europe and North America, drawing such large attendances as, for instance, 25,000 and 35,000 in Denmark in 1961 and 1962 (Boserup and Iversen, 1966: 345). As superpower relations eased in the 1970s peace movements receded as well, but the onset of the Second Cold War in the 1980s brought them back into the streets, and research on the movements of the 1980s tended to stress the transnational links that united movements across state borders (Walker, 1988). Most Peace Researchers shared the normative goals of the peace movements: nuclear disarmament, arms control or nuclear free zones, but some did critically interrogate their tactics.

In assessing the impact of peace movements, a major question that divided Peace Researchers was the extent to which they had been instrumental in bringing about change, such as the Partial Test Ban Treaty in 1963 (Boserup and Iversen, 1966: 328; Wiberg, 1988: 44). Kenneth E. Boulding's 'snowball theory' held that small protests might grow to activate a large population. Against this optimistic vision of how passive, but latently critical, individuals would be awakened by the vanguard, stood the view (Boserup and Iversen, 1966; Galtung, 1964) that inactive populations may very well be more conservative than 'their' governments (who had better access to the mass media) and peace demonstrations may thus paradoxically strengthen the opponent. Another discussion concerned the pros and cons of peace movements becoming like 'real' political parties (Krasner and Petersen, 1986: 155; Wæver, 1989a).

Studies which focused on popular extra-parliamentarian contestations at the domestic level (situated in the lower left corner of Table 5.1.) worked along a similar structural logic, questioning the claim that societal contestations could be contained within the existing formal political structures. The main case studied within this line of research was the so-called 'Negro movement' and 'ghetto riots' that took place in America in the 1960s (Goldberg, 1968; von Eschen et al., 1969; Monti, 1979). Moving into the 1970s, these movements faded from the American political scene, and so did their coverage by Peace Researchers. This body of literature is worth noting, however, because it foreshadows later post-Cold War concerns, empirically and analytically, with societal security problems on the inside of Western states. It also, as hinted above, ties in with a long-standing Realist anxiety about the production of domestic identity, whether from a Conservative or a more Liberal perspective.

Peace Researchers also studied societal cohesion and parliamentary settings. Popular opinion research combined with the Political Science sub-discipline of election studies in generating complex models linking attitudes to social, economic, cultural and later, gendered factors, identifying for instance a 'gender gap' in women's and men's foreign policy attitudes (Boulding, 1984; Togeby, 1994). Opinion polls and surveying techniques underwent a significant development in the 1960s as part of the general behavioural revolution in the social sciences, and their adoption by Peace Researchers was based on the ideal – drawn from Classical democracy models of direct participation – that public opinion should be reflected in the policies adopted (Galtung, 1964). The relevance of public opinion – and more specifically, the ability to poll on questions of peace and security – was clear: if 'the public' was more prone to conflict resolution and peace than 'its' politicians, the latter would be pressured by the former in the direction of peace. This push was built, first, on the normative assumption that leaders would listen to their citizenry, and second, on the strategic assumption that politicians would seek re-election and therefore have to be responsive to the views of (the majority of) the population. The general belief that the US withdrawal from Vietnam was due to a massive popular mobilisation underscored the possibility of popular opinion to influence such 'high politics' questions as those of warfare (Verba *et al.*, 1967; Hamilton, 1968; Modigliani, 1972; Russett and Nincic, 1976). As the Cold War faded, this line of research expanded into democratic peace theory (see chapter 6): the unwillingness of democracies to go to war, at least against other democracies (Russett, 1975; Doyle, 1986).

Structural violence, economics and the environment

The conceptualisation of positive peace as integration was reworked in 1969 in Galtung's seminal article on structural violence, defined as 'the distance between the potential and the actual, and that which impedes the decrease of this distance' (Galtung, 1969: 168, 171). Structural violence entailed a more conflictual view of the world than peace as integration and opened up for an incorporation of a host of issues related to economic inequality and differences between the global North and South. It provided a bridge between Classical Liberal–Idealist Peace Research on the one hand and the new agenda of 'Critical Peace Research', which drew upon theories in the Marxist tradition, on the other (Wiberg, 1988: 53). Although Marxian in some of its analytical form, structural violence was opposed to violence, and therefore countered that strand in radical politics that sought to legitimise it as a response to oppression and exploitation. As a consequence, most Critical Peace Researchers did not think that structural violence was sufficiently 'critical' (Schmid, 1968). Galtung's insistence on non-violence resonated, however, with a longer Gandhian tradition in Peace Research as well as with the work by other prominent Peace Researchers, such as Gene Sharp (1973), who held that since the state depended on the obedience of its citizens, it could be resisted through non-violent means.

Structural violence referred to manifest injustices with physical material consequences, for instance hunger-related deaths in the Third World, but also to phenomena with a less immediate bodily impact such as illiteracy (which could have been prevented) (Galtung, 1969: 169). Crucially, particularly in the light of later debates over the concept of individual security, Galtung located the concept of structural violence at the level of collectives, not individuals: 'when one husband beats his wife there is a clear case of personal violence, but when one million husbands keep one million wives in ignorance there is structural violence' (Galtung, 1969: 171). The referent object in Galtung's conceptualisation of structural violence was thus human collectivities, neither states nor individuals, and the primary sectoral expansion was to include (critical Marxist) economics. The delineation of the collective referent object in this body of Peace Research differed from Strategic Studies and its (predominant) focus on external security in two specific respects: it argued, first and in retrospect prophetically, that conflicts at the sub-state or trans-state level may be equally as explosive, and hence threatening to the state, as those at the interstate level; second, that groups needed to be given the normative possibility of being referent objects, whether the threat in question came in the form of states, other groups or global imperialist/economic structures. And where negative Peace Research constituted the referent object in relation to the absence of war or violent conflict, structural violence theory constituted it in relation to a longer list of issues.

It is important to stress – especially in the light of the 1990s debates over 'individual security' – that structural violence was a concept located at the structural level and that it was distinct from interpersonal conflict and from personal violence. True, there was a radical expansion of the possible threats to peace/security, but the referent object was constituted through its structurally disadvantaged position. An individual starving to death was not by her- or himself a victim of structural violence, but one who starves because of the global economic structures of imperialism was. What this implies is an ambiguous constitution of the individual–collective referent object dynamics: 'individuals' can appear in a way that is impossible in state-centric Strategic Studies, but they do so because their 'individuality' is constituted in a way that has a particular structural–political meaning, whether that meaning is religious, ethnic, racial, class-based or gendered.

Debates between Galtung and his supporters and radicals like Schmid were heated in the late 1960s and early 1970s, yet, by the mid-1970s, and taking a broader view of the field, there was sufficient commonality between 'the Scandinavian school' (Galtung, Eide), 'the West German school' (Senghaas, Jahn, Krippendorff, Gantzel) and 'the Neo-Marxist school' (Schmid, Dencik), argued Reid and Yanarella (1976: 317), that they could all be seen as belonging to a Marxist Peace Research tradition.

This tradition had its stronghold in Scandinavia and West Germany (Senghaas, 1975: 252; Reid and Yanarella, 1976: 329) and the *Journal of Peace Research*, founded by Galtung in 1964, provided the main outlet for its dissemination (Chatfield, 1979: 174). The link between development and structural violence was based on a critical Marxist/post-Marxist analysis of global economic, particularly capitalist, structures. Galtung drew upon early Frankfurt School theorist Marcuse in criticising capitalist consumer society for promising 'euphoria', but this (apparent) providence of 'pleasure rather than pain' might be 'worse in terms of being more manipulatory' than more overtly repressive societies (Galtung, 1969: 170). In later works, including 'A Structural Theory of Imperialism' (Galtung, 1971), the links to dependency theory were made explicit. *Dependencia* theory was developed in a Latin American context by Cardoso and Faletto (1979) and Gunder Frank (1967), and in an African setting by Amin (1972, 1975, 1976). It held that 'underdevelopment' was not simply a sign of non-Western countries being at a less advanced stage of modernisation, but a structurally determined condition. Third World countries played a particular role within global capitalist structures as they were the suppliers of raw materials or a few commodities on conditions set by the extracting countries and companies of the West. As Western capitalism went through stages of crisis – as predicted by classic Marxist–Leninist theory – these crises were transposed onto the global South (Senghaas, 1975; Jackson and Sørensen, 1999: 200–201). Broadening the scope of imperialism beyond the economic, Galtung (1971) argued that political, military, communication and cultural imperialisms supported an exploitative North–South global structure. Neoliberal regimes would perpetuate and deepen the conditions of structural dependency to the detriment of the populations, if not the elites, of Third World countries.

The call for the inclusion of development issues in Peace Research was further supported by the argument that the number of deaths due to malnutrition, hunger and human-induced disasters in the periphery rivalled the hypothetical body count of a nuclear war – a logic subsequently reiterated by many widening perspectives. Moreover, reasoned Senghaas (1975: 252), the poverty of the Third World constituted an 'explosive potential for conflict and violence', and although such conflicts had so far been confined to the Third World itself, they were likely to start spreading to the West and the socialist East. That Senghaas, Galtung and other critical 'development' Peace Researchers were at least partially successful in setting a broader Peace Research agenda is evidenced by the many articles on structural violence, imperialism and development published in the *Journal of Peace Research* in the 1960s and 1970s (Klausen, 1964; Höivik, 1971, 1972; Hveem, 1973, 1979). Institutionally, the convergence of Development Studies and Peace Research was illustrated by the establishment of PADRIGU, the Department for Peace and Development Research, at the University of Gothenburg in 1971.

Comparing Marxist Peace Research – and understanding 'Marxist' as comprising both Neo-Marxist and Critical as well as softer Marxist German and Scandinavian approaches – to the literature on Third World security mentioned in chapter 4, there is thus a more fundamental challenge to the Strategic Studies agenda. Those in Strategic Studies who studied Third World security in its own right, and not just for its implications for the Cold War, did for the most part not challenge the focus on national security, mainly wanting this concept to be applied to the particular positions and problems of Third World states (Ayoob, 1984; Azar and Moon, 1988). The literature on structural violence, by contrast, took a highly critical view of the Western (and to some extent the Third World) state as the producer of Third World insecurity.

Situating Marxist Peace Research within the larger story of the evolution of ISS, it is clear that this was linked to a series of constitutive *events*. The most prominent of these was the general trickling effect of decolonisation that began in the 1940s, sometimes peacefully, sometimes not, as in the case of the Indochina War between the French and the Viet Minh (Rogers, 2007: 37); the protracted wars in Korea and Vietnam (Boulding, 1978: 345; Wiberg, 1988: 44); the covert, and sometimes not so covert, US political and economic involvement in Latin and South America; and the adoption of development as a key priority within the UN system more broadly (Rogers, 2007: 40). While these events directly boosted the calls for giving attention to the Third World, the oil crisis in 1973 became a particular impetus to focus on the relationship between global economics and peace/war/security, particularly in how the resource-rich parts of the Third World held a bargaining power vis-à-vis the First World.

The easing of superpower confrontation in the latter part of the 1960s and 1970s was also seen as opening up space for non-military security/peace concerns in Peace Research more broadly. The incoming editors of the *Journal of Conflict Resolution*, Russett and Kramer, wrote in 1973 that they wanted to shift the balance a bit from the journal's traditional primary focus on international conflict, particularly the danger of nuclear war, to 'justice, equality, human dignity' and 'ecological balance and control', as 'other problems are competing with deterrence and disarmament studies for our attention' (Russett and Kramer,

1973: 5). Kenneth E. Boulding held that there 'was the feeling, certainly in the 1960s and early 1970s, that nuclear deterrence was actually succeeding as deterrence and that the problem of nuclear war had receded into the background' (Boulding, 1978: 346; Lopez, 1985: 125). With the election of Ronald Reagan in 1980 and the Second Cold War of the 1980s, the relative balance between military and development issues shifted back again in the direction of the former (Gleditsch, 1989: 3; Rogers, 2007: 44), and Third World countries were pushed towards the adoption of Liberal policies which 'emphasized the role of free market forces and the downsizing of state bureaucracies and state regulations' (Jackson and Sørensen, 1999: 201).

The broadening and deepening of the Peace Research agenda in the late 1960s and 1970s, and in particular the form that this took, was also influenced by the way in which events interacted with the *internal dynamics of academic debates*. The import of Marxist economic theory was in part attributable to a general wave of Marxist and post-Marxist theory in the social sciences in Western Europe in the wake of student radicalism in the late 1960s (Gleditsch, 1989: 2). Scandinavian and especially West German Peace Researchers drew on the older Frankfurt School theorists Adorno, Horkheimer and Marcuse in pointing to the alienation and manipulation of citizens in late-modern Western societies, and, younger 'radical' Peace Researchers went further back to classical Marxists and Leninist writings (Gleditsch, 2004: 17). The older Frankfurt School held a rather pessimistic view of the possibility of genuine democracy and popular resistance to the machinations of political, financial and cultural elites, whereas the younger Frankfurt School, represented by Habermas, allowed for a more positive view of civil society, of the so-called 'life world's' ability to resist systemic interests and of the possibility of emancipation. The more pessimistic and radical branch of Neo-Marxist theory was the stronger influence on 1970s Peace Research, whereas it was Habermas's theory that informed early Poststructuralist writings (Ashley, 1981) and later Critical Security Studies (see chapter 7), which singled out 'emancipation' as its core parallel concept (Alker, 1988; Booth, 1991, 1997, 2005a; Wyn Jones, 1995, 1999, 2005).

During the 1980s, Peace Research becomes gradually more specialised (Wiberg, 1981; Gleditsch, 1989: 2) and less is published on 'pure' economic and development issues in key journals such as the *Journal of Peace Research*. There is a growing division of labour between Peace Research and Development Studies as the latter becomes a distinct specialism, and a bigger differentiation between the sub-disciplines of IR and IPE. Peace

Research remains the home of conflict studies, whereas development economics become a part of IPE (Liberal or Neo-Marxist). As a consequence, by the close of the Cold War, Peace Research is heavily dominated by political scientists compared to its multidisciplinary make-up in the 1960s (Gleditsch, 1989: 3). But this does not mean, as we shall see in chapter 7, that development disappears from the security–peace agenda forever. In fact, one of the most successful new political concepts of the 1990s is *Human Security*, coined by the United Nations Development Programme (UNDP) to locate questions of poverty and health more firmly on the global security agenda.

Galtung's structural violence theory did not explicitly foreground the environment, but concern with the extraction of resources from the Third World and a general worry about the impact of Western policies on future generations clearly resonated with concerns about the environment which arose in the 1960s and 1970s. Rachel Carson's book *Silent Spring* (1962) described the accumulation of pesticides through the food chain, and the belief that industrialisation had such significant side-effects that local and planetary environments were dramatically endangered gained hold (Barnett, 2007: 184–188). Parts of the environmental literature linked quite explicitly with the traditional agenda of Strategic Studies by identifying environmental 'resource wars', particularly in the Third World (Ullman, 1983). Others, such as Deudney (1990), argued that there was a low probability that environmental conflicts would lead to war. Here the referent object was still the state, and the environment a strategic resource that might precipitate conflict. Peace Researchers, by contrast, who approached the environment from a Galtungian perspective, called for industrialised countries to reduce their energy consumption (Gjessing, 1967; Poleszynski, 1977), or for seeing the environment as an arena susceptible to conflict resolution (Westing, 1988). A particular line of 'environmental literature' linked to nuclear warfighting, as in Sagan's (1983/4) path-breaking critique of how it would precipitate an environmental crisis in the form of a 'nuclear winter' (Nye, 1986). A more fundamental reorientation of the ISS agenda was undertaken by those who incorporated the environment as a referent object itself, seeing some of the bigger environmental problems as threatening to human civilisation as a whole.

The broader constitution of environmental security as threatened through climatic changes or through the degradation of land, biodiversity, the atmosphere, water, forests, coastal areas and rivers (Barnett, 2007: 189) arose mainly from overlapping scientific and political agendas that had little to do with the superpower military rivalry (Brundtland Commission, 1987; Nye and Lynn-Jones, 1988; Nye, 1989; Mathews, 1989; Buzan *et al.*, 1998: 71–72). In terms of the driving forces, this happened mainly as a response to *events* in the slow-moving sense: a generally rising concern about the (in)stability of the ecosphere. But processes of *institutionalisation*, such as the joint organising of a programme on Environmental Security in the 1980s by PRIO and the United Nations Environment Programme (UNEP) also worked to situate environmental security as one of the first sectoral expansions of national security beyond the military.

The internal dynamics of debates in Peace Research

The expansion of the concept of 'peace' from negative to positive was not, however, uncontested. Peace Research in the 1970s features heated, conceptually focused, debates over the concept of peace, the sectors to which it is applicable and its epistemology. This stands in contrast to Strategic Studies, which contained fierce discussions of the logics of deterrence, but which hardly examined the concept of security itself. The conceptual debates within Peace Research are further significant to the evolution of ISS in that several of them were to be continued in – or mirrored by – subsequent widening decades, particular in the 1990s.

'Broadeners' such as Galtung were challenged by other leading Peace Researchers who protested the move from military security to development. Kenneth E. Boulding strongly opposed this shift since most Peace Researchers were not, in his view, particularly well qualified to speak on the subject of development (Boulding, 1978: 346). More important still was Boulding's argument that military threats came with an urgency that exceeded that of 'positive peace': nuclear weapons had the potential to incinerate the entire planet, thereby making them the biggest threat to humankind. 'It still remains true', held Boulding, 'that war, the breakdown of Galtung's "negative peace," remains the greatest clear and present danger to the human race, a danger to human survival far greater than poverty, or injustice, or oppression, desirable and necessary as it is to eliminate these things' (Boulding, 1978: 348). Without a solution to the problem of nuclear war – and 'negative peace' – all other problems would become irrelevant.

Boulding's stressing of the urgency and different modality of military security was not the only criticism aimed at positive peace and structural violence. Foreshadowing later traditionalist concerns, other critics pointed to the conceptual imprecision of structural violence: it could not be 'differentiated from related and equally important concepts' and there were no criteria on which researchers could decide whether positive peace was attained (Sylvester, 1980: 307). Boulding (1978: 346) put it more bluntly arguing that to critics the concept of structural violence included 'anything that Galtung did not like'. Concepts, sceptics held, are only meaningful if they can be distinguished from other concepts and if they can be identified empirically. With structural violence 'everything became peace'.

That the positive–negative peace debate was a fixture in Peace Research is evidenced by the frequency with which the terms are used in publications, particularly in the late 1960s and 1970s. Another indication of the constitutive nature of this distinction is that it features prominently in studies of the field of Peace Research's institutionalisation. In 1971, Everts conducted a thorough study of Peace Research institutions on behalf of UNESCO, a key promoter of Peace Research in the 1960s and 1970s. In addition to Everts's study, UNESCO sponsored a similar report in 1966, and the committee under which Chatfield (1979) analysed the growth of Peace Research journals. Everts found that 11% of the 140 Peace Research institutions asked favoured the study of negative peace, 44% the study of positive peace and 28% the study of both (18% provided no answer or a different one). The significant change from 1966 was that at that time 25% favoured positive peace, while 43% answered both; the 11% for negative peace remained constant.

The debates over the concept of peace integrated normative, political and epistemological concerns. Interestingly, when looking back on Cold War Peace Research, there are striking similarities with contemporary debates in ISS. There was an explicit debate on which epistemology should be chosen, and on the normative implications thereof. There was an engagement with the role that Peace Researchers should adopt vis-à-vis the state apparatus, not least how Peace Researchers compare to strategic experts. There was a strong sense that epistemological distinctions followed a US–European divide. When comparing Cold War Peace Research to Strategic Studies there was more explicit debate within the former on epistemology and the identity of the discipline and its practitioners/ activists. This in part may be attributable to Peace Research being the weaker player on the broader ISS terrain as concerns institutionalisation in universities, think-tanks and government offices (if not necessarily in terms of journals). But it may also be an outcome of Peace Research's double genesis as part mathematical and behavioural, and part philosophical, historical and sociological.

The dual epistemological roots of Peace Research go back to the found-ing of the field itself. It was crucial to its self-identity that it was inter-or even transdisciplinary, as evidenced for example by the listing of the editorial board on the inside cover of *Journal of Peace Research*, which announced the discipline of each member. In addition to the predictable ones of Political Science, International Relations and Sociology, board members came from Physics, Economics, Law, Psychology, Anthropol-ogy, Biology, Philosophy, International Law and Chemistry. Beginning with the mathematical, behavioural tradition, the first contributors usu-ally identified as modern forefathers are Sorokin (1937), Quincy Wright (1942), Lentz (1955) and Richardson (1960a, 1960b). Richardson was a meteorologist and partly self-taught mathematician, who turned to the study of war, particularly of arms racing, after having experienced the trauma of the French battlefields during the First World War (Richard-son, 1957: 301). Most of his work was not published until after his death in 1953, but it drew the attention of other researchers such as Kenneth E. Boulding (1978: 344; 1962), Rapoport (1957), Smoker (1964) and Singer (1979, 1980). The next group of contributors were game theorists, and game theory quickly became a key topic of concern in the jour-nal *Conflict Resolution*, later *Journal of Conflict Resolution*, which from 1965 featured a special section on gaming edited by Anatol Rapoport. The last group of contributors (Boulding, 1978: 345) came from Social Psychology and worked on conflict processes and resolution in groups (Osgood, 1953, 1959, 1962; Kelman, 1965; Gurr, 1970). Institutionally, *Conflict Resolution* in 1957 located itself with the 'sociologists, psycholo-gists, educators, and pioneers of behavioral science' (*Conflict Resolution*, 1957: 1–2), but interestingly also placed itself within the field of *Inter-disciplinaris internationalis*, holding that 'conflict resolution' was a better term, since '"peace" is a word too much abused in our day'. The *Journal of Conflict Resolution* became the central launching pad for, in the words of the incoming 1973 editors, Bruce Russett and Marguerite Kramer, '"hard-nosed peace research", primarily formal theory and quantitative research', which formed the core of the field of Conflict Resolution (Rus-sett and Kramer, 1973: 4). Taking stock of disciplinary developments, Russett and Kramer (1973: 3) held that IR journals had seemed 'hostile or at best indifferent' to quantitative research when the *Journal of Con-flict Resolution* had been launched, thus giving Peace Research a stronger behavioural foundation than IR or Strategic Studies. Russett and Kramer (1973: 5) also argued – in keeping with the general 1970's détente-related turn – that they wanted to shift the balance from international conflict and nuclear war to ecological balance, and class, ethnic, racial and societal conflict. Crucially though, this expansion of the substantial topic was not followed by a broadening of the epistemological agenda. A little closer to the middle of the epistemological spectrum, the Arms Control literature was traditional, although there was much of it that was built on counting military hardware. This literature was concerned with numbers and material, quantifiable factors, but did not necessarily adopt more sophisticated research designs seeking to demonstrate causal relationships. The task was to work through the intricate balances between East and West across a large set of elaborate classifications.

The other epistemological Peace Research tradition stretched back to political theorists such as Kant's *Perpetual Peace* and in the twentieth century, writers such as Angell (1910, 1938) and Mitrany (1933, 1966) (de Wilde, 1991). A broader historical agenda and epistemology was adopted by the journal *Peace and Change*, first published in 1976 (Chatfield, 1979: 172–173), and the journal *Alternatives*, edited by Rajni Kathari and Richard Falk from the World Order Model Project, launched in 1975 and described by Chatfield (Chatfield, 1979: 174; see also Vasquez, 1976: 708) as 'normative and policy-oriented'. Yet also Critical-positive Peace Researchers were in favour of 'disciplined methodology' (*Journal of Peace Research*, 1964: 4) even if it was not a formal, quantitative one, and Scandinavian and German Peace Research were devoted to developing key concepts and terminology. Epistemologically, this came closest to a qualitative, sociological tradition with an empiricist, soft-positivist leaning (Patomäki, 2001: 728) in that concepts had to be distinct and be applicable to – or found in – the real world (Lawler, 1995; Väyrynen, 2004: 32). Theories referred to measurable material objects and actions, and were structural rather than hermeneutic. When Galtung called for an incorporation of case-studies, for instance, these were to be situated inside structural analysis of economic and cultural imperialism. They were not designed to uncover local constitutions of peace, development and security issues. Nor were linguistic or discursive phenomena going to be given much concern, as Galtung (1984: 128) put it: 'Thoughts and words come and go, actions depend on what is objectively possible, given by the constraints of natural laws only.'

This epistemological diversity led to a concern in the 1970s with 'the two cultures problem', that Peace Research might bifurcate into two epistemological camps unable to speak to each other, training students who either would be 'unable to read, let alone critically assess, a number of socially important pieces of quantitative research' or alternatively 'be

insensitive to the suffering that can occur from the violation of ethical norms' (Vasquez, 1976: 710–711). This two cultures problem was
– as today (see chapters 8 and 9) – also seen in geographical terms:
Western Europe was humanistic and post-Marxist, the United States was
behavioural and quantitative (Onuf, 1975; Reid and Yanarella, 1976). The
Europeans had, held Boulding (1978: 347), retreated from reality into
'fantasies of justice', whereas Americans had succumbed to a 'niggling scientism, with sophisticated methodologies and not very many new ideas'.
Then, as now, researchers in the critical-European tradition were more
concerned with engaging the US-behavioural mainstream than vice versa
(Reid and Yanarella, 1976: 317). But European-Marxist Peace Researchers
were also rebutted for being 'a closed, complete system of thought' and
for seeking to explain all conflict of the global South with economic structures in the North (Onuf, 1975: 72; Reid and Yanarella, 1976: 316). Some
individuals did not, of course, fall into these rigid categories, and the
most important European journal, the *Journal of Peace Research*, continuously published articles from all corners of Peace Research (Gleditsch,
1993).

Worth noting in this debate is that the criteria for what constitutes a
humanistic epistemology are not at all fixed. Vasquez (1976: 710) defines
for instance the *Journal of Peace Research* as having shifted to 'a more
humanist approach by publishing radical and normative work', while
Reid and Yanarella (1976: 322) argue that this approach 'tacitly share[s]
a scientistic foundation with establishment figures'. Certainly, to a contemporary audience, the 'radical' writings of the 1960s and 1970s would
in most cases not look particularly radical compared to how the epistemological fault-lines became established from the late 1980s onwards.
How a field is understood and divided into epistemological perspectives is
thus not based on trans-historical objective factors, but is itself something
that can change in hindsight as other approaches appear. Epistemological
differences and commonalities are, in short, socially constituted.

There are also numerous discussions of the normativity of Peace
Research, but no consensus on what that means. Sometimes human-
ism and normative theory are linked and opposed to quantitative studies
(Vasquez, 1976: 710; Lopez, 1985: 118) or it is held that the scientism
of behavioural approaches depoliticises the normative issues that should
be confronted (Reid and Yanarella, 1976). The latter position became
increasingly common as epistemological debates gained hold of IR and
ISS in the late 1980s and after the Cold War (see, for instance, Walker,
1987; Patomäki, 2001) and we will return to it in coming chapters. But

many Peace Researchers in the scientific camp *did* conceive of themselves as normative. Kenneth E. Boulding (1978: 343) argued that Peace Research had always been normative and Richardson's son described how his father had been strongly motivated by his Quaker faith, foregoing wealth, vacations, hobbies and a professorship in his search for the causes of war (Richardson, 1957). Gleditsch (2004: 17) also notes how Norwegian Peace Researchers in the early 1960s linked behaviouralism to a radical agenda – as did Finnish Peace Researchers (Väyrynen, 2004: 31) – only to constitute it as a symbol of imperialism and US dominance by the late 1960s. Marxist Peace Research at that time still adopted a soft positivist epistemology, only not the quantitative, statistical one of behaviourally influenced approaches. As both scientific and softer positivist Peace Research had normative foundations, their difference lay not in <u>whether</u> normativity was involved, but <u>where</u> and <u>how</u> it entered the research process. Peace Researchers should, according to Boulding, choose important political problems, but subject them to scientific scrutiny. The lessons learned should then be normatively assessed, but the scientific testing should not be influenced by normative concerns. To Critical Theorists, this cutting up of the research process was problematic at best.

The view of Peace Research as normative also had consequences for the conception of the role that Peace Researchers adopted – and should adopt – vis-à-vis other disciplines and the political structures in place. Galtung repeatedly described Peace Research as akin to medicine and Peace Researchers as doctors: against the eradication of illness and in favour of health. Many others held that Peace Research should have a policy relevance (*Journal of Peace Research*, 1964: 4; Gleditsch, 1989: 4), or act in 'the dual capacities of scientists and reformers' (Burtan, quoted in Chaudri, 1968: 367). Yet as Wiberg (1981: 111) noted, this often took on 'a highly artificial impression', with authors trying to squeeze out general policy implications from quite specific studies. Particularly to Peace Researchers in the Marxist tradition, there was a sense of being different from 'war researchers' (Reid and Yanarella, 1976: 318), not only in substantial research focus, but in one's willingness to be complicit with the state. Controversy arose, for instance, over Peace Researchers who offered their advice to the US government during the Vietnam War (Olsen and Jarvad, 1970). To others working on concrete questions of arms reduction, conflict resolution and game theory, the disciplinary distinctions and the self-identities of Peace Researcher versus security strategist seemed less significant and more pragmatic.

From peace to security: Common Security, Feminism and Poststructuralism

During the 1980s there is a gradual shift from 'peace' to 'security' as the guiding concept of approaches critical of the Strategic Studies mainstream. Gleditsch notes in 1989 that 'most authors avoid the word peace, possibly because it sounds too grand and pretentious' (Gleditsch, 1989: 3). At the close of the 1980s, it seems thus as if Buzan's (1983, 1984a) call for changing the status of 'security' from underdeveloped to the conceptual common ground between Strategic Studies and Peace Research has been heard. This section explores three approaches – Common Security, Feminism and Poststructuralism – which grew out of early 1980s Peace Research, yet, particulary in the case of the latter two, intersected with social, political and feminist theories that propelled them away from the mainstream of Peace Research as the Cold War ended.

Foregrounding 'security'

Picking up the concept from Wolfers's old article on security as an ambiguous symbol, Buzan (1983: 6) looked back on thirty years of 'security' as an unexplored and essentially contested concept. This was unfortunate, argued Buzan (1983, 1984a), because 'security' had the ability to act as a conceptual meeting ground between the extremes of Realist Strategic Studies 'power' on the one side, and the 'peace' of Peace Research on the other. Moreover, Buzan pointed to '[t]he hazards of a weakly conceptualised, ambiguously defined, but politically powerful concept like national security', which 'offers scope for power-maximising strategies to political and military elites, because of the considerable leverage over domestic affairs which can be obtained by invoking it' (Buzan, 1983: 4, 9). Since 'security' was already in widespread high-politics use, one would for academic as well as political–normative reasons be better off engaging it directly.

Coining the terminology of 'referent objects', Buzan stressed the interlinkages and tensions across levels of analysis. As the subtitle of his book *People, States and Fear: The National Security Problem in International Relations* indicated, 'national security' stood at the centre of the analysis, but it was simultaneously stressed that 'people represent, in one sense, the irreducible basic unit to which the concept of security can be applied' (Buzan, 1983: 18). Echoing the view of security as always an individualising and a collectivising concept laid out in chapter 2, Buzan (1983: 20, 31) held that there was a tension between the state as the protector of 'its' citizens' security and the state as a threat to its own individuals, and that this was an inherent one rooted in the 'nature of political collectivities'. This did not mean that individual security should not be taken into account, but rather that there would be no abstract 'individual security solution' that could be laid out a priori. Security scholars needed therefore to theorise the relationship between individual and collective security and to analyse its empirical manifestations. Building on this tension, Buzan opened up the concept of the state to see it as constituted by its physical base, the idea supporting it and its institutional expression. A central point here, which was later developed into the theory on societal security, was to stress that the idea of the state might be more, or less, accepted and that questions of nationality might either support it (in a nation-state) or weaken it (in multinational states where minority nations feel repressed or maltreated). National security thus has an 'inside dimension' and unless this is relatively stable, 'the image of the state as a referent object for security fades into a meaningless blur' (Buzan, 1983: 69). The question of the weakness/strength of the state should therefore be separated from the question of the power that a state wields against other states. On the outside, international security is dependent upon the character of the international system, not only, as Neorealists pointed out, on the polarity of the system, but also on whether its character is one of immature anarchy (an unmediated Hobbesian world) or a mature anarchy where states have developed in Bull's terms an international society of norms, rules and institutions to mediate the effects of the anarchical, fragmented system (Buzan, 1983: 96). Buzan's conceptualisation of security as individual, national and international pointed to a deepening of security along the axis of referent objects. The second significant expansion advocated by *People, States and Fear* was along the axis of sectors, where the traditional military sector that Strategic Studies had concentrated on should be widened to include the economic, the political and the ecological.

In parallel with this new agenda, criticism of traditional national security rhetoric triggered a discussion about new concepts: *Common Security* (Independent Commission on Disarmament and Security Issues, 1982; Väyrynen, 1985; Windass, 1985; Buzan, 1987b; Dewitt, 1994) and *comprehensive security* (Chapman et al., 1983; Akaha, 1991; Dewitt, 1994). Comprehensive security, particularly linked to thinking in Japan, but also elsewhere in East Asia, retained a national security focus but widened the agenda away from just military security to other concerns, particularly economic, political and environmental threats.

The single most successful 'expansive' concept of the 1980s, is, however, probably 'Common Security', coined by the Independent Commission on Disarmament and Security Issues chaired by Olof Palme in 1982. Common Security was picked up by Peace Researchers, particularly perhaps in Germany, where the concept resonated with central policy debates (Meyer, 1989; Wæver, 1989b) The underlying assumption of Common Security was that 'the main threats to international security come not from individual states but from global problems shared by the entire international community: nuclear war, the heavy economic burden of militarism and war, disparities in living standards within and among nations, and global environmental degradation' (Porter and Brown, 1991: 109). Starting from national security, the report stressed that many aspects of the security agenda were collective and pointed to the 'less tangible dimensions to security'. It held that 'Citizens of all nations want to be able to remain true to the principles and ideals upon which their country was founded, free to chart futures in a manner of their own choosing' (Independent Commission on Disarmament and Security Issues, 1982: 4). Clearly, this should be read against the backdrop of the Second Cold War. To say that citizens wanted to be true to their countries' ideals was to reiterate not only the (fictitious) harmony between state and individual held by state-centric conceptions of security, but also to invoke the principle of 'non-interference in domestic affairs': state sovereignty protected states from others meddling in their domestic ideological, religious, political or economic choices. The Palme Commission was thus firmly embedded within the bipolar confrontation where states were seen as the key to a more peaceful world. Suggesting that states could override the principle of non-interference in domestic affairs to defend the insecurities of threatened populations, as became the norm in humanitarian operations/wars in the 1990s (Kosovo being the strongest example), was not on the agenda. The way in which questions of military technology saturated critical security thinking in the early 1980s is also evidenced in that after the first 12 pages laying out more general links between Common Security, national security, development and the Third World, the rest of the Palme Commission Report's 177 pages are devoted to detailed discussions of different disarmament and arms control scenarios. 'True security' was defined as 'ending the danger of nuclear war, reducing the frequency and destructiveness of conventional conflicts, easing the social and economic burdens of armaments' (Independent Commission on Disarmament and Security Issues, 1982: 6) and underdevelopment was considered through its relationship to military conflict: either because the militarisation of

Third World countries tied up resources that could have been spent on welfare and poverty reduction, or because scarcity, hunger and underdevelopment may cause conflict.

Yet, to articulate citizens' ability to chart their own future introduced a certain ambiguity: did this refer to citizens happily applauding 'their' government's choices, or did it refer to each individual's right to choose a future different from the one sanctioned by the state? This ambiguity, as well as the remark that the 'furtherance of human rights must continue' (Independent Commission on Disarmament and Security Issues, 1982: 6) makes it possible to read the Palme Commission as sowing the seeds of a concept of individual security. Although the state was supposedly the guarantee of citizens' security, this may not always be the case in real life. This ambiguity has made Common Security a concept that is often used in opposition to state-centric security, and viewed as setting the scene for individual security. It becomes in this respect the forerunner to Human Security, launched in 1994 by UNDP, which explicitly constituted the individual as the referent object for security.

Women as a particular group: the birth of Feminist Security Studies

A particularly noteworthy case of the negotiation of the tension between an individual and a collective–structural concept of security was the one over 'women' which began in the late 1970s and developed into the 1980s. Of the long list of issues falling under the rubric of structural violence, or linking to questions of conflict and group-formation, gender was not one given pride of place. Gleditsch (1989: 4) summed up the state of affairs in 1989: 'Only 8% of the articles in the JPR's [Journal of Peace Research] first 25 years were written by women; this figure shows little change over time. Moreover, we have not had very much to say on such issues as feminist approaches to peace.' In this the JPR was not alone: of the eighty subjects of research identified by Peace Research institutions in Everts's 1972 study none included gender, while class, imperialism, religion and race are prominently mentioned (Everts, 1972: 500–501). The absence of gender in Galtung's theory on structural violence may also be related to the downplaying of gender in post-Marxist theory in the late 1960s and 1970s. Marxists held that class relations were more fundamental, hence solving the problems of capitalist societies would also bring gender equality. In the 1960s and 1970s a few game-theoretical studies of women's behaviour in prisoner's dilemma appeared (Lutzker, 1961; Ingram and Berger, 1977), but these were situated inside a general game-theoretical research agenda and were concerned neither with women's contributions to Peace Research nor with the question of whether women might be facing particular security problems.

The absence of gender was not a particular feature of ISS, but a general trait of IR as a whole, and the writings on gender, peace and security that first materialised in the early 1980s grew out of Peace Research. These works were particularly concerned with how women's role as nurturer gave them a different view of war, peace and security. Opinion polls showed, argued Elise Boulding (1984), that women to a greater extent than men oppose military spending, intervention and environmental exploitation, while being in favour of aid to the poor at home and abroad. But the significance of gender goes beyond mobilising women in the electoral process: women hold different values, behave more cooperatively, favour holistic critical epistemologies and are 'more interested in identifying alternative security systems than in studying arms control' (Boulding, 1984: 2–3). Women are, in short, more peaceful than men.

Another first stage security feminist was Ruddick, who in *Maternal Thinking: Toward a Politics of Peace* (1989) argued that 'women have a cognitive style distinctly more concrete than men's' and that the military is built on notions of masculinity, not only because most soldiers are men, but because military thinking – including just war theory – turns our attention 'from bodies and their fate to abstract causes and rules for achieving them' (Ruddick, 1989: 95, see also 150; see also Cohn, 1987: 715, 717). First stage security feminists were careful to point out that gender is not a fixed biological identity, but produced through practices of socialisation: 'a boy is not born, but rather becomes, a soldier' (Ruddick, 1989: 145). 'Gender' therefore refers to cultural, political, social and discursive structures: the concepts of masculinity and femininity do not represent how 'women' and 'men' actually are, but how they have been formed through a complex political history that situates women within the private sphere and men within the public (Elshtain, 1981; Pateman, 1988). Men are constructed as protectors, domestically of the patriarchal family and internationally of the body politic, as self-sacrificing, patriotic, brave, aggressive and heroic. Women, by contrast, are in Elshtain's words 'Beautiful Souls', who offer emotional support and bestow romantic validation on the bravery of their Just Warrior men (Elshtain, 1987).

The second stage in developing a feminist approach to security involved an explicit challenge to women's peacefulness and thus, in Sylvester's (1987) words, a pointing to the dangers of merging feminist and peace projects. This also entailed a shift from to what extent peace-proneness was biological or cultural or not at all, to the argument that 'women' should be seen as a separate referent object for security. The first book to include an extensive conceptual engagement with security from a feminist perspective was Tickner's *Gender in International Relations* which explicitly acknowledged the influence of Scandinavian Peace Research (Tickner, 1992: xiii). Her conceptualisation of the referent object implied a shift from the state and towards the individual: 'national security often takes precedence over the social security of individuals' (Tickner, 1992: 28). Thus to 'consider security from the perspective of the individual' is to argue in favour of 'definitions of security that are less state-centered and less militaristic' (Tickner, 1992: 53). Situating Feminist Security Studies on the broader terrain of ISS, feminists broke with the positivist epistemology of quantitative Peace Research and adopted a 'multilevel and multidimensional' conceptualisation based on the experiences of women (Tickner, 1992: 66). Cynthia Enloe showed, for example, how military bases depend on the unpaid work of military wives, how a gendered economy of prostitution is tolerated in the name of 'national' security and how the global politics of nuclear deployment was countered by women protesting at Greenham Common (Enloe, 1989).

Locating Feminism within the general debates on security in the 1980s, it makes a strong call to include 'women' and 'gender' as referent objects for security. Looking more closely at the way in which those two referent objects are defined, Tickner sees gender as social, not biological, yet she maintains 'women' as a referent object with a real-world existence, a conceptualisation that concurs with standpoint feminism's view of women as pre-given subjects who are structurally disadvantaged. Work in this tradition has generated important accounts of how women are being adversely affected by a multitude of state practices, for instance of how women and children suffer disproportionately as refugees, how domestic violence is deemed acceptable in a manner that 'public' violence is not and how states until recently have constituted wartime rape as an expectable 'by-product' of conquering soldiers (for an overview see Blanchard, 2003). State security is supposed to provide security for all citizens, yet there is a gendered difference in how men and women are affected and what problems are considered 'proper' security problems. Women are not inherently peaceful or necessarily more likely to die, but they are threatened in other ways than men and their insecurities are validated differently within state-centric security discourses – women and men are not in other words equal referent objects before the state. It is also shown that many of the insecurities experienced by women have no direct connection with military state-centric security: women die from malnutrition, impoverished health care, environmental hazards and economic deprivation, issues that only figure within Strategic Studies to the extent that they impact on the military capabilities of the state.

What drove the arrival of Feminism to ISS in the 1980s and why did it take the form that it did? *Great power politics* and nuclear *technology* were significant in that bipolar confrontation formed the particular political context that Feminist writings addressed. Militarism, nuclear and conventional, was a central concern as was the way in which militarised societies marginalised women's security problems economically, socially and politically. There were also constitutive *events* that linked in with these concerns, most clearly when women played a key role in peace movements, as at the women's camp at Greenham Common. Yet the most significant driving factor for Feminist Security Studies was in all likelihood the *internal dynamics of academic debates* which was, again, linked to broader societal processes of women's liberation in the 1960s and 1970s. The late 1970s and early 1980s had witnessed a growth in Feminist literature in the humanities and the fields of the sociology of science and Political Theory, and this started to make an impact on IR around 1987–88. In 1988, a symposium on Women and International Relations was hosted at the London School of Economics and Political Science (LSE) which led to a special issue of *Millennium*, and in 1990 the Feminist Theory and Gender Studies Section of the International Studies Association was founded.

Linguistic approaches and Poststructuralism

The study of in-groups and out-groups has always been a key part of Peace Research, particularly under the heading of conflict resolution, but by the mid-1980s a distinct, more linguistic approach appeared. Drawing on linguistic philosophers such as Austin and Searle (Austin, 1962; Searle, 1969), Hook (1984, 1985) and Chilton (1985, 1987) held that language has a structuring and influencing capacity that provides it with 'social power' (Hook, 1984: 260). The central claim was that the choice of different metaphors, euphemisms or analogies had fundamental consequences for how 'reality' was understood, and hence also for which policies should be adopted. In keeping with the general focus on nuclear deterrence in the 1980s, most analyses dealt with how nuclear issues were represented through terms such as 'collateral damage' (Cohn, 1987; Cardiff Text Analysis Group, 1988). As Carol Cohn (1987: 711) made clear, 'collateral damage' was part of a larger technostrategic discourse where the reference point was the weapons themselves rather than the death of human beings. Nuclear language was furthermore shot through with gendered imagery: it was a 'patriarchal language' and 'both a product and an expression of the power of men in science, nuclear war planning and politics' (Hook, 1985: 71; Cohn, 1987).

Linguistic analysis in the 1980s came out of or had affinities to Critical Peace Research and would (still) in most cases echo the early Frankfurt School's post-Marxist concern with how modern media manipulated and structured reality, creating in Marcuse's words a *One Dimensional Man* (Marcuse, 1964). This rested upon an understanding of language as more or less able to represent, or misrepresent, reality. For those who drew upon French poststructuralist philosophers, most prominently Jacques Derrida and Michel Foucault, this view was modified in that to Poststructuralists, no materiality would ever be able to present itself outside of a discursive representation (Shapiro, 1981; Dillon, 1990: 103). While parting epistemologically with Peace Research's positivist agenda, 1980s Poststructuralism grew out of (the fringes) of Peace Research: institutionally, authors such as R. B. J. Walker and Ashley had ties to the World Order Models Project, as had the journal *Alternatives*, a key outlet for Poststructuralist research. Wæver and Joenniemi worked as Peace Researchers at COPRI and the Tampere Peace Research Institute (TAPRI), and the latter's journal *Current Research on Peace and Violence* also published Poststructuralist writings. Politically and substantially, Poststructuralists shared Peace Researchers' concern with the dangers of nuclear bipolarity and the need to change it, yet they also adopted epistemologies and methodologies radically different from both quantitative and soft-positivist Peace Research. In terms of the driving forces, the advent and first development of the Poststructuralist approach was impacted by *internal academic debates* in the form of disciplines (Political Theory, Philosophy, Linguistics and Sociology) and theories from outside ISS and IR, and by unfolding internal debates over epistemologies and methodologies within ISS itself. Yet, since Poststructuralism was equally formed by its historical context – the Second Cold War of the 1980s – it was also influenced by *great power politics* and the general fear and opposition that nuclear *technology* and arms racing generated on the academic and political left.

To Poststructuralists, to see security – or peace – as discourse involved a shift from an objective conception of security where threats could be assessed – at least in hindsight (Wolfers, 1952) – to a practice through which subjects were constituted. This implied a significant turn in security

thinking in that actors or identities were no longer stable and given entities to which Peace Researchers or security theorists could refer. National
security was not, in short, something that could be assessed through
an analysis of which threats a nation confronted, but rather a process
through which 'the nation' came to be produced and reproduced with a
particular identity. Threats themselves were therefore also discursive: to
constitute something as threatening was to invoke 'discourses of danger
and security', and to situate that 'something' as of a particular importance to the threatened Self (Dillon, 1990: 102). Drawing upon Foucault,
Poststructuralists furthermore emphasised the significance of power and
knowledge, of security discourses as 'plays of power which mobilize rules,
codes and procedures to assert a particular understanding, through the
construction of knowledge' (Dalby, 1988: 416). Knowledge in turn was
not free of value judgements, and the claim to objectivity that Classical
positivists and ISS traditionalists espouse was thus problematised.

Security politics, argued Poststructuralism, was fundamentally about
the construction of a radically different, inferior and threatening Other,
but also, since identity is always relational, about the Self. The focus on the
constitution of the Other broadened the scope of traditional security analysis in that Poststructuralists argued that security policies were directed
not only against an external Other – usually other states and alliances –
but also against internal Others as these were 'located in different sites
of ethnicity, race, class, gender, or locale' (Campbell, 1990: 270). Linking
back to the central questions at the heart of ISS laid out in chapter 2,
Poststructuralists advocated a critical scrutiny of the ways in which policy
discourse as well as (parts of) Realism and Strategic Studies pointed to
the need for societal cohesion as this 'need' produced the objects of fear
and difference which were to be eradicated or transformed.

Poststructuralism in the 1980s explored these themes through two –
sometimes intersecting – routes: one which dealt with security as an
abstract practice situated within the larger structures of state sovereignty,
and one which engaged the political context of the antagonistic superpower relationship. As one of the key theorists in the first tradition, Walker
traced the historical evolution of state sovereignty and its link to modern
conceptions of security (Walker, 1987, 1990). Walker held that the principle of state sovereignty provided a very powerful answer to the problem
of political identity in that it offered a spatial solution, where citizens
were located within the sharply demarcated territory of the state, and
a temporal solution, where progress and 'universalizing standards' were
possible on the inside, whereas power and conflict made global, universal

principles impossible (Walker, 1990: 10–12). The challenge, according to Walker, was to find an alternative conception of security flexible enough that it could deconstruct the rigid claims of national security, allow those subjects whose security was not identical to that of the state to come into focus, and to define modes of differentiation that escaped both the friend–foe distinction and the tempting trap of universalism as one global conflict-free state.

Other Poststructuralists turned to contemporary events, and the Second Cold War was the subject of several early Poststructuralist analyses (Dalby, 1988; Nathanson, 1988; Campbell, 1990). Campbell (1990) located the constitution of the Soviet Other inside a longer American history of difference that comprised American Indians, gender relations and environmental degradation. Dalby (1988: 423) offered a critical analysis of Sovietology as a discipline of knowledge and power. The emphasis on structure and the wider discursive context that actors or texts are situated within also made Poststructuralists suspicious of what may at first look like changing structures. Challenging concepts of state sovereignty and security was made difficult by the discursive and political 'work' that had gone into reproducing these over several centuries, not least because other, alternative conceptions had been silenced. Yet resistance might also come from unlikely corners. Shapiro and Der Derian in particular argued in favour of expanding the understanding of how security politics was produced to include how popular culture represented such practices as surveillance (Der Derian, 1990) and espionage (Shapiro, 1988, 1990; Der Derian, 1992).

Situating Poststructuralism within the evolution of ISS, it was noteworthy for how it explicitly adopted and engaged the concept of security – and to a lesser extent peace – hence reinforcing the idea that security was the key concept around which Strategic Studies and Peace Research could meet. Early Poststructuralist works, particularly by Walker, Ashley, Der Derian and Wæver came out of a Peace Research tradition, yet explicitly recognised their debt to Classical Realism – Der Derian (1987: 4) to the extent that he labelled his approach a 'neo- or post-classical' one. Their insistence on the impossibility of moving from national security and state sovereignty to 'peace' and universal arrangements located them in an interesting space between the Cold War extremes of Strategic Studies and Peace Research. Poststructuralism's insistence on theorising security as discourse did, however, also draw much criticism from Realists as well as Peace Researchers, particularly as IR and ISS debates at the end of the 1980s and 1990s focused on epistemology and assumptions about 'reality', materiality and ideas. Since most Poststructuralist analyses of Western security discourse refrained from assessing (discursively constituted) Soviet capabilities or the 'discourses of the Other', they often appeared as internally driven. As the Cold War came to a close and the Soviet Union dismantled, these events pressured Poststructuralism, as we shall see in chapter 7, to further engage questions of change, events and non-radical constructions of identity. Looking to how Poststructuralism was *institutionalised*, the rather limited amount of literature and writers at this point make it a shorter story. Key outlets for Poststructuralist work were the journals *Alternatives* and *Millennium*, and ISA's flagship journal *International Studies Quarterly* published a special issue titled 'Speaking the Language of Exile: Dissidence in International Studies' in 1990. As this title indicated, a central Poststructuralist self-understanding was of being marginalised, exiled and silenced.

The internal structure and main offshoots of Peace Research are mapped in Figure 5.2. The full lines show a stonger connection, the dotted lines a weaker one.

Institutionalisation

We have already covered some aspects of Peace Research's institutionalisation above (for Poststructuralism, Feminist Security Studies and the views on the institutionalisation of the positive–negative peace debate). This section will focus on organisational structures, funding patterns and the outlets for the dissemination of research for Peace Research as a whole. The institutionalisation of Peace Research and Arms Control was not as big or as extensive as that for Strategic Studies, but it was nevertheless substantial, and broadly followed the same form. Given its oppositional character, there was a surprising amount of state backing for it, even in the US. That said, there can be no question that while interest in Arms Control was distributed fairly evenly across the Atlantic, Peace Research was considerably stronger in Europe, a difference closely related to Europe being the front line of the Cold War. In Europe there was more room for public concern that nuclear strategy was mainly about the defence of the US, and therefore room for differences of interest/policy vis-à-vis what was good for Europe and Europeans (Gleditsch, 2004; Väyrynen, 2004). The domestic difference, as noted, had partly to do with the existence of a strong political left in Europe (and its relative absence in the US), and partly with a larger room for critical Marxist perspectives within the academic world. Perhaps also the relative weakness of IR in continental

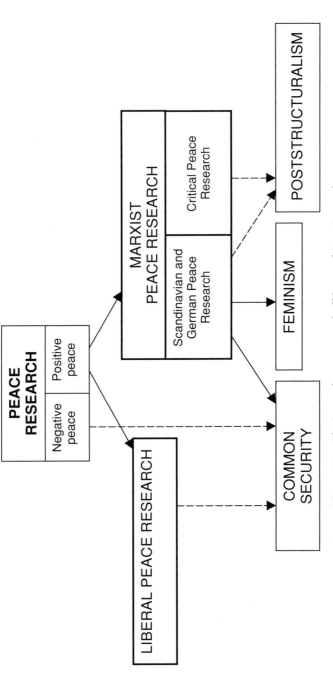

Figure 5.2. The internal structure and offshoots of Peace Research

Europe left more of a niche for Peace Research than was the case in the US and Britain.

Thinking about peace is almost as old as thinking about war, and there are general traditions of pacifism, anti-militarism, non-violence and anti-war stretching far back and having many different roots, whether religious (Bhuddist, Christian, Hindu), political (mainly liberal and socialist) or ethical (humanist). Specific institutionalisation in pursuit of peace seems to be a largely twentieth-century phenomenon, with perhaps the earliest manifestation being the Carnegie Endowment for International Peace, founded in 1910 as a private, non-profit organisation dedicated to advancing cooperation between nations and promoting active international engagement by the United States. Although there were many activist peace movements and organisations of various sorts during the inter-war years, the self-reflexive constitution of an academic discipline devoted to the study of peace is a post-Second World War phenomenon that mirrored that of Strategic Studies (Rogers, 2007: 36). Given the 'utopian' reputation of inter-war IR, there was perhaps less need for a distinctive Peace Research until IR took its Realist turn after the Second World War.

The main institutionalisation of Peace Research has thus almost all taken place since the Second World War, and not surprisingly its story runs in rough parallel with that of Strategic Studies. It got going during the 1950s and 1960s as the superpower nuclear arms race was moving into high gear, and maintained an impressive rate of growth right through the Cold War. It manifested itself in think-tanks, standing conferences, academic associations, journals, university departments and institutes, and even a whole university (Wiberg, 1988). Lenz founded his Peace Research Laboratory in St Louis in 1945, and the French Institut Français Polémologie was also established that year (Rogers, 2007: 37). The long-running Pugwash Conferences, starting in 1957, stemmed from the manifesto issued in 1955 by Bertrand Russell and Albert Einstein. Pugwash aimed to bring together scientists from many countries to discuss the threat posed to civilisation by the advent of thermonuclear weapons, and to explore, and make available to policy-makers, alternative approaches to arms control and tension reduction. In 1959 the Richardson Institute was set up as a Peace Research centre at Lancaster University in Britain, dedicated to pioneering research in peace and conflict studies, in the spirit of the Quaker meteorologist and mathematician, Lewis Fry Richardson. The same year saw the opening of PRIO, which was followed by a series of other Nordic Peace Research Institutes supported by public funding: in

Sweden (SIPRI, 1966), in Finland (TAPRI, 1969) and somewhat later in Denmark (COPRI, 1985). A smaller private Danish Institute for Peace and Conflict Research had, however, been founded in 1965. Along somewhat similar lines, the Peace Research Institute Frankfurt (PRIF) was founded in 1970 by the government of the state of Hessen as an independent foundation. Other central West German institutes founded in the late 1960s to early 1970s (Everts, 1972: 487) were the Arbeitsgemeinschaft für Friedens- und Konfliktforschung (AFK), Bonn (1968); Arbeitsgemeinschaft für Friedens- und Konfliktforschung, Heidelberg (1970); and Projektbereich Friedens- und Konfliktforschung, Freie Universität Berlin (1971). The Netherlands was also among the first countries to witness the establishment of Peace Research Institutes, the Polemological Institute at the University of Groningen in 1961 (identified by Wiberg, 1988: 39 as one of the three early growth poles of Peace Research) and the Peace Research Center, University of Nijmegen in 1965. All of these northern European institutes had research as their main activity, and like many Strategic Studies think-tanks, usually had a practical, policy-orientated mission. They were largely government funded, though some also received outside money for particular projects.

The Canadian Peace Research and Education Association (CPREA) was founded in 1966, and 1970 saw the setting up of the UN-linked International Peace Academy as an independent think-tank aimed at promoting peace policies. The Cornell University Peace Studies Program began in 1970. The Institute for Peace Research and Security Policy at Hamburg University (IFSH) started in 1971. Also in 1971, three university departments for peace and conflict research were established in Sweden, at Uppsala, Gothenburg and Lund, not just to do research, but to teach peace and conflict studies, and chairs were created and appointed at the two former universities in 1985 (Gleditsch, 2004: 20–21). Along similar lines, but with funding from the Society of Friends (Quakers) rather than the government, a Department of Peace Studies was established at Bradford University in the UK in 1973, and this department grew to become the world's largest university peace studies centre with 200 postgraduate students and five associated research institutes by 2003 (Rogers, 2007: 38). The Institute for Peace Science Hiroshima University (IPSHU) started in 1975 and was the first academic research body of its kind in Japan. In general, notes Wiberg (1988: 35–37), the period of growth has been around 1970 and may be attributed to the expansion of the social sciences as a whole in the 1960s and the subsequent stagnation of the 1970s.

That said, new institutions were still being founded during the 1980s. A University for Peace was established in Costa Rica in 1980 by the UN General Assembly. In the UK, the Council for Arms Control (CAC) started work in 1981 as an independent research and educational organisation for disseminating ideas and information on arms control and disarmament. CAC worked in part to support arms control as a counter to the nuclear disarmers in the British peace movement. When its funding ran out in the early 1990s as a result of the great decline in the military agenda consequent on the ending of the Cold War, CAC merged into the Centre for Defence Studies at Kings College London. The Geneva International Peace Research Institute (GIPRI) was founded in 1980 and it collaborates with the UN Institute of Disarmament Research (UNIDIR) and the Université Libre de Bruxelles (www.gipriwaterproject.ch/ – last accessed 6 December 2007). UNIDIR was established by the First Special Session of the UN General Assembly Devoted to Disarmament in 1978 at the behest of the French government and began work in 1980. Most of UNIDIR's activities are in the area of arms reduction and military conflict management (http://www.unidir.org/html/en/background. html – last accessed 6 December 2007). Perhaps surprisingly, the United States Institute of Peace (USIP) was set up by and remains funded by the US Congress, and was signed into law by President Reagan in 1984. USIP has invested 58 million dollars since 1986 in some 1,700 grants for research and peacebuilding projects in 76 countries around the world (www.usip.org/aboutus/faqs.html – last accessed 21 December 2007). Even towards the end of the Cold War new institutions were being founded. There was the Centre for Peace Studies at McMaster University and the Center for Nonproliferation Studies (CNS) at the Monterey Institute of International Studies, both in 1989. At present, the Peace Institutes Database lists 600 research and training institutes in 90 countries (http://databases.unesco.org/peace/PeaceWEBintro. shtml).

Peace Research in the US was, as noted above, mostly within the behaviouralist tradition, and was mainly institutionalised through particular leading university professors and their departments. The strongest institutional basis for the first wave of behavioural Peace Research was the Center for Research on Conflict Resolution set up at the University of Michigan in 1956. The Center hosted several members of the 'invisible college' inspired by Richardson's work, including Kenneth E. Boulding, Katz, Rapoport and Singer (Wiberg, 1998: 39). The Center published the *Journal of Conflict Resolution (JCR)* until 1971, when it was disbanded due to a lack of funding, and *JCR* moved to Yale University where Bruce Russett has been an editor ever since.

As early as 1964, Peace Research was sufficiently well established to enable the founding of the International Peace Research Association (IPRA). This created a global network of Peace Research institutions and eventually comprised five regional associations. The Peace Studies section of the ISA was founded in 1972,[5] and by 1987 it is described as one of the oldest sections of the ISA (memo dated 4 March 1987). There has also been steady growth in Peace Research journals and periodicals from *Conflict Resolution*, later the *Journal of Conflict Resolution* in 1957, *Peace Research Abstracts* (1963), the *Journal of Peace Research* (1964), *SIPRI Yearbook* (1968), *Bulletin of Peace Proposals* (published by PRIO, 1970), *Instant Research on Peace and Violence* (published by TAPRI from 1970, later changed to *Current Research on Peace and Violence*), *Alternatives* (1975), *Peace and Change* (1976), *NOD: Non-Offensive Defence – International Research Newsletter* (1987–1999, later changed to *NOD and Conversion*) published by COPRI and edited by Bjørn Møller, and the general journal of the ISA, *International Studies Quarterly*, described in 1979 by Chatfield (1979: 173) as 'the major broad-gauged organ of peace research in North America'.

A crucial component in the institutionalisation of academic fields is the development of a curriculum, a body of texts that can be taught to new students (Lopez, 1985). As Vasquez (1976) laid out, the 'two cultures problem' also had ramifications in the classroom in that there was a tendency to teach Peace Research along either behavioural or humanistic lines. A thoroughly integrated introduction to Peace Research which covered both of the two epistemological traditions was, argued Lopez (1985: 118) in his survey of Peace Studies curricula, only offered by Michael Washburn's (1976) *Peace and World Order Studies*. Wiberg (1988: 48) recommends *Peace and World Order Studies: A Curriculum Guide* for those teaching undergraduate courses in Peace Research (Institute for World Order, 1981). Other works from which Peace Research could be taught were Boulding and Boulding (1974) *Introduction to the Global Society*; Bremer *et al.* (1975) *The Scientific Study of War*; and in Swedish, Wiberg (1976) *Konfliktteori och fredsforskning*.

Turning to the impact of foundations and think-tanks on the institutionalisation of Peace Research and Arms Control, this is a theme much less covered in the self-reflective Peace Research literature than the topics

---

[5] According to papers from the ISA Headquarters inviting members to a meeting to establish the section at the annual conference.

of founding institutions, key forefathers, curricula, journals and associations. Benedict (1989: 91), the then associate director of the Program
on Peace and International Cooperation at the MacArthur Foundation,
argues nevertheless that foundations have played a major role in funding
and shaping peace studies. Focusing on the 1980s, the following foundations are deemed crucial: Carnegie, Hewlett, W. Alton Jones, MacArthur,
Rockefeller and Sloan. Reaching back to the 1970s, Wallerstein (2002: 83)
holds that a small group of foundations have systematically given grants to
institutions and researchers working in the fields of peace studies, conflict
resolution, arms control, non-proliferation and regional security: Ford,
MacArthur, W. Alton Jones, Rockefeller, Carnegie, Crompton, Prospect
Hill, Samuel Rubin, Scherman and Winston, and the Ploughshares Fund.
Benedict (1989: 93) notes that of grants given by MacArthur to institutions
between 1985 and 1988, '69 percent were awarded for projects on U.S.–
Soviet relations and issues of nuclear and military policy, 14 percent were
devoted to work on regional conflict, 9 percent to global issues such as the
development of an international economy, and 7 percent to the process of
U.S. policymaking in peace and security'. A broader epistemological and
substantive agenda is reflected in grants to discourse analysis, historical
and anthropological studies, global and economic change, ethnic conflict,
migration and resource-based conflicts (Benedict, 1989: 94).

   Think-tanks have been partially covered by the discussion of university
centres and research institutes mentioned above in that several of these
(SIPRI, PRIO and COPRI for instance) have such independent institutional identities that they would qualify as think-tanks, although it should
be noted that these are think-tanks with a strong emphasis on research.
Peace Research institutions would thus often engage in policy debates,
but usually from the vantage point of the (left-leaning) intellectual rather
than the policy advisor or consultant.

   Think-tanks which should be mentioned include the Brookings Institution established in 1927 by the merger of the Institute for Government
Research (1916), the Institute of Economics (1922) and a graduate
school (1924) (www.tni.org/detail'page.phtml?&publish=Y&int02=
&pub_niv=&workgroup=&text06=&text03=&keywords=&_lang=&
text00=&text10=history-index&menu=07a – last accessed 8 December
2007). Brookings associates played central roles in drafting the plans for
the UN and the Marshall Plan after the Second World War and is usually
located at the centre-left of the US policy spectrum. Another think-tank
with links to Arms Control is the Carnegie Endowment for International
Peace, which during the Cold War conducted research on the UN, founded

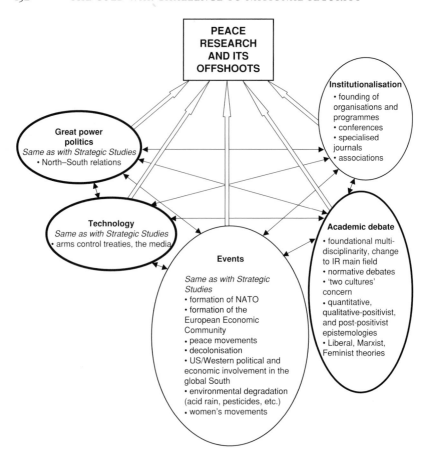

Figure 5.3.   The main drivers behind Peace Research and its offshoots

the Arms Control Association in 1971 and became the publisher of *Foreign Policy* (www.carnegieendowment.org/about/index.cfm?fa=history – last accessed 8 December 2007). The Social Science Research Council (SSRC) has also played a major role as an institution mostly funded by large Liberal foundations: the Ford Foundation, the MacArthur Foundation and the Andrew W. Mellon Foundation. In the Nordic area, the Nordic Cooperation Committee for International Politics, including Conflict and Peace Research (NORDSAM), funded smaller Peace Research projects and the joint committees of the Nordic Social Science Research Councils sponsored the publication of the *JPR* (Gleditsch, 2004: 15).

The main drivers of Peace Research and its offshoots are shown in Figure 5.3. One should note that the main box at the top centre,

'Peace Research and its offshoots', comprises all of the approaches shown in Figure 5.2. As laid out above, there were important differences between the impact of the driving forces on each of these offshoots, and Figure 5.3 therefore provides a general overview of the main development, not specific details.

Conclusions

As this chapter shows, there is quite strong evidence for seeing Cold War Strategic Studies, Arms Control and Peace Research as a single conversation despite their obvious political differences. There was a lot of substantive overlap, very similar drivers, a parallel profile of institutionalisation and not much in the way of epistemological differences, at least not in ways that correlate with Strategic Studies and Peace Research orientations. There were certainly disagreements, bordering at times on overt antagonism and contempt, about preferred priorities and policies, and at the extremes there were different views of how to define the problem. But across a broad middle range, both Strategists and Peace Researchers were responding to the same problem: how to pursue security in the context of a nuclear-armed bipolar superpower confrontation.

The evolutionary story told in this chapter is in several ways a more complex one than that of chapter 4, which was concerned with the birth of ISS and its Strategic Studies core. This chapter has traced how Arms Control to a lesser extent and Peace Research in more fundamental ways criticised Strategic Studies and how crucial political, normative and epistemological divisions within Peace Research generated separate approaches with distinct identities: negative versus positive peace researchers, and within the positive camp between the Liberal Deutschian approach and the Critical Neo-Marxists, while bridging them a Galtungian position incorporated Liberal as well as Marxist ideas. During the 1980s, Common Security grew out of an Arms Control agenda that resonated with negative Peace Research, but it simultaneously opened the door to the wider agenda of positive Peace Research. In the same decade, two other approaches, Feminism and Poststructuralism, had their roots in positive Peace Research, but they gained momentum and took directions that generated an understanding of them as being approaches in their own right rather than sub-branches of Peace Research. Debates evolved around the fundamental questions at the heart of ISS: the possibility of transforming Realist dynamics between states, the question of domestic stability and which epistemologies to adopt. The story of this chapter is thus one that brings in more approaches and labels on the terrain of ISS and therefore also to a larger extent than in chapter 4, one of interactions and academic debates.

In terms of the driving forces, the shared concern across Strategic Studies, Arms Control and Peace Research with nuclear deterrence and bipolar relations indicated that *great power politics* and *technology* were highly influential also for this part of the ISS story. Even to positive Peace Researchers, nuclear stalemate was significant both as a subject in its own right and as an economic and political drain on the world's resources. In terms of *events*, both Arms Control and Peace Research thus shared with Strategic Studies the Cold War and the thawing and cooling of super-power relations as foundational events. To positive Peace Researchers, their expanded agenda was in part formulated as a response to events in the Third World, both sudden ones, such as the waves of decolonialisation, and more slow-moving ones, like the economic exploitation that North–South structures entailed. The stronger focus on debate within this chapter implies that the *internal dynamics of academic debates* played a major role in explaining the evolution of Peace Research. Peace Research not only imported from other disciplines (game theory, Mathematics, Philosophy, social theory, Development Studies and Feminist Theory among them), as did Strategic Studies, but constituted itself as thoroughly interdisciplinary. Peace Research was also concerned with epistemology and 'the two cultures problem' as well as with the political and normative stances that being a scholar entailed. Finally, *institutionalisation* implied that Peace Research put down its own roots in terms of organisations, educational institutions, venues for publication and networks.

The similar patterns of institutionalisation and focus on the Cold War meant that the ending of the Cold War posed a parallel crisis in both Peace Research and Arms Control to that for Strategic Studies. The main exception here was those who had been challenging not just the national security orientation of ISS, but also its confinement to the military sector. This had happened both under the conceptual banner of positive peace, and from the early 1980s increasingly under the label of securities other than national security. For them the ending of the Cold War was not a crisis but an opportunity. As we shall see in chapter 6, the success of the 1980s widening attempts was evidenced in traditional

Strategic Studies theorists coming out to <u>defend</u> a concept of military, state security which had hitherto been so hegemonic that it did not have to justify itself. Chapter 7 will analyse the booming academic industry of post-Cold War widening approaches that took off where the 1980s ended.

6

International Security Studies post-Cold War: the traditionalists

This chapter concentrates on those Strategists, Peace Researchers and Arms Controllers who stayed with the military agenda despite the ending of the Cold War, and discusses these together as 'traditionalists'. It thus collapses most of the main distinctions between Strategic Studies and Peace Research used to structure chapters 4 and 5. This chapter and the next are organised around a new division between traditionalists collectively, and those who wanted to widen and deepen the meaning of security. Our argument that Cold War ISS can be seen as a single conversation as far as military security was concerned remains just as strong, or even stronger, after the end of the Cold War.

Yet one might wonder what produced this convergence between Strategic Studies and 'negative' Peace Research considering their heated normative and analytical exchanges during the Cold War? Building on our analysis in the previous two chapters, we would argue that this convergence, illustrated in Figure 6.1, was facilitated in part by the shift towards 'security' within Peace Research. As Gleditsch noted in 1989, by then peace was no longer the concept that guided Peace Research (Gleditsch, 1989). In addition, although negative Peace Research understood itself as normatively driven, it was a normativity that entered the analysis through the choice of research subject. Once the research question had been formulated, it was up to social science to determine its validity and the research process was therefore objective as far as the results produced were concerned. This created an analytical meeting ground with Strategic Studies which worked from a similar epistemology. If anything, Peace Researchers were more hard-core game theory, rational choice and large-scale quantitative data-sets, compared to much of Strategic Studies' preference for historical and comparative case-studies (Walt, 1991, 1999a). The fact that epistemological convergence was deemed important and could be the basis for common research agendas was itself an indication that epistemology was given pride of place in IR debates in the late 1980s and the 1990s (Keohane, 1988). The ending of the Cold War also implied that

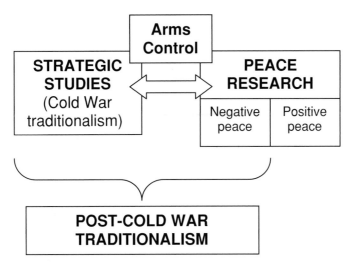

Figure 6.1.   The composition of Post-Cold War traditionalism

Peace Research's sense of nuclear urgency – the *Bulletin of the Atomic Scientists*' 'Doomsday Clock' showing five minutes to midnight was an apt indication – was replaced by a greater variety of issues. This generated more specific research agendas along which Peace Researchers and strategists could more easily converge on substance, for instance on the democratic peace and proliferation. And in terms of disciplinary sociology there might have been a shared sense that wideners and deepeners were presenting more of a common challenge to be confronted, in that the post-Cold War agenda might look, at least to politicians, journalists and other non-specialists, as being less about military security than had been the case during the Cold War. The widening–deepening challenge was aimed not only at the military state-centrism that negative peace researchers and strategists shared, but also at their common rationalist epistemological position.

   In terms of the four basic questions that guide ISS, the convergence is thus brought about through a downplaying of the question 'what is the view of security politics?' Peace Researchers and Strategists might continue to disagree on this, but the declining nuclear urgency made this less of an issue, and the shared epistemology made this a question that could be posed empirically. In terms of the referent object, the state held centre-stage; in terms of the security sector, the military did too; and in terms of the location of threats, Strategic Studies opened up for a broader view that may have previously given Peace Research a bit of an 'internal threats' advantage.

The post-Cold War era was defined by the fact that bipolarity, in both its material and ideological senses, disappeared as the Soviet Union first changed its identity to an ideological and military form less threatening to the West, and then imploded, taking with it the main legitimising reason for the massive military competition. But what exactly replaced it – unipolarity? multipolarity? globalisation? – remained a matter of debate throughout the IR literature. Whatever the answer, it was clear for ISS that, from the late 1980s onwards, the priority attached to the Cold War political–military security agenda of how to deal with superpower confrontation, both nuclear and NATO central front, had plummeted. The ending of the Cold War thus raised big questions about the basic nature of a Strategic Studies and Peace Resarch agenda that had long been dominated by superpower rivalry and the fear of nuclear war (Jervis, 1991/2; Gaddis, 1992/3; Lebow, 1994). The sharp decline in military security concerns was in part what opened the way for the expansion of the wider security agenda already visible during the 1980s, a story we pick up in chapter 7. As we shall see in this chapter, while some big parts of the Cold War military agenda did indeed largely drop out of interest, other parts remained robust, and new topics quickly emerged. The traditional agenda lost some of its dominance of ISS, faced new challengers, and for a few years suffered some intellectual pressure and institutional retrenchment. But perhaps surprisingly, given the magnitude of change in its environment, it underwent no major existential crisis. Realists would not find this lack of crisis surprising, since for them it was just a matter of time before the relevance of the military agenda would again become apparent.

Looking to the five driving forces, how did they produce the convergence between Strategic Studies and Peace Reseach as well as the directions that 'traditionalist' military security took? The Cold War had been the *meta-event* upon which ISS had been founded, and great power politics and technology had been the two most significant forces shaping the evolution inside of that 'event framework'. Post-Cold War, traditional ISS was compelled to answer two fundamental questions that concerned the focus on and explanatory power of *great power politics*: why did the Cold War end? And would traditional military state-centric approaches be of much use with bipolarity gone? The first two sections below examine how answering these questions pushed Realist ISS to consider some of its ontological, analytical and epistemological assumptions. This in turn also indicates the significance of *internal academic debates*, both within

ISS and on ISS as it was impacted by IR. As the 1990s unfolded, a patchwork of conflicts and crises framed a third question for traditional ISS: what polarity had replaced bipolarity? We look to the responses in a section below as well as to the manner in which regional security and non-Western events gained an increased saliency.

The preoccupation with *technology*, particularly nuclear technology, during the Cold War had been enormous, and with the ending of the Cold War the link between technology development and superpower rivalry was broken. Yet the material reality of nuclear technology was still there to be dealt with, even though its political context had changed radically, and technology remained therefore a significant driving force for traditionalist post-Cold War ISS. One result, which we examine in a separate section, was that the literature on nuclear proliferation, already large during the Cold War, became more prominent, and there were similar continuities on other technology-driven topics. The chapter ends by looking to the consequences that the ending of the Cold War had on the *institutionalisation* of traditional, military approaches.

The loss of a meta-event: surviving the Soviet Union

The specific characteristics of the Cold War – bipolarity, nuclear weaponry and deterrence in the context of an oscillation between confrontation and détente – played an integral role in how security was conceptualised and institutionalised within ISS. With the Cold War now history, the traditional core of ISS faced the simple and potentially devastating question of *how to survive in the face of the peaceful, voluntary dismantling of the bipolar order*. How could traditional ISS explain the ending of the Cold War, and would there be a role for Strategic Studies, and indeed the military side of Peace Research, to play in the post-Cold War order? Linking back to our four basic questions, the challenges posed to Strategic Studies and more broadly, Realist and state-centric approaches, came in a number of more specific forms targeting different parts of the Strategic Studies and Realist edifice.

The breakdown of bipolarity challenged Neorealist assumptions that this system was particularly durable. The Neorealist (and Realist more generally) response, to be further examined below, held that while bipolarity was assumed to be durable, it was not presumed to be permanent. Kennan's (1947) account of how the populations of the Soviet Union would come to topple 'their' Communist leadership was repeatedly invoked as a testament to Realist forewarnings of the changing global

structure. Moreover, Realists also approached the changing global structure as an empirical fact that should be addressed analytically: the end
of bipolarity did not prove that polarity did not matter, but, held Neorealists, rather that a new politically and academically pertinent research
agenda was produced. What followed in the 1990s was thus a concern with
establishing what the new polarity of the system was (Kegley and Raymond, 1992, 1994; Huntington, 1993b; Jervis, 1993; Layne, 1993; Waltz,
1993; Kapstein and Mastanduno, 1999; Wohlforth, 1999). This was no
easy question. The Cold War definition of polarity had been based on the
military having the clear upper hand, but also on a convergence of the
military, political, economic and cultural sectors. In the early 1990s, it was
no longer obvious that military capabilities were more significant than
economic or political ones, nor was it clear how to compare across sectors:
were Japan (economically strong, militarily not) or the EU (economically
strong, militarily and politically fragmented) potential poles?

The end of bipolarity was one thing, but the manner in which it came
about, peacefully and voluntarily rather than through military confrontation, formed a challenge of its own. Realism's understanding of the state
as driven by its own utility, power, security and interests seemed to resonate poorly with the Soviet leadership's decision to allow a dismantling of the Warsaw Pact, the end of communism, German reunification
and the disintegration of the Soviet Union itself. This process seemed
to prove Deutschian transactionists, Liberal interdependency economists
and peace researchers right that security politics need not be based on the
Realist assumption of permanent political–military rivalry. If this was the
case, a series of key normative and political assumptions at the heart of
Strategic Studies were thrown into possibly unsalvageable doubt. A major
debate therefore ensued around domestic versus systemic, and material versus ideational explanations for Soviet behaviour (Deudney and
Ikenberry, 1991, 1991/2; Perle, 1991; Risse-Kappen, 1991; Dolan, 1992;
Lebow and Risse-Kappen, 1997; Forsberg, 1999; Brooks and Wohlforth,
2000/1).

Realists rose to the ontological challenge, and many argued that Gorbachev's decisions were in fact driven by Western security policies which
had pushed the Soviet Union to such economic and military overexten-
sion that it stood on the brink of internal collapse. Its choice was one of
non-violent defeat or being faced with violent domestic opposition. Or,
in two-level game terminology, Soviet leaders were pushed by domestic
forces to make the international adjustments necessary. Yes, the inability
of the Soviet leadership to provide welfare to its citizens undermined

the communist system, but this showed pressure being applied on the economic sector through the military sector and thus the military as the causal factor impacting the economic. Furthermore, nuclear deterrence might be said to have worked in the sense that Gorbachev could have chosen to remain within a US–Soviet competitive and mutually deterring logic, but that this would have run the risk of escalating confrontation to the point where the nuclear threshold was passed, or that domestic turmoil would eventually become so severe that nuclear weapons would be procured by opponents of the regime (for actual use or for bargaining power). According to this line of reasoning, nuclear deterrence did, in short, apply external and internal pressure and the fact that Gorbachev realised this shows that state leaders can make rational decisions, not that they are utopian, altruistic or motivated by world peace.

A slightly different line of Realist defence moved from the second level of analysis – the foreign policy of the Soviet Union – to the third, structural, level arguing that the case of the peaceful dismantling of the Soviet Union may be explainable, but nevertheless unusual. It should not in other words be interpreted as a fundamental break with the dynamics of international relations or as a sign that one had now progressed beyond the power struggles of an anarchic system. International politics goes through periods of accommodation and fewer wars, but there is always the lurking shadow of conflicts to come, and if states do not prepare for this – the lesson of the inter-war period – they will learn the hard way that others do (Mearsheimer, 1990; C. S. Gray, 1992, 1999; Waltz, 2000b). By making claims about the future, but not specifying how long it might take before conflicts reoccurred, this Realist ontology became in principle immune to empirical challenges.

Did the ending of the Cold War challenge the understanding of security as concerned primarily with external threats? Yes, in that the ending seemed to stem as much or more from internal dissolution and transformation, not only of the Soviet Union, but throughout the Eastern bloc as Hungarians crossed the border into Austria and the Berlin Wall fell. No, in that these events could be seen as linked to the external pressure applied. Looking past the explanation of the end of the Cold War and into the events – particularly the military conflicts – that were to be at the top of the political and ISS agenda in the 1990s, the need to shift from external threats to internal ones was, however, apparent as evidenced by the upsurge in so-called ethnic or civil conflicts, and in the ensuing series of humanitarian interventions discussed below. The Strategists' response was not to relinquish intra-state wars to Peace Researchers, sociologists or anthropologists used to working at the sub-state level, but to move Realist analysis down one step and apply it to warring sub-state groups (Posen, 1993; Van Evera, 1994; Kaufmann, 1996). Looking back to the formative early years of ISS, there were indeed elements of that tradition which facilitated a broadening of the research agenda to include intra-state conflict. Kennan had been concerned with domestic cohesion at home and abroad, Herz's security dilemma was applicable across levels of analysis, and Neorealism's understanding of the state was built on the rational actor assumption of micro-economic theory and hence could quite easily be transferred to sub-state collectivities.

Internal academic debates: state-centrism and epistemology

The dwindling of the Cold War registered on traditionalist ISS in that it generated a series of explicit discussions of what should be the research agenda of ISS, which concept of security should be employed and which epistemology should be adopted in its study. Such conceptual and theoretical engagements had been largely absent from the field since the immediate post-Second World War decade when Wolfers (1952) and Herz (1950) had produced their seminal works on security as an ambiguous symbol and the security dilemma (Walt, 1991; Baldwin, 1995). This turn to basic theoretical and conceptual questions was not only a consequence of the ending of the Cold War, but also of factors related to the driving force of internal academic debates. It seems safe to say that widening approaches were starting to make an impact on the Strategic Studies mainstream by the close of the 1980s. While those speaking from that position might still be strongly committed to a state-centric, military conception of security as '*the study of the threat, use, and control of military force*' (Walt, 1991: 212), they were now more pressured to defend this position. In terms of the sociology of academic debates, a perspective's diminishing hegemonic status may be identified through its need to define what was previously seen as common sense or natural. Although engaging challengers may grant the latter more visibility, ignoring them risks marginalising the older, hegemonic perspective even further. In terms of traditional approaches and their defences against challengers in the late 1980s and 1990s, orthodox wideners became 'contestants to be addressed', and up to a point the process of explicit defence hardened and narrowed the traditionalist position around its military core. But there were also challengers that remained largely ignored by the traditionalist mainstream. *International Security*, for instance, did not publish a single article on gender, Poststructuralism, or Post-colonial approaches, and Kolodziej's *Security and International Relations* (2005), which effectively summed up and spoke to the traditionalist-widening agenda of the 1990s, defined Conventional Constructivism (see chapter 7) as the most radical widening perspective to be addressed.

Why did traditionalists stick by their state-centric military guns? In addition to subscribing to Realist ontological assumptions about the inability of states to transform the anarchical international system – or in the case of Peace Research making this a testable research question – traditionalists pointed to the need for a concept that was analytically clearly defined. Probably the clearest statement of this position was made by Walt in his 1991 article on the state of the field of Security Studies, where he pointed to those wanting to broaden the concept of security 'to include topics such as poverty, AIDS, environmental hazards, drug abuse, and the like'. Such calls were important, argued Walt, in that they showed that

> nonmilitary issues deserve sustained attention from scholars and policy-makers, and that military power does not guarantee well-being. But this prescription runs the risk of expanding 'security studies' excessively; by this logic, issues such as pollution, disease, child abuse, or economic recessions could all be viewed as threats to 'security.' Defining the field in this way would destroy its intellectual coherence and make it more difficult to devise solutions to any of these important problems.   (Walt, 1991: 213)

Walt's repudiation of widening approaches echoed Kenneth E. Boulding's (1978) defence of negative peace thirteen years earlier, and was based on a combination of ontological, analytical and political considerations: the state was considered the best defence against external and domestic insecurity in an imperfect world, and the threat of military force a fact that ISS should be devoted to studying (Betts, 1997; Williams, 1998) and a coherent subject around which expertise could be accumulated. This, however, did not mean that traditionalists were uncritical of the way in which security policy was conducted, or more specifically of the relationship between policy-making and the academic institution of ISS. Walt (1991: 212–213) was adamant that ISS should be devoted to 'central policy problems' and 'phenomena that can be controlled by national leaders'. But he was equally concerned with the academic quality of the work that went on inside think-tanks or was supported by defence contractors and the US Defense Department. Much of it was 'propaganda' that did not meet 'the standards of logic and evidence in the social sciences', held Walt (1991: 213), who noted that 'there is a difference between the scholarly side of security studies and works that are largely political advocacy, just as there is a difference between scholarship in criminology and the public debate on gun control'. The concern for the standing and solidity of security research was also central to Nye and Lynn-Jones (1988: 12–13) who held that the policy-oriented nature of ISS meant that the field was theoretically underdeveloped. This was linked both to 'Foundation funding patterns and the policy fads of the day' and to analysts being constantly involved in policy-making and advising. This was not only weakening ISS itself, in that good theory is what allows a field to take on a constantly changing empirical world, as deterrence theory had done for Strategic Studies during the golden age. It would also put ISS at a structural disadvantage within the broader institutional structures of academe, undermine scholarly respect for research in Security Studies and weaken its status inside and across departments.

Epistemology played a crucial part in Walt's defence against widening approaches, and this in turn linked in with broader IR debates in the late 1980s and 1990s. Keohane's Presidential address at the ISA in 1988 used the labels of *rationalism* and *reflectivism* and this both testified to and further cemented the status of epistemology – rather than the ontological views of IR – as the most important way in which to view IR positions and debates (Keohane, 1988; chapters 2 and 3; Wæver, 1997; Katzenstein *et al.*, 1998). Interestingly, Walt differentiated his position against epistemologies at both ends of the rationalist–reflectivist spectrum. In terms of 'epistemological wideners', Walt (1991: 223) warned against Poststructuralists who 'have seduced other areas of international studies' in spite of being 'mostly criticism and not much theory'. As a consequence, 'issues of war and peace are too important for the field to be diverted into a prolix and self-indulgent discourse that is divorced from the real world'.

Looking in the opposite epistemological direction, Walt (1991: 223) held that formal models, in spite of being more useful than Poststructuralism, should also be viewed with caution: 'impressive technical firepower' notwithstanding, 'their ability to illuminate important national security problems has been disappointing'. Eight years later – and with Poststructuralism apparently off the agenda – Walt (1999a) expanded this criticism of rational choice theory (including mathematical models and game theory), holding that while this approach scored high on logical consistency, it had failed to produce much original work, nor had it done much to test the empirical validity of its hypotheses. Formal theorists, almost all of whom had published in the *Journal of Conflict Resolution*, the main outlet for 'hard-nosed' quantitative Peace Research, naturally contested this assessment, arguing first that logical consistency was superior to originality and empirical validity, and second that formal theories were original and tested to a greater extent than acknowledged by Walt (de Mesquita and Morrow, 1999; Niou and Ordeshook, 1999; Powell, 1999; Zagare, 1999). Yet Walt stuck to his original analysis and ended his response on a rare explicit note: 'Let us be candid. There is a widespread perception that formal modelers are less tolerant of other approaches than virtually any other group in the field of political science' (Walt, 1999b: 128–129).

Linking back to the analysis of 'the two cultures problem' in Peace Research in chapter 5, and what seems to be an ongoing concern that ISS (and Peace Research) was or would be developing into disconnected streams of analysis, Walt's criticism of formal modelling is a good indication that in the 1980s and 1990s, formal theory was stronger in the area of conflict resolution. It also shows that labels such as Peace Researchers, Strategists and Realists, are of less significance – at least in this context – than epistemological and methodological distinctions. Depending on whether the glass is half full or half empty, this exchange can be seen as indicating a fundamental gap between formal and qualitative approaches or as evidence of there being a conversation across the Conflict Resolution–Security Studies divide.

Great power politics: a replacement for the Soviet Union?

With the challenge of the Soviet Union gone, there was a transitional question about how to manage its decline (Hopf, 1992), and a temporary boom in Arms Control (on which more below). But the end of bipolarity triggered bigger questions for ISS. Would other superpowers arise, and if so when? As the most likely candidates, how long would it take before China or the EU could bid for superpower status? Should the US adjust to this or resist it? Should the US seize its historical moment to impose its values and visions on the world or, given that its own military security was no longer threatened, should it take the opportunity to withdraw and play a lower-profile role as offshore balancer?

At the beginning of the Cold War this type of 'grand strategy' question had been settled relatively early. The ending of the Cold War produced a much murkier international situation in which the nature and identity of the challenger(s) to the US, if any, remained unclear. Indeed, for much of the 1990s the US security establishment seemed almost nostalgic for the certainties and simplicities of the Cold War in general, and particularly for the way in which the existence of an unquestioned superpower rival gave long-term direction, clarity and domestic support to US foreign and security policy-making. This problem was well illustrated by the way in which the rather vague strategy of the Clinton administrations to enlarge the sphere of liberal (market) democracy, in marked contrast to the Cold War, failed to overcome domestic resistance in the US to foreign engagements. Japan, China, 'rogue states' and radical Islam all at times drifted into focus as possible rivals, perhaps most famously, and more or less all together, in Huntington's (1993a, 1996) 'clash of civilizations' thesis. But none had either the military or ideological standing to come anywhere close to replacing the Soviet Union as Washington's significant Other, and while 'clash of civilizations' was much discussed, it failed to fill Washington's threat void. The question of appropriate US strategy thus remained more open for a longer time, and the debate about US grand strategy became a major feature of the ISS literature (Nye, 1989; Carpenter, 1991; Huntington, 1993b, 1999; Waltz, 1993; Posen and Ross, 1996/7; Layne, 1997; Kupchan, 1998; Kapstein and Mastanduno, 1999; Lake, 1999; Wohlforth, 1999; Ikenberry, 2001b). Indeed, the grand strategy debate carried on through and past 9/11 (Bacevich, 2002; Hassner, 2002; Kagan, 2002; Nye, 2002; Daalder and Lindsay, 2003; Prestowitz, 2003; Buzan, 2004a). The initial assumption in this literature that US unipolarity would be short-lived – 'the unipolar moment' – was strongly rooted in Neorealist theory's central idea that great power relations must be dominated by balancing. But as the 1990s wore on, this view steadily gave way to the assumption that unipolarity would be quite durable, and to discussions about why there was no balancing against the US (Kapstein, 1999; Ikenberry, 2002) and what this meant for US policy.

The uncertainties about how to focus US grand strategy, and how to respond to what the US government actually did, were mainly the concern of American writers. But they were about, and in part accompanied by, more widely held concerns about the future of the Atlantic partnership in general, and NATO in particular. Was 'the West' itself simply an artefact of the Cold War, meaning that the US and Europe would increasingly go their separate ways now that there was no common threat to keep them together? Mearsheimer's (1990) 'back to the future' argument exemplified the Neorealist view that NATO and the EU, being products of bipolarity, should soon disappear along with the Cold War, and a similar argument from a different direction was made by Calleo (1996). Or had the Cold War forged a durable Western security community, whose common culture, economic interests, institutions and commitment to liberal democracy would long outlast the Cold War? This view was expressed in two closely related literatures. One was on democratic peace theory, which kicked off towards the end of the Cold War (Doyle, 1986). This literature revived classic Liberal thinking on the conditions for peace, and during the 1990s rapidly became both influential in US foreign policy and a substantial subject of debate across the IR literature (Lake, 1992; Schweller, 1992; Maoz and Russett, 1993; Russett, 1993; R. Cohen, 1994; Porter, 1995; Gates *et al.*, 1996; Oneal and Russett, 1997, 1999; Starr, 1997; Kahl, 1998/9; Mousseau and Shi, 1999), sometimes filling up all or nearly all of whole issues of journals (*Journal of Peace Research*, 29:4, 1992; *International Security*, 19:2, 1994; *European Journal of International Relations*, 1:4, 1995). If the Cold War had been won by the liberal democracies, and if these now had no great power challengers, then international relations would be profoundly transformed by the permanent marginalisation of the fear of great power wars. The other literature was on the 'two-worlds' formation of the post-Cold War world. This put the democratic peace in context by proposing a kind of twin-track international system comprising a democratic zone of peace amongst the capitalist core states, and a zone of conflict in the periphery (Buzan 1991b: 432; Goldgeier and McFaul 1992; Singer and Wildavsky 1993; and implicitly in the earlier work of Deutsch *et al.*, 1957; Keohane and Nye 1977). In this view the new world order was only in the core, while the periphery remained subject to the old Realist rules of the game.

For the first decade after the Cold War, the democratic peace advocates seemed to have the better of this argument. The EU enlarged and deepened, and NATO not only endured but expanded. But while the EU clearly had an internal logic of its own, however contested, it was much less clear what the purpose of NATO now was. Did an unopposed West need an armed wing or could that job be left to the sole superpower? Could and should Europe now stand more on its own in defence matters, especially via the EU, which during the 1990s and early 2000s, like ISS itself, enjoyed something of a spurt in both widening and deepening? The 1990s opened with many general ruminations on the implications of the new state of affairs for the existing institutions and arrangements (Hettne, 1991; Glaser, 1993; MacFarlane, 1993; Williams *et al.*, 1993; Duffield, 1994/5). Various themes emerged out of this as the Cold War receded into history and NATO remained standing. One was about the policy choices for Europe and the US in the absence of a common threat, and the possibility of a widening Atlantic and a weakening West (Treverton, 1992; Snider, 1992/3; Gebhard, 1994; Sloan, 1995; Daalder, 2001). Another was about the wisdom (or not) of NATO's enlargement into the former Soviet space in Eastern (now Central) Europe (Ball, 1998; MccGwire, 1998; Waltz, 2000a), and about the general way in which NATO was adapting to the post-Cold War world through its Partnership for Peace and ot'.er outreach programmes (Borawski, 1995; Wallander, 2000). Like the democratic peace, the debates about NATO also filled up whole issues of journals (*Journal of Strategic Studies*, 17:4, 1994 and 23:3, 2000). Alongside the talk about NATO was a discussion of the possibilities for more European self-reliance in defence (Taylor, 1994) or even, during the later 90s when the EU seemed to be on a roll, the rise of a European superpower (Buchan, 1993; Walton, 1997; Hodge, 1998/9).

The Atlantic relationships, for all of their difficulties, generally fitted within the democratic peace/two worlds framework. If there was a potential threat to the idea that great power wars had gone into the dustbin of history it was the rise of China. Although it was clear during the 1990s that the West had no immediate military or ideological challengers of any weight, it was equally clear that somewhere down the line China was a possible candidate for that role. During the 1990s, China's rapid and sustained economic growth contrasted sharply with Japan's seemingly interminable stagnation. Despite its move to embrace the market, China remained politically authoritarian and prickly about US hegemony. In some senses, US–China relations were in part a carry-over of the Cold War in which the containment of China had been one element of the overall US strategy against the communist bloc. More so than in Europe, US alliances in East Asia remained militarily significant, and while NATO, despite its new members, became militarily and politically weaker and less central, the US–Japan alliance held steady despite economic frictions between the two and speculations about a widening Pacific (Stokes, 1996). There was much musing about the nature of post-Cold War international relations in East Asia, the US role there and whether China should be contained, as during the Cold War, or engaged, in the hope that market liberalisation would eventually generate a more liberal politics and society in China, or both.[1] Within this general debate, the rise of China became a

---

[1] Xinghao, 1991; Betts, 1993; Friedberg, 1993; Pollack, 1993; Simon, 1994; Dibb, 1995; Nye, 1995; Roy, 1996; Shambaugh, 1996; Segal, 1997; Carpenter, 1998; Christensen, 1999; Dibb *et al.*, 1999; Ross, 1999; Berger, 2000; Friedberg, 2000.

substantial theme in its own right (Cable and Ferdinand, 1994; Roy, 1994; Shan, 1994; To, 1997; Rozman, 1999), including the possibility of conflict with the US (Bernstein and Munro, 1997).

Somewhat parallel to the debates about Atlantic relations, there was speculation about whether Japan would retain both the US alliance and its highly circumscribed military posture, or move towards being a more 'normal' type of great power.[2] Realists tended to assume that Japan would become more normal, while those looking more inside Japan argued that its pacifism was deeply internalised. Since many Asian economies were growing fast, there was also concern about regional arms racing (Ball, 1993; Gong and Segal, 1993; Klare, 1993; Huxley and Willett, 1999), the weakness of regional institutions in East Asia (Aggarwal, 1993; J. S. Duffield, 2001; McDougall, 2002), and the impact of economic relations and their disruption by the 1997 financial crisis on regional security (Harris, 1993; Cossa and Khanna, 1997; Dibb *et al.*, 1998). The main concern was that East Asia's rising powers might easily fall into a Classical Realist model of unstable interstate rivalry and balance of power.

Despite concerns about Asia, the ending of the Cold War was not just treated as the conclusion of a specific conflict, but also possibly as the end of wars amongst the great powers generally. In addition to the democratic peace, unipolarity left no challengers to the US, 'the end of history' (Fukuyama, 1992) seemingly left no ideological differences worthy of world wars, and the main possible challengers, China and Russia, were both relatively weak and themselves engaged in a conversion to market economies. If great power wars had indeed come to an end, then this was a matter of very great interest not just for ISS, but for IR as a whole. Ever since its emergence after the First World War, IR theory (Waltz, 1988, 1993; Gaddis, 1992/3) had been rooted in the problem of war. If great power war had indeed become history, then both IR and ISS faced radical transformations in their core subject matters and *raisons d'être*.

The response in the ISS literature was varied. Some just carried on with traditional themes about the nature of war generally (Biddle, 1998; Howard, 1999; McInnes, 1999; Avant, 2000; Clarke, 2001), the perennial debates about the use of force (Haas, 1994; Orme, 1997; Farrell and Lambert, 2001) and the balance between offensive and defensive strategies

[2] Funabashi, 1991; Holbrooke, 1991; Berger, 1993; Katzenstein and Okawara, 1993; Mochizuki, 1994; Akaha, 1998; Spruyt, 1998; Drifte, 1999; Twomy, 2000; Liberman, 2000/1; Rozman, 2002a.

(Van Evera, 1997; Lieber, 2000). A newer theme – or at least a new label for an old theme about the impact of technology on war – was about the changing nature of war arising partly from the Revolution in Military Affairs (RMA – more on this below – Luttwak, 1995, 1996; McInnes, 1999), and partly from other factors such as globalisation (Guehenno, 1998/9; Van Ness, 1999; Cha, 2000b; Brooks and Wohlforth, 2000/1; Willett, 2001). The apparent obsolescence of great power wars, suggesting a major transformation in international relations, was discussed (Coker, 1992; Mandelbaum, 1998/9; Luttwak, 1999; *Survival*, 1999), though with suspicions that the end of war might be only a Western phenomenon (the 'zone of peace') and perhaps not applicable to Asia (Bracken, 1994). Given its implications, this debate had surprisingly little impact on ISS, though perhaps more on IR generally.

The technological imperative

Despite the doubts about the future of war aired above, the post-Cold War ISS literature concerned with technology was marked by a surprising amount of continuity, albeit with some significant changes of emphasis. Even with the driver of superpower rivalry removed, nuclear weapons and the technologies associated with them continued to dominate the agenda. Concern about nuclear proliferation took up the slack left by the defunct US–Soviet arms race with everything else adjusting to fit this new priority.

Interest in deterrence theory was perhaps the main casualty of the collapse of bipolarity, although there was still some ongoing concern (Huth, 1997; Mercer, 1997; Goldfischer, 1998; Harvey, 1998; Sagan, 2000), even with extended deterrence and Europe (Tertrais, 1999; Yost, 1999). There was also a new twist in that the empirical focus moved somewhat away from Western states and into the Third World. In effect, quite a bit of the thinking about deterrence merged into the literature on nuclear proliferation and new nuclear powers, particularly in South Asia (more on this below) and the Middle East (Cimbala, 1995; Lieberman, 1995; Stein, 1996; Mares, 1996/7; Steinberg, 1997; Bar-Joseph, 1998).

As the 1990s unfolded, and particularly in the US, interest in deterrence was overtaken by debates about BMD. The BMD issue had deep roots in the Cold War. But up to a point during the 1990s, and very noticeably after the arrival of the Bush administration in 2000, BMD was increasingly reorientated towards US concerns with so-called rogue states, and in the background China. China could be handled within the framework of deterrence, but the very term 'rogue states' by definition invited scepticism about the rationality criteria on which deterrence depended. While the Cold War discussions of BMD were driven by desire to escape the MAD relationship of deterrence, the post-Cold War one was more moved by the desires both to have some defence against possibly irrational actors and to underpin US claims to sole superpower status. This latter motive continued the Cold War tradition of using massive military superiority to differentiate superpowers from the lesser ranks. The rogue state focus meant that the BMD debate, like much else in post-Cold War Strategic Studies, became tied into concerns about the proliferation of both nuclear and missile technology. As the US once again got more serious about BMD, the general debate about the pros and cons was re-enlivened (Harvey, 2000; Payne, 2000; Wilkening, 2000b; Center for Nonproliferation Studies, 2001; Levine, 2001; Miller, 2001; Sokolsky, 2001; *Survival*, 2001), as were analyses of US policy (Daalder *et al.*, 2000; Glaser and Fetter, 2001). There were concerns about the impact of BMD on international politics generally (Valentino, 1997/8) and particularly on Europe (Bowen, 2001; Gordon, 2001; Kenyon *et al.*, 2001) and East Asia (Roberts *et al.*, 2000; Urayama, 2000). Another focus was the consequences of US moves towards deployment of BMD on arms control, most obviously the ABM Treaty (Wilkening, 2000a; Coyle and Rhinelander, 2001). The subject broadened out beyond just ballistic missiles to take into account how to deal with cruise missiles (Gormley, 2001). Other than updating to the new international conditions and the not very impressive improvements in the technology, this literature delivered little in the way of basic new insights about the political and strategic consequences of deploying BMD. It was largely just a response to changes in US policy and the spread of missile and nuclear technological capabilities.

Yet BMD development was just one element in a broader fascination with military technological advance that marked the post-Cold War Strategic Studies literature, not least because the US continued to maintain an enormous military budget and huge expenditures on military research and development. Whereas bipolarity and rivalry was once used to explain high US military expenditure, post-Cold War the US need to maintain unipolarity seemed to have the same consequence: keeping a wide technological gap between the US and all other military powers was a badge of sole superpower status regardless of whether there was any pressing need for such capability. This continuity offered grounds for suspicion reminiscent of the Cold War literature on the MIC, which looked to domestic political and economic drivers to explain military expenditure. A lot of this discussion went under the heading of the RMA (Cohen, 1996; C. S. Gray, 1997; Lambeth, 1997; Freedman, 1998; O'Hanlon, 1998; Goldman and Andres, 1999). It was about many things, but mainly the impact of improvements in the technologies of surveillance, guidance, communication and data processing, which taken together seemed to open the way to a transformation in both battlefield management specifically and the conduct of war more generally. The potential of the RMA to transform war was demonstrated to considerable effect by the US performance in the 1991 war against Iraq, and subsequently in the interventions in the former Yugoslavia, on which more below. Among other things, the RMA offered the prospect of battlefield dominance for US forces, and of zero-casualty wars (for the US) that would ease the political problems for Washington of fighting limited wars. This in turn stimulated interest in 'asymmetric' war (Arreguin-Toft, 2001, 2005; Barnett, 2003): if the US was going to be untouchable in normal types of battle, then those hostile to it, or threatened by it, would have to find other forms of conflict that sidestepped the military advantages that the RMA gave to US forces. The RMA also raised questions about whether the growing qualitative gap between the US armed forces and those of its allies would undermine the Western alliances. Were allies needed? If so, could the interoperability of allied forces be maintained? In this sense the RMA was one of several factors feeding into the US shift towards greater unilateralism in the later 1990s. Along with the apparent ending of any near- or medium-term prospect for great power war, the RMA opened up a more general discussion about the changing nature of war examined above.

But the main focus of concern about technology shifted to horizontal nuclear proliferation. This was, of course a lively topic throughout the Cold War, but then it played second fiddle to the star act of vertical proliferation by the superpowers, and the deterrence, BMD and arms control literatures that revolved around that. Post-Cold War, with the strategic emphasis shifting more to so-called rogue states and terrorists, nuclear proliferation becomes almost the main focus of the traditionalist literature.

In many ways, this literature retained the general shape and pattern of concerns developed during the Cold War. One core of it was the general literature updating developments in the non-proliferation regime and the spread of nuclear technology, and discussing prospects, consequences and policy options for both.[3] The subject was now sufficiently long-standing and embedded to support not only introductory textbooks

---

[3] Fisher, 1992; Scheinmann, 1992; Davis and Frankel, 1993; Imai, 1993; van Creveld, 1993; Simpson, 1994; Simpson and Howlett, 1994; Thayer, 1995a; El-Baradei, 1996; Jones and McDonough, 1998; Kurihara, 1998; Mutimer, 1998; Howlett *et al.*, 1999; Walker, 2000; Schmitt, 2001.

(van Ham, 1993; Gardner, 1994), but also a stab at theory (Ogilvie-White, 1996). Concern about the link between civil nuclear power and the potential for nuclear weapons remained an ongoing theme (Dauvergne, 1993; Perkovich, 1993a; Kokoski, 1996; Yamanouchi, 1997; Harrison, 1998), as was missile proliferation (Frye, 1992; Harvey, 1992; Pedatzur, 1994). The debate opened by Waltz about whether or not nuclear proliferation was a good or bad thing also continued (Lee, 1995; Sagan and Waltz, 1995; Thayer, 1995b; Feaver, 1997), as did that about why states want nuclear weapons (Sagan, 1996/7) and the linkage between the ongoing possession of nuclear weapons by some states (substantial cuts in nuclear arsenals post-Cold War notwithstanding) and the dynamics of proliferation in non-nuclear weapon states (Quinlan, 1993). Although certainly not absent from the Cold War literature, there was more of a tone of pessimism in much of this literature, with some authors assuming the erosion of the non-proliferation regime and moving to think about the nature of a proliferated world (Feaver, 1992/3; van Creveld, 1993; Karl, 1996/7; Posen, 1997; Preston, 1997; Delpech, 1998/9; Thakur, 2000). As the history of this subject lengthened, there was also the beginnings of attempts to apply the lessons of history to the new proliferants (Blight and Welch, 1995). Against this pessimism there was some good news in the abandonment of nuclear weapons in South Africa and the winding down of apparent nuclear weapons programmes in Brazil and Argentina (Spector, 1992; Howlett and Simpson, 1993).

Notable new themes were the perceived threats and problems from new nuclear weapon states (Deutch, 1992; Karl, 1996/7; Preston, 1997; Glaser, 1998), including the spreading problem of increasing numbers of states with short or very short lead times separating them from a possible shift from non-nuclear to nuclear weapon status (Fortmann, 1992/3; Mazarr, 1995a; Cohen and Pilat, 1998). Some of this literature blended proliferation with issues of deterrence (Feaver, 1992/3; Sagan, 1994; Joseph and Reichart, 1998) so, along with Israel, rescuing that topic from near oblivion. There was concern about the pros and cons of the US shift from the non-proliferation policy of the Cold War to a more unilateralist and potentially military anti-proliferation policy (Roberts, 1993; Schneider, 1994; Feaver and Niou, 1996; Joseph, 1996; Kristensen and Handler, 1996; Posen, 1997; Andreani, 1999/2000). There was also increased focus on terrorism, not just with nuclear weapons, but also, especially given the advances in biological technology, with other weapons of mass destruction (WMD) (Failey, 1995; Tucker, 1996, 1999, 2000; Steinbruner, 1997/8; Betts, 1998; Carter *et al.*, 1998; Falkenrath, 1998, 2001; *Survival*, 1998/9).

Within this general literature there continued to be many studies of particular countries and regions. This was mainly empirical and policy-orientated work providing updates on technological and political developments, and mainly it stemmed from worry about the decay of the non-proliferation regime. As pessimism spread about the prospects for more proliferation, and as specific countries moved towards, or crossed, the nuclear threshold, this part of the literature expanded dramatically. There were some global surveys (Goldblat, 2000), and some with a regional focus, mainly on Asia (East and South) (Delpech, 1998/9; Bracken, 1999; Cirincione, 2000; Cha, 2001) or the Middle East (Fahmy, 1998). There was still some interest in Europe generally (Croft, 1996; Tertrais, 1999), and in individual European states.[4] Post-Soviet Russia and the other successor states were new entrants into the proliferation literature (Hopf, 1992; Walker, 1992; Zagorski, 1992; Gottemoeller, 1996; Baker, 1997), Russia about becoming a source of nuclear weapons for other proliferants (Blank, 2000), and Ukraine and others as possible new nuclear weapon states (S. E. Miller, 1993). In the event, the other successor states soon gave up their nuclear weapons, but a potentially leaky Russia remained a source of worry.

In Asia, in addition to the general concern about proliferation chains, there were many more specific studies, again with a largely empirical and policy focus updating technological and political developments. As China moved closer to international society, interest picked up in its role within the non-proliferation regime (Wallerstein, 1996; Gill and Medeiros, 2000; Malik, 2000). Elsewhere in Northeast Asia, North Korea became a major focus as it moved to break away from its obligations under the NPT (Mack, 1991, 1993, 1994; Bracken, 1993; Cotton, 1993; Kang, 1994; Masaki, 1994/5; Mazarr, 1995b; Hughes, 1996; Kim, 1996; Moltz and Mansourov, 2000; Lee, 2001). Southeast Asia made a brief entry because of its nuclear weapon free zone agreement, even although there were no states there suspected of interest in going nuclear (Dewitt and Bow, 1996; Acharya and Boutin, 1998). So, too, did Africa, following on from the denuclearisation of South Africa (Ogunbanwo, 1996).

The other major focus of proliferation attention in Asia was the ever fractious relationship between India and Pakistan as they drifted towards the nuclear threshold (Chellaney, 1993; Perkovich, 1993b; Reiss, 1993;

---

[4] France (S. Cohen, 1994; Gordon, 1995; Yost, 1996; Jabko and Weber, 1998), Germany (Kötter and Müller, 1991) and Britain (Bailes, 1993; Heuser, 1993; Croft, 1994; O'Neill, 1995; Chalmers, 1999).

Gordon, 1994; Mattoo, 1996), and then with the Indian and Pakistani tests in 1998, over their nuclear status.[5] The reality of a new nuclear dyad in South Asia triggered discussions about the implications for the stability of the India–Pakistan relationship, and how deterrence would work, or not, in this context (Bhimaya, 1994; Hagerty, 1995/6; Joeck, 1997; Heisbourg, 1998/9; Zook, 2000; Quinlan, 2000/1; Basrur, 2001). Beyond South Asia what would be the implications for the Sino–Indian relationship (Garver, 2001) and India's strategic position generally (Tellis, 2002)? Although neither India nor Pakistan was a member of the NPT, there was widespread concern about how the arrival of two new nuclear weapons states might damage the non-proliferation regime generally (Singh, 1998; Gupta, 1999; Talbott, 1999; Thakur, 1999; Vivekanandan, 1999; Mahapatra, 2000; Mutimer, 2000; Nizamani, 2001; Shaikh, 2002), and challenge US non-proliferation policy in particular (Mahmudul, 1997; Singer *et al.*, 1998; Ayoob, 1999; Mistry, 1999; Carranza, 2002).

The other region of intense interest regarding proliferation was the Middle East, where Israel was a long-standing nuclear weapon state and subject of interest (Sayed, 1993; Inbar and Sandler, 1993/4; Keeley, 1993/4; Cochran, 1996; Cohen, 1998). During the 1990s, Iraq (Kelly, 1996) and increasingly Iran (Chubin, 1995; Eisenstadt, 1999) were widely suspected of aspiring to that status. In this region, as elsewhere, concern about nuclear proliferation was accompanied by that about the proliferation of missile capability and the Missile Technology Control Regime (MTCR) (A. Karp, 1991; Pedatzur, 1994; Pikayev *et al.*, 1998). And, as in South Asia, the seeming approach of states crossing the nuclear threshold revived interest in proliferation chains (Russell, 2001), and the implications and prospects for arms control (Oxenstierna, 1999; Solingen, 2001). By the 1990s, Latin America was no longer of much concern as a possible site of proliferation, but it still attracted some attention in the literature, mainly as historical retrospectives (Carasales, 1996; Wrobel, 1996; Hymans, 2001).

Like the literature on non-proliferation, other technology-driven concerns also showed a lot of continuity. Long-standing debates about the MIC (Hartung, 2001) and arms racing (Gray, 1996; Sample, 1997; Diehl and Crescenzi, 1998; Koubi, 1999) simply carried on without much impact from the ending of the Cold War. The debates on NoD lost their NATO

[5] Ahmed *et al.*, 1998; Chellaney, 1998/9; Ahmed, 1999; Ahrari, 1999; Chellaney, 1999; Ganguly, 1999; Gizweski, 1999; Hagerty, 1999; Huntley, 1999; Synnott, 1999; Yasmeen, 1999; Ahmed, 2000; Bajpai, 2000; Kampani, 2001.

central front focus, but adapted to post-Cold War circumstances (Møller, 1992, 1998; Huysmans, 1994; Møller and Wiberg, 1994; Bellany, 1996; Martin, 1999).

As noted in chapter 5, after its seeming collapse at the end of the 1970s, arms control underwent a revival from the mid-1980s, but increasingly as the mechanism for demobilising a Cold War that was ending for other reasons rather than for managing an ongoing superpower rivalry. Post-Cold War both the practice and the literature therefore saw out the dismantling of the Soviet Union and the Cold War well into the 1990s (Schimmelfennig, 1994; McCausland, 1996; Baglione, 1997; Collins, 1998). Part of this was keeping an eye on China in relation to the post-Cold War disarmament and arms control (Garrett and Glaser, 1995/6). But this settling of Cold War issues was inevitably a time-limited agenda so, as always, there was worrying about the future of arms control (Daalder, 1992). Given the changed strategic context, and the shift to more Third World concerns, there was also quite a bit of effort to find new foundations for arms control: in cooperative security now that MAD was no longer the problem (Desjardins, 1996; Krepon, 2001; Larsen, 2002); or in coordinated unilateralism (Dunn and Alessi, 2000/1). Thus, along with much else on the military security agenda, arms control turned towards the Third World generally, and particularly to issues connected to nuclear proliferation, such as ballistic missile proliferation and the MTCR, and BMD and the ABM Treaty discussed above, but also to long-established regional rivalries (Dixit, 1995). There were some perennial topics such as the debate about disarmament (Glaser, 1998) and chemical weapons (Robinson, 1996), and some new ones, such as concern about the proliferation of light weapons, which seemed an important factor in the many internal wars that marked the 1990s (Lumpe, 1999).

Regional security and non-Western events

The shift to interest in war in the Third World (Biddle and Zinkle, 1996) also created a turn from interstate war to wars within states (Berdal, 1996; Snow, 1996; Wallensteen and Solenberg, 1996; Kaldor, 1999, 2001). This interest in domestic conflict was closely linked to concerns about weak and failed states (Adibe, 1994; Mazrui, 1995; Krause, 1996; Herbst, 1996/7; Williams and Brooks, 1999; Sørensen, 2001; *Journal of Peace Research*, 2002), thus reinforcing the long-standing interest within Peace Research about the relationship between development and (in)security. Other related themes in this literature were the rise of interventions and peace-keeping (Sesay, 1995; Howe, 1996/7; Glynne, 1997; Freedman, 1998/9) and 'humanitarian wars' (Roberts, 1996), as a result of various attempts by the West to intervene (or sometimes not) in the name of human rights. In this section we focus on the regional international events that began with the US-led war against Iraq in 1991, through the wars accompanying the dissolution of Yugoslavia, and the humanitarian intervention in Somalia, up to, but not including, 9/11. As with the shift in the nuclear agenda towards the Third World, here, too, one sees that a main consequence of the disappearance of bipolarity was that regional and local security problems gained in prominence. The 'two worlds' formulation noted above seemed to split the world into a peaceful core, where perhaps the traditional agenda was no longer relevant, and a turbulent periphery, where the old rules of the game carried on. This formulation itself explains much of the turn of the military security agenda towards the Third World. It also explains the two themes that emerged, one with the Third World as the focus of concern in its own right, as for example in the concerns about nuclear proliferation in South Asia, or humanitarian crises in various places; and the other, especially with the rise of the rogue state and terrorism agendas in the US, about the possible threats from the zone of conflict to the zone of peace. As noted above, worries about rogue states and terrorists were strongly linked to the issue of proliferation of WMD.

Within this was another literature calling for ISS to pay more specific attention to the regional level of security itself as something that was neglected (or subordinated to the global level) during the Cold War, and which post-Cold War was of increasing importance (Buzan, 1991a: 186–229; Alagappa, 1995: 363; Ayoob, 1995: 56–59; Lake and Morgan, 1997; Maoz, 1997: 2–8; Buzan et al., 1998; Buzan and Wæver, 2003; Hettne, 2005: 553–554). Even some hard-line Neorealists took up the regional implications of unipolarity (Hansen, 2000). Regional security as something reflecting indigenous dynamics additional to superpower interventionism had been a persistent, if relatively marginal, topic in ISS that went well back into the Cold War (Buzan, 1983: 105–115; Väyrynen, 1984; Ayoob, 1986). As well as this more theoretical literature stressing the importance of the regional level generally, there was of course a great deal written about the security affairs and dynamics of specific regions. Some of this literature has already been noted in the discussion of nuclear proliferation, particularly for East and South Asia and the Middle East. But there was much more that was not specifically connected to proliferation.

Not least because of the Gulf War of 1990–91, and the ongoing night-mare in and around Israel/Palestine, the Middle East was a popular topic. There were general ruminations on the region's position in the post-Cold War world (Karsh, 1997; Lustick, 1997; Maoz, 1997) and on the Gulf War and its aftermath (more on this below). In addition to Iraq, three coun-tries attracted most of the attention: Iran (Chubin, 1992; Chubin and Tripp, 1996), Israel (Alpher, 1992/3; Cohen *et al.*, 1998; Merom, 1999; Heller, 2000) and Turkey (Hale, 1992; Tunander, 1995; Rubin and Kirisci, 2001), with particular interest in the emergence of a strategic partnership between Turkey and Israel (Gresh, 1998; Müftüler, 1998; Jung and Piccoli, 2000; Israeli, 2001). Overarching all this was discussion of the intensified US policy engagement in the Middle East that followed the Soviet with-drawal, specifically the Peace Process between Israel and its neighbours and 'dual containment' in the Gulf (Khalilzad, 1995; Mor, 1997; Watkins, 1997; Sick, 1998; Kemp, 1998/9; Lewis, 1999). The Middle East also fea-tured as one of the sources of tension negatively afflicting post-Cold War US–Europe relations (Hollis, 1997; Gordon, 1998; Serfaty, 1998).

The 1990–91 war against Iraq was both part of the turn towards regional security and the opening event of the post-Cold War 'unipolar' era. This war seemed to send a number of signals. As already mentioned, it served as a powerful demonstrator for the RMA, not only because of the ease with which US forces were able to destroy what was thought to be quite a substantial regional military power, but also because of the difficulty its allies had in operating with the high-tech US forces. The war laid down a US claim to military exceptionalism, and also did something to leave behind the legacy of the Vietnam syndrome, which had inhibited US military engagements in the Third World. There was also, of course, a literature on the war itself and on its impact in the region (Hale, 1992; Stein, 1992; Fuller, 1993; Joffe, 1993; Bengio, 1995; Khalilzad, 1995).

But more interesting in some ways was the political discourse stemming from the war. In the absence of superpower rivalry, the US had managed to create a spectacular international coalition against Iraq, and this seemed to espouse the possibility of the 'new world order' unwisely mooted by US president George W. Bush shortly after it. At the centre of the coalition were the US and a group of allies ready to fight against Saddam Hussein (principally Britain, France, Egypt and Saudi Arabia). Supporting them were allies prepared to pay but not to fight (principally Germany and Japan). Around them was a large group not prepared to fight or to pay, but willing to give political support (including the Soviet Union and China). Most of the rest of international society was prepared to be neutral. Only a handful of states (Cuba and some Arab states) were prepared to give Iraq political support, and Iraq had no military allies. This looked like a foreshadowing of the likely nature of unipolar international relations, in which something like a logic of collective security could be used by the US both to defend principles of international society (the illegitimacy of annexation in the case of Kuwait), and to support US interests (preventing the rise of monopoly control over Middle East oil). It quickly became clear that this was a false dawn, and that at least from a US perspective the 1990s were unfolding more as a 'new world disorder' (Carpenter, 1991; Rubinstein, 1991; Freedman, 1992; Nye, 1992; Slaughter, 1997).

East and South Asia have been substantially covered in the discussions of great power politics and nuclear proliferation above. In addition to these themes, the Association of Southeast Asian Nations (ASEAN), and its development of the ASEAN Regional Forum (ARF) and ASEAN-plus-3 as wider security institutions attracted some attention, not least because they seemed a beginning to remedy the institution-poor nature of East Asian regional international relations (Acharya, 1993; Stubbs, 1993; Leifer, 1996; Wanandi, 1996; Shaun, 1997; Kivimäki, 2001). This promising development was shaken by the late 1990s regional economic crisis (Ahmad and Ghoshal, 1999; Henderson, 1999), which exposed the linkage between economic and traditional security relations. For South Asia, the long-standing rivalry between India and Pakistan in South Asia continued to be a subject that was of wider strategic interest than just its nuclear dimension (Ayoob, 1991; Varshney, 1991; Ganguly, 1993; Thomas, 1993; Oren, 1994).

Africa was very much part of the discussion about failed states noted above. In addition, the local conflicts and regional security politics there attracted some attention both in themselves (Keller and Rothchild, 1996; Vale, 1996; Shearer, 1999; Breytenbach, 2000; Weinstein, 2000), and more generally in terms of the rights and wrongs and ifs and whens of intervention (Evans, 1997; Greenhill, 2001), and in terms of the problems of peacekeeping operations (Sesay, 1995; Howe, 1996/7). Having neither military crises nor strategic centrality, Latin America attracted relatively little interest in the ISS literature (Hurrell, 1998).

One interesting feature of this turn to the regions was that both Europe and the former Soviet Union and its Eastern European satellites shifted from being the seemingly permanent front line of the Cold War to being regions with security dynamics in their own right. Some of this has been discussed under great power politics, NATO and nuclear proliferation above, but post-Cold War interest grew in European regional security as such (Buzan *et al.*, 1990; Richmond, 2000). Much of what had been referred to as Eastern Europe moved West and became Central and Eastern Europe (CEE), and the former Soviet Union (FSU) became a new international sub-system of states. There was some jostling for position, especially over the Balkans (L. J. Cohen, 1994), before things settled down into what might be called EU-Europe (former Western and Eastern Europe, the Baltic states and the Balkans) and the FSU (minus the three Baltic states). The Balkans, and especially the conflicts around the disintegration of the former Republic of Yugoslavia (FRY) became a landmark crisis of the immediate post-Cold War period. Literatures sprang up to deal with the new security relations in both CEE[6] and the FSU.[7]

Within the literature focusing on intra-state, ethnic or civil wars, the wars in the former Yugoslavia were constitutive events. Authors such as Posen (1993) and Van Evera (1994) argued that Neorealist – and Realist – theory and the 'ethnic' security dilemma held at the sub-state level as well. In terms of the strategic aspect of the Bosnian war, a key debate was whether the policy of 'lift and strike' – lifting the arms embargo imposed on the Bosnian government and conducting air strikes against Bosnian Serbian positions – could be adopted as long as there were United Nations Protection Force (UNPROFOR) peacekeepers on the ground and whether air strikes alone would significantly impact the outcome of the war (Gati, 1992: Doder, 1993; Roberts, 1995: Rieff, 1996; Gow, 1997). This debate coincided with a US and European policy divide, where American politicians and academics took a much more positive view of lift and strike than did Europeans (Mearsheimer and Pape, 1993; Wood, 1994; Mearsheimer and Van Evera, 1995; Maull, 1995/6; Cushman and Mestrovic, 1996; Kaufmann, 1996: Mousavizadeh, 1996; Campbell, 1998a; Daalder, 2000; Simms, 2001; Hansen, 2006).

The relative success of NATO's bombing campaigns in 1995, that facilitated the Dayton Peace Accord, and the general convergence between Tony Blair and George W. Bush's interventionist and morally driven foreign policy agendas, supported the intervention in Kosovo in 1999, where NATO bombed Serbian leaders into withdrawing from the province. NATO relied exclusively on aerial bombardment – although a threat of ground intervention was at times ambiguously raised – and did not lose one life in

---

[6] Dienstbien, 1991; Zielonka, 1992; Joffe, 1992/3; Brezezinski, 1993; Chalmers, 1993; on the Balkans in particular, see Larrabee, 1992; Pettifer, 1992; Zametica, 1992; Glenny, 1995; V. Gray, 1999; King, 2001.

[7] Menon and Barkey, 1992/3; Allison, 1993; Dunlop, 1993/4; Chopra and Weiss, 1995; Petersen, 1995; Larrabee, 1996; Sherr, 1997; Kuzio, 2000; Ambrosio, 2001.

combat. Since this was the first time air strikes alone had secured victory, and since strategic observers had remained sceptical of the coercive power of aerial bombardment, a debate over what lessons could be drawn ensued (Pape, 1996; Byman and Waxman, 2000; Posen, 2000).

As noted in the technology section above, there was a post-Cold War discussion of terrorism driven by concerns about the possible conjuncture of extremist political motives and methods with WMD. Underpinning this was not a particular signature event, but a steady background noise of terrorist incidents. As during the Cold War, many of these were embedded in long-established domestic or local conflicts or issues and were there-fore not mainly understood as being of systemic security significance (various bombs in France; Britain and the IRA; Spain and the Basques; Israel/Palestine; the Sri Lankan civil war). But during the 1990s, some, even if with local roots, took on wider significance either because they impacted directly on the US and/or because they suggested the existence of transnational terrorist networks. The highlight terrorist events of the 1990s included:

1993	– bombing of the World Trade Center in New York City
1995	– Aum Shinri Kyo gas attack in Tokyo
1995	– bombing of a military training building in Riyadh
1995	– Oklahoma City bombing (home-grown, but initially thought of as international terrorism)
1996	– truck bomb at US Air Force base near Dhahran, Saudi Arabia
1998	– US embassy bombings in Tanzania and Kenya
2000	– attack on the USS *Cole* in Aden

The seeming rise of terrorist networks that were more global in organi-sation and motive, and more extreme in method, fed concerns about the potential links between such groups and the possible availability of WMD. This concern was further amplified both by the worry prevalent during much of the 1990s that WMD might leak out of the corpse of the former Soviet Union, and by the fear of some that in the light of the 1993 attack on the World Trade Center, the US homeland was becoming a target. There was both general discussion of terrorism (St. John, 1991; Schmid and Crelinsten, 1993; Crenshaw, 1995; Laqueur, 1996, 1998; Carr, 1996/7; Hoffman, 1998; *Terrorism and Political Violence*, 1999) and a debate about how seriously the US should take the threat to itself (Tucker, 1996, 2000; Sprinzak, 1998; Roy *et al.*, 2000; Falkenrath, 2001). Until 9/11, terrorism remained a steady, but not central concern in the ISS literature. It was somewhat on the fringes of the mainstream, and more part of the general 'new world disorder' than a dominant threat to international security. The same could be said for a smaller literature about transnational crime (Williams, 1994).

Partly in response to both the 'clash of civilizations' discourse and to long-standing concerns about the Middle East, the security implications of Islam became a notable post-Cold War topic (J. Miller, 1993; Salame, 1993; Ahrari, 1994; Hashemi, 1996; Karawan, 1997; Dawisha, 2000; Rabasa, 2003), At this point, the security interest in Islam was not specifically because of any link to terrorism, which unlike during the Cold War was mainly being discussed in more general and global terms. It did, however, seem to be part of a growing concern not just amongst traditionalists (Seul, 1999; S. M. Thomas, 2000; Fox, 2001, 2007; Haynes, 2008), but also amongst wideners (Lausten and Wæver, 2000), about the political and security implications of religion. There were special issues on this at both ends of the spectrum: *Orbis*, 43:2 (1998) 'Religion in World Affairs' and *Millennium* 29:3 (2000) 'Religion and International Relations'. This more general interest played as much to concerns about the influence of the religious right in US politics as it did to worries about Third World Islamic extremism.

Aside from interest in current events, the ISS literature of the 1990s began to show its age. The so-called post-Cold War era was its second distinct era, and some literature reflected a growing element of history in ISS, looking back on some Cold War events, most notably the Cuba Missile Crisis (Scott and Smith, 1994; Bernstein, 2000; Pressman, 2001).

Institutionalisation

In chapters 4 and 5, we recorded the very successful institutionalisation of both Strategic Studies and Peace Research, and speculated that this very success would generate a problem of overcapacity in a post-Cold War world in which much of the military agenda had either shrunk or disappeared. In fact, although there was some shrinkage of funding and a transitional period of anxiety and uncertainty, there was no generalised institutional crisis. As can be seen from the story in this chapter so far, the traditionalist wing of ISS still found plenty on its agenda, and most felt secure enough to resist the temptation to widen it. Substantively, ISS recovered very quickly from the loss of its Cold War core, and most of its institutional structure remained intact. The content of university courses in ISS changed, but the courses themselves mostly did not disappear, and the subject certainly did not. Much the same was true of think-tanks. A few, such as the Council for Arms Control in the UK, lost support and did not long survive the end of the Cold War. Some failed to sustain funding for reasons other than the end of the Cold War: despite being very successful, for example, the Programme for Promoting Nuclear Non-Proliferation at Southampton University and the Copenhagen Peace Research Institute were both wound up in 2002 because of the withdrawal of their main funding. Accompanying the robustness of ISS organisations was a similar strength in publications. Hardly any expired, and there were several new startups: *European Security* (1991), *Nuclear Proliferation Journal* (1991), *The Nonproliferation Review* (1993), *International Peacekeeping* (1994), *The International Journal of Peace Studies* (1996) and *Arms Control Today* (1997). This pattern was broadly in line with the continued expansion in the number of IR journals generally. It remained the case, in line with the Cold War pattern, that the ISS debates took place in both the specialist journals and the more general IR ones.

Failure was thus the exception and properly seen mostly in the drop in grant-making foundations and a shift in foundation priorities from arms control and non-proliferation to environmental questions (Wallerstein, 2002: 86–89). The great bulk of the existing ISS establishment carried on successfully, and there was significant new growth, mainly outside the Europe–US core. This reflected both the general robustness of the military security agenda and the shift of interest to regional security that followed from the end of the Cold War. The Mountbatten Centre for International Studies was established at Southampton University in 1990 to focus on WMD issues, and reflected the rising importance of this topic post-Cold War. The Centre for Strategic Studies in New Zealand, and the Centre for European Security Studies (CESS) in the Netherlands were both founded in 1993. The Geneva Centre for Security Policy (GCSP) started in 1995 as a Swiss contribution to NATO's Partnership for Peace (PfP). The Institute of Defence and Strategic Studies (IDSS) at Nanyang Technological University in Singapore, and the Institute of Peace and Conflict Studies in India, linked to the Indian Ministries of Defence and External Affairs, were both established in 1996. The Malaviya Centre for Peace Research was established in 1997 at the Banaras Hindu University, and the Peace Research Institute in the Middle East (PRIME) in 1998. The Centre for Defence and Strategic Studies (CDSS) opened in 2001 as part of the reorganised Australian Defence College, and the European Union Institute for Security Studies (EUISS) started work in 2001. Some of these were linked to universities and some to government ministries.

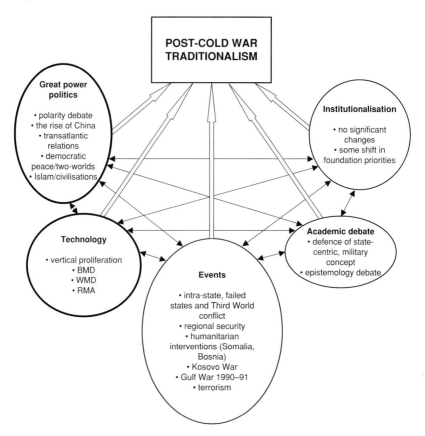

Figure 6.2.   The main drivers behind Post-Cold War traditionalism

Figure 6.2. sums up the main drivers behind post-Cold War tradition-alism.

Conclusions

ISS had evolved with superpower nuclear rivalry at its core and the ending of the Cold War thus raised fundamental questions about the field's survivability. Yet, as this chapter has shown, even with the loss of this 'meta-event' and framing, and the seeming marginalisation of the military–political agenda, the traditionalist wing of ISS, including neg-ative Peace Research, showed considerable continuity and noteworthy robustness. General continuity was reflected in ongoing themes ranging from deterrence and arms racing, through BMD and terrorism, to military technology and war. Perhaps the central continuity was on nuclear pro-liferation, which in some respects took over from superpower nuclear rivalry as the core problematique of this agenda. The robustness of the traditionalist agenda was not just a matter of hanging on to old themes regardless of changing times. There was a good deal of adaptation to the new realities of the post-Cold War era, most notably the shift of focus from East–West to South (and up to a point North–South). New tech-nological possibilities continued to emerge and demand comment and analysis, with the RMA at one end of this spectrum and the worrying possibilities of a conjuncture between nihilistic terrorists and WMD at the other. In the absence of superpower rivalry, the relative independence of the technology variable from the great power politics one became clearer during this period. Even without the driver of superpower rivalry, technological advances with military implications continued to roll out of the laboratories and factories. Emblematic of this, and only one of many examples, was the development of small cheap digital cameras, which could be used both as consumer toys and as guidance systems for precision-guided munitions. There was, of course, also a steady stream of events to take on board, and some of these opened up new questions about the use/utility of force, most obviously whether military intervention was an appropriate response to humanitarian crises.

What is interesting about the 1990s is the impressive amount of conti-nuity in the traditional agenda despite the loss of the Cold War organising frame. It did not require some new great power conflict to regenerate the military agenda, though it might to restore it to its former unquestioned dominance of ISS.

How did the driving forces explain this robustness and adaptability of the state-centric, military wing of ISS? It is clear first of all that *institution-alisation* in itself works as a conservative factor. Programmes in Strategic and Security Studies would shift in emphasis, but not in kind, journals would continue to publish along the lines previously set out, and research networks would mobilise to generate funding proposals, new projects and graduating PhDs. *Internal dynamics of academic debates* also played a role, not least in how the privileging of epistemology over ontology allowed a convergence – as well as debate – between Strategists and negative Peace Researchers. The loss of the meta-event and framing of the Cold War did have an impact on traditionalist approaches. This intersected with the driving forces of *great power* and *technology*: it opened debate on which polarity had replaced bipolarity and what the consequences were as well as on the implications for proliferation, and it allowed for an increased emphasis on regional and sub-state conflicts. Great power politics and technology might be said to provide slightly more room for the other driving forces than during the Cold War, where they were the dominant ones, but they were still very important and allowed for the production of a new set of research questions as well as for some continuity.

The general robustness and adaptability of military state-centric approaches goes part way to explaining why the institutional crisis for ISS that seemed inevitable at the end of the Cold War largely did not happen. The other half of that story concerns the successful expansion of the ISS agenda beyond both the military–political agenda and the materialist, positivist epistemology of the traditionalists. This is the subject of chapter 7.

7

Widening and deepening security

The previous chapter showed how traditionalists repositioned themselves after the end of the Cold War and how they argued that their military, state-centric agenda had in no way been harmed. Yet this claim was not universally accepted by 'wideners' and 'deepeners', some of whom grew out of positive Peace Research, Poststructuralism and Feminism (laid out in chapter 5), and some of whom came to ISS as the Cold War ended. To those seeking to expand the concept of security, the narrowness of the military state-centric agenda was analytically, politically and normatively problematic. Such things as the peaceful ending of the Cold War, the growth in intra-state conflicts, Western societies' fear of immigration, the decaying environment and the acceleration of the HIV/AIDS epidemic demonstrated that traditionalism was unable to meet the challenges of the post-Cold War era. Moreover, wideners and deepeners held that the 1990s failed to produce a constitutive military event or a defining great power problematic that traditionalists could claim should take centre-stage.

To challenge military-state centrism was, of course, not new, but what reconfigured the terrain of ISS in the late 1980s and 1990s was that challengers were no longer identified as 'Peace Researchers' – and thus as having a particular political position on the contested academic and political landscape of the Cold War – but as people doing Security Studies or IR. Some more specific labels – Poststructuralism and Human Security in particular – were politicised within ISS, but this rarely translated into broader non-academic circles, as Peace Research had done. ISS became as a consequence more of an even playing field and the fact that the media and policy discourses in many countries and global settings articulated a wider security agenda provided further support for widening–deepening approaches within ISS. If we look to processes of institutionalisation, there was a steady stream of books, conferences, PhD theses, journal articles – and even journals – on why and how security should be expanded beyond the military and the state-centric. If we look to the sociology of academic debates, the perceived need for traditionalists to engage broader conceptions rather than ignore them was an indirect testimony to how widening and deepening approaches had been strengthened.

Taking a broad look at ISS, the post-Cold War terrain was thus char-acterised by debate across the traditionalist and widening–deepening divide, but also, crucially, within the widening–deepening camp itself. Turning to the four questions that structure debates about ISS, widener–deepeners argued, to different extents and in different combinations, in favour of deepening the referent object beyond the state, widening the concept of security to include other sectors than the military, giving equal emphasis to domestic and trans-border threats, and allowing for a transformation of the Realist, conflictual logic of international secu-rity. Yet while united in their challenge to military state-centrism, the widening–deepening position was in reality made up by such diverse approaches that as much – and sometimes more – time was taken up debating differences within the widening–deepening position as across the traditionalist–expansionist distinction. An important feature of intra-widening debates in the 1990s and 2000s is thus the rapid growth in labels that identify a distinct widening–deepening perspective: Constructivism, which later divided into Conventional and Critical; Human Security; Post-colonialism; Critical Security Studies; and the Copenhagen School are added to Poststructuralism and Feminism.

Looking to the driving forces, widening–deepening debates were impacted by *great power politics* insofar as the disappearance of the Cold War had changed both the questions on the security agenda and the actors who could engage them, and this in turn allowed for a longer list of *events* to be felt on ISS debates. Looking at particular approaches, *tech-nology* was a driving force in some cases, such as in Poststructuralism's concern with the impact of new media technology, while being less sig-nificant in others. Yet, in terms of driving forces, the strongest impact was exerted by *internal academic debates*. This force impacted in numer-ous ways, not least by making the discussion of schools and labels rather than, for example, particular events or technologies, the central organ-ising dynamic. These school discussions were furthermore impacted by internal academic debate dynamics in three respects. First, they were influ-enced by epistemological and methodological debates in IR, as was the convergence between negative Peace Researchers and Strategists laid out in chapter 6. Second, there was a marked difference in the extent to which specific widening–deepening approaches grew out of the Peace Research agenda of the 1970s and 1980s or came to ISS through IR debates or social and Political Theory. And third, there was as a consequence a difference in the extent to which they foregrounded and discussed the concept of security.

The schools-driven character of widening–deepening post-Cold War ISS, shown in Figure 7.1, indicates that not only was there disagreement over whether and how security should be expanded, but also over who counted as legitimate contestants on the ISS terrain. To take the example of textbooks, whereas Kolodziej (2005) presents Wendtian Constructivism as the most radical challenger to the mainstream, it is given little notice in European textbooks like Collins (2007), Fierke (2007), Sheehan (2005) and Hough (2004), which are more concerned with Feminism, Human Security, Critical Security Studies and the Copenhagen School. In fact, as this chapter will show, the European–US divide that had concerned peace researchers worried about 'the two cultures problem' during the Cold War was also prominent during the 1990s (Wæver, 2004a).

This chapter looks primarily to those approaches that combined widening and deepening. That part of the widening debate that consisted of the largely empirical calls that gathered force during the 1970s and 1980s for addressing economic and especially environmental issues as part of international security has been noted in various chapters above (Nye, 1974; Maull, 1975; Buzan, 1983; Ullman, 1983; Mayall, 1984; Brundtland Commission, 1987; Nye and Lynn-Jones, 1988; Mathews, 1989; Nye, 1989; Deudney, 1990). From the late 1980s, widening and deepening merged in the explicit debates on the concept of security that became prominent within ISS, and which opened the way for a much more thorough debate about this concept than had occurred during the Cold War (Buzan, 1991a; Haftendorn, 1991; Dewitt, 1994; Baldwin, 1995, 1997; Cable, 1995; Caporaso, 1995; Rothschild, 1995; Wæver, 1995; Ayoob, 1997; Buzan et al., 1998; Smith, 1999; Walt, 1999a; Farrell, 2002). In this chapter we look to the way in which schools deepened and widened security – or not – thus bringing in a wider agenda around economic, environmental, societal and regional security and a deepening of the referent object beyond the state. Put simply, while there was an earlier literature on, for instance, environmental security, there was not an environmental security school but rather different ways in which environmental security appeared, or was excluded, by different approaches. On the subject of widening, one should note also that to widen security is to consider specific non-military sectoral dynamics as phenomena in their own right. To say, as did the founding editors of International Security (International Security, 1976) for instance, that military force is impacted by economic factors, energy supplies, food and natural resources, expands the list of

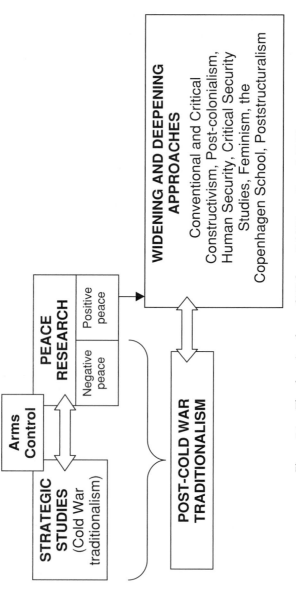

Figure 7.1. The changing shape of ISS from Cold War to Post-Cold War

capabilities which should be included in the study of state security, but remains within a military optic.

The chapter begins with the least radical perspective, where Constructivism in both its Conventional and Critical forms is presented and discussed; second, we look at those approaches that picked up the development theme and 'structural violence' from the 1970s and which argued in favour of 'human', 'gendered' or 'individual' security, namely Postcolonialism, Human Security, Critical Security Studies and Feminism; third, the discussion turns to the two main discursive approaches to security, the Copenhagen School and Poststructuralism. Each section lays out how these perspectives challenged traditional conceptions of security as well as what were the most common criticisms raised against them from other wideners (the response from the traditionalists is covered in the section 'Internal academic debates: state-centrism and epistemology' in chapter 6). This chapter deviates slightly from the chronological division of labour that we have used so far in that it moves into the post-9/11 period as far as general theory building and criticism that does not raise specific questions related to 9/11 and the 'War on Terror' is concerned. This avoids artificially cutting our presentation of theoretical debates in half and foreshadows the conclusion in chapter 8 that not everything in ISS post-2001 was driven by the Global War on Terrorism.

Constructivisms: norms, identities and narratives

The introduction of Constructivism as a self-identified perspective into ISS was largely a consequence of the general IR debate in the early 1990s between so-called rationalist and reflectivist approaches (Keohane, 1988). As this distinction reflected American social science traditions more than European ones (where rationalist epistemologies had never had the same privileged position), there was a distinct US–Europe flavour to the map of the 1990s security debates: European approaches (Critical Security Studies and the Copenhagen School in particular) were more strongly linked with the political, critical and normative concerns of Peace Research, while most of US Constructivism developed from the rationalism–reflectivism debate with no similar connection to past normative approaches. Poststructuralism started out most strongly as a North American perspective but gradually gained more ground in Europe, while Feminism provided a counterpoint to traditional approaches in both Europe and the United States. As the 1990s went on, Constructivism branched off into a Conventional and a Critical branch, where the latter had some interesting affinities to earlier Peace Research themes and concepts (Adler, 1997b; Katzenstein *et al.*, 1998; Wendt, 1999). These developments are illustrated in Figure 7.2.

Conventional Constructivism

Conventional Constructivism was the least radical widening approach, locating itself within 'a traditional, narrow definition of security studies' in which the task was to take the 'hard case' of national, military state-centric security, but to explain it through ideational rather than material factors (Katzenstein, 1996b: 10–11). This contrasted to European approaches; Feminism and Poststructuralism focused explicitly on the conceptualisation of security, debating whether it should be 'individual', 'national', 'gendered' or 'societal', a deepening which in turn facilitated widening across economic, societal, cultural, environmental and political sectors (Walker, 1992; Rothschild, 1995; Wæver, 1995; Krause and Williams, 1996; Smith, 2005). If, argued Katzenstein (1996b: 11), in what became the landmark Conventional Constructivist study, *The Culture of National Security*, Constructivists could prove that ideational explanations could account for outcomes missed by materialist Realist – and to a lesser extent Liberal – theories, then 'it should be relatively easy to apply this book's analytical perspective to broader conceptions of security that are not restricted to military issues or to the state'. As this statement illustrates, Conventional Constructivists were traditionalists not only insofar as they accepted a concept of military-state security, but in that they conformed to a substantive and epistemological traditionalist research agenda which held that ISS and IR should be devoted to explanations of state behaviour. Security, in short, is a behaviour to be explained, not, as argued by most other deepening approaches, a concept which is inherently contested and political (Der Derian, 1995; Wæver, 1995). Hence Katzenstein's suggestion that widening and deepening approaches could easily apply Constructivism's ideational conclusions missed, according to other deepeners, the deeper political nature of the concept of security. That there was something more at stake than convincing traditionalists by 'choosing the hard case' was also indicated by Conventional Constructivists' desire to distance themselves from Poststructuralism, from 'exotic (presumably Parisian) social theory' (Jepperson *et al.*, 1996: 34; Adler, 1997b).

The confluence between Conventional Constructivism and traditional Realist approaches was further indicated by the choice of research design,

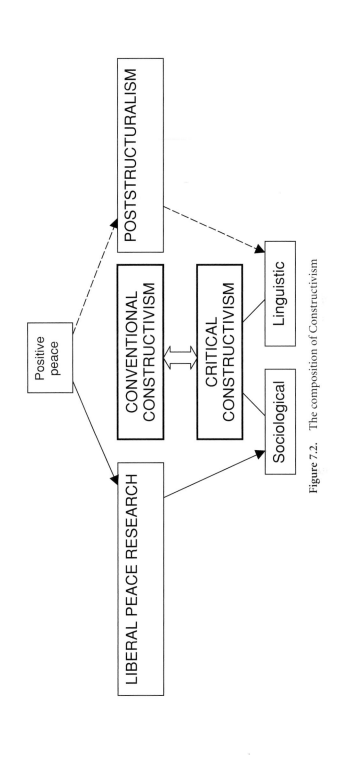

Figure 7.2.   The composition of Constructivism

where Constructivists often took the inability of Realists to explain particular phenomena as the starting point for showing the causal or semi-causal significance of ideational factors such as beliefs, norms, values and culture. While most Constructivists at first advocated the use of both positivist and post-positivist approaches, Conventional Constructivists, led by Wendt, gradually moved towards a positivist research agenda (Laffey and Weldes, 1997; Desch, 1998; Wendt, 1999; S. Smith, 2005: 39–40). Moreover, prominent Conventional Constructivists published their work in *International Security*, the most prestigious traditional ISS journal, and they often adopted the same structured case-study design as did traditionalists – or the other way around, the choice of traditionalist epistemology and methodology increased the chances of Constructivist articles being accepted. Articles in *International Security* have traditionally fallen into two broad categories: the structured (often historical) case-study and more policy-oriented, less theoretically explicit articles on contemporary security issues. Conventional Constructivist works belong largely to the first category: the historical case-study applied in the service of a more general theoretical argument. As noted in chapter 3, journals are an important aspect of academic institutionalisation, and the incorporation of Constructivism in *International Security* thus had a double effect: it legitimised Constructivism as an ISS perspective to be recognised (at least in the American context) and it allowed the editors to constitute *International Security* as a broad and inclusive journal irrespective of its virtual silence on any other widening approach (Critical Constructivism, the Copenhagen School, Critical Security Studies, Feminism, etc.). Thus at the journal's twenty-fifth anniversary, editor-in-chief Steven E. Miller (2001a: 8, 12) characterised *International Security* as 'multidisciplinary' and adhering 'to no political, substantive, or methodological line' – perhaps not a view that would be shared by those outside its coterie of contributors.

This is turn indicates that the driving force of internal academic debates – the rationalist–reflectivist discussions in IR more specifically – has had a stronger impact on Conventional Constructivism than have events, technology or great power politics. That said, all of those three driving forces have played some role in Constructivism's evolution. A significant proportion of Conventional Constructivist works adopted, as noted above, the historical case-study as its methodological strategy and hence has not been driven by contemporary events to a similar extent as, for instance, Cold War Strategic Studies, Human Security or Poststructuralism. Events did nevertheless play a role in some studies, particularly in those which dealt with the implications of the end of the Cold War, for instance for NATO (Risse-Kappen, 1996), Japan (Katzenstein and Okawara, 1993) or humanitarian interventions (Finnemore, 1996, 2003). Turning to the driving force of great power politics, many of the historical case-studies did involve great powers, probably since these have always been privileged by traditional ISS. Most Conventional Constructivists were furthermore American-based, hence probably more likely to adopt a great power focus, and to the extent that contemporary events were covered, they often had a great power component. Although technology was not usually cast as a driving force in itself, there were several studies that dealt with its development, its social constitution and the norms surrounding it, for instance the cases of the non-use of chemical and nuclear weapons (Price, 1995, 1997; Price and Tannenwald, 1996; Tannenwald, 1999, 2005).

Moving to the substantial claims of Conventional Constructivism, it offers analysis that attacks traditional ISS, particularly Neorealism, at several different points. One group of works focused on international norms, particularly those that appear to contravene the assumption of Neorealism and Neoliberalism that states are rational, self-help actors in an anarchic system. These studies were usually constituted around a Realist puzzle: why do states accept constraints on their ability to conduct warfare, such as providing aid for the wounded according the Geneva Conventions (Finnemore, 1996)? Why are chemical weapons not used, when these may be effective, and militaries are prepared to use them (Price, 1995)? Or why is the assassination of political and military leaders considered inappropriate, even though these might be effective, easy to carry out and a preferable moral alternative to waging war against an entire army or population (W. Thomas, 2000)? These questions, argue Constructivists, cannot be answered by Realist materialist explanations, but only through an ideational analysis that traces the genesis and evolution of norms. The non-use of chemical weapons during the Second World War, for example, was, argues Richard Price (1995), coupled to a constitution of 'civilised' and 'uncivilised' nations. Where the 'civilised' found chemical weapons morally abhorrent, it was simultaneously their same (constructed) 'civility' which allowed them to use chemical weapons against 'non-civilised' peoples.

A second group of Constructivist work moved from the level of the international system to the foreign policies of particular states or institutions. These studies also point to phenomena which cannot be explained by Neorealist theories located at the level of the international structure, arguing that these require a foreign policy level explanation <u>and</u> the incorporation of an ideational variable. Kier's (1995) analysis of French military doctrine claims that the choice of either offensive or defensive doctrine can only be explained through a combination of civilian concerns over the military's power and military culture itself (Kier, 1995: 68). Katzenstein and Okawara (1993) hold that since the international structure had changed, but not Japan's understanding of its security, domestic factors have to be brought in (see also Berger, 1993, 1996). Turning from states to international institutions, Risse-Kappen (1996) argues that Neorealism's (Mearsheimer, 1990; Waltz, 1993) inability to explain NATO's post-Cold War survival is due to this theory's exclusion of ideational variables such as values and identity. Rather than being formed against an external threat and hence, as Neorealists predicted, due to dissolve as this threat withers away, NATO, held Risse-Kappen, was founded upon a set of democratic, liberal values which would guarantee the institution's survival.

Conventional Constructivism has, not surprisingly, been criticised by traditionalists as well as by other wideners. The main traditionalist criticism has been that Constructivist theories have failed 'to demonstrate that their theories outperform [R]ealist theories in "hard cases"' (Desch, 1998: 144). Hence, while Constructivism can supplement Realism it cannot supplant it. More interesting, perhaps, is the way in which other widening approaches have attacked Conventional Constructivism for being 'essentially a form of rationalism' focused on states and military security (S. Smith, 2005: 39; see also Campbell, 1998b: 218). Conventional Constructivism, in this view, fails to engage 'security' critically, and it pushes to the background the normative implications of accepting the state as the referent object and the military as the privileged realm.

To say that Constructivists comply analytically with state-centrism is not to say, however, that Constructivist analysis cannot be critical of particular state policies. Kier's analysis of the US military's ban on openly homosexual service personnel argues, for instance, that the military's justification – that open integration of gays and lesbians would hinder the primary group cohesion which is critical to military effectiveness – is false (Kier, 1998; Barnett, 1996). As laid out in chapter 5, to adopt a positivist epistemology does not by itself foreclose a normative engagement, and while the study of norms may not necessarily be normatively explicit, it often produces a demand for a more explicit normative and political assessment: is the norm against the use of chemical weapons/assassinations/nuclear proliferation applied to all or just against some subjects? What are the consequences, and for whom?

Perhaps most importantly, there is an ambiguity or an opening in Conventional Constructivism in terms of how it constitutes the basic logic of international relations. Contrary to what some critics have held, Constructivist ideational explanations do not imply peaceful outcomes: ideas, norms and culture might spur as well as dampen expansionist and aggressive behaviour. Constructivism is thus neutral as far as Classical Liberal and Realist ontological assumptions are concerned. Yet if, as Wendt (1999) holds, states might exist in a Kantian rather than a Hobbesian anarchical culture, then a more fundamental shift away from the Realist understanding of the state is possible, and 'security' might change accordingly. Or, when the morally engaged individuals and networks studied by Finnemore (1996) change state practices, they also move the understanding of 'security' in a less Realist direction.

Critical Constructivism

Critical Constructivism branched off during the latter half of the 1990s, distinguishing itself from Conventional Constructivism by analysing discourses and the linkages between the historical and discursive constitution of identities on the one hand and security policies on the other (Katzenstein *et al.*, 1998: 677). Critical Constructivists argued that Conventional Constructivism reified the state as the object of analysis, and that this entailed a normative privileging of the state as the preferable referent object for security (Weldes, 1996; Zehfuss, 2001; Rumelili, 2004). Epistemologically, Critical Constructivists challenged Conventional Constructivism's increasing embrace of positivism (Laffey and Weldes, 1997).

Exactly where to draw the line between Critical Constructivism and Conventional Constructivism, as well as between Critical Constructivism and Poststructuralism, is a difficult question: both boundary drawings are to a significant extent a question of overlapping zones rather than insurmountable differences (see, for instance, Price, 1995). On that note of caution, we can identify two main bodies of work within Critical Constructivism, each of which has some interesting affinities to Cold War Peace Research. One body of Critical Constructivist work brought social theory and historical sociology to bear on Classical Peace Research and ISS themes and concepts. This body of work included Adler's (1992) account of the significance of the American strategic epistemic community and its ideas about arms control for bringing about the end of the

Cold War, and his and Barnett's reinvigoration of Deutsch's security community theory (Adler, 1997a; Adler and Barnett, 1998). As in Deutsch's original formulation, Adler (1997a: 250) theorised security communities as forming through a bottom-up process, where citizens from different countries came to realise that their values and hence their destinies were shared. The optimism that flowed from Liberal Deutschian Peace Research was echoed by Adler's description of the Organisation for Security and Co-operation in Europe (OSCE) as a security community-building institution empowering individuals, non-government organisations (NGOs), social movements and civil society actors (Adler, 1997a: 274–276).

Other Constructivists were more critical of Liberal assumptions, for example of the explanatory power of democratic systems as well as of the normative privilege accorded to the (allegedly) democratic West. Democratic peace theory was challenged by Oren (1995, 2003) who held that the definition of what makes a state democratic has evolved historically as a consequence of which countries the United States has thought of as its enemies. Hence, since democracy is the dependent rather than the independent viable, it is hardly surprising that democratic peace theory in the 1980s and 1990s would discover that democratic states do not go to war against each other. Williams and Neumann's analysis of NATO enlargement (2000) suggested that enlargement was an exercise of symbolic power rather than a Liberal, security community project driven by universal democratic values. The idea of symbolic power also resonated with Mattern's (2001, 2005) analysis of security communities as built upon representational or narrative force.

The other main body of Critical Constructivist work has affinities with linguistic Peace Research analysis (see chapter 5), and describes itself as taking a deeper, more discursive approach to identity and security, drawing in some cases on Poststructuralism. Significantly, however, most linguistic Critical Constructivists mirror Conventional Constructivism in that they do not explicitly engage the concept of security. Critical Constructivists working in the linguistic tradition argue that key Realist concepts like the national interest are discursively constituted through representations (of countries, peoples, etc.) and linguistic elements (nouns, adjectives, metaphors and analogies) (Weldes, 1996, 1999). Foreign and security policies therefore do not arise from objective national interests but become legitimated through particular constructions which are not free-floating or 'just words', but follow a specific set of rule-bound games (Fierke, 1996, 1998, 1999, 2000). Fierke shows, for instance, how the Western responses to the Bosnian War situated the war inside a particular language game (Fierke, 1996: 473). Comparing the war to 'the Second World War', 'Vietnam', the 'Gulf War' or 'the First World War' thus constituted different identities for the Bosnian parties and for the West and suggested which policies could or should be carried out. Conducting a historical case-study, Weldes (1996, 1999) contrasted the official US discourse on the Cuba Missile Crisis with Cuban and Soviet representations to illustrate the contestability of material facts, such as missiles. And Mutimer (1998) analysed how practices and narratives of proliferation control spread from nuclear proliferation to chemical, biological and chemical weapons after the end of the Cold War. Crucially, to constitute these weapons through 'disarmament', 'market economy' or 'a war on drugs' discourse rather than 'proliferation' would reorient the constitutions of objects, identities and interests and hence what policies should be adopted.

The concern with the construction of identity and the link between representations and policy in Critical Constructivism means that there are obvious similarities to Poststructuralism (see chapter 5 and the section below). There are, however, also differences between the two approaches. First, in that Critical Constructivists often examine language games or narratives from a logical or hypothetical perspective rather than, as do most Poststructuralists, from an empirical one (Wæver, 2004a). This logical deduction provides the language games identified with a free-standing or self-contained quality which makes transitions and variations harder to explain (Fierke, 2000 seeks to address this). Second, the conception of identity is slightly more Constructivist than Poststructuralist. Critical Constructivists speak about states as actors, not as discursively constituted subjects, and there is sometimes a slippage between 'identity' and 'role' (Mutimer, 1998: 113). This implies that identity is something that a state (or others) has, and which 'it' explicitly defines and pursues (Mitzen, 2006), or a property that it can decide to protect or 'kill off' (Mattern, 2001). For Poststructuralists identity is discursively constituted, and while states (or rather those speaking on behalf of states) construct and mobilise identity when legitimating foreign policies, identity is not an entity that can be fully controlled. Third, Critical Constructivists often establish identities on the basis of explicit words or concepts found in the texts examined; Mutimer (1998), for example, identifies the identities of the proliferation discourse as 'suppliers' and 'recipients'. Poststructuralists usually trace how such terms are linked to more deep-seated identities such as civilised/barbaric, Western/Oriental, democratic/despotic and rational/irrational.

Beyond the (Western) state

The Constructivists dealt with in the section above did not explicitly advocate an expansion of the referent object beyond the state or outline a theory that went beyond the military-political sector. This is not to say that Constructivism cannot be critical: to point to the ability of transcending the Realist view of security politics and interstate relations goes to the core of central normative debates in ISS. But Constructivism's scope differs from those widening approaches that explicitly engage the concept of security, and this section deals with the latter, particularly those which claimed the need for an expansion of the referent beyond the (Western) state: Post-colonial approaches (to which some Critical Constructivists contributed), Human Security, Critical Security Studies and Feminism. With this widening of the referent object came also a widening of the sectors or areas to which security analysis should be applied, adding development, the environment, economics and social-welfare issues.

Post-colonialism

The status of the Western state has been an issue in ISS since the 1970s. More traditional security scholars, such as Ayoob (1984, 1997), pointed to the specificities of the Third World while insisting on the need for a strong state and maintaining it as the referent object. Critical Peace Researchers, on the other hand, employed Marxist and *dependencia* theories to their analysis of the economic, political and cultural exploitation that the Liberal world order entailed. In the 1990s, the calls for critical scrutiny of the Western-centric conception of the state at the heart of ISS became more frequent and an explicit Post-colonial ISS perspective began to crystallise. This was in part a consequence of the advent and growth of Post-colonialism in the social sciences and humanities more broadly (Said, 1978; Spivak, 1999; Grovogui, 2007), in part supported by the overlap between Post-colonialism and other widening approaches which drew upon each other to generate critical momentum.

Post-colonial theory comprises a broad range of perspectives (Grovogui, 2007), and one body of Post-colonial ISS overlapped with social theory and historical sociology, and hence with Critical Constructivism, in pointing to the need for conceptualisations of security that acknowledged the specificity of the Third World. Drawing on the work of Charles Tilly, Krause (1996), for example, held that the state-centric concept of security advocated by traditionalist Realist approaches was based on a particular European history of state formation. The European state had been built on an understanding of security as oriented towards external threats, and rested upon 'a strong identification of the security of the *state* with the security of *its citizens*' (Krause, 1996: 320, emphasis in original). This understanding of security implies that state-centric conceptions of security provide neither an analytical nor a normative position from which to identify the threats that regimes may pose to their own citizens.

Post-colonialism holds that the non-Western state has followed a different trajectory, but takes issue with the view of this as 'failed' or 'underdeveloped'. The failed states literature discussed in chapter 6 looked at the 'failed' state as lacking in some respects in comparison with the West, and hence in need of 'catching up'. Post-colonialists argue in response that these 'failures' are 'the after-effects of the unequal encounter with Western colonialism' (Niva, 1999: 150; Barkawi and Laffey, 2006) and that there is a recurring economic, social and military unequal relationship between the West and the rest. This line of Post-colonial ISS emphasises 'the material and ideological struggles of historically situated agents in a neoliberal world order' (Agathangelou and Ling, 2004: 518) and resonates with critical IPE as well as with Marxist Peace Researchers' accounts of imperialism and structural violence in the 1960s and 1970s.

Another strain of Post-colonial theory diverged from 1970s Marxist Peace Research by emphasising the discursive constitution of identities rather than material structures. In this literature, Post-colonialism and Poststructuralism drew upon each other, pointing to the Western political and academic construction of 'the Southern', 'the Oriental', the 'underdeveloped' and the 'failed' Other (Doty, 1996; Muppidi, 1999; Niva, 1999). These inferior identities assume 'an unchanging "precolonial" cultural essence' that can be mobilised by the West, for instance in arguments against nuclear proliferation to the Third World (Mutimer, 1998; Niva, 1999: 150; Biswas, 2001; Grovogui, 2007: 240–241), but also by the non-Western elites seeking to boost their position domestically and abroad (Niva, 1999: 150–152). A crucial implication of Post-colonialism is thus that a different understanding of the non-Western subject appears, and since identity is relational, of the West itself (Bilgin, 2008). This means that other referent objects may come into analytical focus, but also that 'security' itself may be constituted in distinct non-Western terms that require the adoption of new epistemologies and methodologies (Grovogui, 2007: 232–233).

Post-colonialism's reconstitution of the referent object and its deployment of a broader set of contextualised epistemologies concur with calls for bringing Anthropology to bear on ISS. This call was prominently made by a group of Critical Constructivists in *Cultures of Insecurity: States, Communities, and the Production of Danger* (Weldes *et al.*, 1999) which, as indicated by the title, was an explicit attempt to define a Critical Constructivism that differed from that of *The Culture of National Security* (Katzenstein, 1996a). Weldes *et al.* argued more specifically for a research agenda focused on the production of insecurity across multiple levels of analysis, across different sectors, and as applicable to collective referent objects below and across state boundaries (Weldes *et al.*, 1999: 1–10). This perspective was brought to bear not only on non-Western contexts (Litzinger, 1999; Muppidi, 1999; Niva, 1999) but also on domestic, Western settings, as in Masco's (1999) account of how different ethnic groups around Los Alamos, New Mexico, confronted the economic consequences of the downscaling of nuclear facilities at the end of the Cold War. These groups articulated societal, economic and environmental security concerns, thus linking security across a wider set of sectors.

Anthropologists working from a Post-colonial perspective warn against assuming that a universal, globally shared concept of security exists. They argue that ethnographic field studies can identify local constructions of security that differ from what is commonly assumed in (Western-centric) ISS, that '[it] cannot, for instance, be assumed that the objective of security is to ensure the survival of either the individual or the state' (Kent, 2006: 347; see also Bubandt, 2005). These differences are not simply semantic but indicate profound variation in how societies are organised and how key political principles such as governance, violence and legitimacy are understood. These local constructions also have significant implications for the epistemology and methodology of security analysis, particularly for discursive approaches, in that the word 'security' may not identify the 'logic of security' as we know it from Realist definitions of national security and, vice versa, that 'logics of national security' might be invoked by other concepts and practices (see also the discussion of the Copenhagen School below).

Human Security

Post-colonial approaches draw attention to the specificities of the non-Western state, to global economic structures and hence also to development issues. A more straightforward expansion of security to include development was made with the United Nations Development Pro-gramme's concept of Human Security, launched in 1994. Human Security has the advantage of being promoted from a strong institutional base and, like Common Security in the early 1980s, combines political-activist and academic agendas. The original UNDP formulation opted for an expan-sion of security along several dimensions. The 'logic of security' should be broadened beyond territorial defence, national interests and nuclear deterrence to include 'universal concerns' and the prevention of conflicts, but also crucially a cooperative global effort to eradicate poverty and underdevelopment (UNDP, 1994: 22). The referent object was shifted from nation-states to that of 'people', and to be 'people-centred' was to be 'concerned with how people live and breathe in a society, how freely they exercise their many choices, how much access they have to mar-ket and social opportunities – and whether they live in conflict or in peace' (UNDP, 1994: 23). This implied a radical widening of the types of threats and sectors to which security was applicable to food, health, the environment, population growth, disparities in economic opportunities, migration, drug trafficking and terrorism.

The UNDP's conceptualisation of Human Security is probably the most encompassing expansion of the concept since Galtung launched structural violence and, like Marxist Peace Research, it sought to bring development and North–South issues into ISS. As in the case of structural violence, Human Security has also been attacked for being so broad that it becomes academically and politically vacuous (Special Section of *Security Dialogue*, 2004). As Roland Paris puts it, 'if human security means almost anything, then it effectively means nothing' (2001: 93). Other critics question the wisdom of adding 'security' to what they hold is essentially a human rights agenda (Buzan, 2004b), and point to the ease with which states co-opt Human Security rhetoric without actually changing their behaviour (Booth, 2007: 321–327).

The common expansive ambitions notwithstanding, there are, how-ever, important differences between Human Security and the concept of structural violence. Human Security in UNDP's founding formulation articulates a much less conflictual relationship between the West and the South, and between regimes and citizens, and hence offers less of a sys-tematic critique of the global economic structure than did *dependencia* theory. Moreover, Critical Peace Researchers were highly critical of the (Western) state, while the state's inability to provide security for 'its' peo-ple is only briefly mentioned by the UNDP. These absences – criticism of the state and the Neoliberal economic order – are perhaps not too surprising considering the document's status as a UNDP text which by its very nature and institutional location has to be acceptable to states. Subsequent appropriations of Human Security have, however, used the concept in different ways to challenge the state and the current political–economic structure.

Tracing the evolution of Human Security since its UNDP inception, one might first point to its adoption by states, most prominently Norway, Canada and Japan, and to academic literature analysing this shift in state discourse (Suhrke, 1999; Axworthy, 2001; Neufeld, 2004). These governments have linked Human Security with 'the pre-eminent progressive values of the 1990s: human rights, international humanitarian law, and socio-economic development based on equity' (Suhrke, 1999: 266). The Canadian government has furthermore provided funding for the Canadian Consortium on Human Security, 'an academic-based network promoting policy relevant research on human security', which since 2002 has published the *Human Security Bulletin* (www.humansecurity.info/ – last accessed 29 January 2008). Taking a Constructivist perspective that combines interests and ideas, Suhrke (1999) holds that this progressive conception of Human Security suited Canadian aspirations for a middle-power status and Norwegian ambitions about a UN Security Council seat in 2001–2003 (Newman, 2001; McDonald, 2002). These aspirations and ambitions coalesced with global structural shifts in the 1990s that made more room for normative foreign policies based on humanitarian concerns (Suhrke 1999: 268–270). The coupling of Human Security to a 'humanitarian foreign policy' modifies the Classical Realist understanding of the state as concerned exclusively with territorial defence and national interests. Yet, critics argue, Norwegian and Canadian conceptions suffer from the Classical widening problem: how to delimit the concept, and how to judge which insecurities to honour when conflicting concerns are at stake (Suhrke, 1999; Paris, 2001).

Some, for instance Thomas and Tow (2002a: 179), have tried to address these problems by defining Human Security in narrower terms as crossing state borders and assuming 'a truly international significance, affecting other societies and individuals'. Yet, as Bellamy and McDonald note, this conceptualisation provides rigour only by reinstalling the state-centric conception of security that critical advocates of Human Security attacked in the first place (Bellamy and McDonald, 2002; Thomas and Tow, 2002b). Others have approached Human Security from a poverty, development and global health literature rather than from Security Studies, and argued for a 'simple, rigorous, and measurable definition of human security:

the number of years of future life spent outside a state of "generalized poverty"' (King and Murray, 2001/2: 585). Based on an empiricist epistemology, this approach takes the individual as the referent object to such an extent that the political dynamics at the state and international levels are virtually absent (King and Murray, 2001/2: 597).

More critical advocates of Human Security have either tied it to a Critical Security Studies agenda (Dunne and Wheeler, 2004; Booth, 2005b) or linked it with a critique of Neoliberal economics, particularly as this ideology is influencing development policies. As a consequence, argues Caroline Thomas, '[the] globalisation process is resulting in highly uneven distribution of gains and, without concerted action, inequality may deepen further, with all its attendant implications' (Thomas, 2001: 173–174). This in turn creates a link to critical IPE and to the economic, structural inequalities at the heart of the old Marxist Peace Research agenda.

The debates over Human Security read in major respects like a new round of the Classical debate between wide and narrow concepts of security. As wideners point to the political consequences of privileging state security at the expense of marginalised people threatened by poverty and persecution by their own state, those advocating narrow approaches stress the need for security concepts to make distinct academic arguments and be a guide towards making policy priorities. What is perhaps crucial and distinct about the Human Security debate is that it shows both the value of institutionalisation (its genesis in the UNDP and its adoption as a concept by states such as Norway and Canada) and that academic criteria are not always what determine a concept's success or failure. Human Security did articulate a very broad agenda, but this simultaneously provided a rallying point for a diversity of political actors seeking to boost support for development issues and humanitarian foreign policies.

Critical Security Studies

Human Security was also, as noted above, picked up by Critical Security Studies, which shared the former's concern with 'people' rather than states and which also envisaged a more just, peaceful world order. Although quantitatively small, Critical Security Studies has managed to institutionalise itself on the European Security Studies arena to quite a remarkable extent. Critical Security Studies is usually defined as the Frankfurt School inspired work by Booth and Wyn Jones and their Aberystwyth students and collaborators (Booth, 1991, 2005a, 2007; Wyn Jones, 1995, 1999, 2005; Bilgin, 2003, 2004a; Dunne and Wheeler, 2004; Mutimer, 2007: 62–65; Van

Munster, 2007). In the mid-1990s a broader definition of Critical Security Studies which also covered Poststructuralism and Constructivism was put forward by Krause and Williams (1997), yet this never gained hold and the narrower 'Aberystwyth definition' of Critical Security Studies became (re)established (Booth, 2005b; CASE, 2006). Critical Security Studies has made a significant impact on the widening discussions in that it has been the perspective to most explicitly pick up the Critical Theory Frankfurt School tradition that was part of Peace Research in the 1970s. This, however, did not happen as an explicit engagement with the latter literature, but through a reading of the Frankfurt School itself. Conceptually, Critical Security Studies argued that 'individual humans are the ultimate referent' for security, as states are unreliable providers of security and too diverse to provide for 'a comprehensive theory of security' (Booth, 1991: 319–320). To Wyn Jones (1995: 309), Critical Security Studies implies 'placing the experience of those men and women and communities for whom the present world order is a cause of insecurity rather than security, at the centre of our agenda'. Critical Security Studies' vocal call for an individual referent object is furthermore linked to an empirical–political assessment of interstate war as far less real and threatening than 'environmental security, food security and economic security', and to a view of the vast majority of states as generating insecurity rather than stability and prosperity (Wyn Jones, 1995: 310).

This makes for a very pessimistic view of global security: states make individuals insecure and the Neoliberal economic structure further exacerbates this condition. Booth (2007: 395 ff.) speaks of a 'new twenty years' crisis' to be soon followed by a range of environmental, political and humanitarian disasters which he labels 'the great reckoning', unless radical changes are made in many basic aspects of human conduct. The transformation of individual/global security away from this pessimistic account of the present is facilitated by the concept of emancipation. Emancipation functions as the goal of individual security as well as the analytical and political engine, and is defined by Booth (in terms reminiscent of Galtung's structural violence) as 'the freeing of people (as individuals and groups) from those physical and human constraints which stop them carrying out what they would freely choose to do' (Booth, 1991: 319). This, in Booth's view, is a highly desirable situation: if people are emancipated, what they freely choose to do is peaceful. The emancipated solution at the level of individual security therefore has positive consequences at the level of collective security: 'individual security' is deeply connected to 'global security', which is when all individuals and groups have been emancipated and more organic constructions of political community have replaced the state (see also McSweeney, 1999).

Critical Security Studies' concept of emancipation draws explicitly on the Frankfurt School, particularly on Habermas's account of the emancipatory potential in interaction and communication (Wyn Jones, 2005: 223). This in turn establishes a link both to Cold War Peace Research and to early Poststructuralist interest in emancipatory forms of knowledge (Ashley, 1981, 1984; Alker, 1988). The degree to which contemporary Critical Security Studies shares common ground with other widening approaches is, however, debatable: Wyn Jones (2005) holds that a notion of emancipation is implicit in Poststructuralism, the Copenhagen School and Feminism, and the CASE collective has recently called for a common Copenhagen–Paris–Aberystwyth agenda (Aradau, 2004b, 2006; CASE, 2006; Taureck, 2006; Floyd, 2007; Van Munster, 2007). Booth (2005b), however, has sharpened his views of the distance between Critical Security Studies on the one hand and Poststructuralism, the Copenhagen School and Constructivism on the other (Mutimer, 2007: 62–65). In Booth's opinion, the point of Security Studies is to awaken and create security audiences, and not, like the Copenhagen School, just to analyse how audiences respond to securitising moves (Booth, 2007: 163–169).

Such positioning debates are a crucial part of the sociology of ISS, particularly perhaps in Europe after the end of the Cold War, and critics of Critical Security Studies argue that to insist on an individual referent object dichotomously opposed to the state repeats the Classical fallacy, laid out in chapter 2, of constituting the options as a choice between the two. All political concepts articulate a relationship between the individual and the collective, and an exclusively individual referent object is thus impossible. Emancipated individuals are in need of a resolution at the collective level, and to envisage this as unproblematically flowing from the individual level leads one back to a Classical utopian position. Critical Security Studies argues in favour of an objective definition of security insofar as the critical security theorist can determine which security problems are particularly threatening, and a subjective definition insofar as an individual's own definition of security problems should be taken into account. In this respect, Critical Security Studies confronts similar problems to Feminists working with an epistemology of experience, to be discussed below. It also points to a Classical tendency in (post-)Marxist theory to explain away repressed peoples' failure to see their 'objective' security interests as a case of false consciousness. The concept and strategy of emancipation has also been criticised for being vague. As Wyn Jones (2005: 222) points out, 'Adorno and Horkheimer cannot point to any concrete examples of what types of institutions and relationships might characterize a more emancipated society', and later theorists have not come much further in terms of defining the steps towards an emancipated society, nor what it would ultimately look like.

Feminism

Feminist Security Studies, to a greater extent than the other widening–deepening perspectives covered in this chapter, comprises sub-approaches which adopt different referent objects, epistemologies and methodologies. With the exception of traditional military-state centric approaches which leave no room for gender and security, Feminist Security Studies can thus be seen as a microcosm of ISS itself. The most significant questions on the post-Cold War Feminist Security Studies agenda were: first, how to further develop the standpoint Feminist approach associated with J. Ann Tickner and Cynthia Enloe presented in chapter 5, particularly how to tackle the problems connected to its epistemology of experience; second, how to integrate a new set of events; and third, how to respond to Constructivism and quantitative Feminism.

The Tickner approach has been the most prevalent one within Feminist Security Studies, in terms of which conceptualisation of security is adopted and how it is introduced by most textbooks (Pettman, 2005; Kennedy-Pipe, 2007; Tickner and Sjoberg, 2007). This approach has much in common with Critical Security Studies and Human Security in calling for an expansion of the referent object to include 'women' and non-military security sectors (Hoogensen and Rottem, 2004; Hudson, 2005; Hoogensen and Stuvøy, 2006). In Tickner's words, Feminists adopt 'a multidimensional, multilevel approach' committed to 'emancipatory visions of security' that seek to 'understand how the security of individuals and groups is compromised by violence, both physical and structural, at all levels' (Tickner, 2001: 48). Feminist analysis has as a consequence 'generally taken a bottom-up approach, analyzing the impact of war at the microlevel' (Tickner, 2001: 48), deepened the referent object and widened the sectors to which security is applicable.

Epistemologically, those working in the Tickner tradition have usually adopted 'experiences' as their key concept. The absence of women in traditional ISS approaches and the form that gender-specific threats to women's security take are closely connected to the fact that '[too] often, women's experiences have been deemed trivial or only important in so far as they relate to the experiences of men and the questions they typically ask' (Tickner, 2005: 7). Feminist research, according to Tickner, is thus informed by the assumption that 'women's lives are important' and that 'the routine aspects of everyday life that help sustain gender inequality' should be brought out (Tickner, 2005: 7). This leads to a preference for methodologies that embrace an 'ethnographic style of individually oriented story-telling typical of anthropology' (Tickner, 1997: 615) or 'hermeneutic and interpretative methodologies' that 'allow subjects to document their own experiences in their own terms' (Tickner, 2005: 19).

The attraction of an epistemology of experience for Feminist Security Studies – as well as for Critical Security Studies – is that it brings in subjects marginalised by state-centric – and other collective – concepts of security, for instance victims of wartime rape or sex-trafficking (Stiglmayer, 1994; Pickup, 1998; Denov, 2006; Jackson, 2006). Yet the weakness of an epistemology of experience is that it rests on standpoint feminism's view of women as forming a coherent subject distinct from that of 'men'. Many standpoint feminists therefore developed diversity feminism that understands identity as informed not only by gender but by ethnicity, class and race (Dietz, 2003: 408). This opened up a bigger variety of gendered referent objects and experiences, but it also created the problem of how to unite a feminist movement and consciousness across multiple experiences. The problem was in short that 'Feminist epistemology in the realm of international security must either decide to curtail the admission of all "women's experiences" or accept, as other fields have done, that there is a need to judge and select, even within the feminist perspective' (Grant, 1992: 95).

This is not only a matter of selecting which women to include. Rather, the more fundamental problem is that 'experience' relies upon an ambiguous construction of the individual subject, gendered structures and the privileged status of the researcher. 'Experience' is on the one hand a concept that promises a direct link to (marginalised) subjects' everyday lives and to a deeply subjective, narrative and often emotional form of knowledge. Yet this subject is on the other hand constituted through a gendered structure: it is only conceivable as a 'gendered experience' if gender is already accepted as a frame of reference. As Joan Scott (1992: 27) explains, experience 'leads us to take the existence of individuals for granted (experience is something people have) rather than to ask how conceptions of selves (of subjects and their identities) are produced'.

Accepting Scott's call for giving the production of identity centre-stage, some Feminists moved in a more Poststructuralist direction (Sylvester,

1994; Weber, 1998). As chapter 5 and the section below lay out, this implies a concern with the construction of identity, and in the specific context of Feminism and gender with the often ambiguous and multi-faceted articulation of gendered subjects. Gender comes into Feminist Poststructuralist focus, first, as the way in which other referent objects – states, nations or, for instance, religious groups – are gendered, that is constituted as masculine or feminine. Feminists working in this tradition resonate with Poststructuralist and Critical Constructivist analyses which trace the use of gendering representations as part of their broader study of security discourses and narratives (Campbell, 1992; Weldes, 1996). Second, gender comes into focus through an account of competing constructions of the gendered referent object itself and of the policy spaces – or silences – that ensue (Hansen, 2001; Berman, 2003). To take the example of sex-trafficking in women, one of the key themes on the post-Cold War Feminist Security Studies agenda, Feminist researchers point to the constitution of trafficked women as either the victims of kingpins and manipulation or as illegal migrants seeking entrance into the labour market of the EU (Pickup, 1998; Petersen, 2001; Berman, 2003; Aradau, 2004a; Jackson, 2006). 'Victims' are to be assisted, although not necessarily given asylum, while the 'illegal migrants' are scheming subjects to be deported. The key point for a Poststructuralist Feminist analysis is here not to identify the 'real' representation, but to explore and criticise how subject constructions condition how 'women' can appear (Hansen, 2001).

Yet not all those working in the field of gender and security would self-identify as Feminists or adopt a Tickner–Human Security–Critical Security Studies or a Poststructuralist position. Expanding the scope of Feminist/gender research in Security Studies, Caprioli (2004a) and R. Charli Carpenter (2002) argue that Feminist Security Studies has been dominated by the Tickner–Enloe approach to such an extent that quantitative, positivist and Constructivist scholarship has been marginalised. Coming from the quantitative tradition of Peace Research, Mary Caprioli (2004a) pointed to how Feminist theorists such as Sandra Harding have called for all methodologies to be included, and specifically to the significance of causal analyses of how gender impacts state behaviour, for instance in a Feminist version of the democratic peace theory that examines the relationship between gender equality, democracy and conflict (Keohane, 1989; Caprioli, 2000, 2003, 2004b; Caprioli and Boyer, 2001; Caprioli and Trumbore, 2003; Regan and Paskeviciute, 2003). Other quantitative studies did not, as Caprioli, self-identify as Feminist, but adopted

gender as a variable in explaining public attitudes to foreign and security policy (Togeby, 1994; Eichenberg, 2003). Shifting from explaining
state behaviour to women as a referent object for security, other studies
explored the correlation between polity type and human rights on the
one hand and women's security on the other (Caprioli, 2004b).

Caprioli self-identified her work as Feminist, whereas Carpenter (2002)
argued in favour of a non-Feminist Conventional Constructivism that
examines the importance of norms for national security but does not share
the political commitments of Feminism. Based on a study of humanitarian evacuations during the Bosnian War, Carpenter (2003) concluded that
norms about the vulnerability of women and children conditioned the
policy options available to protection workers from the United Nations
High Commissioner for Refugees (UNHCR). Hence, although adult males
and male adolescents were more likely to be massacred when besieged
enclaves fell to Serbian forces, women and children were the ones evacu-
ated. Put in the language of referent objects, men were more likely victims
of gender-based violence and hence should be granted more concern by
Feminist security scholars (Jones, 1994, 1996, 1998; R. C. Carpenter, 2003,
2006). The general Feminist response to quantitative and Constructivist
(non-)Feminist analysis was that these did not consider women as a referent object for security, and hence could not address the gender-specific
threats that women face (Carver, 2003; Bilgin, 2004c). Nor had Feminists
claimed that men and masculinity were not significant or indeed that men
were not more likely to die in combat, but rather that it was the constructions of masculine and feminine identities and the protector/protected
dichotomies that made it seem warranted that men went to the line of
fire and women stayed at home (Enloe, 1983, 1989; Elshtain, 1987; Carver
et al., 1998; Locher and Prügl, 2001; Carver, 2003; Sjoberg, 2006). What
a Feminist expansion of the referent object revealed was that women's
security problems were privatised, marginalised or even silenced, and
that their deaths were validated differently from that of military men's,
not that men were not threatened.

This section has emphasised the analytical and epistemological debates
over how the gendered referent object might be broadened or deepened.
Yet it should be stressed that much, if not most, of the work on gender and
security is not explicitly theoretical or engaging directly with the concept
of security, but written in an empirical low-theory style. As a consequence,
analysis often combines elements from several approaches. This empirical focus also means that Feminism has to a large extent been driven by
events. Some of the key themes on the Feminist research agenda were:

sex-trafficking across old East–West boundaries (Pickup, 1998; Petersen, 2001; Berman, 2003; Aradau, 2004a; Jackson, 2006); rape as a weapon of war and other forms of wartime sexual violence (Rogers 1998; Stanley, 1999; Hansen, 2001; Skjelsbæk, 2001; Denov, 2006); masculinities, peacekeeping, humanitarian intervention and post-conflict reconstruction including the difficulties of negotiating a traditional Feminist preference for non-military solutions with women's demands for protection, particularly in the light of scandals where UN peacekeepers had kept prostitutes or committed rape (Handrahan, 2004; Higate and Henry, 2004); women and children as combatants and men as victims of sexual violence (Jones, 1994; R. C. Carpenter, 2003, 2006; Alison, 2004; Fox, 2004; Sjoberg, 2006; Sjoberg and Gentry, 2007); and the impact of the adoption of UN Security Council Resolution 1325 on gender and security in 2000 (Cohn et al., 2004). In terms of institutionalising these debates, the key outlets were the *International Feminist Journal of Politics*, published from 1999, *Millennium*, with an anniversary special issue in 1998, *Alternatives* and, from the mid-2000s, *Security Dialogue*.

Discursive security: the Copenhagen School and Poststructuralism

The Copenhagen School and its critics

The Copenhagen School has at its core Barry Buzan and Ole Wæver, who, with different collaborators at COPRI, published books and articles on regional security complex theory (RSCT), European security, and the relationship between regions and global security (Jahn et al., 1987; Buzan et al., 1990; Buzan, 1991a; Buzan et al., 1998; Buzan and Wæver, 2003; for an overview see Huysmans, 1998a). In terms of the widening–deepening debate, the most distinctive contributions of the Copenhagen School have, however, been the concepts of societal security and securitisation. In keeping with the US–European difference in the extent to which the concept of security is explicitly addressed, the Copenhagen School has been much more discussed within Europe than in the US, although it has to an increasing extent been applied to non-Western settings (Jackson, 2006; Kent, 2006; Wilkinson, 2007).

The concept of societal security was launched in *Identity, Migration and the New Security Agenda in Europe* (Wæver et al., 1993), and initially developed in response to a series of national conflicts, most violently in the former Yugoslavia, but also in Transylvania and the former Soviet Union (Roe, 2005). It constituted a specific sectoral addition to the earlier widening literatures from the 1980s that had mainly focused on the economic and environmental sectors. In Western Europe, increased integration within the EU made 'European integration' a threat to national constituencies fearing the loss of political sovereignty as well as cultural autonomy, and immigration was also presented as a threat to national identity. 'Societal security' was defined as 'the ability of a society to persist in its essential character under changing conditions and possible or actual threats' (Wæver *et al.*, 1993: 23). While the state was the referent object for political, military, environmental and economic security, it was 'society' that constituted the referent object for societal security (Wæver *et al.*, 1993: 26). This opened up for the study of 'identity security' and pointed to cases where state and societies did not align, for instance when national minorities were threatened by 'their' state, or where the state, or other political actors, mobilised society to confront internal or external threats.

The Copenhagen School explicitly constituted this as a middle position between traditionalist state-centrism on the one hand and equally traditional Peace Research's and Critical Security Studies' calls for 'individual' or 'global security' on the other. 'Societal security' limited the possible referent object to two collective units, state and society, and excluded the individual and the global. According to Wæver, 'it seems reasonable to be conservative along this [referent object] axis, accepting that "security" is influenced in important ways by *dynamics* at the level of individuals and the global system, but not by propagating unclear terms such as individual security and global security' (Wæver, 1995: 49; McSweeney, 1996, 1998; Buzan and Wæver, 1997).

Societal security theory made reference to 'possible or actual threats' and was still to some extent linked to an objective definition of security, although the emphasis on how political actors pointed to identity as being threatened had a Constructivist element to it. This ambiguity was later resolved in favour of a discursive conception of security in that the 'securitisation' approach, developed by Wæver, made the definition of security dependent on its successful construction in discourse. Securitisation theory has three main roots: one in speech act theory, one in a Schmittian understanding of security and exceptional politics, and one in traditionalist security debates (Williams, 2003; Huysmans, 2006b: 124–144). Combining these three, the general concept of 'security' is drawn from its constitution within *national* security discourse, which implies an emphasis on authority, the confronting – and construction – of threats and enemies, an ability to make decisions and the adoption of emergency measures. Security has a particular discursive and political force and is a concept that does something – *securitise* – rather than an objective (or subjective) condition.

Securitisation refers more precisely to the process of presenting an issue in security terms, in other words as an existential threat:

> The way to study securitization is to study discourse and political con-
> stellations: When does an argument with this particular rhetorical and
> semiotic structure achieve sufficient effect to make an audience tolerate
> violations of rules that would otherwise have to be obeyed? If by means
> of an argument about the priority and urgency of an existential threat the
> securitizing actor has managed to break free of procedures or rules he or
> she would otherwise be bound by, we are witnessing a case of securitization.
> (Buzan *et al.*, 1998: 25)

Security 'frames the issue either as a special kind of politics or as above politics' and a spectrum can therefore be defined ranging public issues from the *non-politicised* ('the state does not deal with it and it is not in any other way made an issue of public debate and decision'), through *politi-cised* ('the issue is part of public policy, requiring government decision and resource allocations or, more rarely, some other form of communal governance') to *securitisation* (in which case an issue is no longer debated as a political question, but dealt with at an accelerated pace and in ways that may violate normal legal and social rules) (Buzan *et al.*, 1998: 23). It is the discursive power of securitisation which brings together actors and objects: *securitising actors* are defined as 'actors who securitize issues by declaring something – a referent object – existentially threatened', *referent objects* as 'things that are seen to be existentially threatened and that have a legitimate claim to survival' (Buzan *et al.*, 1998: 36). At first glance this seems to make for a very open conceptualisation of security, but the Copenhagen School explicitly positioned securitisation as a way of limiting the excessive widening of security, and thus responding to a key traditionalist criticism of the wideners (Buzan *et al.*, 1998: 1–5). While securitisation theory was in principle open for anyone to make the securitising move, in practice the most common securitising actors are 'political leaders, bureaucracies, governments, lobbyists, and pressure groups', and referent objects usually middle-range collectivities (Buzan *et al.*, 1998: 40–41). More recently the School has pushed this thinking beyond the middle-range referent object to consider *macrosecuritisations*, which aim at structuring international politics on a larger scale (Buzan and Wæver, 2009).

'Securitisation' has been a very successful concept, at least in Europe. As a consequence, it has not surprisingly generated criticisms, particularly from approaches that advocate a more radical expansion of the concept of security (state-centric traditionalists have on the other hand tended to avoid discussing the concept). One of the most significant challengers has been Critical Security Studies, where Booth has argued that the Copenhagen School does not move far enough in the direction of 'real people in real places', that it mistakenly ties together security and survival, and that it is state-centric, elite-centric, discourse-dominated, conservative, politically passive, and neither progressive nor radical (Booth, 2005b: 271; 2007: 106–107, 163–169). Since the Copenhagen School is a constitutive, non-causal theory, criticism has not been concerned with whether the School can explain phenomena in a positivist (American) social science sense, but with the analytical, political and normative implications of adopting the School's perspective.

The most prominent criticism of societal security has been that it builds upon a conceptualisation of identity as fixed rather than constructed (McSweeney, 1996; Huysmans, 1998a). This implies, as in Conventional Constructivism, a focus on the (causal) consequences of identities rather than on the discursive and political processes through which these identities are (unstably) constituted. The Copenhagen School has replied (Buzan and Wæver, 1997) that one may separate analytically the process of identity constitution from the point where identities have become fortified to such an extent that they function as fixed in security discourse. This is, on the one hand, a legitimate analytical decision, but on the other hand it does indicate that the Copenhagen School is closer to a Constructivist than to a Poststructuralist perspective, at least insofar as its conception of identity is concerned (Campbell, 1998a: 222–223).

The Copenhagen School's separation of 'social security' and 'international security' has also been challenged. To the Copenhagen School, the articulation of urgency and extreme measures is what establishes a boundary between 'security proper' and concepts that bear only a semantic resemblance to 'security'. 'Social security' is defined as 'about individuals' (and thus not about collective referent objects as in 'international security') and 'largely economic' (rather than 'security') (Buzan et al., 1998: 120), and 'investment securities', or insecurities related to crime or unemployment are not securities in the sense carried by 'international security' (Buzan et al., 1998: 104). These distinctions have been challenged by Neocleous (2006a) who argues – as did Wolfers

(1952: 482) – that New Deal policy in the 1930s constituted social–economic security with precisely the drama and urgency required by the Copenhagen School. 'Economic' and 'social' security were therefore key factors in shaping the Cold War concept of 'national security', a concept which could then in turn be mobilised to de-privilege the concerns raised under the rubric of 'social security' (Neocleous, 2006a: 380–381). Coming from a Constructivist sociological perspective, Krause's analysis of insecurity and state formation in the Middle East presented above also makes a call for incorporating social security into security studies in that questions of welfare and the relationship between militarisation and the economic sphere are central to questions of state and regime legitimation (Krause, 1996: 346).

The concept of securitisation has been criticised for its inability to identify, in Lene Hansen's terms, 'the silent security dilemma' (Hansen, 2000a; Elbe, 2006; Stern, 2006; Wilkinson, 2007). 'Security as silence' occurs when the potential subject of (in)security has no, or limited, possibility of speaking its security problems. Methodologically, there is a certain ambiguity in securitisation theory, as it argues that the utterance of the word 'security' is not the decisive criterion and that a securitisation might consist of 'only a metaphorical security reference' (Buzan *et al.*, 1998: 27). Yet what this entails has not been further explored, and the majority of the theory leans in the direction of a more explicit verbal speech act methodology. Since the explicit articulation of 'security' – or other signs which have a similar status – is an epistemological and methodological criterion for 'security problems' to be identified, if explicit articulations cannot be identified a potential security problem does not register in the analysis. This is the case, for instance, in certain Muslim settings where women who have been the victims of rape might actually endanger themselves by bringing attention to the offence (Hansen, 2000a), or in parts of Africa, where discourses on HIV/AIDS constitute those infected as threats to society, hence preventing victims from seeking treatment (Elbe, 2006). Wilkinson argues that the 'security as silence' problem points more generally to an unacknowledged Western-centric assumption in securitisation theory, in that it presupposes the possibility of free speech and political structures that guarantee individuals protection against random as well as systematic violence (Wilkinson, 2007; Kent, 2006).

A corollary to the 'security as silence' problem concerns the Copenhagen School's normative privileging of desecuritisation, that is the movement of an issue out of the threat–danger modality of security and into the logic of politics, where compromise, solutions and debate is made possible to a much larger extent. Constituting something as a security problem might be a problematic or even dangerous strategy in that it grants privilege to official leaders and legitimises the suspension of civil and liberal rights (see also Deudney, 1990, for a similar point). But, critics argue, desecuritisation may not be normatively desirable if it merely illustrates the repression of an issue (Huysmans, 1998b; Aradau, 2004b, 2006; Alker, 2006; Behnke, 2006; Elbe, 2006; Taureck, 2006; Floyd, 2007). It is crucial, therefore, that desecuritisation is contextualised and that it is replaced by the possibility of politicisation, rather than mere silence. Another set of articles have responded to these issues by deepening the linguistic foundations of securitisation theory (Balzacq, 2005; Stritzel, 2007; McDonald, 2008; Vuori, 2008), its attention to media and 'visual securitisation' (Williams, 2003: 527; Möller, 2007; Hansen, forthcoming), or by exploring the role of 'violisations' that take security from the speech act to acts of physical violence (Neumann, 1998).

A related critique has come from Bigo (2002: 73) and Huysmans (2006b: 5), who argue that the conceptualisation of securitisation through discourses of drama and emergency misses the bureaucratic routines and the 'effects of power that are continuous rather than exceptional', for instance the concrete everyday practices undertaken by the police and groups of 'security professionals' patrolling the border. Drawing on Foucault and Bourdieu, Bigo's conceptualisation of security is, like the Copenhagen School's, discursive, but with more explicit links to Poststructuralism and an emphasis on the importance of the institutionalisation of the field of security. Networks of surveillance and data-mining help to create a 'security state' where everybody is under electronic surveillance, and Bigo emphasises the way in which governments and their bureaucracies have managed to gain control over the political process at the expense of parliaments and oppositional political actors (Bigo, 2002).

Finally, as noted above, the Copenhagen School rests on a Schmittian understanding of security as danger and the exceptional character of security politics (Huysmans, 1998b; Williams, 2003). Since this is a particular set of political and normative assumptions, rather than objective, empirical facts, this in turn leads the Copenhagen School to confront a similar set of questions to those which have been asked of both Realism and Poststructuralism: what are the implications of this conception of security and state identity? Does the state rely upon enemies to maintain identity/control over its population? How may this logic be changed, and what would a post-Schmittian security scenario look like?

Poststructuralism

Poststructuralism was already, like Feminism, a distinct approach during the Cold War. As chapter 5 laid out, Poststructuralism was highly critical of the way in which Strategic Studies had adopted a state-centric military conception of security without problematising the historical, normative and political implications that, Poststructuralists held, were embedded in this concept. Yet Poststructuralists also constituted themselves as indebted to the Classical Realist tradition and, like Realism, argued that state sovereignty and security were not easily transformed. The parallels between Poststructuralism and Realism meant, furthermore, that while Constructivists had come to security mainly through general IR debates, Poststructuralists had been engaged in debates on peace and security since the early 1980s. Although critical of Western security policies, Cold War Poststructuralism had always maintained the possibility of rethinking security, and hence was not faced by the crisis of traditional approaches when the Cold War ended. However, the ending of the Cold War was, if not a 'meta-event', then at least a constitutive event that threw some of its central analytical assumptions into question.

The most important challenge that Poststructuralism confronted coming out of the Cold War was whether states needed enemies. The central text in this debate was Campbell's study of American discourses of danger from 'its' discovery to the end of the Cold War. Campbell's *Writing Security* (1992) explicitly foregrounded the importance of the Other – that is the construction of states, groups and other non-Selves – arguing that while state identity could in principle be constituted through relations of difference, in reality the pressure to turn difference into radical, threatening Otherness was overwhelming (Connolly, 1991: 64–65, 209–210; Campbell, 1992: 55; Klein, 1994). 'Security' thus became an ontological double requirement: the state needed to be secure, but it also needed the threatening Other to define its identity, thereby giving it ontological security. The problem with Campbell's conception was, argued (sympathetic) critics, that it reified state identity ('the state needs enemies') and that it effectively adopted the same view of the state as did Realism ('the state is surrounded by potential enemies'). Both perspectives assumed an ontological inseparability between states and enemies, and a conception of the Other as monolithic and dangerous (Neumann, 1996a; Milliken, 1999: 94; Rumelili, 2004; Hansen, 2006: 38–39). Methodologically, the problem of assuming state identity as radical Otherness was that, if this was taken to be the only form of identity that states could adopt, this would be what was identified in empirical studies, in spite of there being potential other forms of less radical identity, such as that of being 'Nordic' (Joenniemi, 1990; Hansen, 2006: 38–41). Since the Poststructuralist conceptualisation of security is dependent upon the construction of identity, if identity is given, security would be as well, and Poststructuralism would be unable to find a way out of Realist security.

Although frequently accused of being detached from the real world (Katzenstein *et al.*, 1998), or for not providing a workable foundation for political action (Booth, 2007: 175–178), Poststructuralism is in fact more driven by the force of 'events' than many other widening approaches, not least Constructivism. Since several major events on the security agenda of the 1990s were linked to (debates over) great power politics, the latter driving force also made an impact on the evolution of post-Cold War Poststructuralism – the fact that a significant number of influential 1980s and 1990s Poststructuralists were either North Americans or based in the US also spurred an interest in great powers, particularly the US. The internal academic debates on identity and security thus intersected with events and great power politics to produce a series of empirical–analytical focal points.

The Gulf War of 1990–91 was the first event to instigate debate over how the West legitimated interventions and wars (Luke, 1991; Der Derian, 1992: 173–202; Shapiro, 1992; Campbell, 1993; Kuusisto, 1998). This raised a specific concern with military operations undertaken in defence of Others, whether countries (Kuwait), regions (Kosovo) or peoples (Bosnians, Somalis), rather than to deter or threaten the Other, as had been the main identity–policy dynamic during the Cold War. Although dealing with historical cases set before and during the Cold War, Weber's *Simulating Sovereignty* (1995) was an important theoretical contribution to 1990s Poststructuralist debates over interventionism. Weber showed that those intervening legitimated their actions by arguing that these were made on behalf of 'the people' of the Other state to protect it from 'its' government and thus that Western states had a proclivity for constituting their security policies inside a moral and value-based discourse. Security policies benefited not only the (selfish) 'national interest', but universal values and the peoples of other (less civilised and democratic) states.

The 1990–91 Gulf War was undertaken in defence of Kuwait's territorial sovereignty, was supported by a UN mandate and was described by Western powers as a 'war'. With the 'internal conflict/wars' in Somalia, Bosnia and Kosovo, the discourse changed from one of 'war' to 'humanitarian intervention'. The consequences of that representational shift for how 'the West' constituted itself, particularly how governments legitimated themselves to the international community, to besieged parties to the conflicts and to the media and citizens of their own countries who demanded that 'something must be done', was a key theme in several Poststructuralist analyses (Campbell, 1996, 1998a, 2002a, 2002b; Ó Tuathail, 1996; Crawford and Lipschutz, 1997; Kuusisto, 1998; Hansen, 2000b, 2001, 2006; Malmvig, 2001, 2006). A big question was whether such interventions shifted the Cold War constitution of the Other as antagonistic, threatening and radically different and of the ensuing identity of the Self as superior, threatened and the embodiment of universal values. Several Poststructuralists argued that the central Other was no longer a radically different threat, but a humanitarian 'victim' in need of a 'rescue', but that this subject construction depoliticised the conflicts and allowed the West the appearance of 'doing something' without fundamentally acknowledging its responsibility (Campbell, 1998a; Debrix, 1999: 159). The ambiguity of humanitarianism was also at the heart of Campbell's attempt to develop a Poststructuralist ethics drawing on the 1990–91 Gulf War, the war in Bosnia (1993; 1998a) and the philosophies of Levinas and Derrida. Campbell argued in favour of recognising the Other as Other without constituting it either as radically different, a 'victim' or an underdeveloped version of the Self, and of recognising one's responsibility for its well-being. Campbell's ethical security project was also an attempt to counter the frequent criticism that Poststructuralism merely observed and deconstructed the policies in place, rather than formulate a pro-active and constructive approach (Walt, 1991; Adler, 1997b; Katzenstein *et al.*, 1998).

The question of whether a non-radical Other could be the ontological foundation for state identity was also at the heart of debates over the EU. Wæver (1996) argued that the main constitutive Other was that of Europe's own past, and hence that the main threat in discourses supporting EU integration was the reappearance of conflict between France and Germany (Wendt, 2003). Turning from the 'Self as temporal Other' to Europe's relationship to its 'new' border regions, other studies focused on the competing constructions of Turkey, the Balkans, Russia and the Mediterranean as not only radically different, but as bridges or ambiguous zones between East and West (Neumann and Welsh, 1991; Hansen, 1996; Neumann, 1996b, 1999; Rumelili, 2004; Malmvig, 2006; Pace, 2006). Looking to the institutional centre of Western security, the possibility of NATO moving beyond a dichotomous construction of Western civilised

Self and antagonistic Eastern Other was also discussed (Klein, 1990, 1994; Constantinou, 1995; Williams and Neumann, 2000).

The 1990–91 Gulf War was, furthermore, a significant event in that it spurred a Poststructuralist concern with modern technology, particularly for how wars were conducted and brought to global media audiences. The combination of precision-guided weaponry, computerised warfare, bombing from afar (see also the discussion of RMA in chapter 6) and real-time CNN broadcasts led Baudrillard (1995) to declare that 'the Gulf War did not take place'. Der Derian (1992, 2001) expanded upon this, arguing that the significance of video games, exercises and simulations intersected with 'the real' to create a military environment where soldiers no longer clearly separated between gaming and 'fighting on the ground' (Krishna, 1993; C. H. Gray, 1997). To global audiences who watched 'war' in the skies over Baghdad or videos of bombers locking onto physical targets in Kosovo, this implied a disembodied form of warfare where neither soldiers nor civilian populations were in sight. As laid out in the section on Poststructuralism in chapter 5, such disembodied discourse allows for the constitution of death and destruction as something that does not really take place or happen to real human beings. Since global audiences often respond to visual representations of individuals who are captured, tortured or, as in Somalia, killed and dragged through the streets by angry mobs, Poststructuralists devoted attention to the visual politics of television news and advertisements, press photography and popular culture (Der Derian, 1992, 2001; Shapiro, 1997; Debrix, 1999; Campbell, 2002a, 2002b). As we shall see in chapter 8, this concern was further boosted by the events on 9/11 and the 'War on Terror'. Another theme which was part of Poststructuralist analysis in the 1990s, but which became more strongly stressed after 9/11, was that of surveillance and its societal consequences (Klein, 1990, 1994; Campbell, 1992).

The main approaches on the widening–deepening terrain of ISS are mapped out in Figure 7.3. Even though there are many links between them, one should note that these are only the most important ones, as debates within and across widening–deepening approaches are a main feature of non-traditionalist ISS.

Institutionalisation

The thriving widening–deepening debate is itself a good indication of the successful institutionalisation of the approaches discussed above. There were numerous conferences and projects, funding opportunities

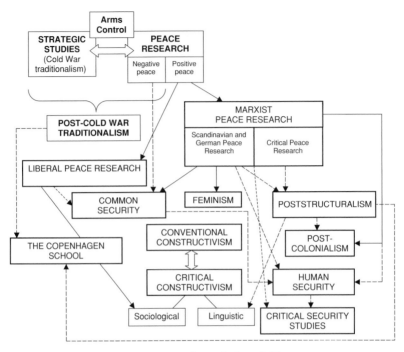

Figure 7.3.   The evolution of ISS

and journal publications and a growing number of graduate students and post-docs to give expansion approaches momentum. Particular noteworthy were foundation support from the Social Science Research Council and the MacArthur Foundation, for instance for *The Culture of National Security* (Katzenstein, 1996a). Other important Constructivist works that lay further towards Critical Constructivism, such as Adler and Barnett's (1998) *Security Communities,* were supported by the Global Studies Program at the University of Wisconsin-Madison and the Carnegie Council on Ethics and International Affairs. A specific and crucial source of funding was the MacArthur Foundation/Social Science Research Council's International Peace and Security Fellowship programme. This programme ran from 1985 to 2000 and offered support for Security Studies as a whole (217 dissertation and postdoctoral fellowships were awarded), but perhaps particularly for widening–deepening approaches in that it funded such (later) prominent scholars as Ronnie Lipschutz, Alastair Johnston, Audie Klotz, Neta Crawford, Hugh Gusterson, Christian Reus-Smit, Michael Barnett, Martha Finnemore, Jonathan Mercer, Ido

Oren, Ole Wæver, Tarak Barkawi, Cecelia Lynch and Elisabeth Kier (GSC Newsletter, 2001: 6–13). This influential programme was designed to support PhD students and scholars in the early stages of their careers. But institutionalisation, especially of new perspectives, is also facilitated by the support of more senior scholars, who boost the authority of new approaches and build research environments that educate and promote PhD students. Constructivism in both its Conventional and Critical forms was significantly aided in this respect by Peter J. Katzenstein, who incidentally dedicated *The Culture of National Security* to his graduate students at Cornell, by Friedrich Kratochwil, Nicholas Onuf, Hayward Alker, Thomas Biersteker and Raymond Duvall, the father of the Minnesota School (Wendt, 1999: xv).

Looking to the most radical end of the spectrum, Poststructuralism had been part of the debates of the 1980s and came into the post-Cold War 1990s with a significant degree of institutionalisation. This was perhaps most strongly shown by how Ashley and Walker were allowed to guest edit a 1990 special issue of *International Studies Quarterly* on 'Speaking the Language of Exile: Dissidence in International Studies'. At least in Europe, Poststructuralism was mentioned in introductions to Security Studies, and as noted in chapter 6, Walt's famous 1991 state of the field article singled out Poststructuralism as the main widening perspective to be opposed. But there were also processes that worked against an ongoing institutionalisation of Poststructuralism. First, as the widening agenda became more crowded with the blossoming of new approaches, the battle for attention became more acute, and Poststructuralism had to share some of its space with a range of newcomers. Second, the increasingly fierce attacks from traditionalists and Conventional Constructivists did work, particularly in the US, to delegitimise Poststructuralism as a perspective that should be taken seriously.

Significant parts of the institutionalisation of widening–deepening approaches applied generally, but there were also ways in which the substantial differences and disagreements played themselves out. Crucial here was a tendency for Conventional Constructivism to come to security through IR rather than Peace Research or Security Studies, and for the degree of expansionism to correlate with a US–European divide. This was, as noted above, evidenced both in the way textbooks covered non-traditionalist security and in different patterns of journal publication. Conventional Constructivists published in mainstream ISS and IR journals such as *International Security* and *International Organization*, and Critical Constructivists also had a strong IR trajectory, as indicated by their preference for the *European Journal of International Relations*, a general IR journal published from 1995, rather than *Alternatives* (more Poststructuralist and Post-colonial) or *Security Dialogue* (more 'European security debates', Copenhagen School, Critical Security Studies, Feminism, Poststructuralism and Human Security). The steady stream of North American Critical Constructivists moving to the UK in the 1990s – perhaps in response to the privilege bestowed upon positivist epistemologies in US Political Science – complicates, however, a clear US–European distinction.

Figure 7.4 shows how the driving forces have impacted the evolution of widening–deepening approaches within ISS. As with Figure 5.3, since the 'widening–deepening' box at the centre comprises the complex mapping of Figure 7.3, what is presented is a general overview.

Conclusions

This chapter has traced the growth and evolution of the widening–deepening side of ISS after the ending of the Cold War. These approaches were already making their mark during the 1980s, but the ending of the Cold War opened up analytical and political space that benefited their growth. This chapter has shown that there were crucial and deeply held differences in how these approaches constituted referent objects, the sectors to which security is applicable and the possibility of moving from a Realist logic of security and into a more cooperative one. There is, in other words, no one shared definition of what 'expanding security' should entail.

In terms of the driving forces, *internal academic debates* were crucial insofar as they were the primary key to how debates were organised. Crucial differences between European and American approaches meant that Constructivists came to ISS through general IR debates, Europeans came to it from Peace Research and ISS itself; Constructivists did not explicitly discuss the concept of security, while this was what drove European debates. The disappearance of the Cold War as a meta-event might have exacerbated this tendency in that there was no longer one overarching conflict that all ISS approaches had to engage. This meant that some perspectives were driven by a mixed 'events agenda', especially Poststructuralism and Feminism. Towards the other end of the spectrum, Constructivists were much more concerned with engaging epistemological IR debates and were therefore more prone to pick historical case-studies. *Great power politics* and *technology* played – with the exception of Poststructuralism – less

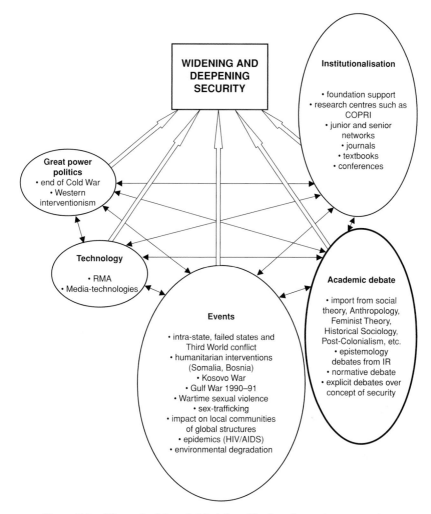

Figure 7.4.   The main drivers behind the widening–deepening approaches

of a role for widening perspectives than for traditionalist ISS. The question to be analysed in the next chapter is whether the events of 9/11 and the subsequent 'War on Terror' were able to provide a new 'meta-event' focus, whether this would boost traditional Realist approaches and their calls for military security, territorial attacks and antagonistic Others, and how this might bring back great power politics and technology.

8

Responding to 9/11: a return to national security?

This chapter uses the events of 9/11 in two ways. In a general sense we use 9/11 as a temporal benchmark in the same way as we used the ending of the Cold War. In a more specific sense, we ask whether 9/11 and the subsequent unfolding 'Global War on Terrorism' (GWoT) have been taken as an 'event' of sufficient importance to reshape the agenda of ISS in some ways. How did the different strands within ISS respond (or not) to all this, and what do their responses tell us about the sub-field as it moves deeper into the twenty-first century? We should bear in mind that chapter 7 dealt with those theoretical and conceptual discussions in the widening and deepening wing of ISS that were carried over from the 1990s and into the post-9/11 era and which proceeded relatively unaffected by the attacks and the ensuing GWoT. Thus we begin this chapter from the partial conclusion that not *all* of ISS changed pace and direction in response to these events. Still, there are important analytical as well as political reasons for asking whether and how the field of ISS was impacted by the GWoT. Analytically, this tells us something about the extent to which ISS is driven by events, a sociology of science debate laid out in chapter 3. Politically, the GWoT has had important consequences for the relationship between 'the West and the rest' as well as for a number of domestic policies in the US and Europe. It has also been promoted as a replacement for the Cold War as the central organising issue for international security.

The GWoT spans a wide array of linked events, interventions and practices. Many of the policies adopted by Western governments in their defence against 'terrorism' were either in place or on the drawing board prior to 9/11, but the GWoT accelerated their introduction and legitimised their application across a wider set of issues and areas than would otherwise have been the case. As Realists, Liberals and critical widening perspectives all pointed out: in times of (discursively constituted) war, the money and manpower allocated to the military increase, and encroachments on civil, liberal and human rights are more likely to meet with public acceptance.

Concern with terrorism is, of course, not new, with the literature stretching back into the Cold War (see chapters 4 and 6). But the earlier literature dealt with terrorism as a peripheral problem to the main core of ISS concerns, not the central one. The events of 9/11 and the responses to them certainly elevated the existing literature on terrorism to a new prominence and also spurred a concern with religion that was already under way (Philpott, 2002; Thomas, 2005). This shift challenged both the wideners, by seeming to move the core of security back towards political violence, and the traditionalists, by moving the focus of war from interstate to relations between states and non-state actors. Yet while the GWoT changed the balance of ISS literature, it did not sweep away all earlier concerns and debates: chapter 7 dealt with those theoretically driven widening debates that continued relatively unaffected by 9/11, and this chapter will show that there were also significant parts of the traditional agenda that were only tangentially touched by the GWoT.

Within the structure of this book, framing a full chapter around 9/11 makes a strong call for seeing events as the dominant driving force for this period. This diverges from the structure of chapters 4 to 7, where we contrasted traditionalist and widening perspectives first during the Cold War (chapters 4 and 5) and then in the aftermath of the ending of the Cold War (chapters 6 and 7). Chapter 8 is the first chapter to bring the whole of ISS together. This is not to say that 9/11 brought academic or political consensus to ISS, or to foreshadow the conclusion that ISS was thoroughly changed by it. But it does mean that the GWoT functioned for parts of ISS as a set of dominating common events constituting a shared focal point for debate. Whatever else the GWoT did or did not accomplish, it certainly created a boom in the literature on terrorism, one publisher (Edward Elgar) even going so far as to relabel his book list 'terrorism and security studies'!

That said, it is also true that the different perspectives within ISS were not influenced by – or engaged with – 9/11 to a similar extent. A major part of traditional, military ISS dealt with the GWoT, since this was widely seen as the new overarching security problematic that either already had, or had the potential to, influence the general security agenda for years if not decades. Because traditionalist perspectives have been so decisively impacted by the driving forces of great power politics and technology, the question is how the relationship between ISS and these two were, and were not, impacted by the GWoT. Widening approaches varied more, with Poststructuralists, Feminists and Post-colonialists making the strongest call for critical analysis of the GWoT, whereas Conventional Constructivists at the other end of the spectrum maintained their historical, social theory research agenda. These differences were not just coincidentally connected to the choice of empirical research focus prior to 9/11. They related to fundamental differences in how the basic questions about the policy identity of ISS were answered. Should ISS stress policy relevance or scientific understanding? Should it seek influence through explicit policy advice or did it have an obligation to pursue an oppositional and critical agenda? Could a critical agenda ever be merged with advising the state? These questions have been active in ISS debates since the field's inception but, as crises often do, 9/11 cast a stronger light upon them.

To say that 9/11 had an impact on ISS does not, however, necessarily mean that it changed it. Events may change the balance between existing perspectives, or they may spur the establishment of new approaches and cause (although less likely) the abandonment of others. But events may also impact a field by solidifying existing perspectives and hence its broader sociological make-up. Whether 9/11 could or should change ISS was also explicitly debated within the field itself, as some pointed to revolutions brought about at the level of actor rationality (non-state, non-rational 'terrorists') and technology (military and civil) (Der Derian, 2004), while others held that 9/11 might change the current research agenda of ISS, but not the basic paradigms (Kupchan, 2004).

The first part of the chapter is divided into two sections, one addressing the traditionalist response to 9/11, and the other addressing those areas in which the traditionalists carried on earlier debates in a manner little or not at all affected by 9/11 and the GWoT. The second part of the chapter looks at the way in which 9/11 impacted widening–deepening approaches, examining first how discursive approaches were employed in critical analysis of policies and discourses on 'terrorism', and then how the specific concern with risk, cyber- and bio-security was boosted by the GWoT. Widening–deepening discussions were primarily concerned with the question of how 'terrorism' and the GWoT impacted on the referent object discussion: to what extent were 'terrorists' akin to states and did the securitising logic at the heart of Western official discourse invoke a return of the state as the central referent object in need of deconstruction? Depending on which perspective was adopted, this discussion had consequences for widening: the military responses in Afghanistan and Iraq clearly showed the significance of the military, but the concern with the consequences of the GWoT along an array of issues also raised questions in the areas of gender, religion, development, and economic and societal security. The last part of the chapter turns to questions of internal academic debate and institutionalisation. In addition to the question of how the institutional backbone of ISS – that is journals, institutions, programmes, curricula and funding – was impacted by the GWoT, we draw attention to the way in which security scholars from different parts of ISS engaged politically, raising questions about the political–academic double identity that has been at the core of the field since its inception.

Traditionalist ISS post-9/11

The traditionalist response to the Global War on Terrorism

The most natural assumption might be that 9/11 and the policy responses that ensued played into a Realist, traditional agenda insofar as this was an attack on American/Western territory that brought in the words of Carter (2001/2: 5–6) the return of 'A-list' security problems after the humanitarian B- and C-list concerns of the 1990s. From a Realist point of view, 9/11 would thus bring home the perennial truth that the absence of international conflict was no indication of an irreversible qualitative change, but a temporary lapse in the ebb and flow of tensions within an anarchical system. This view had already resonated in American military circles prior to 9/11, where the fear was that the post-Cold War 1990s was not a Liberal, unipolar peaceful order, but a replay of the inter-war period (Der Derian, 2001). But other factors complicate the picture of 9/11 and the subsequent GWoT as simply playing into the hands of Realists (of all types: Classical, Neoclassical, Neorealist, Offensive, Defensive). While Realists had, as described in chapter 6, pointed to the conflictual potential of a seemingly (from a Western perspective) benign unipolar order, they had not envisaged the scenario which unfolded on 9/11 – the attacks on US soil using box cutters and civilian airliners – nor had they any premonition that these events would engender two major US-led wars into Afghanistan and Iraq.

The events of 9/11 and the GWoT impacted on traditionalist ISS in several respects. The prominence of globally networked non-state actors raised questions about both state-centrism and the rationality assumptions that underpinned traditionalist thought. The declaration of 'war' on terrorism rekindled interest in the use of force generally, and the whole topic of war in particular. And since both 9/11 and the GWoT had strong links to the Middle East, the security literature on that region was in part concerned with those issues.

Realism, particularly Neorealism, and with them most of traditionalist ISS, had been largely devoted to the study of states and external threats and 9/11 complicated this in two major ways. First in that those attacking were not states, but nineteen individuals situated inside a terrorist network that did not have the centre or the official structure of states or even of traditional nationalist separatist or guerrilla movements. The Bush administration invested significant discursive resources in the first days following 9/11 on linking this non-state, decentred 'actor' to a state, but this did not erase the discussions of whether Islamic terrorism/al-Qaeda/bin Laden resembled traditional state actors sufficiently for Realist theories to be applicable. Particularly central to Neorealist theories was the discussion of whether al-Qaeda, bin Laden, and later Saddam Hussein, were sufficiently 'rational' for Neorealist premises to hold (Carter, 2001/2; Posen, 2001/2; Walt, 2001/2). Waltzian Neorealism had drawn its ontological assumptions about rational state identity from micro-economic theory and hence defined the state as maximising its utility, pursuing its own interests and fundamentally preoccupied by its own survival. Much Cold War debate in Strategic Studies had evolved around whether the Soviet Union shared the strategic reasoning of the US, and hence whether deterrence theory could be based on identical sets of actor assumptions, or whether the two opponents were too different for this to be plausible. Such concerns were taken to a different level post-9/11. Prominent Neorealists such as Posen (2001/2) and Walt (2001/2) were quick to develop analyses which argued in favour of bin Laden as a rational actor and the attacks on 9/11 as part of his larger Middle Eastern policy, and Saddam Hussein was, according to Mearsheimer and Walt (2003), eminently capable of understanding force and hence could be deterred by means other than war. This view of 'terrorism' and Hussein as sufficiently 'rational' to warrant the continued use of Realist/Neorealist theory clashed with the Bush administration, which constituted Hussein as irrational and untrustworthy.

One striking effect of the GWoT is that it brought out a political and analytical difference between Realists on the one hand and Neo-Conservatives and Liberal Institutionalists on the other (Boot, 2004; Der Derian, 2004; Williams, 2005). Neo-Conservatives had played a key role during the Reagan administration, and took an activist, ideas- and values-based approach to foreign policy (Mearsheimer, 2005: 3). The question of how to characterise Neo-Conservativism as well as measure its impact on the Bush administration was itself a topic of debate, with some seeing a clear overlap between the two in terms of both personal networks and policy doctrines (Williams, 2005; Elden, 2007; Owens, 2007), while others claimed a more sceptical position (Boot, 2004). Realism has a history of scepticism against values- and ideas-based foreign policy (Morgenthau, 1946, 1951), and Mearsheimer's (2005: 6) blunt conclusion was that Iraq proved Realists right and Neo-Conservatives wrong. Overall, there was a noticeable rise in concern about the possible strategic irrationality of the US itself because of apparent dysfunctionalities in its foreign-policy-making processes (Cavanaugh, 2007; Krebs and Lobasz, 2007; Mearsheimer and Walt, 2007; Thrall, 2007; Desch, 2007/8). Some argued that the whole centre of US policy had shifted durably to the right, and that there would be no post-Bush return to the liberal internationalism that had underpinned Atlantic relations during the second half of the twentieth century (Kupchan and Trubowitz, 2007).

Another impact of 9/11 on the traditionalist literature was the way in which it revived concerns about the use of force as the central theme of security. As indicated above, however, the GWoT took the traditional core of the ISS agenda in quite different directions from interstate war, nuclear deterrence and arms control. The elevation of terrorism from the marginal position it had occupied during the Cold War and the 1990s to being the central issue, triggered a wide-ranging debate aimed at relating this new challenge to many of the main aspects of the traditional security agenda. Opinions varied as to whether the GWoT marked an epochal change or something less dramatic in the landscape of international security (Freedman, 2001; Hurrell, 2002; Jervis, 2002a; Roberts, 2005; Kennedy-Pipe and Rengger, 2006). Could it be understood as a dark side of globalisation, where liberalisation opened opportunities not just for civil society but also for uncivil transnational actors, or was a more Huntingtonian 'clash of civilizations' perspective more appropriate (Rasmussen, 2002; Cronin, 2002/3; Mousseau, 2002/3)? What kind of war was this given that one side was a non-state actor (Betts, 2002; Nacos, 2003; Barkawi, 2004; Howard, 2006), and was it a good idea to frame it as a 'war' at all (Andreani, 2004/5)? Who was the enemy, what kinds of strengths and weaknesses did 'terrorism' have, and how was it to be understood (Hellmich, 2005; Neumann and Smith, 2005; Abrahms, 2006; Cronin, 2006; Enders and Sandler, 2006; Kydd and Walter, 2006)? Perhaps of most concern was how to devise appropriate alliances, tactics and strategies for fighting such a strange type of war.[1]

---

[1] Simon and Benjamin, 2001; Stevenson, 2001; Roberts, 2002; Winer and Roule, 2002; Freeman, 2003; Kenney, 2003; Stevenson, 2004; Kilcullen, 2005; Nincic, 2005; Trager and Zagorcheva, 2005/6; Auerswald, 2006; Badey, 2006; Byman, 2006a, 2006b; Cassidy, 2006; Clunan, 2006; Frisch, 2006; Slater, 2006; Stevenson, 2006; Aradau and Van Munster, 2007; Betz, 2007; Schwartz, 2007.

The implications of 9/11 and the GWoT, and especially the prominence of non-state actors, penetrated into traditional debates about the use of force (Ulfstein, 2003; Rasmussen, 2004), and the proliferation of WMD, particularly nuclear and biological weapons and their arms control regimes (Busch, 2002; Roman, 2002; Chyba, 2004; Gahlaut and Bertsch, 2004; A. Newman, 2004; Frost, 2005; Bellany, 2007; Byman, 2007). It raised not just general questions about how US grand strategy should respond to the new threat (Ikenberry, 2001a, 2001b; Boyle, 2008), but also specific ones about how its relations to China, Europe and Russia would be affected by how they responded to the GWoT.[2] There were concerns about the negative impact of the GWoT on human rights (Foot, 2004, 2006b) and of terrorism on particular countries and regions (Ayoob, 2002; Judah, 2002; Rabasa, 2003; Menkhaus, 2004; Berger and Borer, 2007; Jones, 2007). There was also reflection on what the GWoT meant for Western societies. How did such societies, and their media, play into the construction of the GWoT, and with what effects on them (Hoskins, 2006; Prozorov, 2006; Vinci, 2008)? How could essentially open societies be hardened against the sort of theats posed by terrorists of the al-Qaeda sort (Coaffee and Wood, 2006)?

Not surprisingly, the GWoT and the Anglo-American invasion of Iraq triggered a large extension of the discussion about war that had marked the 1990s. Now, though, this was driven by events rather than, as previously, by great power politics and so, like the debates about proliferation, shifted the focus away from great powers and towards the Third World. For that reason it mostly went in different directions from those of the 1990s literature, signified by the application of sociological ideas about war and state-making to Third World states (Sørensen, 2001; Dannreuther, 2007b; Taylor and Botea, 2008).

Tradition was maintained by the endless adaptation of Clausewitz to new situations (Holmes, 2007). Newer approaches to ISS opened an interest in the use of force/power to impose or shape norms (Gentry, 2006; De Nevers, 2007b). The much more aggressive statements of US national security strategy that appeared after 9/11 seemed to end the debate about whether war itself was fading away. The US claims to a right of preemptive and preventive war in the context of the GWoT restored focus to the discussion (Nichols, 2005; Dombrowski and Payne, 2006), and the

---

[2] China (Friedberg, 2002; Roy, 2002), Europe and NATO (Boukhars and Yetiv, 2003; Katzenstein, 2003; Rees and Aldrich, 2005; De Nevers, 2007a; Rees, 2007; De Goede, 2008) and Russia (Antonenko, 2001).

GWoT itself stimulated interest in what war would look like, and what role it would play in international politics in the future (Dick, 2002; Jervis, 2002b; Kroenig and Stowsky, 2006; Taliaferro, 2006; P. Jackson, 2007).

Another line of debate about war predated the GWoT, picking up from the 1990s literature on the transformation of war (van Creveld, 1991; Snow, 1996). This literature was more driven by events in the periphery, particularly the increase in intra- as opposed to interstate wars, and the debate was about whether the dominant form of war had changed from so-called 'old wars' (mainly interstate, fought largely by formal armies under central political control for political objectives) to 'new' ones (mainly intra-state, often many-sided, fought by a variety of entities including private military companies, militias, warlord gangs and 'government' armies, and often with economic and criminal rather than political motives) (Brzoska, 2004). The main argument was between those who argued for a general change towards new wars after 1990 (M. Duffield, 2001; Kaldor, 2001; Cooper, 2002; Münkler, 2004), and those who argued that these apparent changes did not represent anything really new (Kalyvas, 2001; Gantzel, 2002; Berdal, 2003; Matthies, 2003; E. Newman, 2004; Chojnacki, 2006). The GWoT neither triggered nor shaped this debate, but because of the prominence of non-state actors, it did help both to reinforce the 'new war' view and to heighten the prominence of this debate within ISS. There was particular interest in the array of actors in play in 'new wars', both private military companies on the one side (Singer, 2001/2; Percy, 2006; Carmola, 2007; Kinsey, 2007; Wolf et al., 2007; Rosén, 2008) and the array of militias, warlords and other non-state political actors on the other (Fowler, 2005; Shultz and Dew, 2006; Marten, 2007). This literature also began to branch out into what rules should apply to such conflicts (De Nevers, 2006), and how 'new wars' should be approached theoretically (Heng, 2006).

A third line, related both to the GWoT and 'new wars', was an unusual degree of concern with operations and the process of warfighting (Douglas, 2007). Discussion of warfighting and operations is not, of course, in itself new, but in the post-1945 period has tended to reside in professional military literatures. Under the pressure of events, however, there was now concern about civilian targets and casualties generally (Gross, 2005/6; W. Thomas, 2006; Eck and Hultman, 2007). There were studies of both why soldiers fight (Henriksen, 2007) and how fewer of them than previously were dying in the process (Lacina et al., 2006). Older themes such as counterinsurgency (Kilcullen, 2006) and asymmetric war (P. Sullivan, 2007) enjoyed new relevance.

For obvious reasons the themes of war generally and the GWoT in particular played strongly into long-standing and ongoing concerns about the Middle East. There had for decades been a volatile mix of security issues at play in the Middle East, and the GWoT both added to them and sometimes changed their significance. The US rivalries with Iraq and Iran, its strong tie to Israel, and its anxieties about nuclear proliferation in the region all long predated 9/11. But once the GWoT got under way, all of these staples of Middle East security politics were reinterpreted in its new light. Proliferation looked much more dangerous if the next possessors of nuclear weapons were going to be entities like al-Qaeda. Accusations of support for terrorism, and fears that such support might include access to WMD, were added to the list of US grievances against Iran and Iraq (more on this below), and in the case of the latter were instrumental in justifying the Anglo-American invasion and occupation in 2003 in pursuit of regime change. All of this could be seen in the light of ongoing general interest in the US and regional security (Press-Barnathan, 2001) and the question of intervention (MacFarlane, 2002).

As key elements in the US's GWoT, the war in Iraq and, to a lesser extent, that in Afghanistan, quite quickly generated their own literatures, particularly so once the consensus that the Iraq War was a disaster began to take hold (Hodes and Sedra, 2007; Johnson and Mason, 2007; D. P. Sullivan, 2007; P. Sullivan, 2007). There was some analysis of operations and situations in Iraq (Andres, 2006; Bensahel, 2006; Egnell, 2006; Malkasian, 2006; Mowle, 2006), and of the consequences of the war for Iraq (Dodge and Simon, 2003; Dodge, 2005). There was of course a vigorous post-mortem on the US policy-making process that generated the disaster and on what to do next (R. A. Clarke, 2004; Kaufmann, 2004; Flibbert, 2006; Jervis, 2006; Dodge, 2007; Simon, 2007). Once the likelihood of failure in Iraq became the near consensus position, there was much analysis of the consequences (Gordon, 2006; Saunders, 2007; Telhami, 2007) and much looking ahead to learn the lessons for US and Western security policy (Barnett, 2006; Dobbins, 2006; Fitzsimmons, 2006; Freedman, 2006a; Lesser, 2006; Miller, 2006; Strachan, 2006; Allin, 2007; Steel, 2007).

Continuities in traditionalist ISS after 2001

Although 9/11 and the GWoT clearly made a substantial impact on traditionalist work, there were many areas in which earlier debates carried on largely undisturbed by concerns about 'terrorism'. Theoretical analysis about the causes of war (Caprioli and Trumbore, 2006; Toft, 2006; Atzili,

2007; Hassner, 2007) provides one example of this continuity, and the debate about democratic peace another (Daxecker, 2007, Gibler, 2007; Adler, 2008; Ish-Shalom, 2008). Although, as noted above, some aspects of regional security and concerns about technology were influenced by 9/11 and the GWoT, as might be expected, many others were not.

Despite the particular impact of the GWoT and the wars in Iraq and Afghanistan, there was much continuity in the literature on Middle East security: the GWoT simply added to the long list of reasons why regional security in the Middle East remained a key concern within ISS both generally (Buzan and Wæver, 2003; Bilgin, 2004a, 2004b; Leenders, 2007), and in relation to specific countries such as Iran (Ekovich, 2004) and its new prominence in the war against Israel (Bahgat, 2006; Takeyh, 2006) and Saudi Arabia (Peterson, 2002). Old staples such as water (Selby, 2005) and democracy (Kurth, 2005) continued to be of interest, and theorists used the region as a case to test balance of power theories (Cooper, 2004; Gause, 2004; Lebovic, 2004; Miller, 2006). More attention was paid to the political significance of Islam (Murden, 2002; Ayoob, 2004), and to the divisive effects of the Middle East on Euro-American relations (Boukhars and Yetiv, 2003; Gordon, 2005). Similarly, even though the US and Israel had found a stronger sense of community as victims of terrorism, the debates about Israel and Palestine still continued in much the same way as before (Allin and Simon, 2003; Slater, 2003).

Continuity was also the rule for other discussions of regional security, both generally (Acharya, 2007; Kelly, 2007; Solingen, 2007) and more specifically on South Asia (Paul, 2006), Southeast Asia (Emmers, 2005; Goh, 2007/8), Central Asia (Buszynski, 2005) and Africa (Brown *et al.*, 2007; P. Jackson, 2007; Kaplan, 2007; Mazzitelli, 2007; P. D. Williams, 2007).

One set of debates that remained largely outside the GWoT was the traditionalist's ongoing obsession with great power politics. After September 2001, debates about the rise of China, US grand strategy and position in the world, and the future of the EU as a great power all drew upon discussions well under way during the 1990s (see chapter 6). Of these three, the discussion of the US and Atlantic relations was the most affected by the GWoT, while the two others were comparatively less impacted.

The rise of China debate, at least in its military–strategic sense, was mainly a preoccupation of the US and of China's neighbours. Since early in the 1990s there had been a well-entrenched view in Washington that China was, in the long run, the main threat to the sole superpower position of the US. If the unipolar world that had emerged after the Cold

War was going to be pushed back to bipolarity, then China was the most plausible engine of change. This view was given more edge both by the continued rapid growth of the Chinese economy, and by the harder line on national security developed by the Bush administration. Its 2002 National Security Strategy made explicit that the US would not tolerate any rivals to its power, a policy that was clearly aimed at China, and could also be read as including the EU. Yet because China was broadly onside with the US in the GWoT, linking its own securitisation of dissident Muslims in its northwestern province to the broader US securitisation of terrorism, there was little or no scope for the US to link its GWoT and China securitisations. Islamists had few, if any, grievances with Northeast Asia and therefore the main strand of terrorism played weakly in this region in comparison with familiar concerns such as the rise of China, local instabilities and nuclear proliferation. This debate thus continued largely in terms of US–China relations, China's relations with its neighbours and the interplay between these two given the long-standing US position and alliances in East Asia. There was also a new theme on the rise of China in relation to energy (Andrews-Speed *et al.*, 2002; Downs, 2004). While the rise of China, and the evolution of China's security policy, was often a subject in its own right (Goldstein, 2001; Bitzinger, 2003; Johnston, 2003; Xuetong, 2006), it was also inseparable from the East Asian regional context (*Journal of Strategic Studies*, 2001; Shambaugh, 2004; Xiang, 2004; Fravel, 2005; Ross, 2006; Gilson, 2007). Regional security in East Asia was a substantial topic in its own right,[3] and a major theme within this was the linkage between multilateral regional institutions and security in East Asia.[4]

Within this general framing there were many specific themes. There was, of course, much analysis of Sino–American relations, both specifically,[5] and in the context of their implications for East Asia as a whole.[6] Taiwan, and its impact on US–China relations, remained an abiding concern (Ross, 2002; Thies and Bratton, 2004; Yang, 2006; Kennedy, 2007), as did its implications for Japanese security policy (Soeya, 2001). Japan's slow but seemingly steady drift towards a more robust military

[3] Dittmer, 2002; Acharya, 2003; Buzan and Wæver, 2003; Kang, 2003a, 2003b; Kim, 2003; Manosevitz, 2004; Rozman, 2004; Taniguchi, 2005.
[4] J. S. Duffield, 2001; Webber, 2001; Hemmer and Katzenstein, 2002; Ikenberry and Tsuchiyama, 2002; McDougall, 2002; Nabers, 2002; Stubbs, 2002.
[5] Xiang, 2001; Van Ness, 2002; Casetti, 2003; Pollack, 2003; Roy, 2003; Ward, 2003; Van Ness, 2004/5; Gries, 2005a; Chan, 2006; Erickson and Goldstein, 2006; Foot, 2006a; Tammen and Kugler, 2006; Zongyou, 2006.
[6] Christoferrersen, 2002; Khoo and Smith, 2002; Beeson, 2006; Christensen, 2006.

posture made its strategy increasingly interesting in itself,[7] though the US–Japan alliance remained the dominant framing,[8] not least because of its implications for China (Wang, 2003; Midford, 2004). Given the rise of China, and signs of greater independence in Japan's security policy, more consideration was given to Japan's relations with Korea (Cha, 2000a; Auslin, 2005). In this context, a long overdue development was the increase of interest in the relationship of Northeast Asia's two great powers, China and Japan, which even through the 1990s had remained masked by Japan's self-subordination to the US in security matters and relations with China.[9] North Korea remained an abiding concern,[10] both because of its implications for regional stability and because of the particular crisis about its nuclear weapons programme (on which more below). Analysis of the implications of China's rise also extended to the wider context of its relationships with India and Russia (Garver, 2001; Sidhu and Yuan, 2003; Pant, 2004; Rangsimaporn, 2006; Ferdinand, 2007; Scott, 2008).

The debate about US grand strategy that had been a feature of the post-Cold War decade not only continued unabated, but also diversified under the impact of both 9/11 and the Bush administration's more aggressive foreign policy.[11] The 1990s debate had mainly focused around the emergence of a dominant view that unipolarity would be considerably more than a transitional moment following the end of bipolarity. Post-9/11, the debate was more about the nature of the unipolar order, though some remained sceptical about its durability (Layne, 2006) and there was some interest in the political economy aspects of the subject (Caverley, 2007; Stokes, 2007). Whether because of the particular impact of the Bush administration and the GWoT, or whether because the Neorealists seemed to be correct in their prediction (if not in its timing or intensity) that a unipolar power structure would foment opposition, much of this debate was about the weakening of the Atlantic community.

---

[7] Midford, 2002; Hughes, 2004a, 2004b, 2004c, 2006; Lind, 2004; Inoguchi and Bacon, 2006; Arase, 2007; Hughes, 2007; Hughes and Krauss, 2007; Samuels, 2007/8.

[8] Oka, 2001; Ohtomo, 2002; Van Ness, 2002; Midford, 2003; Rowan, 2005; Yoda, 2006.

[9] Rozman, 2002a, 2002b; Reilly, 2004; Wan, 2004; Chiba and Xiang, 2005; Gries, 2005b; Roy, 2005; Tamamoto, 2005; Dreyer, 2006; Hsiung, 2007; Mochizuki, 2007.

[10] Kihl, 2002; Miles, 2002; Pinkston and Saunders, 2003; Rozman, 2003; Cha and Kang, 2005; Kerr, 2005; H. Smith, 2005; Michishita, 2006.

[11] Cronin, 2002; Hendrickson, 2002; Daalder and Lindsay, 2003; Jervis, 2003b, 2005; Layne, 2003; Lobell, 2003; Posen, 2003; Dueck, 2003/4, 2004a, 2004b; Bacevich and Prodromou, 2004; A. Newman, 2004; Dunn, 2005; Mastanduno, 2005; Calleo, 2007; Posen, 2007.

There was a general sense that 9/11 and the GWoT amplified the differences between the US and Europe (Kagan, 2002, 2003; Cox, 2003a; Toje, 2003; Lindley-French, 2004; Berenskoetter, 2005). In the immediate aftermath of the attacks on 9/11, there was widespread global support for the US, and the war against the Taleban regime and al-Qaeda in Afghanistan was backed by a concerted NATO response. The war against Iraq proved much different and met with opposition from Germany and France as well as many non-Western countries who conceived of the war as based on inadequate proof of Iraq having weapons of mass destruction and more broadly of an American willingness to use unipolarity to bully through its policies with whatever means it thought necessary.

The post-9/11 difference between the US and Europe in both power, especially military power, and outlook and policy meant that the Atlantic was getting wider (Daalder, 2001; T. G. Carpenter, 2003; Allin, 2004; van Oudenaren, 2005) and 'the West' weaker (Calleo, 2004; Clark, 2004). Although a bit slow to materialise, this weakening of the West was again in line with Neorealist predictions for the post-bipolar world, making 'the West' look more like a specific product of the Cold War than a historic and deeply embedded cultural community. A widening Atlantic raised questions about the (in)stability of NATO and the core US alliance with Europe,[12] including the divisive effect of US–European differences over policy in the Middle East (Boukhars and Yetiv, 2003; Talentino, 2004). It also raised the possibility of balancing against the US in some form of counterpole coalition, as predicted earlier by Neorealists (Ahrari, 2001; Posen, 2006). More broadly, a debate sprang up about whether a more aggressive, more unilateralist US unipole should now be thought of in terms of empire.[13] Generally this 'empire' debate had a critical tone, though some (mainly on the right in the US) thought it a good thing. It is interesting to note the sharply Atlanticist focus of the debate about the weakening West, which took place largely (but not completely: Liberman 2000/1; Ohtomo, 2002; Katzenstein, 2003) in disconnect from the generally strengthening trend in the US–Japan alliance resulting from the rise of China. A key background condition for all this was the perception of Russia as basically down and out for at least the medium term, though

---

[12] Liberman, 2000/1; Coker, 2002; Moore, 2002; Calleo, 2003; Krahmann, 2003; Cottey, 2004; Weede, 2005; Press-Barnathan, 2006; Allin et al., 2007; Michta, 2007.

[13] Bacevich, 2002; Brooks and Wohlforth, 2002; Hassner, 2002; Ikenberry, 2002; Lafeber, 2002; Nye, 2002; Chace, 2003; Cox, 2003b; Layne, 2003; Prestowitz, 2003; Buzan, 2004a; Crawford, 2004; Hurrell, 2005; Inoguchi and Bacon, 2006.

there was some interest in Russia's reactions to both NATO developments and US hegemony more generally (Monaghan, 2006; White *et al.*, 2006; Sakwa, 2008). As this book goes to press, it seems a reliable prediction that Russia's more assertive foreign policy will increase discussion of it in the ISS literature.

The third key part in this reconsideration of global polarity was the EU. If the EU was becoming a pole of power in world politics, or even a superpower, then this was both a parallel development to the rise of China, and a complement to the widening Atlantic being driven by the unilateralist turn in US policy. Against the background of the EU's rather feeble performance as a security actor, there was still a surprising amount of interest in the idea from the 1990s debates of the EU as a coming superpower (Guttman, 2001; Rotfeld, 2001; Kupchan, 2003; Buzan, 2004a; McCormick, 2006; Yeilada *et al.*, 2006). The main focus, however, was less ambitious, looking at the military–political capability of the EU,[14] and its attempt to find a more coherent security and defence policy.[15] Side themes included the security implications of the EU's eastern enlargement (Higashino, 2004; O'Brennan, 2006), the strategic relations of the EU with Russia (Averre, 2005; Giegerich *et al.*, 2006) and the implications of EU security developments for NATO (Peters, 2004; Whitman, 2004). 9/11 and the GWoT made little impact on this discussion, which was mainly driven by developments, or the lack of them, in the EU's internal structures, and by enlargement.

Technology has been the other main driving force for traditionalist ISS and, like great power politics, it remained important. This side of the ISS literature maintained a very similar overall structure of debate to that in the 1990s. Under its key headings of BMD, RMA, deterrence, proliferation, arms racing and arms control there was mainly continuity. The key difference that the GWoT made was to further boost the concern about rogue states, strengthening the linking of debates about nuclear proliferation and debates about deterrence that was already becoming evident during the 1990s. The GWoT of course amplified concerns about the proliferation of nuclear weapons and other WMD, but it created nothing like the obsession with military technology that had marked the Cold War. One of the curious twists of 9/11 was the way it put emphasis

---

[14] Ortega, 2001; Hagman, 2002; Salmon and Shepherd, 2003; Giegerich and Wallace, 2004; Kupchan, 2004/5.

[15] Hunter, 2002; Webber *et al.*, 2002; Youngs, 2002; Jones, 2003; Becher, 2004; Menon, 2004; Cornish and Edwards, 2005; Smith *et al.*, 2005; Hills, 2006; Jones, 2006; Posen, 2006; Salmon, 2006; Kaldor *et al.*, 2007; Bailes, 2008.

on the vulnerability of open societies to the use of readily available civil technologies as weapons, and to the vulnerability of civil infrastructure to attack using low-technology weapons.

Some topics just trickled on in familiar tracks, for example arms racing (Kinsella, 2002; Glaser, 2004) and the general concerns with the offensive/defensive military implications of technological change (Jin, 2006). Some, like NoD, rather dwindled away, seeming less relevant in an age of 'new wars' and the GWoT. The Arms Control literature became rather sporadic and marginal (e.g. Fehl, 2008; Robinson, 2008), but also edged into non-military aspects of security, such as the environment (Lindley, 2006). Interestingly, the Strategic Offensive Reductions Treaty (SORT), better known as the Moscow Treaty, of 2002 between Russia and the United States, limiting their nuclear arsenals to 1,700–2,200 operationally deployed warheads each, attracted little attention. But given ongoing US concerns about both nuclear rogue states and the rise of China, BMD remained a hot enough topic to fill whole issues of journals (*Contemporary Security Policy*, 2005), even though only marginally influenced by the GWoT (Gormley, 2002). The debates about it largely followed familiar themes from the 1990s: the technology itself (Ghosh, 2003), the arguments about whether it was a good idea or not (Peoples, 2006; M. Smith, 2006), the linkage to deterrence and proliferation (Utgoff, 2002; Powell, 2003; Karp, 2004) and the particularities of its implications for different regions (Russell, 2002; Freedman and Gray, 2004). The proposed US BMD deployments in former Warsaw Pact countries created a flutter of concern about the impact of BMD on US and NATO relations with Russia (Samson, 2007; Slocombe, 2008). The RMA also remained popular (Cohen, 2004; Paarlberg 2004; Stone, 2004; Freedman, 2006b), though here there was some branching out into new concerns about biotechnology (Koblentz, 2003/4; Chari and Chandran, 2005; Tucker, 2006), information warfare (Morgan, 2003) and space weapons (DeBlois *et al.*, 2004). This last topic also emerged as part of the more specialised debates about arms control (Altmann and Scheffran, 2003; Goldblat, 2003).

The pattern of debate about deterrence carried on in much the same track as during the 1990s, partly linked to BMD as noted above, and with the emphasis shifted to the Third World and the link with nuclear proliferation (Cimbala, 2002) (on which more below). There was considerable discussion of both deterrence theory generally,[16] and US nuclear policy

---

[16] Jervis, 2003a; Freedman, 2004, 2005; Lebow, 2005; Morgan, 2005; Sperandei, 2006; Zagare and Kilgour, 2006.

specifically.[17] There was even a bit of history on the nuclear taboo (Tannenwald, 2005). The nuclear policies of Britain and France continued to attract a surprising amount of interest, the former because of debates about renewing (or not) the small but expensive fleet of ballistic missile carrying submarines.[18] Less surprising, given the concerns about proliferation, was the interest in the deterrence logic of small/new nuclear arsenals (Goldstein, 2003; Ghosh, 2004), and nuclear weapons as a way for rogue states such as North Korea, Iraq and Iran to deter the US from threatening them with regime change (D. D. Smith, 2006). The impact of the GWoT was visible in a new concern with deterring non-state actors (Auerswald, 2006).

As during the 1990s, horizontal proliferation of WMD was the central concern driven by technology. The links to deterrence and BMD have been noted immediately above, and the link to the post-9/11 concern with terrorism noted in the discussion under events at the beginning of this chapter. Although worries about terrorism infused and reinforced the general agenda of nuclear proliferation, they did not change the overall shape and direction of the literature, which had already undergone a turn towards rogue states. A more formalised sense now emerged of a so-called 'second nuclear age' (Cha, 2001; Schmitt, 2001; Bracken, 2003; Gavin, 2004), in which a new wave of mainly Third World states was acquiring nuclear weapons. These developments provided fuel for the long-established debates between optimists and pessimists about the effects of nuclear proliferation (Woods, 2002; Knopf, 2003; Asal and Beardsley, 2007; Rendall, 2007; Singer, 2007). Either way, along with the GWoT, this second nuclear age was clearly putting heavy pressure on the non-proliferation regime, and opened a substantial discussion about the opportunities and challenges for the existing components of the non-proliferation regime from the new wave of nuclear weapon and missile proliferation.[19] A whole issue of *International Affairs* (2007) was devoted to this topic. Within this debate, new initiatives such as the 'proliferation security initiative' (Cotton, 2005; Valencia, 2005) and other measures to curb the trade in nuclear technology (Montgomery, 2005) also attracted attention. The existing debates about US counter-proliferation policies

---

[17] Butfoy, 2002; Ross, 2002; Russell and Wirtz, 2004; Yost, 2005a; Cimbala, 2006; Gormley, 2006; Lieber and Press, 2006; Colby, 2007.

[18] On Britain: M. Clarke, 2004; Simpson, 2004; Yost, 2005a; Lewis, 2006; MccGwire, 2006; Quinlan, 2006; Stocker, 2007. On France: Simpson, 2004; Yost, 2005a, 2005b.

[19] Deibel, 2002; Levite, 2002/3; Mistry, 2003a, 2003b; Paul, 2003; Braun and Chyba, 2004; Gahlaut and Bertsch, 2004; D. D. Smith, 2006; Quinlan, 2007; O'Hanlon, 2008.

were given added edge by the even harder stance on intervention and preventive war taken by the Bush administration as part of the GWoT (Hartung, 2002/3; Litwak, 2003; Carranza, 2006; Byman, 2007; Dunn, 2007), and there was even some spillover into IR theory (Roth, 2007). The GWoT also enlivened existing worries about the security of nuclear weapons and materials in Russia in relation to proliferation to both rogue states and terrorists (Busch, 2002; Weiner, 2002; Wolfsthal and Collina, 2002; Moltz *et al.*, 2004; Ball and Gerber, 2005).

A technological influence of a completely different kind came from the rise of 'green' interest in nuclear power as one solution to the problem of carbon emissions. On this basis, there was some revival of the interest in the link between nuclear power and nuclear weapons, which had been largely dormant since nuclear power went out of fashion in the 1980s (Deutch *et al.*, 2004/5).

The general shape of regional concerns about nuclear proliferation largely carried on from the 1990s, with the main subjects being the unfolding nuclear balance in South Asia; the seemingly intractable problem of North Korea's steady acquisition of missile and nuclear weapon capability; and, with the removal of Saddam Hussein from the picture, the mounting evidence that Iran was moving towards nuclear weapons capability.

For South Asia, the main interest was in how the deterrence relationship between India and Pakistan was developing,[20] and what the wider strategic implications of a nuclear India would be (Tellis, 2002; Berlin, 2004). There was also a focus on how the US was responding to the two new nuclear weapons states in South Asia, and especially whether US policy towards India had shifted away from a general opposition to proliferation, and towards a position more like that which it held towards Israel, in which some new nuclear weapons states would be de facto accepted and up to a point supported.[21] Since US policy could be read as a major defection from the non-proliferation regime, this aspect tied into the broader literature noted above about whether the regime was collapsing and, if so, whether effort should be made to revive it, or whether the conditions of the second nuclear age called for more robust and less consensual approaches to non-proliferation.

For the Middle East, Israel continued to get some attention (Maoz, 2003; Beres and Maoz, 2004; Raas and Long, 2007), and Libya's nuclear

---

[20] Winner and Yoshihara, 2002; Kapur, 2003, 2005; Batcher, 2004; Davies, 2004; Ganguly and Wagner, 2004; Salik, 2004; Sidhu, 2004; Quinlan, 2005; Riedel, 2008.

[21] Carranza, 2002, 2007; Ganguly and Mistry, 2006; Tellis, 2006; Thyagaraj and Thomas, 2006; Pant, 2007; Paul and Shankar, 2007.

reversal was noteworthy (Bowen, 2006; Bahgat, 2008). But the main interest was in tracking Iran's nuclear developments, their implications for other states in the region, and the possibilities and consequences of a pre-emptive strike against Iran's nuclear facilities by the US and/or Israel.[22] For East Asia, North Korea's missile and nuclear tests ensured that it got the lion's share of attention.[23] The implications of North Korea's going nuclear also generated a flutter of interest in Japan's position on nuclear weapons (W. Walker, 2006; Hughes, 2007).

Widening perspectives and the Global War on Terrorism

As mentioned in the introduction, widening and deepening perspectives responded to the GWoT in two ways. Some claimed it as a major political event that revolutionised international politics and hence that it should have a similar impact on ISS (Der Derian, 2004). Others either downplayed its significance, or, as discussed in chapter 7, simply went on with their theoretical and empirical research without devoting the GWoT much attention. In this section we examine those widening perspectives most directly engaged with the consequences of 9/11, the war in Afghanistan and the war against/in Iraq. Here the most active perspectives were Post-structuralism, Feminism and Post-colonialism, and their analyses often overlapped. Since the GWoT was to a large extent a question of how the US (and the coalition supporting the war in Iraq) conducted its foreign policy, these analyses were, of course, also driven by great power politics.

Discourses and terrorist subjects

Discursive conceptions of security have, as laid out in chapter 5 and 7, been a central part of widening approaches since the 1980s. Poststructuralists, Feminists, Post-colonialists, Critical Constructivists and the Copenhagen School have all – although in slightly different ways – argued in favour of seeing security as a discourse through which identities and threats are constituted rather than as an objective, material condition. Building on

---

[22] Einhord and Samore, 2002; Takeyh, 2003, 2004/5; Bowen and Kidd, 2004; Taremi, 2005; Fitzpatrick, 2006a, 2006b, 2007; Huntley, 2006; Tarock, 2006; Dueck and Takeyh, 2007; Guldimann, 2007; Kaye and Wehrey, 2007; Pedatzur, 2007; Raas and Long, 2007; Shoham, 2007; Litwak, 2008.

[23] Lee, 2001; Cha, 2002; Martin, 2002; Lee and Moon, 2003; Samore, 2003; Cotton, 2005; Fitzpatrick, 2006a; Huntley, 2006; Reiss, 2006; Bi, 2007; Rozman, 2007; Litwak, 2008; Moore, 2008

these insights, 'terrorism' and 'terrorists' were seen not as threats, actions or actors that could be objectively identified, but as signs that constituted a radical Other (Der Derian, 1992, 2005). 'Terrorists' were not legitimate opponents, but evil, sneaky, barbaric and irrational. Discursive approaches showed both how the actions on 9/11 were constituted as 'terror', 'acts of war' and 'orchestrated', rather than 'accidents' or 'crimes' committed by a few individuals, and what political consequences these subject constructions entailed (Der Derian, 2001; Owens, 2003). The coalition's failure to find the WMD that were the most immediate reason for going to war in Iraq caused a shift within Western discourse to emphasise that war was undertaken in defence of the Iraqi population, universal human rights and civilisation. Later, as armed opposition to the US–UK led 'occupation', 'nation-building' or 'reconstruction' grew, this was constituted as 'terrorism', 'insurgency' and/or 'Islamic fundamentalism'. Discursive widening approaches analysed the ways in which these discourses sought to legitimate the GWoT fought in Iraq through a mobilisation of universally good categories – civilisation, democracy, human rights, development and reconstruction. This was simultaneously a discourse which legitimated war through a development discourse; which made the identification of the 'universally good' the sole prerogative of the superior West, thus repeating the colonial and Orientalist tradition; and which depoliticised Iraqi actors, either by constituting them as passive 'victims' of Saddam Hussein, or by their opposition as 'insurgency' or 'terror' (Agathangelou and Ling, 2004; Barkawi, 2004; Debrix, 2005; Barkawi and Laffey, 2006; Hansen, 2006: 28–33; Mgbeoji, 2006; Nayak, 2006; R. Jackson, 2007; Sovacool and Halfon, 2007; Zehfuss, 2007). This constitution of the Iraqi Other as either terrorist or victim relied upon a construction of the Western Self as superior, strong, moral and civilised. Even those discourses that tried explicitly to break with this construction – such as those responding to the London bombings in July 2005 – ultimately, it was argued, had difficulties coming up with something genuinely multicultural and critical–political (Weber, 2006a; Stephens, 2007).

The concern with what kind of an actor 'terrorists' were also spoke to a general Poststructuralist and Constructivist call for theorising the importance of emotion, passion and feelings (Crawford, 2000; Der Derian, 2004, 2005; Bleiker, 2006; Mitzen, 2006; Ross, 2006). Emotion complicates rationality assumptions, not only about the terrorist subject, but in state (and collective) interactions more broadly. Linking back to the discussion of deterrence theory in chapter 4, the applicability of rationality assumptions to security politics has always been a subject of discussion, but Cold War critical views usually focused on psychological explanations, how bureaucracies complicated 'rational decision-making', or the difficulty of signalling and decoding (rational) intentions. Emotions or subjective factors were thus generally treated as noise, complicating the assumptions that researchers could make about 'rational action', but the notion that rationality existed underneath was maintained. Post-Cold War wideners held that emotions were not simply noise, but integral, if undertheorised, to foreign policy. This claim was not specific to 9/11, but the 'foreign policy' actions of 'terrorists' as well as the responses in the US and the West became an apt illustration.

Comparing widening perspectives with Neorealism as well as US policy discourse, the argument was thus not that 'terrorists' were either rational or irrational, but about the way in which rationality assumptions were employed in different discourses. The challenge to the rationality/irrationality dichotomy was also brought out in analyses which highlighted the different epistemological reasoning adopted by central terrorist actors. Der Derian (2003, 2005), for example, pointed out that bin Laden and his cohort spoke within a discourse of faith and dreams. If actions could be mobilised by divine, rather than worldly, communities, and if dreams could be an indication of attacks, the ontological, political and epistemological domain of ISS would be radically reconfigured.

The largest challenge to the constitution of a superior, benign and rational Western identity came in the spring of 2004, when photographs showing American prison guards at Abu Ghraib humiliating and torturing Iraqi inmates hit the Western media. The Abu Ghraib scandal forced US policy-makers and military officials to rely upon a 'few bad apples' explanation of the events, in spite of evidence pointing to these practices having migrated from the prison at Guantanamo to Abu Ghraib. A series of wider institutional practices and oversights also pointed to this as not only a few 'bad' or 'un-American' soldiers, and there was a growing concern with the US use of torture in defence of liberal societies (R. Jackson, 2007; Kennedy-Pipe and Mumford, 2007; Linklater, 2007). Furthermore, critical analysis pointed to the significance of new media technology, both for taking the photos and for disseminating them. The photos documented the abuses taking place, but the posing for the camera and the process of having the pictures taken was simultaneously a part of the torture and humiliation (Sontag, 2004). The double status of the photos as both evidence and enactment of abuse led Critical Theorists to discuss how visual material might be used to generate resistance, and what the ethical implications of making such material public are (Campbell, 2003; Weber, 2006a, 2006b; Beier, 2007; Dauphinée, 2007).

The concern with media technology and the way in which it may impact the public's understanding of war stretched back, as laid out in chapter 7, to at least the CNN-effect of the 1990–91 Gulf War, but what coincided with the post-9/11 age was the radical shift in the relationship between producers and consumers. During the 1990–91 Gulf War, established television networks had been the dominant provider of images – now the ubiquity of videophones, digital cameras and laptops made everyone in New York on 9/11 (Möller, 2007), or in Iraq, a potential producer for a worldwide audience. Abu Ghraib also showed that images have an ability to trigger emotional responses and that there was a need for studying processes of visual securitisation (Williams, 2003; Hansen, 2006, forthcoming; Campbell and Shapiro, 2007; Möller, 2007). In addition to photography, this literature pointed to different media and genres as places where security policies were articulated and negotiated.[24] The significance of visual representations was also brought out by the Danish Cartoon Crisis of early 2006 which, although initially driven more by domestic Danish debates on immigration and the status of Danish Muslims, escalated into a global concern with Western/Islamic relations. Interestingly, in terms of how ISS is constituted as an academic institution, some scholars, Der Derian and Weber prominently among them, incorporated documentary film making into their work and course designs (http://watsoninstitute.org/globalmedia/ – last accessed 11 February 2008).

That Feminism had become a well-institutionalised sub-field of ISS was shown by a significant number of analyses dealing with the GWoT. Feminists provided critical analysis of policy discourses, the way the war was fought, the process of post-conflict reconstruction and the representation of soldiers and civilians. Those working within a discourse analytical tradition pointed to the mobilisation of gender within the Bush administration's discourse and how the war against Afghanistan was legitimated through references, not only to al-Qaeda and bin Laden as threats to Western and global security, but to the plight of women living under the (non-Western, barbaric, masculine) Taleban regime (Hunt, 2002; Tickner, 2002; Ferguson, 2005; Nayak, 2006; Shepherd, 2006).

---

[24] Film and television fictional shows (Croft, 2006; Debrix, 2006; Weber, 2006b; Amoore, 2007; Erickson, 2007); video games (Power, 2007); murals (Lisle, 2006); museums (Sylvester, 2005; Lisle, 2007); music (Bleiker, 2006); poetry (Burke, 2000); and editorial cartoons (Diamond, 2002; Dodds, 2007; Hansen, forthcoming).

Although in favour of addressing the insecurities that Afghan women faced, the problem was, argued Feminists, that Western discourse constructed women as victims, as helpless and without agency. As a consequence a number of female actors that had opposed the regime, but also disagreed with each other, were overlooked. Women had fought before the war, for instance in the Revolutionary Association of the Women of Afghanistan (RAWA) but also by adopting everyday life strategies that circumvented the restrictions of the regime. The exclusion of 'women as active agents' from Western discourse allowed for a depoliticised understanding of women and concretely for their omission from the post-war political and legislative bodies, a pattern repeated in Iraq (Enloe, 2004a: 268–305). The Bush administration's alleged concern for women was further undermined by the way this had been ignored prior to 9/11, thus making 'women' a strategic, discursive chip to be played, rather than a genuine concern. The hollowness of the West's gender commitment was underlined by its collaboration with the Northern Alliance in Afghanistan, who had a poor track record on women's rights; the inattention to the increase in post-conflict rapes; and the silence on the insecure conditions in the refugee camps generated by the wars (Tickner, 2002; Khattak, 2003; Enloe, 2004a).

Feminist analysis also traced the constitution of masculinity and femininity across a variety of GWoT themes and subjects. The construction of the gender of the Taleban/fundamentalist male played, for example, an important role in Western discourse. This subject was simultaneously inferior and Oriental, embodying a different masculinity from Western soldiers, a masculinity that was tainted by weak and irrational femininity. Masculinity was also at stake in the West itself, in that the GWoT brought a resurgence of men as political and military actors and a virtual eradication of women (Tickner, 2002: 335). A particular form of masculinity was validated, especially in the US, with the Bush administration constituting 'hard'-military policies like warfighting as masculine and humanitarian actions as 'soft' and effeminate (Tickner, 2002; Shepherd, 2006: 29). Femininity and masculinity were also central, first in the much publicised rescue and homecoming of Jessica Lynch and then in the events and photos from Abu Ghraib (Enloe, 2004b; Pin-Fat and Stern, 2005; Kaufmann-Osborn, 2006). The humiliation of prisoners by female US soldiers was clearly linked to strategies of effemination, and the reception of the photos in the US where audiences were shocked that women could engage in such actions also showed deeply entrenched gender views. Female soldiers were assumed to behave as 'good' people, even in war, not as humiliating, torturing or gloating in the pain of others. A similar concern with women who transgressed traditional feminine constructions arose with the advent and increase in the number of female suicide bombers, in the Palestinian–Israeli conflict, Chechnya, Sri Lanka, Turkey and Iraq (Alison, 2004; Brunner, 2005; Gonzalez-Perez, 2007; Ness, 2007).

Information technology, bio-security and risk

One group of widening scholars linked the politics of identity at the heart of the discursive, Constructivist, Feminist and Poststructuralist agenda to an explicit concern with technology (Der Derian, 2004: 92; 2005). Technology came into the picture through the RMA, particularly the US use of 'global surveillance, networked communication, smart weapons, robotic aircraft, real-time simulation, and rapid deployment of special forces', a form of warfare that was 'low-casualty, long-distance, good visuals' (Der Derian, 2004: 92). Other studies examined terrorist use of networked technologies, and how the Internet became a site for antiwar/peace movements as well as targeted by government surveillance. The significance of cyberspace for critical infrastructures as well as for building communities – including groups fighting totalitarian regimes – predated 9/11 in that the Clinton administration had recognised 'cybersecurity' as an issue in the 1990s, but the GWoT took this concern to a new, more complex and heightened level (Arquilla and Ronfeldt, 1993, 1996, 1997, 2001; C. H. Gray, 1997; Deibert, 2000, 2003; Bendrath, 2003; Der Derian, 2003; Latham, 2003; Nissenbaum, 2005; Hansen and Nissenbaum, forthcoming). What set Poststructuralists and those working in a critical sociological vein apart from more traditional analyses of RMA was a stronger concern with how networked technologies change the ways in which non-territorial communities and referent objects can be constructed.

A particular concern was the way in which information technology and securitisations were linked in the discourses and practices of Western governments. The securitisation of 'terrorism' at the heart of the GWoT discourses worked, argued Critical scholars, to legitimise the transgression of a host of civil and human rights, most noticeably perhaps in the treatment of prisoners at Guantanamo and in the clandestine programmes of so-called extraordinary rendition through which suspected terrorists were believed to be transferred to regimes suspected of using torture. One group of scholars drew upon the Classical work on the exception by Carl Schmitt, as well as the more recent and influential Italian political philosopher Giorgio Agamben, the Copenhagen School and Foucault, in discussions of how these practices accentuated the tension between security and liberty at the heart of Liberal discourse (Huysmans, 2006b; Jabri, 2006; Neal, 2006; Neocleous, 2006b; R. B. J. Walker, 2006; Burke, 2007). Linking back to the central questions at the heart of ISS laid out in chapter 1, this literature pointed to the difficulties within modern Liberalism of reconciling the need to provide security and hence a sovereign authority on the one hand and the belief in individual liberty on the other.

Critical Security scholars working on bio-security analysed the shift from a territorial, well-defined enemy during the Cold War to the terrorist who moves anonymously until the moment he/she strikes (Dillon and Reid, 2001; Dillon, 2003; Salter, 2006; Epstein, 2007; Vaughan-Williams, 2007). Governmental authorities engage as a consequence in practices that seek to define the likely terrorist through profiling. The constitution of terrorist profiles is, however, intimately interwoven with the political discourses on insecurity that are in place, and hence always prophetic, seeking to identify the future threat, and thereby ultimately producing its own subject (Bigo, 2002; Jabri, 2006). The effect of such profiling and surveillance is the creation of a 'society of insecurity', where each citizen is taught to be alert and on the lookout for suspicious packages, activities and people. On a deeper analytical level it means that bodies are seen as potential carriers of insecurity (Campbell, 1992; Dillon and Reid, 2001; Dillon, 2003). One concrete consequence of this society of suspicion was the shooting of Brazilian electrician Jean Charles de Menezes in the London tube by police officers who mistook him for a terrorist (Weber, 2006a; Vaughan-Williams, 2007). The concern with the control of bodies and bio-security also came out in analyses of infectious diseases, particularly HIV/AIDS, the avian flu and other (potentially) global health hazards (Singer, 2002; Peterson, 2002/3; Elbe, 2006; McInnes and Lee, 2006; Davies, 2008; Sjöstedt, 2008). This literature was not driven by 9/11 as such – and the question of catastrophic infectious diseases was a policy concern prior to the GWoT – but there was a concern with how funding might be diverted from global health due to the financial strains caused by the GWoT, and how global patterns of mobility and responsibility would be affected by the regimes set in place to identify and prevent not just 'terrorists', but 'dangerous bodies' from entering the West (Bell, 2006; Epstein, 2007).

A related element in the GWoT generated surveillance regime is the practices through which borders are secured and bodies are categorised and disciplined through visa regimes and biometric passports (Bell, 2006;

Salter, 2006; Epstein, 2007), or by civilian border patrols, for instance on the US–Mexican border (Doty, 2007). As Bigo and Huysman's criticism of the Copenhagen School pointed out (see chapter 7), such regimes show that the big Schmittian exception – the declaration of war – has now been accompanied by 'everyday exceptions' carried out by bureaucracies and 'security workers' (R. B. J. Walker, 2006).

Another, often related, body of work criticised the focus on grand narratives of threat and survival at the heart of the majority of ISS, arguing that *risk* rather than security captured the nature of the post-Cold War era (Rasmussen, 2001, 2004; Beck, 2002; Coker, 2002; Griner, 2002; Heng, 2002, 2006; M. J. Williams, 2008). This literature drew upon the influential writings by German sociologist Ulrik Beck (1992, 1999), who argues that the advent of risk society is deeply connected with late-industrial society which produces a host of risks, predominantly in the environmental sector, which are integral to the workings of society itself and hence not easily avoided or controlled. On top of the immanent 'everyday' risks comes the risk of catastrophes that have irreversible effects, but which are difficult, if not impossible, to calculate, and hence uninsurable (Albert, 2000; Aradau and Van Munster, 2007). Crucial to Beck's analysis is the Frankfurt School–Habermasian emphasis on reflexivity: risk societies are capable of understanding themselves as constituted through 'risk dynamics', and hence of negotiating how best to meet the material and political consequences that arise from 'everyday risk management' as well as catastrophic risks. Risk analysis had been brought into ISS prior to 9/11, but the surprise attacks on 9/11 as well as the utility of 'everyday risk management' to identify the enactment of anti-terrorism and anti-migration policies made risk theorists hold that they offered a better account of security and terrorism (Rasmussen, 2001: 308). Risk certainly became popular enough to fill whole journals: *Global Society* (2007); *Security Dialogue* (2008).

One may discuss whether the risk literature falls within or outside ISS. On the one hand it seeks to shift the conceptual centre from 'security' to 'risk', proposing the latter as an oppositional concept that may drive risk analysis away from ISS. What speaks in favour of seeing the risk literature as part of ISS is that it engages with largely the same security–war–terrorism problematic as ISS, that it constitutes itself in relation to ISS rather than just ignores it, and that it publishes in most of the same journals as other Critical widening approaches. The fact that the exact difference between security and risk is often not made crystal clear is a further indication that the risk–security literature is part of ISS even if written across its boundaries. Whether this will remain the case is, however, a different question, and since 'security' is not the guiding concept, risk theorists may decide to leave ISS debates rather than try to change them.

Institutionalisation and the Global War on Terrorism

To ask the question whether the GWoT functioned as a meta-event for ISS is, of course, also to ask how this impacted – or was reflected in – the institutionalisation of ISS. The first thing to point out in this respect was that the GWoT generated an unusually high level of policy intervention by parts of ISS. A group of Realists fought adamantly against the US invasion of Iraq, and in an unusual display of public interventionism warned against going to war in Iraq through policy journals like *Foreign Policy* (Mearsheimer and Walt, 2003) and a large paid advertisement in the *New York Times* (26 September 2002). The headline of the *New York Times* advertisement was 'War with Iraq is not in America's national interest' and it argued that while 'war is sometimes necessary to ensure our national security', a war against Iraq would not meet this standard. Among the reasons listed were the lack of evidence linking Iraq to al-Qaeda, the instability it would generate in the Middle East, the diversion of resources from the war against al-Qaeda, the lack of an exit strategy, the divided nature of Iraqi society, and the need for an occupying force for 'many years to create a viable state'. The signatories made up a Realism Hall of Fame, including Robert J. Art, Richard K. Betts, Michael C. Desch, Alexander L. George, Charles L. Glaser, Robert Jervis, Chaim Kaufmann, Jack S. Levy, John J. Mearsheimer, Steven E. Miller, Robert A. Pape, Barry R. Posen, Richard Rosecrance, Thomas C. Schelling, Glenn H. and Jack L. Snyder, Stephen Van Evera, Stephen M. Walt and Kenneth N. Waltz. Elizabeth Kier, a prominent Conventional Constructivist, was also on the list.

The double identities of ISS as an academic institution and as giving policy advice has been a key element of the field since its inception, and the GWoT brought that out in a major way. The intensity with which the Realists' response was made shows that a prominent part of traditional US ISS conceives of itself as politically engaged and – although not expressed directly in those terms – of the role of the Security scholar as coming with a normative obligation to speak 'truth to power'. It also showed that this obligation comes out more forcefully during times of war where political and normative issues are brought to the forefront.

The American Anthropological Association's Executive Board's official disapproval of the Human Terrain System, a US military programme that employs anthropologists in the field in Afghanistan and Iraq, is a related case in point (AAA, 2007; AAA Commission, 2007; Rhode, 2007). The GWoT also showed that different parts of ISS constitute this science/policy interface differently: Conventional and Critical Constructivists came out of IR debates (see chapter 7) and were generally less concerned with the GWoT than were Realists, Poststructuralists and Feminists.

The debates over the GWoT also brought out, as noted above, a critical concern with the importance of think-tanks and foundations, particularly of the Neo-Conservative think-tanks the American Enterprise Institute and the Project for the New American Century, which received support from the Bradley, John M. Olin and Smith Richardson foundations (Boot, 2004: 22). Writers from these think-tanks were at the margin of ISS publishing in *Foreign Affairs* and *Foreign Policy*, but their much discussed influence on Bush's foreign policy made them the subject of increasing ISS Realist as well as Critical Constructivist/Poststructuralist analysis (Mearsheimer, 2005; Williams, 2005; Elden, 2007; Owens, 2007). Linking back to the discussion of post-Cold War traditionalism in chapter 6, it is worth noting that although there is a long tradition of prominent Security scholars entering (and leaving) US administrations, there are also Realist scholars such as Walt (1991), who have long been critical of the way in which Washington think-tanks are trying to influence US foreign and security policy.

In terms of the specific elements of institutionalisation of ISS that we have discussed in chapters 4 to 7, the impact of 9/11 certainly had some impact on funding patterns, degree programmes and publications. This is not too surprising: ISS has always had to keep an eye on the policy questions at the top of the agendas of politicians, the media and foundations, and these agendas are generally more influenced by the ebb and flow of contemporary events than academic disciplines, which are slower to shift around. One should note also that there were institutionalised research communities devoted to terrorism prior to 9/11 that were able to pick up the challenge and expand their research agenda, while others, for instance in the Critical widening camp of ISS, were quick to incorporate a concern with the consequences of the GWoT across a range of issues. Providing an exhaustive account of the institutional impact of 9/11 in terms of how existing centres and programmes were strengthened or newly created is beyond the scope of this book, but indications of this growth are found in the expansion of the Centre for the Study of Terrorism and Political Violence at the University of St Andrews, the first centre of its kind in Europe, established in 1994, which also offers an MLitt in Terrorism Studies (www.st-andrews.ac.uk/~wwwir/research/cstpv/ – last accessed 17 February 2008). Another example is the Infopeace project at the Watson Institute at Brown, supported by a Ford Foundation grant, which started in 1999, but grew after 9/11 as it became devoted to critical engagements with the GWoT through a series of conferences, films, blogging and an expansive website in addition to more traditional academic forms of dissemination (www.watsoninstitute.org/infopeace/index2. cfm – last accessed 17 February 2008). This project has been continued in the Global Media Project that deals with the links between conflict and media, not least the terrorist use thereof. In addition to the Ford Foundation, other foundations active, particularly in supporting critical research, were the Social Science Research Council (Latham, 2003) and in the UK the Economic and Social Research Council (ESRC). The ESRC has provided support through its initiative on the Domestic Responses to Terrorism and its New Security Challenges Programme. Running from 2003 to 2007, it brought together more than 120 researchers, many of them working on questions related to terrorism and the GWoT and it produced a long list of conferences and publications (www.newsecurity.bham.ac.uk/projects/ – last accessed 18 February 2008). Another major project that has underpinned critical research and conferences on securitisation, internal/external security, liberalism and security is CHALLENGE, the Changing Landscape of European Liberty and Security, funded by the EU Commission's 6th Framework Programme (www.prio.no/Research-and-Publications/Project/?oid=63990). Some of the institutionalisation effects are harder to quantify, but significant nonetheless: there is no doubt that the number of conference papers, PhD dissertations and courses on terrorism (critical or conventional) have increased. The impact of 9/11 also intersected with a general growth in journal publications where new journals were founded – *International Political Sociology* (2007), *Critical Studies on Terrorism* (2008) and *Asian Security* (2005) – and others were relaunched (*International Relations*, 2002) or moved to larger publishers (*International Politics*, 2003; *Journal of International Relations and Development*, 2004; *Millennium*, 2008).

Conclusions

Did 9/11 change ISS? The answer is both yes and no. There was a lot of continuity, particularly in long-standing debates about great power polarity and nuclear weapons, and even the significant changes in the debates about war were not dominated by the GWoT. Linking back to chapter 7, a significant part of the widening debate was concerned with theoretical and conceptual issues driven by internal academic debates not much impacted by 9/11. Yet, as this chapter has shown, there was also a significant concern with the way in which 'the event' of 9/11 impacted great power politics and technology and what the consequences should be for the concept of security, assumptions about 'security actor rationality' and the role that ISS scholars should adopt. Within ISS itself the status of 9/11 is debated, some seeing it as a revolution (Der Derian, 2004), others as a continuation of older paradigms (Kupchan, 2004; Wæver, 2008).

In terms of the four questions that structure ISS, the GWoT questioned the state as the referent object insofar as 'terrorists' operate in ways that differ from the sovereign rational state with a well-defined decision-making centre. But the policies put in place were also widely seen as reinforcing the state, hence the need to critically examine discourses of national security. A similar logic applied to the question of internal/external threats, in that terrorism worked precisely through an ability to transgress borders. Yet the GWoT was simultaneously about states trying to secure not only physical borders, but biometric and digital ones. In terms of the widening of security, military security certainly held a prominent place, while other more empirical widening lines of analysis continued on their own tracks, particularly in the areas of gender security, environmental security, societal security, and religion and security. Whether the GWoT should be read as a testimony to the inevitability of Realist security dynamics or not was, as always, debated.

Looking to the future, whether the GWoT will define a new era of international security remains an open question. The case that it does rests on whether or not the GWoT will be deep and durable enough as a new global macrosecuritisation to replace the Cold War. If so (and at the time of writing the possibility is still plausible, though by no means certain, or even the most likely probability), then the GWoT could provide a new core framing for ISS of a kind that has been absent since the ending of the Cold War. The situation, however, is nothing like that at the early stages of the Cold War, when the identity of 'the enemy' crystallised quickly and attracted broad support in the West. The GWoT itself, and particularly the characterisation of 'terrorism', and the identity of 'terrorists', remain heavily contested, and the Bush administration's portrait of it/them has done as much to divide the West as to unite it.

Against the idea of a new era in ISS is the fact that its traditional preoccupations with great power politics and technology remain independently strong. The ongoing debate about US grand strategy dating from the 1990s is much less concerned with terrorism than with the thoroughly traditional fixation on the balance of power, and the possible rise of great power challengers to the US, principally China and the EU. Great power politics could easily return to dominate the security agenda, though given the arguments for democratic peace that is not inevitable either. Nevertheless, whether seen from a traditional or discursive perspective, terrorists do pose a potentially severe threat to public peace and order. For traditionalists they do so both because they question the primacy of the state and because if they could get hold of WMD they might actually use them. For discursive deepeners, they do so because of 'their' ability to generate discourses powerful enough to disturb the balance and even the legitimacy of the liberal ideological order. But they do not represent a plausible alternative political order in the way that the Soviet Union did, and future great power challengers may do (or be seen as doing). Unless the direst predictions about terrorists and weapons of mass destruction come to pass, it may well be that the concern with terrorism that acquired prominence post-9/11 will prove to be a transitory obsession rather than something that defines a strategic era (Buzan, 2006).

If the GWoT does prove durable, what does this signify for the direction of ISS? Was the agenda-widening of the 1990s just a response to the temporary eclipse of military concerns, or do the ideas of democratic peace and globalisation suggest a deeper transformation? Perhaps the question from looking at ISS as a whole is whether the impact of 9/11 reveals that ISS still remains essentially one single conversation, as we argued it was during the Cold War, or whether it reveals that the ontological and epistemological differences introduced by widening and deepening approaches have fundamentally fragmented it into several separate, largely unrelated streams. Our reading, to be laid out in more detail in chapter 9, is that ISS remains to an important degree a single conversation, but one that now has a much wider, deeper and more sophisticated take on how to interpret any given event or issue.

9

Conclusions

It is twenty years since Nye and Lynn-Jones (1988: 8) described ISS as a young field whose 'progress has been halting' and with a 'definitive intellectual history' yet to be written. The sheer quantitative magnitude of ISS is perhaps a good explanation of why nobody has picked up the Nye and Lynn-Jones challenge. Since 1988, the ISS archive has expanded even further with the rapid growth of widening perspectives in the 1990s and the vast body of literature dealing with 9/11 and the GWoT. Leaving the intellectual merits of ISS aside, in the past twenty years, the field has been productive, generating an extraordinary number and range of books, reports, journals, students, conferences, think-tanks and policy advocates. Crucially, in terms of Nye and Lynn-Jones's late-1980s diagnosis of ISS as a theoretically underdeveloped enterprise, there has been a rapid growth in conceptual and analytical work examining, adopting or rejecting new conceptualisations of security.

There may be good reasons other than the daunting scale of the ISS archive for why a historical sociology of ISS has not yet been written. Both Political Science and other sub-fields like International Relations and Political Theory have, as laid out in chapter 3, generated at least some disciplinary sociologies, but ISS has not. One explanation might be that security scholars are in the business of the contemporary: if security is about the urgent, then why spend years digging up the past? Historical case-studies are plentiful in ISS and history is the basis for aggregated data-sets, but both are deployed in the attempt to generate theories for the present and the future. Historical disciplinary sociology, by contrast, claims the importance of the past as a worthy subject in its own right.

Another reason why we have not yet seen an intellectual history of ISS may well be that in order to write such a history, one has to have a clear idea of what is part of ISS and what is not, yet the delineation of ISS has been contested, particularly from the late 1980s onwards. A certain truce was made between Strategic Studies and Peace Research, and up to a point between them and some wideners, but the mainstream never accepted 'all' of the widening perspectives as we have described them in chapters 5 and 7. These battles imply that the object under study – the history of ISS – cannot be defined independently of the ISS debate itself. The stories we tell about the past are necessarily part of producing a contemporary disciplinary identity and this makes writing a disciplinary sociology more difficult and contestable than if we could observe the object from afar or start from a universally agreed concept or archive.

A central normative concern underlying this book – and which has informed the construction and application of its three key analytical frameworks: the driving forces, the four structuring questions, and the notion of 'security' and its three adjacent concepts – is how conversations and dialogues are facilitated across different ISS perspectives. As we will argue below, it is possible to see ISS as moving towards becoming one conversation, but a different interpretation of ISS as moving towards fragmented self-centred camps can also be made (Sylvester, 2007b; Wæver, 2007). Although these interpretations differ in their assessment of where ISS is at, they share two views: first, that no ISS perspective is going to conquer the field; and second, the normative assumption that it is good to have dialogue across perspectives/camps. A major advantage of a disciplinary history that is both inclusive (allowing for all potential participants to join) and located at a rather deep analytical, conceptual level (showing where the underlying points of convergence and divergence lie) is that it facilitates dialogue. It is through accounts of where concepts might link back to 'security', and how deeper questions are guiding debates, that a vocabulary and a 'meta-dialogical' field of conversation might be generated.

Put concretely, our hope is that everyone who participates in the great conversation of ISS will be able to see the relationships among what they and others have contributed. This has certainly been our experience as authors who came to this project from very different backgrounds, and who leave it with a much greater appreciation of the whole. We hope that at least some will share our view that the evolution of ISS has not just made it wider, deeper and more varied, but has also generated a certain division of labour which should be welcomed. We certainly do not expect or want that everyone should agree. Disagreement, as we have shown, has been an important driving force in how ISS has developed. But it might be hoped that a larger conception of ISS will encourage those within it to be more aware of the limits of their own approaches, and more open to how contributions from other perspectives can deepen understanding about shared concerns. A lesson along these lines might be taken from the fact that, in retrospect, there was much less difference between Strategic Studies and negative Peace Reseach than seemed to be the case at the time.

The first task of this chapter is to sum up the main stages and themes in the evolution of ISS. This discussion also includes a consideration of the interplay between ISS and IR. The second section focuses on the five driving forces, and we discuss the specific empirical conclusions that can be made as well as the analytical value they have contributed. The third section looks to the current state of ISS. We begin by identifying views of ISS as either conversation or camps, and we make the call for finding ways to deepen the conversational features. We also confront the obvious but tricky question of whether ISS can be seen as progressive, and point to the different takes in ISS on what 'progress' might entail. Finally, we use the driving forces framework to reflect upon the future of ISS.

The changing shape of ISS

Looking back upon the previous five chapters, the first conclusion is that the subject matter of ISS, and even its conceptual structure, has been rather fluid. In terms of subject matter, the sub-field has moved away from its initial concentration on military issues and national security. It has taken on a much wider range of referent objects for security, still with the state in a strong position, but now with much more space for individual human beings (human security), non-human things and entities (aspects of environmental security), and social structures (the world economy, collective identities of various sorts). This broadening of subject matter has in turn put pressure on the concept of security. In the early days after the Second World War, the new concept of national security was intended to broaden thinking away from the tradition of war and national defence. But although the concept of security survived as the core idea of ISS, its wider implications were quickly lost in the urgency to deal with the burgeoning military confrontation between the US and the Soviet Union. It was not until the 1970s, when nuclear paralysis and the onset of the oil crisis opened the way, that economic issues began again to appear independently on the security agenda.

Peace Research and Strategic Studies were pitching themselves against each other during the Cold War, and within Peace Research there was a further division between those working on 'positive peace' and those doing 'negative' Peace Research. In hindsight, there were strong commonalities between Strategic Studies, particularly its Arms Control wing, and negative Peace Research, in terms of agreed focus on military security, armament and conflict. The main disagreement lay in the basic belief among Peace Researchers in the possibility of overcoming Realist dynamics. 'Positive' Peace Researchers, by contrast, focused on integration dynamics, within and across societies, and later in a more critical tradition on structural violence. Looking back upon the evolution of ISS, this positive Peace Research tradition was significant for Liberal and Constructivist scholars who picked up the Deutschian sociological tradition and its concern with international institutions, communication and the patterns of civic interaction below the state level. Scandinavian, German and Neo-Marxist Peace Research was equally important as an input into the critical widening literature – Poststructuralism, Postcolonialism, Feminism and Critical Security Studies – which by the mid-1980s started to shift the conceptual terrain from 'peace' to 'security'.

Most of what was written in ISS during the Cold War did not explicitly go through the concept of security. After the first seminal conceptual articles by Wolfers (1952) and Herz (1950), the concept was largely taken for granted – security was national (state) security; it was about military threats, capabilities and the use of force; it was about external threats; and it was to be achieved through the balance of power, or simply the overwhelming display of power – and hence was not much discussed. Significant concepts – and theories to match – came instead in the form of general 'parallel concepts' (most prominently power and strategy) that linked into general IR Realism. Or, they were more specific, 'complementary concepts', such as 'deterrence' and 'containment'. Peace Research, on the other hand, was constituted around 'peace', an oppositional concept, although as just argued, the distance between 'security' and 'negative peace' was often not as wide as perceived by participants at the time.

What ties Peace Research into ISS, and what ties ISS together, is first of all a commonality in concepts. But when such commonality is not to be found because different concepts (e.g. 'peace' versus 'power') play the parallel, supporting or oppositional role, the convergence stems from a shared concern with the four structuring questions laid out in chapter 1: how the referent object is defined, whether threats are internal or external, whether the military is the sole security sector or others are included, and whether or not there is a belief in the transformation of international relations beyond Realist recurrence of war and conflict. Of course, the fact that these are questions rather than givens is only brought out as different perspectives, first Strategic Studies and Peace Research, later the manifold approaches on the post-Cold War widening agenda, contest these issues by answering the questions differently.

In addition to these four questions, we have shown that epistemological discussions have been significant both to Cold War Peace Research and to discussions in all of ISS from the late 1980s onwards (to a large extent as a consequence of the general IR concern with epistemology). Here, interestingly, the story of Peace Research and ISS has some interesting twists compared to how IR perspectives are usually situated along a positivist–post-positivist axis. First, where rational choice theories have held a strong – if not superior – position within Political Science for the past decades, they have never been particularly strong in ISS (Walt, 1999a; Wæver and Buzan, 2007). Not even if we expand to look at quantitative, causal, large data-set studies, do we find much explicit ISS. Negative Peace Research has, on the other hand, a long history of quantitative research, but this has been situated mainly within the sub-field of Conflict Resolution or in general quantitative IR. Hence one of the (potential) conversations that we have not seen emerge to the extent that might have been expected by the end of the Cold War is between this body of work and ISS. Second, most Marxist Peace Research during the Cold War shared negative Peace Research's positivist epistemology to the extent that it looked for causal connections, concepts with clear material referents, and behaviour rather than words or discourses. This should remind us that there is no automatic one-to-one relationship between the concept of security/peace, the epistemology chosen and the normative belief in the role of research and researchers.

Does ISS move from a single mainstream to a river delta? Yes, in that the ending of the Cold War pushed military concerns into the background, allowing much more room for the wider security agenda to come into play. This in turn precipitated the struggle for the soul of security, with traditionalists defending a narrow military meaning, wideners wanting to expand the agenda, and those like the Copenhagen School in the middle, allowing some widening but retaining the specific sense of (inter)national security as being an exceptional and extreme form of politics. There were definitely many more voices seeking to be heard in post-Cold War ISS, and the response to 9/11 and the GWoT showed that the multi-perspective nature of ISS had been institutionalised to such an extent that no political event would be likely to kill it off. One may also conceive of the increased extent to which the field is united by a concern with 'security' as the way in which cohesion can be built. To stay with the river delta analogy, during the Cold War negative Peace Researchers and ISS traditionalists may have been travelling on the same river without knowing it, while after the Cold War the expanding delta is recognised, mapped and discussed to a much larger extent.

As ISS has become wider, deeper and more multi-channelled, this has changed not just the sub-field of ISS itself, but also how it relates to the wider field of IR. Some boundary zones and crossover points remain pretty stable, e.g. Strategic Studies and (Neo)realism, and Strategic Studies and area studies. The old links between Peace Research and both Liberalism and Marxism have mainly been taken over by Critical Security Studies, Post-colonialism and Human Security, and the latter threaten/promise to move a chunk of the IR agenda (human rights, development) into ISS. Some new crossover points have been created, e.g. with Feminism, the environment, development and identity, and ISS is much more concerned with philosophy of knowledge questions than it was during the Cold War. The boundary/crossover between ISS and IPE remains, on the other hand, relatively weak, still largely focused on a few 'strategic' resources, principally oil. This reflects the ongoing institutional power of the split that took place within IR between ISS and IPE during the 1970s.

Driving forces reconsidered

Recall that we set up our framing of driving forces at the beginning on the basis of a pragmatic mix of general ideas from sociology of knowledge with our empirical sense of what factors were particularly influential within the specific domain of ISS. In a general sense, one would expect the evolution of any body of thought to be influenced by standard factors such as money, power, ideas, history and institutionalisation. Given the subject matter of ISS, and the history out of which it emerged, it did not seem controversial to focus on great power politics and technology as specific factors of relevance to this sub-field. Neither, given the strong commitment to engage with public policy questions that has been a feature of ISS since the beginning, did it seem controversial to give a specific place to events. In general, we think the framing of our discussion in terms of five driving forces has worked pretty well to explain why and how ISS has evolved as it has. Our confidence in this approach is sufficient that we will use it below to stick our necks out a bit in thinking about where ISS might go from here. Our general conclusion is that the operation of the five driving forces has remained visibly in play throughout, and that there is no reason to expect that this will change as the main background to ISS. That said, however, the mix and impact among them have changed over time. As we hope is clear from the preceding chapters, different driving forces have been more or less dominant at different times. Great power politics and technology were very strong during the Cold War, and weaker during the 1990s. Academic debates became more prominent during the 1980s and 1990s than they had been before. Events assumed particular prominence from 2001.

Although we think this framing has worked, it has not been without some problems of application. It proved difficult, for example, to draw clear lines between 'events' and various movements within the great power politics and technology headings. In some senses, the ending of the Cold War was an 'event', as were various technological breakthroughs such as the launching of Sputnik and the spreading of nuclear weapons to China and India. Although problematic for us in deciding how to locate different discussions, we do not think that this problem has posed any fundamental difficulties for our analysis of the evolution of ISS.

The state and future of ISS: conversation or camps?

Telling the story about the evolution of ISS from the present vantage point makes it possible to conceive of it as a conversation. One may say with Foucault's genealogy that history is always a history of the present where the past is constructed and hence reconstructed as the present changes. But one may also just point more concretely to how changes in the conceptualisation of security and the shift from 'peace' to 'security' that began in the 1980s reconfigured the way in which ISS is constituted and how it constitutes its past. We would get quite a different answer to the question 'what is ISS?' in the 1960s, where 'ISS' meant Strategic Studies and deterrence theory, and 'Peace Studies' meant positive–negative peace debates over concepts as well as epistemology. The bringing together of widening–deepening perspectives on the one hand and the traditionalist concept of security on the other after the Cold War means that 'security' to a much larger extent becomes the conceptual and disciplinary terrain of both. The history of ISS therefore also changes: Peace Research, particularly 'positive peace' research in both the Marxist and the Liberal tradition, is a crucial ancestor connected through complicated strains of literature to present widening approaches. Had there been, on the other hand, no conceptual convergence between the two main Cold War fields, telling the story of ISS today would have been a different thing: it would have been one of two fields nursing (to a larger extent than today) distinct identities, debates and institutions. It would have been more appropriate in that case to analyse ISS – and Peace Research – as free-standing, if opposed, enterprises with a narrower scope than is the case now.

Telling the story from the point of the present also allows for a critical or at least a different interpretation of ISS than may have been the one harboured by the participants at the time. In the throes of the heated academic moment, it is often easier to zoom in on what separates than what unites – and academia is after all an institution that defines contestation and falsification as the modes through which to progress and excel. By our adopting a longer historical perspective, the commonalities are allowed to come forth precisely because the point of comparison changes.

The crucial question is to what extent it is possible to have 'a field' in a disciplinary sociological sense if there is no conversation between the different perspectives. Does it not, we may fear/celebrate, fragment into a new system of 'sub-fields'? There are several current studies which identify IR as moving into camps, and their reasoning is applicable to ISS as well (Sylvester, 2007a, 2007b; Wæver, 2007). Often a US–European divide is identified as an important fracture line within ISS. Europe has had more Peace Research, more Critical Theory and more post-positivism of all sorts. The US has had more Strategic Studies and more positivism. After Wolfers, the US mainstream has had little interest in thinking about the concept of security, whereas this is big business in Europe. The institutionalisation of sub-perspectives in separate journals, book series and conference sections laid out in chapter 7 certainly supports the view of ISS as withdrawing from shared conversation (Sylvester, 2007b).

On the one hand, we applaud the diversification of ISS which has been one of the main empirical observations of this book. If we see the single conversation of ISS during its Cold War years as based primarily on how Strategic Studies called the shots, this was a 'conversation' that came at the expense of wider approaches. In that reading, there were already ghettos during the Cold War and what has changed is not that the field has lost its 'coherence', but that Strategic Studies is no longer capable of controlling the field to the same extent as before. On the other hand, the disadvantage of a field that fragments into non-communicating camps is that important engagements are missed (Walt, 1999a: 7; Sylvester, 2007b). We should remember also that 'conversation' does not spell agreement, but 'only' a common view of what it is important to discuss and a basic consensus on through which venues and with what kind of means discussion can take place. This implies also that those who call for other perspectives to be evicted – like the traditionalists with respect to Poststructuralism discussed in chapter 6 (Walt, 1991) – are hard to imagine as 'conversational partners'.

The possibility of seeing the evolution of ISS as engaged with answering four structuring questions may itself facilitate dialogue insofar as it brings out the conceptual themes of conversation at the heart of the field. Human Security and Neorealism are not, for instance, from different planets, but constitute referent objects, individual–collective relationships, the role of violence and politics, the urgency of development versus military issues, the internal versus the external, and so on. These constitutions are different – even opposed – but they are about the same things. Putting the current camp-assessment into the historical disciplinary sociology context of this book, there are three other things that complicate – or ameliorate – this view and that allow us to end on a more positive note. First, the fact that ISS has a tradition of debating through concepts may in itself facilitate conversation in that conceptual discussions function as catalysts for bringing different theories together – think, for example, of how 'democracy' or 'freedom' structure Political Theory.

Second, our longer historical view allows us to point out that the identification of ISS as fragmenting is not new. As chapter 5 laid out in some detail, Cold War Peace Researchers were concerned to the point of being alarmed about the 'two cultures problem': that Peace Research would split into 'positive' and 'negative' peace, into quantitative and critical epistemologies, and into American and European perspectives, and quite a lot of work went into thinking about how to counteract this tendency, not least in terms of how Peace Research was taught (Vasquez, 1976). That the concern with fragmentation is not new tells us two things: that the present might not be as unique (and hence as fragmented) as one might think, and that the concern with the status of the field is itself a healthy sign of the desire for things to be different.

Third, although ISS can point to an impressive (or depressing, depending on one's view) list of sub-perspectives, it is noteworthy that rational choice has not established itself as strong perspective (Walt, 1991, 1999a, 1999b). Hard-core rational choice has continued as part of Peace Research, but has not made nearly the impact on post-Cold War ISS as it has on Political Science as a general field (Walt, 1999a: 5). If Walt (1999b: 128) is right that 'formal modelers are less tolerant of other approaches than virtually any other group in the field of political science', then the relatively minor role that rational choice has played in ISS might itself generate a more dialogical environment.

But if we cannot produce a clear-cut either–or answer to the question of camps or conversation, can we say that ISS has made progress? As we noted at the beginning, evolution is a process. Environments change and the entities within them adapt or die, without there being any necessary teleology of progress built in. Has there been an accumulation of knowledge and a deepening of understanding (keeping in mind that different perspectives approach the question of progress differently depending on their epistemological, political and normative agendas)? Yes, in the sense that deterrence and arms control and other golden age strategic theory did create deeper understandings of important and ongoing international processes. Yes, in terms of Peace Research's claims about democratic peace theory being a major empirical finding in social science. Yes, in that ISS has successfully created and maintained institutions to develop and reproduce itself.

Has ISS been progressive in the sense of safeguarding and adapting to the liberal values it was originally created to defend? Yes, in the sense that the Cold War was won by the West, and that ISS has both adapted to new threats and opened up more for consideration of Human Security. Yes, in the sense that there is much more discussion and awareness of the concept of security and its political significance, at least in academic circles. Yes, inasmuch as the wider agenda can be seen as a discussion about the security consequences of 'real existing liberalism'.

No, in the sense that the voices of ISS, both Realist and radical, have mainly been ignored (Arms Control, Vietnam, Iraq, GWoT) and that the divide between advice to the prince and speaking truth to power is ongoing and unresolved. In some views the knowledge progress of deterrence theory was bought at the price of liberal values and reduced concern for the lives of citizens. The essential tension between security and liberal values remains, and the specific GWoT securitisation threatens huge and durable erosions in liberal values. In this view, 'progress' of any sort is illusory. ISS is there to cope with an ever-changing agenda of threats. It evolves only in the sense that these threats evolve and it has to keep pace with them. And as its history demonstrates, ISS will always produce a range of responses to any given issue. It should not be judged a failure for failing to produce single consensual answers, but as a success, or not, according to how fully and deeply it sets out the analyses and the alternatives.

The outlook for ISS

Our evolutionary framework necessarily commits us to the view that ISS will remain a work in progress. Whatever else our story tells, it shows how ISS has evolved in response to five driving forces, and it suggests that all of these will remain in play. It would be a step too far at this late stage in the book to speculate about whether the basic framing of the driving forces might itself change. The scope for such change can, however, be indicated just by thinking about the implications of democratic peace theory. If all of the great powers were liberal democracies, and if this theory proved correct in its core prediction that democracies do not go to war with each other, then the great power variable as it has played throughout this study would be either removed or transformed. Similarly, if those arguing that world government is not nearly so remote a possibility as commonly thought (Wendt, 2003; Deudney, 2007) turn out to be correct, then many of the Realist assumptions underpinning much of ISS would disappear. However interesting it might be to go down this route, we will forbear. But we cannot resist ending with a little speculative foray based on the assumption that our five driving forces remain in operation. Given current trends and developments, what sorts of pressures might they generate that would (re)shape the further evolution of ISS in the coming decades?

Great power politics

Even if democratic peace theory eventually eliminates this category it will not do so for some time, and may not do so at all. Within that room for doubt lie two partly linked developments that could significantly reshape ISS.

First is the 'rise of China' already extensively discussed. The simple version of this is that a big (non-democratic) state rises to superpower status on the basis of its growing material capability and returns the international system to a bipolar structure. In the Neorealist view, China and the US must then become rivals, including military rivals, with the result that, among other things, the traditional agenda within ISS returns more to centre-stage. Much can be interpreted as pointing in this direction, from Sino–US rivalry in space to concerns about Chinese influence in Africa and other places. If the rise of China became widely seen as threatening to the capitalist world in the way that the Soviet Union was, then this scenario is plausible.

But there is also much that argues for the rise of China not being seen as threatening, either by its neighbours or by much of the rest of the world, including Europe. China's adoption of capitalism, and its integration into the world economy, its 'peaceful rise' strategy, and its moderate behaviour in many international institutions provide room for a plausible alternative scenario in which China becomes the dominant securitisation for the US – but perhaps not for many or all of the other great powers. From a Neorealist perspective, the rise of China must threaten the US regardless of whether China rises peacefully or not, because it must undermine the current US commitment to remaining the sole superpower and brooking no rivals. If this remains the US view, and the China threat lobby in Washington remains strong, then what would be the dominant security agenda in Washington might not be shared by much, if any, of the rest of the world. Indeed, in those places where multipolarity is called for, many might actually welcome the rise of China as a check on US unilateralism.

A development along these lines could strengthen one of the fault-lines within ISS that we have observed throughout this study: the difference between ISS in Europe and the US. During the Cold War there were significant differences between the two over normative/political and strategy questions (though the latter was largely contained by the dominance of the shared securitisation of the Soviet Union on both sides of the Atlantic), and over epistemological and agenda questions. During the 1990s they split over the whole concept of security, and over different degrees of reaction to 9/11 and how to respond to it. This latter split was amplified by differences over GWoT-linked policy in the Middle East, obviously Iraq, but also picking up on longer-running differences between Europe and the US over Israel/Palestine. If the US made a major securitisation of China, and Europe did not, this would drive their ISS communities even further apart. There is already a noticeable difference between the US academic debate on 'grand strategy', which retains a strongly military flavour, and the emerging European one which, in line with the stronger widening–deepening concerns of European ISS, reflects more the outlook of a civilian power (Solana, 2003).

A development along those lines might make ISS seem, like the West itself, to be an artefact of the Cold War, the product of a temporarily shared macrosecuritisation. In that case, ISS might drift into a more 'nationalised' mode, with each ISS community driven more by the policy concerns of its own polity than by a common agenda. What seemed like differences of style between the US and Europe during the Cold War and after might then begin to look like the emergence of an EU style of security thinking. It is not difficult to imagine that in both the US and Europe as many would welcome such a development as lament it. Neither is it difficult to imagine similar developments elsewhere, as already prefigured by the rise of a 'Chinese school' of IR (Qin, 2007).

Events

We have already shown how the GWoT has impacted on, though not transformed, ISS. If things carry on as they have between 2001 and the time of writing (summer 2008), then the GWoT could easily fade into the margins of security concerns. But if terrorist attacks intensify, and especially if they begin to involve WMD, then the GWoT could become 'the new Cold War', a successful macrosecuritisation that shapes both world politics and ISS for several decades.

But perhaps more interesting than this is the possibility, and arguably the growing probability, that events in the environmental sector will emerge to trump all other security concerns. Environmental issues are the wild card in the security pack. So far they have been rather marginal. But as the sudden upsurge of concern about food security in 2007–2008 showed, when the diversion of agricultural production to biofuels helped, along with high oil prices, to jack up the price of many basic foods, they are capable of changing the game quickly and radically. There are many possibilities. Imagine, for example, the consequences if it is authoritatively announced tomorrow that a two-kilometre-wide chunk of rock has reliably been predicted to be on a collision course with Earth twenty years from now (Mellor, 2007). All priorities would change immediately.

But on present trends the two most likely environmental wild cards are global warming (Dupont, 2008) and the possibility of a rampant and virulent epidemic. As of 2008, the general consciousness about the dangers of global warming was, like the planetary temperature, on the rise. Embedded within the warming scenario are plenty of specific events that would have very major consequences for the present disposition of human habitation on the planet. For example, the already feared rapid collapse of the West Antarctic ice sheet would raise sea levels by at least six metres, and even a substantial partial collapse might cause one or two metres increase. This would flood many low-lying coastal areas, and many coastal cities, displacing tens or possibly hundreds of millions of people. Climate change on this scale would create huge crises in the supply of food, energy and other basic requisites of civilisation. If the event is the emergence of a new disease that combines ease of transmission (like the common cold) with high fatality (like Ebola), then at the very least the impact on the world economy would be huge as quarantines and travel bans shut down vast amounts of trade and tourism. If the impact of the disease was severe enough it could destabilise the social and political order in many places. Although the occurrence of specific scenarios like these is difficult to predict with much accuracy, the general probability that they will occur in the not too distant future is rising. When/if they do, they will reshuffle the cards with which ISS has mainly been played since 1945.

Technology

Technological impacts have been an important shaper of ISS, most obviously during the Cold War with its endless concerns about the impacts of new technological capabilities on the military balance. Also notable has been the very large and continuous presence of nuclear weapons in ISS thinking, whether in the form of worries about deterrence logic or in the form of concerns about nuclear proliferation. It is easy to imagine scenarios that simply extend technology discussions that are already an established part of ISS. There might, for example, be a local or a more general breakdown of the nuclear non-proliferation regime and a rapid move to a proliferated world of many small nuclear weapon states, and possibly nuclear-armed non-state actors. In the other direction, the development of a workable BMD system would still make a noticeable difference to strategic thinking. Similarly, there might be a struggle for the 'high frontier' of space as a means of asserting and resisting strategic dominance, though this development would have to overcome the increasing financial attractions of cooperation for space science and the commercial development of space.

Less conventionally, one might speculate about the impact of more and more sophisticated robot soldiers and pilots – already in limited use – and the implications they have for both ethical and tactical thinking about who uses force and how and when it is used. The tendency of capitalist societies to replace labour with capital pushes in this direction for purposes of destruction as well as production, as does the reluctance of rich, low-birth-rate societies to incur casualties. If the war 'dead' are machines, then the relationship of society to war and warriors is fundamentally transformed. Another technologically driven scenario involves cyber-security threats where terrorists or other malign actors attack physical and digital structures, thereby bringing down critical infrastructures and global communication networks. Clearly, the effects of such concerted attacks would be devastating, but their likelihood is hugely debated with some corners of the cyber-security debate pointing to severe digital vulnerabilities, while others hold that such discourse vastly exaggerates both terrorist capabilities and the weaknesses of Western digital systems (Latham, 2003; Nissenbaum, 2005; Hansen and Nissenbaum, forthcoming).

Extending the logic of the GWoT, environmental, cyber-security and nuclear proliferation scenarios discussed above points to some even more unconventional but important ways to think about possible impacts of technology on ISS. If one assumes that the salience of environmental issues is on the rise, then technologies associated with disease control and climate change could become as central to the ISS discourse as those of nuclear weapons once were. If global warming is the problem, then 'energy security' might well come to mean not access to hydrocarbons, but the availability of energy technologies with low carbon footprints, and/or the availability of technologies for reducing greenhouse gases in the atmosphere. Developments along these lines would, among other things, diminish the strategic significance of oil and gas, and with them the strategic significance of the Gulf and Russia.

Thinking even more deeply, the concern behind nuclear proliferation has been that ever larger numbers of ever smaller (and possibly less reliable/rational) states would get hold of ever larger powers of destruction. The GWoT added to that the worry that some of the new holders might be extremist non-state actors, i.e. even smaller entities and possibly not 'rational' at all. The logical extension of such thinking is nicely demonstrated by Martin Rees (2003), who sets out in detail the well-established technological trend leading to the current situation where huge destructive forces can be wielded by small groups of people or even individuals. This contrasts with the strategic reality behind most of ISS, that large powers of destruction could only be marshalled and wielded by large (state) actors. It is not just nuclear weapons that are becoming more easily available. Viruses, both biological and digital, can be made and distributed by individuals with easily available resources. Physicists and nanotechnologists might accidentally or intentionally unleash catastrophes on the planet. This diffusion of destructive capability is likely to be a constant of the human condition from here on in, and creates questions about democracy and governance that will change the ground on which ISS rests. How to deal politically and socially with a world in which many individuals and small groups can command large powers of destruction raises questions that go well beyond the security competence of ISS and poses chilling and challenging questions for any form of liberal society.

Academic debates

During the 1980s and 1990s, academic debates made a big impact on ISS by introducing a whole range of epistemological and ontological issues that had not previously been of much concern within the sub-field. There is always the possibility that new intellectual fashions will arise, but the safer bet now is that for the time being the dynamics of academic debates have run their course. ISS has now largely absorbed the 'deepening' hit from all the new epistemological fashions. It is now broadly in tune with the social sciences as a whole, and is therefore likely to be in 'working them all through' mode for some time rather than being subject to immediate big new inputs from this source. It is not clear now that there remains anything else out there that has not already been brought into ISS in some way, though this of course does not discount the possibility that socio-biology, or quantum social theory or somesuch might emerge as a new source of intellectual pressure on ISS. The academic world never stands still! The challenge from risk theory to security as the framing idea for ISS might also grow. Conceivably, the sort of massive modelling being developed for extremely complex physical systems such as the atmosphere might at some point begin to spill over into the social world, fulfilling the long-standing dreams of behaviouralists to make social science a branch of physics. But big changes from this driving force look much less likely than those from great powers, events and technology discussed above. The current river delta configuration looks relatively stable as the medium-term framing for ISS.

Institutionalisation

As we have seen, institutional factors can be as much expressions of other driving forces as driving forces in themselves. The institutional establishment of university courses and centres, of think-tanks and of journals, tend to act conservatively, reproducing existing lines of thinking and work, though these, too, can also reflect shifts to new priorities. ISS is now deeply rooted in this institutional sense, and these roots reflect the widening and deepening that has gone on over the last quarter-century. It is difficult to imagine all of this crumbling away, so institutionalisation lends a considerable inertia to ISS. But a moment's reflection on the scenarios above suggests that quite dramatic changes in funding priorities are easy to imagine, perhaps similar to the ones that attended the birth of ISS in the 1940s, 1950s and 1960s, and possibly bigger than the ones generated by the ending of the Cold War. Changes in funding fashions can either promote or reduce the research attention paid to given issues. The diversification of ISS's organisational base under the impact of widening and deepening places it well to respond to such changes when they come, although funding may of course be unevenly distributed across the landscape of ISS.

Whatever changes shape the future of ISS, even if the military agenda does reassert itself as central again, it seems unlikely that all of the widening and deepening developments in ISS will be rolled back. Peace Researchers, Constructivists, Critical Security theorists, Feminists and Post-structuralists have scored deeply in moving the understanding of threat away from purely material calculations towards more social and political understandings. While many developments of the sort sketched above will make changes, possibly big ones, in the agendas that become prominent under the heading of international security, it is difficult to envisage these gains being lost. If anything, the future agenda of ISS is more likely to reinforce, and play to the strengths of, its hard-won widening and deepening, than to push for a return to the narrow Cold War world of Strategic Studies. During its early decades, the pressures of Cold War strategy meant that ISS was largely pushed into the military sector, and consequently did not develop anything like the full potential of the security motif that was its constitutive concept. From the 1970s and 1980s onwards this began to change, and now we begin to see the full range and diversity of what the security concept can do across a range of issues and approaches. ISS has come a long way in the last sixty years, and in the decades to come we are in no doubt that it will remain a lively and disputatious area of study. It will continue to evolve not just in keeping pace with new security concerns, but also in developing new ways to think about them.

REFERENCES

AAA (2007) 'American Anthropological Association Executive Board Statement on the Human Terrain System Project', 31 October 2007.

AAA Commission (2007) 'AAA Commission on the Engagement of Anthropology with the US Security and Intelligence Communities', Final Report, 4 November 2007.

Abel, Elie (1966) *The Missiles of October: The Story of the Cuban Missile Crisis 1962*, London: MacGibbon & Kee.

Abelson, Donald E. (1996) *American Think-tanks and their Role in US Foreign Policy*, New York: St. Martin's Press.

Abrahms, Max (2006) 'Why Terrorism Does Not Work', *International Security*, 31:2, 42–78.

Acharya, Amitav (1993) 'A New Regional Order in South East Asia: ASEAN in the Post-Cold War Era', *Adelphi* 279, London: IISS.

(2003) 'Will Asia's Past be its Future?', *International Security*, 28:3, 149–64.

(2007) 'The Emerging Regional Architecture of World Politics', *World Politics*, 59:4, 629–52.

Acharya, Amitav and J. D. Kenneth Boutin (1998) 'The Southeast Asia Nuclear Weapons-free Zone Treaty', *Security Dialogue*, 29:2, 219–30.

Adelman, Kenneth (1984) 'Arms Control With and Without Agreements', *Foreign Affairs*, 63:2, 240–63.

Adeniran, Tunde (1981) 'Nuclear Proliferation and Black Africa: The Coming Crisis of Choice', *Third World Quarterly*, 3:4, 673–83.

Adibe, Clement (1994) 'Weak States and the Emerging Taxonomy of Security in World Politics', *Futures*, 26:5, 490–505.

Adler, Emanuel (1992) 'The Emergence of Cooperation: National Epistemic Communities and the International Evolution of the Idea of Nuclear Arms Control', *International Organization*, 46:1, 101–45.

(1997a) 'Imagined (Security) Communities: Cognitive Regions in International Relations', *Millennium*, 26:2, 249–77.

(1997b) 'Seizing the Middle Ground: Constructivism in World Politics', *European Journal of International Relations*, 3:3, 319–63.

(2008) 'The Spread of Security Communities: Communities of Practice, Self-Restraint, and NATO's Post-Cold War Transformation', *European Journal of International Relations*, 14:2, 195–230.

Adler, Emanuel and Michael Barnett (eds.) (1998) *Security Communities*, Cambridge: Cambridge University Press.

Agathangelou, Anna M. and L. H. M. Ling (2004) 'Power, Borders, Security, Wealth: Lessons of Violence and Desire from September 11', *International Studies Quarterly*, 48:3, 517–38.

Aggarwal, Vinod (1993) 'Building International Institutions in Asia-Pacific', *Asian Survey*, 33:11, 1021–42.

Agrell, Wilhelm (1987) 'Offensive vs. Defensive: Military Strategy and Alternative Defence', *Journal of Peace Research*, 24:1, 75–85.

Ahmad, Zakaria Haji and Baldas Ghoshal (1999) 'The Political Future of ASEAN after the Asian Crisis', *International Affairs*, 70:1, 759–78.

Ahmed, Samina (1999) 'Pakistan's Nuclear Weapons Program: Turning Points and Nuclear Choices', *International Security*, 23:4, 178–204.

(2000) 'Security Dilemmas of Nuclear-armed Pakistan', *Third World Quarterly*, 21:5, 781–93.

Ahmed, Samina, David Cortright and Amitabh Mattoo (1998) 'Public Opinion and Nuclear Options for South Asia', *Asian Survey*, 38:8, 727–44.

Ahrari, M. Ehsan (1994) 'Islam as a Source of Conflict and Change in the Middle East', *Security Dialogue*, 25:2, 177–98.

(1999) 'Growing Strong: The Nuclear Genie in South Asia', *Security Dialogue*, 30:4, 431–44.

(2001) 'Iran, China and Russia: The Emerging Anti-US Nexus?', *Security Dialogue*, 32:4, 453–66.

Akaha, Tsuneo (1991) 'Japan's Comprehensive Security Policy: A New East Asian Environment', *Asian Survey*, 31:4, 324–40.

(1998) 'Beyond Self-defense: Japan's Elusive Security Role under the New Guidelines for US–Japan Defence Cooperation', *Pacific Review*, 11:4, 461–84.

Alagappa, Muthia (1995) 'Regionalism and Conflict Management: A Framework for Analysis', *Review of International Studies*, 21:4, 359–87.

Albert, Mathias (2000) 'From Defending Borders towards Managing Geographical Risks? Security in a Globalized World', *Geopolitics*, 5:1, 57–80.

Alcock, N. Z. and Keith Lowe (1969) 'The Vietnam War as a Richardson Process', *Journal of Peace Research*, 6:2, 105–12.

Alison, Miranda (2004) 'Women as Agents of Political Violence', *Security Dialogue*, 35:4, 447–64.

Alker, Hayward R. (1988) 'Emancipatory Empiricism: Toward a Renewal of Empirical Peace Research', in Peter Wallensteen (ed.) *Peace Research: Achievements and Challenges*, Boulder: Westview, 219–41.

(2006) 'On Securitization Politics as Contexted Texts and Talk', *Journal of International Relations and Development*, 9:1, 70–80.

Allin, Dana H. (2004) 'The Atlantic Crisis of Confidence', *International Affairs*, 80:4, 649–63.

(2007) 'American Power and Allied Restraint: Lessons of Iraq', *Survival*, 49:1, 123–40.

Allin, Dana H., Gilles Andreani, Philippe Errera and Gary Samore (2007) 'Repairing the Damage: Possibilities and Limits of Transatlantic Consensus', *Adelphi* 389, London: IISS.

Allin, Dana H. and Steven Simon (2003) 'The Moral Psychology of US Support for Israel', *Survival*, 45:3, 123–44.

Allison, Graham (1971) *Essence of Decision: Explaining the Cuba Missile Crisis*, Boston: Little Brown.

Allison, Graham, Albert Carnesale and Joseph S. Nye (1985) 'Hawks, Doves and Owls: A New Perspective on Avoiding Nuclear War', *International Affairs*, 61:4, 581–89.

Allison, Graham and Frederic Morris (1975) 'Armaments and Arms Control: Exploring the Determinants of Military Weapons', *Daedalus*, 104:3, 99–129.

Allison, Roy (1993) 'Military Forces in the Soviet Successor States', *Adelphi* 280, London: IISS.

Allyn, Bruce J., James G. Blight and David A. Welch (1989/90) 'Essence of Revision: Moscow, Havana and the Cuban Missile Crisis', *International Security*, 14:3, 136–72.

Alpher, Joseph (1992/3) 'Security Arrangements for a Palestinian Settlement', *Survival*, 34:4, 49–67.

Altmann Jürgen and Jürgen Scheffran (2003) 'New Rules in Outer Space: Options and Scenarios', *Security Dialogue*, 34:1, 109–16.

Ambrosio, Thomas (2001) 'Russia's Quest for Multipolarity: A Response to US Foreign Policy', *European Security*, 10:1, 45–67.

Amin, Samir (1972) 'Underdevelopment and Dependence in Black Africa: Historical Origin', *Journal of Peace Research*, 9:2, 105–20.

(1975) 'Towards a Structural Crisis of World Capitalism', *Socialist Revolution*, 5:1, 1–25.

(1976) *Unequal Development*, Sussex: Harvester Press.

Amoore, Louise (2007) 'Vigilant Visualities: The Watchful Politics of the War on Terror', *Security Dialogue*, 38:2, 215–32.

Anderson, Benedict (1991) *Imagined Communities: Reflections on the Origin and Spread of Nationalism*, London: Verso.

Andreani, Gilles (1999/2000) 'The Disarray of US Non-proliferation Policy', *Survival*, 41:4, 42–61.

(2004/5) 'The "War on Terror": Good Cause, Wrong Concept', *Survival*, 46:4, 31–50.

Andres, Richard (2006) 'The Afghan Model in Northern Iraq', *Journal of Strategic Studies*, 29:3, 395–422.

Andrews-Speed, Philip, Xuanli Liao and Roland Dannreuther (2002) 'The Strategic Implications of China's Energy Needs', *Adelphi* 346, London: IISS.

Angell, Norman (1910) *The Great Illusion: A Study of the Relation of Military Power to National Advantage*, London: Heinemann.

    (1938) *The Great Illusion – Now*, Harmondsworth: Penguin Books.

Antonenko, Oksana (2001) 'Putin's Gamble', *Survival*, 43:4, 49–59.

Aradau, Claudia (2004a) 'The Perverse Politics of Four-letter Words: Risk and Pity in the Securitisation of Human Trafficking', *Millennium*, 33:2, 251–77.

    (2004b) 'Security and the Democratic Scene: Desecuritisation and Emancipation', *Journal of International Relations and Development*, 7:4, 388–413.

    (2006) 'Limits of Security, Limits of Politics? A Response', *Journal of International Relations and Development*, 9:1, 81–90.

Aradau, Claudia and Rens Van Munster (2007) 'Governing Terrorism Through Risk: Taking Precautions, (Un)Knowing the Future', *European Journal of International Relations*, 13:1, 89–116.

Arase, David (2007) 'Japan, the Active State?: Security Policy after 9/11', *Asian Survey*, 47:4, 560–83.

Aron, Raymond (1965) *The Great Debate*, New York: Doubleday.

Arquilla, John and David Ronfeldt (1993) 'Cyberwar is Coming!', *Comparative Strategy*, 12:2, 141–65.

    (1996) *The Advent of Netwar*, Santa Monica: RAND.

    (1997) 'Looking Ahead: Preparing for Information Age Conflict', in John Arquilla and David Ronfeldt (eds.) *In Athena's Camp: Preparing for Conflict in the Information Age*, Santa Monica: RAND.

    (eds.) (2001) *Networks and Netwars: The Future of Terror, Crime, and Militancy*, Santa Monica: RAND.

Arreguin-Toft, Ivan (2001) 'How the Weak Win Wars: A Theory of Asymmetric Conflict', *International Security*, 26:1, 93–128.

    (2005) *How the Weak Win Wars: A Theory of Asymmetric Conflict*, New York and Cambridge: Cambridge University Press.

Art, Robert (1980), 'To What Ends Military Power?', *International Security*, 4:4, 3–35.

Asal, Victor and Kyle Beardsley (2007) 'Proliferation and International Crisis Behavior', *Journal of Peace Research*, 44:2, 139–55.

Ashley, Richard K. (1981) 'Political Realism and Human Interests', *International Studies Quarterly*, 25:2, 204–36.

    (1984) 'The Poverty of Neorealism', *International Organization*, 38:2, 225–86.

Atzili, Boaz (2007) 'When Good Fences Make Bad Neighbors: Fixed Borders, State Weakness and International Conflict', *International Security*, 31:3, 139–73.

Auerswald, David P. (2006) 'Deterring Nonstate WMD Attacks', *Political Science Quarterly*, 121:4, 543–68.

Auslin, Michael R. (2005) 'Japan and South Korea: The New East Asian Core', *Orbis*, 49:3, 459–73.

Austin, John L. (1962) *How To Do Things With Words*, 2nd edn, Oxford: Oxford University Press.

Avant, Deborah (2000) 'From Mercenaries to Citizen Armies: Explaining Change in the Practice of War', *International Organization*, 54:1, 41–72.

Averre, Derek (2005) 'Russia and the European Union: Convergence or Divergence?', *European Security*, 14:2, 175–202.

Axworthy, Lloyd (2001) 'Human Security and Global Governance: Putting People First', *Global Governance*, 7:1, 19–23.

Ayoob, Mohammed (1984) 'Security in the Third World: The Worm About to Turn?', *International Affairs*, 60:1, 41–51.

(ed.) (1986) *Regional Security in the Third World: Case Studies from Southeast Asia and the Middle East*, London: Croom Helm.

(1991) 'India as a Regional Hegemon', *International Journal*, 46:3, 420–48.

(1995) *The Third World Security Predicament*, Boulder, CO: Lynne Rienner.

(1997) 'Defining Security: A Subaltern Realist Perspective', in Keith Krause and Michael C. Williams (eds.) *Critical Security Studies*, Minneapolis: University of Minnesota Press, 121–46.

(1999) 'Nuclear India and Indian–American Relations', *Orbis*, 43:1, 59–76.

(2002) 'South-west Asia after the Taliban', *Survival*, 44:1, 51–68.

(2004) 'Political Islam: Image and Reality', *World Policy Journal*, 21:3, 1–14.

Azar, Edward E. and Chung-in Moon (1988) *National Security in the Third World: The Management of Internal and External Threats*, Aldershot: Edward Elgar.

Bacevich, Andrew J. (2002) *American Empire: The Realities and Consequences of US Diplomacy*, Cambridge MA: Harvard University Press.

Bacevich, Andrew J. and Elizabeth H. Prodromou (2004) 'God is not Neutral: Religion and US Foreign Policy After 9/11', *Orbis*, 48:1, 43–54.

Badey, Thomas J. (2006) 'US Counter-terrorism: Change in Approach, Continuity in Policy', *Contemporary Security Policy*, 27:2, 308–24.

Baglione, Lisa A. (1997) 'Finishing START and Achieving Unilateral Reductions: Leadership and Arms Control at the End of the Cold War', *Journal of Peace Research*, 34:1, 135–52.

Bahgat, Gawdat (2006) 'Israel and Iran in the New Middle East', *Contemporary Security Policy*, 27:3, 363–75.

(2008) 'Proliferation of Weapons of Mass Destruction: The Case of Libya', *International Relations*, 22:1, 105–26.

Bailes, Alyson J. K. (1993) 'A Nuclear Capable Europe: The Case for the British Deterrent', *Security Dialogue*, 24:3, 323–32.

(2008) 'The EU and a "Better World": What Role for the European Security and Defence Policy?', *International Affairs*, 84:1, 115–30.

Bajpai, Kanti (2000) 'India's Nuclear Posture after Pokhran II', *International Studies*, 37:4, 267–301.

Baker, John C. (1997) 'Non-proliferation Incentives for Russia and Ukraine', *Adelphi* 309, London: IISS.

Baldwin, David A. (1995) 'Security Studies and the End of the Cold War', *World Politics*, 48:1, 117–41.

(1997) 'The Concept of Security', *Review of International Studies*, 23:1, 5–26.

Ball, Christopher L. (1998), 'Nattering NATO Negativism: Reasons Why Expansion may be a Good Thing', *Review of International Studies*, 24:1, 43–67.

Ball, Deborah Yarsike and Theodore P. Gerber (2005) 'Russian Scientists and Rogue States: Does Western Assistance Reduce the Proliferation Threat?', *International Security*, 29:4, 50–77.

Ball, Desmond (1981) 'Can Nuclear War be Controlled?', *Adelphi* 169, London: IISS.

(1993) 'Arms and Affluence: Military Acquisitions in the Asia–Pacific Region', *International Security*, 18:3, 78–112.

Balzacq, Thierry (2005) 'The Three Faces of Securitization: Political Agency, Audience and Context', *European Journal of International Relations*, 11:2, 171–201.

Bar-Joseph, Uri (1998) 'Variations on a Theme: The Conceptualization of Deterrence in Israeli Strategic Thinking', *Security Studies*, 7:3, 145–81.

Barkawi, Tarak (2004) 'On the Pedagogy of "Small Wars"', *International Affairs*, 80:1, 19–37.

Barkawi, Tarak and Mark Laffey (2006) 'The Postcolonial Moment in Security Studies', *Review of International Studies*, 32:2, 329–52.

Barker, John (1987) 'Improving Prospects for Compliance with Arms Control Treaties', *Survival*, 29:5, 430–53.

Barnett, Jon (2007) 'Environmental Security', in Alan R. Collins (ed.) *Contemporary Security Studies*, Oxford: Oxford University Press, 182–203.

Barnett, Michael (1996) 'The Politics of Indifference at the United Nations and Genocide in Rwanda and Bosnia', in Thomas Cushman and Stjepan G. Mestrovic (eds.) *This Time We Knew: Western Responses to the Genocide in Bosnia*, New York: New York University Press, 128–62.

(2006) 'Building a Republican Peace: Stabilizing States after War', *International Security*, 30:4, 87–112.

Barnett, Roger W. (2003) *Asymmetrical Warfare: Today's Challenge to U.S. Military Power*, Washington, DC: Brassey's.

Basrur, Rajesh M. (2001) 'Nuclear Weapons and Indian Strategic Culture', *Journal of Peace Research*, 38:2, 181–98.

Batcher, Robert T. (2004) 'The Consequences of an Indo-Pakistani Nuclear War', *International Studies Review*, 6:4, 135–62.

Baudrillard, Jean (1995) *The Gulf War Did Not Take Place,* Bloomington: Indiana University Press.

Baylis, John, Ken Booth, John Garnett and Phil Williams (1975) *Contemporary Strategy: Theories and Policies,* London: Croom Helm.

(1987) *Contemporary Strategy: Theories and Concepts,* vol. 1, London: Croom Helm.

Beaton, Leonard (1966) *Must the Bomb Spread?* Harmondsworth: Penguin.

Beaufre, Andre (1965) *An Introduction to Strategy,* London: Faber & Faber.

Becher, Klaus (2004) 'Has-been, Wannabe or Leader: Europe's Role in the World After the 2003 European Security Strategy', *European Security,* 13:4, 345–59.

Beck, Ulrich (1992) *Risk Society: Towards a New Modernity,* London: SAGE.

(1999) *World Risk Society,* Cambridge: Polity Press.

(2002) 'The Terrorist Threat: World Risk Society Revisited', *Theory, Culture and Society,* 19:4, 39–55.

Becker, Joerg (1973) 'Racism in Children's and Young People's Literature in the Western World', *Journal of Peace Research,* 10:3, 295–303.

Beeson, Mark (2006) 'American Hegemony and Regionalism: The Rise of East Asia and the End of the Asia–Pacific', *Geopolitics,* 11:4, 541–60.

Behnke, Andreas (2006) 'No Way Out: Desecuritization, Emancipation and the Eternal Return of the Political – A Reply to Aradau', *Journal of International Relations and Development,* 9:1, 62–9.

Beier, J. Marshall (2007) 'Grave Misgivings: Allegory, Catharsis, Composition', *Security Dialogue,* 38:2, 251–70.

Bell, Colleen (2006) 'Biopolitical Governance in Canada's National Security Policy', *Security Dialogue,* 37:2, 147–65.

Bell, J. Bowyer (1975) *Transnational Terror,* Washington, DC; Stanford, CA, American Enterprise Institute for Public Policy Research; Hoover Institution on War, Revolution and Peace (AEI-Hoover Policy Studies, 17. Hoover Institution Studies, 53).

Bellamy, Alex J. and Matt McDonald (2002) '"The Utility of Human Security": Which Humans? What Security? A Reply to Thomas and Tow', *Security Dialogue,* 33:3, 373–77.

Bellany, Ian (1975) 'The Richardson Theory of "Arms Races": Themes and Variations', *British Journal of International Studies,* 1:2, 19–30.

(1996) 'Defensive Arms and the Security Dilemma: A Cybernetic Approach', *Journal of Peace Research,* 33:3, 262–71.

(ed.) (2007) *Terrorism and Weapons of Mass Destruction,* Basingstoke: Palgrave.

Bendrath, Ralph (2003) 'The American Cyber-Angst and the Real World – Any Link?', in Robert Latham (ed.) *Bombs and Bandwith: The Emerging Relationship Between Information Technology and Security,* New York: The New Press, 49–73.

Benedict, Kennette (1989) 'Funding Peace Studies: A Perspective from the Foundation World', *Annals of the American Academy of Political and Social Sciences*, 504:1, 90–7.

Bengio, Ofra (1995) 'The Challenge to the Territorial Integrity of Iraq', *Survival*, 37:2, 74–94.

Bensahel, Nora (2006) 'Mission not Accomplished: What Went Wrong with Iraqi Reconstruction', *Journal of Strategic Studies*, 29:3, 453–73.

Bercovitch, Jacob, Victor Kremenyuk and I. William Zartman (eds.) (2008) *The SAGE Handbook of Conflict Resolution*, London: Sage.

Berdal, Mats R. (1996) 'Disarmament and Demobilisation after Civil Wars', *Adelphi* 303, London: IISS.

(2003) 'How "New" Are "New Wars"? Global Economic Change and the Study of Civil War', *Global Governance*, 9:4, 477–502.

Berenskoetter, Felix Sebastian (2005) 'Mapping the Mind Gap: A Comparison of US and European Security Strategies', *Security Dialogue*, 36:1, 71–92.

Beres, Louis René (1979) '*Hic Sunt Dragones:* The Nuclear Threat of International Terrorism', *Parameters: Journal of the US Army War College*, 9, 11–19.

Beres, Louis René and Zeev Maoz (2004) 'Israel and the Bomb', *International Security*, 29:1, 175–80.

Berg, Per and Sverre Lodgaard (1983) 'Disengagement Zones: A Step Towards Meaningful Defence', *Journal of Peace Research*, 20:1, 5–15.

Berger, Mark T. and Douglas A. Borer (2007) 'The Long War: Insurgency, Counterinsurgency and Collapsing States', *Third World Quarterly*, 28:2, 97–215.

Berger, Thomas U. (1993) 'From Sword to Chrysanthemum: Japan's Culture of Anti-militarism', *International Security*, 17:4, 119–50.

(1996) 'Norms, Identity, and National Security in Germany and Japan', in Peter J. Katzenstein (ed.) *The Culture of National Security: Norms and Identity in World Politics*, New York: Columbia University Press, 317–56.

(2000) 'Set for Stability? Prospects for Conflict and Cooperation in East Asia', *Review of International Studies*, 26:3, 405–28.

Berkowitz, Bruce (1982) 'Proliferation, Deterrence and the Likelihood of Nuclear War', *Journal of Conflict Resolution*, 29:1, 112–36.

Berlin, Donald L. (2004) 'The Indian Ocean and the Second Nuclear Age', *Orbis*, 48:1, 55–70.

Berman, Jacqueline (2003) '(Un)Popular Strangers and Crisis (Un)Bounded: Discourses of Sex-trafficking, the European Political Community and the Panicked State of the Modern State', *European Journal of International Relations*, 9:1, 37–86.

Bernstein, Barton J. (2000) 'Understanding Decision-making, US Foreign Policy, and the Cuba Missile Crisis: A Review Essay', *International Security*, 25:1, 134–64.

Bernstein, Richard and Ross Munro (1997) 'China I: The Coming Conflict with America', *Foreign Affairs*, 76:2, 18–32.

Bertram, Christoph (1981/2) 'The Implications of Theatre Nuclear Weapons in Europe', *Foreign Affairs*, 60:2, 305–26.

Betts, Richard K. (1979a) 'Incentives for Nuclear Weapons: India, Pakistan, Iran', *Asian Survey*, 19:11, 1053–72.

    (1979b) 'A Diplomatic Bomb for South Africa', *International Security*, 4:2, 91–115.

    (1993) 'Wealth, Power and Instability: East Asia and the United States After the Cold War', *International Security*, 18:3, 34–77.

    (1997) 'Should Strategic Studies Survive', *World Politics*, 50:1, 7–33.

    (1998) 'The New Threat of Mass Destruction', *Foreign Affairs*, 77:1, 26–41.

    (2002) 'The Soft Underbelly of American Primacy: Tactical Advantages of Terror', *Political Science Quarterly*, 117:1, 19–36.

Betz, David (2007) 'Redesigning Land Forces for Wars Amongst the People', *Contemporary Security Policy*, 28:2, 221–43.

Bhatia, Shyam (1988) *Nuclear Rivals in the Middle East*, New York: Routledge.

Bhimaya, Kotera (1994) 'Nuclear Deterrence in South Asia: Civil–Military Relations and Decision-making', *Asian Survey*, 34:7, 647–61.

Bhupendra, Jasani and Frank Barnaby (1984) *Verification Technologies: The Case for Surveillance by Consent*, Leamington Spa: Berg.

Bi, Jianxiang (2007) 'The Culture of Self-Destruction: Pyongyang's Struggle for Regime Survival', *Contemporary Security Policy*, 28:2, 244–66.

Biddle, Stephen (1998) 'The Past as Prologue: Assessing Theories of Future Warfare', *Security Studies*, 8:1, 1–74.

Biddle, Stephen and Robert Zinkle (1996) 'Technology, Civil–Military Relations and Warfare in the Developing World', *Journal of Strategic Studies*, 19:2, 171–212.

Bigo, Didier (2002) 'Security and Immigration: Toward a Critique of the Governmentality of Unease', *Alternatives*, 27: Supplement, 63–92.

Bilgin, Pinar (2003) 'Individual and Societal Dimensions of Security', *International Studies Review*, 5:2, 203–22.

    (2004a) *Regional Security in the Middle East: A Critical Perspective*, London: Routledge.

    (2004b) 'Whose "Middle East"? Geopolitical Inventions and Practices of Security', *International Relations*, 18:1, 25–41.

    (2004c) 'International Politics of Women's (In)Security: Rejoinder to Mary Caprioli', *Security Dialogue*, 35:4, 499–504.

    (2008) 'Thinking Past "Western" IR?', *Third World Quarterly*, 29:1, 5–23.

Biswas, Shampa (2001) '"Nuclear Apartheid" as Political Position: Race as a Postcolonial Resource?', *Alternatives*, 26:4, 485–522.

Bitzinger, Richard A. (2003) 'Just the Facts, Ma'am: The Challenge of Analysing and Assessing Chinese Military Expenditures', *China Quarterly*, 173, 164–75.

Blackett, Patrick M. S. (1948) *The Military and Political Consequences of Atomic Energy*, London: Turnstile Press.

(1956) *Atomic Weapons and East–West Relations*, Cambridge: Cambridge University Press.

Blanchard, Eric M. (2003) 'Gender, International Relations, and the Development of Feminist Security Theory', *Signs*, 28:4, 1289–312.

Blank, Stephen (2000) 'Russia as Rogue Proliferator', *Orbis*, 44:1, 91–107.

Blechman, Barry M. (1980) 'Do Negotiated Arms Limitations Have a Future?', *Foreign Affairs*, 59:1, 102–25.

Bleiker, Roland (2006) 'Art After 9/11', *Alternatives*, 31:1, 77–99.

Blight, James and David Welch (1995) 'Risking "The Destruction of Nations": Lessons of the Cuban Missiles Crisis for New and Aspiring Nuclear States', *Security Studies*, 4:4, 811–50.

Boot, Max (2004) 'Think Again: Neocons', *Foreign Policy*, 140, 20–8.

Booth, Ken (1979) *Strategy and Ethnocentrism*, London: Croom Helm.

(1991) 'Strategy and Emancipation', *Review of International Studies*, 17:4, 313–26.

(1997) 'Security and Self: Reflections of a Fallen Realist', in Keith Krause and Michael C. Williams (eds.) *Critical Security Studies*, Minneapolis: University of Minnesota Press, 83–120.

(ed.) (2005a) *Critical Security Studies and World Politics*, Boulder: Lynne Rienner.

(2005b) 'Beyond Critical Security Studies', in Ken Booth (ed.) *Critical Security Studies and World Politics*, Boulder: Lynne Rienner, 259–78.

(2007) *Theory of World Security*, Cambridge: Cambridge University Press.

Booth, Ken and Nicholas Wheeler (2008) *The Security Dilemma: Fear, Cooperation, and Trust in World Politics*, Basingstoke: Palgrave Macmillan.

Borawski, John (1995) 'Partnership for Peace and Beyond', *International Affairs*, 71:2, 233–46.

Boserup, Anders (1985) 'Non-offensive Defence in Europe', *Working Paper 1985/5*, Copenhagen, Centre for Peace and Conflict Research.

Boserup, Anders and Claus Iversen (1966) 'Demonstrations as a Source of Change', *Journal of Peace Research*, 3:4, 328–48.

Boserup, Anders and Andrew Mack (1974) *War Without Weapons: Non-violence in National Defence*, London: Frances Pinter.

Boukhars, Anouar and Steve A. Yetiv (2003) '9/11 and the Growing Euro-American Chasm over the Middle East', *European Security*, 12:1, 64–81.

Boulding, Elise (1984) 'Focus On: The Gender Gap', *Journal of Peace Research*, 21:1, 1–3.

Boulding, Elise and Kenneth E. Boulding (1974) *Introduction to the Global Society: Interdisciplinary Perspectives*, St. Louis: Consortium for International Education, Center for International Studies, University of Missouri-St. Louis.

Boulding, Kenneth E. (1962) *Conflict and Defense: A General Theory*, New York: Harper Brothers.

—— (1978) 'Future Directions in Conflict and Peace Studies', *Journal of Conflict Resolution*, 22:2, 342–54.

Bowen, Wyn Q. (2001) 'Missile Defence and the Transatlantic Security Relationship', *International Affairs*, 77:3, 485–507.

—— (2006) 'Libya and Nuclear Proliferation', *Adelphi* 380, London: IISS.

Bowen, Wyn Q. and Joanna Kidd (2004) 'The Iranian Nuclear Challenge', *International Affairs*, 80:2, 257–76.

Boyle, Michael J. (2008) 'The War on Terror in American Grand Strategy', *International Affairs*, 84:2, 191–209.

Bracken, Paul (1993) 'Nuclear Weapons and State Survival in North Korea', *Survival*, 35:3, 121–36.

—— (1994) 'The Military Crisis of the Nation State: Will Asia be Different from Europe?', *Political Studies*, 42: Special Issue, 97–114.

—— (1999) *Fire in the East: The Rise of Asian Military Power and the Second Nuclear Age*, New York: HarperCollins.

—— (2003) 'The Structure of the Second Nuclear Age', *Orbis*, 47:3, 399–413

Brandt, Willy *et al.* (1980) *North–South: A Programme for Survival* (Independent Commission on International Development Issues: 'Brandt Report'), London: Pan Books.

Braun, Chaim and Christopher F. Chyba (2004) 'Proliferation Rings: New Challenges to the Nuclear Nonproliferation Regime', *International Security*, 29:2, 5–49.

Breitenbauch, Henrik Ø. and Anders Wivel (2004) 'Understanding National IR Disciplines Outside the United States: Political Culture and the Construction of International Relations in Denmark', *Journal of International Relations and Development*, 7:4, 414–43.

Bremer, Stuart, Cynthia Cannizzo, Charles Kegley and J. Ray (1975) *The Scientific Study of War*, New York: Learning Resources in International Studies.

Brennan, Donald G. (ed.) (1961) *Arms Control, Disarmament and National Security*, New York: George Braziller.

Brenner, Michael J. (1981) *Nuclear Power and Non-proliferation*, Cambridge: Cambridge University Press.

Breytenbach, Willie (2000) 'The Failure of Security Cooperation in SADC: The Suspension of the Organ for Politics, Defence and Security', *South African Journal of International Affairs*, 7:1, 85–95.

Brezezinski, Ian (1993) 'Polish–Ukranian Relations : Europe's Neglected Strategic Axis', *Survival*, 35:3, 26–37.

Brodie, Bernard (1946) *The Absolute Weapon: Atomic Power and World Order*, New York: Harcourt Brace.

(1949) 'Strategy as a Science', *World Politics*, 1:4, 467–88.

(1959) *Strategy in the Missile Age*, Princeton: Princeton University Press.

(1965) 'The McNamara Phenomenon', *World Politics*, 17:4, 672–86.

(1976) 'Technological Change, Strategic Doctrine and Political Outcomes', in Klaus Knorr (ed.) *Historical Dimensions of National Security Problems*, Lawrence: University Press of Kansas, 263–306.

(1978) 'The Development of Nuclear Strategy', *International Security*, 2:4, 65–83.

Brooks, Stephen G. and William C. Wohlforth (2000/1) 'Power, Globalization and the End of the Cold War: Reevaluating a Landmark Case for Ideas', *International Security*, 25:3, 5–53.

(2002) 'American Primacy in Perspective', *Foreign Affairs*, 81:4, 20–33.

Brown, Harold and Lynn E. Davis (1984) 'Nuclear Arms Control: Where do we Stand?', *Survival*, 26:4, 146–55.

Brown, Neville (1977) *The Future Global Challenge: A Predictive Study of World Security 1977–1990*, London: Royal United Services Institute.

Brown, Oli, Anne Hammill and Robert McLeman (2007) 'Climate Change as the "New" Security Threat: Implications for Africa', *International Affairs*, 83:6, 1141–54.

Brubaker, Earl R. (1973) 'Economic Models of Arms Races', *Journal of Conflict Resolution*, 17:2, 187–205.

Brundtland Commission (1987) *Our Common Future*, Oxford: Oxford University Press.

Brunner, Claudia (2005) 'Female Suicide Bombers – Male Suicide Bombing? Looking for Gender in Reporting the Suicide Bombings of the Israeli–Palestinian Conflict', *Global Security*, 19:1, 29–48.

Brzoska, Michael (2004) '"New Wars" Discourse in Germany', *Journal of Peace Research*, 41:1, 107–17.

Bubandt, Niels (2005) 'Vernacular Security', *Security Dialogue*, 36:3, 275–96.

Buchan, David (1993) *Europe: The Strange Superpower*, Aldershot: Dartmouth.

Bull, Hedley (1961) *The Control of the Arms Race*, London: Weidenfeld & Nicholson.

(1966) 'International Theory: The Case for a Classical Approach', *World Politics*, 18:3, 361–77.

(1968) 'Strategic Studies and its Critics', *World Politics*, 20:4, 593–605.

(1970) 'Disarmament and the International System', in John Garnett (ed.) *Theories of Peace and Security: A Reader in Contemporary Strategic Thought*, London: Macmillan, 136–48.

(1975) 'Rethinking Nonproliferation', *International Affairs*, 51:2, 175–89.

(1976) 'Arms Control and World Order', *International Security*, 1:1, 3–16.

(1977) *The Anarchical Society*, London: Macmillan.

(1982) 'Civilian Power Europe: A Contradiction in Terms?', *Journal of Common Market Studies*, 21:1, 149–64.

Burke, Anthony (2000) 'Poetry Outside Security', *Alternatives*, 25:3, 307–21.

(2007) *Beyond Security, Ethics and Violence: War Against the Other*, London: Routledge.

Burke, Patrick (2004) *European Nuclear Disarmament (END): A Study of its Successes and Failures with Particular Emphasis on its Work in the UK*, PhD thesis, University of Westminster.

Burt, Richard (1981) 'The Relevance of Arms Control in the 1980s', *Daedalus*, 110:1, 159–77.

Busch, Nathan (2002) 'Risks of Nuclear Terror: Vulnerabilities to Theft and Sabotage at Nuclear Weapons Facilities', *Contemporary Security Policy*, 23:3, 19–60.

Buszynski, Leszek (2005) 'Russia's New Role in Central Asia', *Asian Survey*, 45:4, 546–65.

Butfoy, Andrew (2002) 'Perpetuating US Nuclear "First Use" into the Indefinite Future: Reckless Inertia or Pillar of World Order?', *Contemporary Security Policy*, 23:2, 149–68.

Buzan, Barry (1981) 'Naval Power, the Law of the Sea and the Indian Ocean as a Zone of Peace', *Marine Policy*, 5:3, 194–204.

(1983) *People, States and Fear: The National Security Problem in International Relations*, London: Harvester Wheatsheaf.

(1984a) 'Peace, Power, and Security: Contending Concepts in the Study of International Relations', *Journal of Peace Research*, 21:2, 109–25.

(1984b) 'Economic Structure and International Security: The Limits of the Liberal Case', *International Organization*, 38:4, 597–624.

(1987a) *An Introduction to Strategic Studies: Military Technology and International Relations*, London: Macmillan.

(1987b) 'Common Security, Non-provocative Defence and the Future of Western Europe', *Review of International Studies*, 13:4, 265–80.

(1991a) *People, States and Fear: An Agenda for International Security Studies in the Post-Cold War Era*, 2nd edn, London: Harvester Wheatsheaf.

(1991b) 'New Patterns of Global Security in the Twenty-first Century', *International Affairs*, 67:3, 431–51.

(2004a) *The United States and the Great Powers: World Politics in the Twenty-first Century*, Cambridge: Polity Press.

(2004b) 'A Reductionist, Idealistic Notion that Adds Little Analytical Value', in 'Special Section: What is "Human Security"?', *Security Dialogue*, 35:3, 369–70.

(2006) 'Will the "Global War on Terrorism" be the New Cold War?', *International Affairs*, 82:6, 1101–18.

Buzan, Barry and Lene Hansen (eds.) (2007) *International Security*, London: SAGE.

Buzan, Barry and Eric Herring (1998) *The Arms Dynamic in World Politics*, Boulder: Lynne Rienner.

Buzan, Barry, Morten Kelstrup, Pierre Lemaitre, Elzbieta Tromer and Ole Wæver (1990) *The European Security Order Recast: Scenarios for the Post-Cold War Era*, London: Pinter.

Buzan, Barry and Ole Wæver (1997) 'Slippery? Contradictory? Sociologically Untenable? The Copenhagen School Replies', *Review of International Studies*, 23:2, 211–39.

(2003) *Regions and Powers: The Structure of International Security*, Cambridge: Cambridge University Press.

(2009) 'Macrosecuritization and Security Constellations: Reconsidering Scale in Securitization Theory', *Review of International Studies*, 35:2, 253–76.

Buzan, Barry, Ole Wæver and Jaap de Wilde (1998) *Security: A New Framework for Analysis*, Boulder: Lynne Rienner.

Byman, Daniel (2006a) 'Friends Like These: Counterinsurgency and the War on Terrorism', *International Security*, 31:2, 79–115.

(2006b) 'Remaking Alliances for the War on Terrorism', *Journal of Strategic Studies*, 29:5, 767–811.

(2007) 'Do Counterproliferation and Counterterrorism go Together?', *Political Science Quarterly*, 122:1, 25–46.

Byman, Daniel and Matthew C. Waxman (2000) 'Kosovo and the Great Air Power Debate', *International Security*, 24:4, 5–38.

Cable, Vincent (1995) 'What is International Economic Security?', *International Affairs*, 71:2, 305–24.

Cable, Vincent and Peter Ferdinand (1994) 'China: Enter the Giant', *International Affairs*, 70:2, 243–62.

Calleo, David P. (1996) 'Restarting the Marxist Clock? The Economic Fragility of the West', *World Policy Journal*, 13:2, 57–64.

(2003) 'Transatlantic Folly: NATO vs. the EU', *World Policy Journal*, 20:3, 17–24.

(2004) 'The Broken West', *Survival*, 46:3, 29–38.

(2007) 'Unipolar Illusions', *Survival*, 49:3, 73–8.

Calvocoressi, Peter (1984) 'Nuclear Weapons in the Service of Man', *Review of International Studies*, 10:2, 89–101.

Camilleri, Joseph A. (1977) 'The Myth of the Peaceful Atom', *Millennium*, 6:2, 111–27.

(1984) *The State and Nuclear Power: Conflict and Control in the Western World*, Brighton: Wheatsheaf.

Campbell, David (1990) 'Global Inscription: How Foreign Policy Constitutes the United States', *Alternatives*, 15:3, 263–86.

(1992) *Writing Security: United States Foreign Policy and the Politics of Identity*, Manchester: Manchester University Press.

(1993) *Politics Without Principle: Sovereignty, Ethics and the Narratives of the Gulf War*, Boulder: Lynne Rienner.

(1996) 'Political Prosaics, Transversal Politics and the Anarchical World', in Michael J. Shapiro and Hayward R. Alker (eds.) *Challenging Boundaries: Global Flows, Territorial Identities*, Minneapolis: University of Minnesota Press, 7–31.

(1998a) *National Deconstruction: Violence, Identity and Justice in Bosnia*, Minneapolis: University of Minnesota Press.

(1998b) *Writing Security: United States Foreign Policy and the Politics of Identity*, 2nd and revised edn, Manchester: Manchester University Press.

(2002a) 'Atrocity, Memory, Photography: Imaging the Concentration Camps of Bosnia – The Case of ITN versus *Living Marxism*, Part 1', *Journal of Human Rights*, 1:1, 1–33.

(2002b) 'Atrocity, Memory, Photography: Imaging the Concentration Camps of Bosnia – The Case of ITN versus *Living Marxism*, Part 2', *Journal of Human Rights*, 1:2, 143–72.

(2003) 'Cultural Governance and Pictorial Resistance: Reflections on the Imaging of War', *Review of International Studies*, 29: Special Issue, 57–74.

Campbell, David and Michael J. Shapiro (2007) 'Guest Editors' Introduction', *Security Dialogue*, 38:2, 131–38.

Caporaso, James A. (1995) 'False Divisions: Security Studies and International Political Economy', *Mershon International Studies Review*, 39:1, 117–22.

Caprioli, Mary (2000) 'Gendered Conflict', *Journal of Peace Research*, 37:1, 51–68.

(2003) 'Gender Equality and State Aggression: The Impact of Domestic Gender Equality on State First Use of Force', *International Interactions*, 29:3, 195–214.

(2004a) 'Feminist Theory and Quantitative Methodology: A Critical Analysis', *International Studies Review*, 6:2, 253–69.

(2004b) 'Democracy and Human Rights versus Women's Security: A Contradiction?', *Security Dialogue*, 35:4, 411–28.

Caprioli, Mary and Mark A. Boyer (2001) 'Gender, Violence, and International Crisis', *Journal of Conflict Resolution*, 45:3, 503–18.

Caprioli, Mary and Peter F. Trumbore (2003) 'Identifying "Rogue" States and Testing their Interstate Conflict Behavior', *European Journal of International Relations*, 9:3, 377–406.

(2006) 'First Use of Violent Force in Militarized Interstate Disputes, 1980–2001', *Journal of Peace Research*, 43:6, 741–49.

Carasales, Julio (1996) 'A Surprising About-face: Argentina and the NPT', *Security Dialogue*, 27:3, 325–35.

Cardiff Text Analysis Group (1988) 'Disarming Voices (a Nuclear Exchange)', *Textual Practice*, 2:3, 381–93.

Cardoso, Fernando H. and Enzo Faletto (1979) *Dependency and Development in Latin America*, Berkeley: University of California Press.

Carlton, David (1976) 'Great Britain and Nuclear Weapons', *British Journal of International Studies*, 2:2, 164–72.

Carmola, Kateri (2007) *Private Security Contractors and New Wars: Risk, Law and Ethics*, London: Routledge.

Carpenter, R. Charli (2002) 'Gender Theory in World Politics: Contributions from a Nonfeminist Standpoint?', *International Studies Review*, 4:3, 153–65.

(2003) 'Women and Children First: Gender, Norms, and Humanitarian Evacuation in the Balkans 1991–1995', *International Organization*, 57:4, 661–94.

(2006) 'Recognizing Gender-based Violence Against Civilian Men and Boys in Conflict Situations', *Security Dialogue*, 37:1, 83–104.

Carpenter, Ted G. (1991) 'The New World Disorder', *Foreign Policy*, 84, 24–39.

(1998) 'Managing a Great Power Relationship: The US, China and East Asian Security', *Journal of Strategic Studies*, 21:1, 1–20.

(2003) 'The Bush Administration's Security Strategy: Implications for Transatlantic Relations', *Cambridge Review of International Affairs*, 16:3, 511–24.

Carr, Caleb (1996/7) 'Terrorism as Warfare: The Lessons of Military History', *World Policy Journal*, 13:4, 1–12.

Carr, E. H. (1946) *The Twenty Years' Crisis, 1919–1939: An Introduction to the Study of International Relations*, 2nd edn, London: Macmillan.

Carranza, Mario E. (2002) 'At the Crossroads: US Non-proliferation Policy Towards South Asia After the Indian and Pakistani Tests', *Contemporary Security Policy*, 23:1, 93–128.

(2006) 'Can the NPT Survive? The Theory and Practice of US Nuclear Non-proliferation Policy after September 11', *Contemporary Security Policy*, 27:3, 489–525.

(2007) 'From Non-Proliferation to Post-Proliferation: Explaining the US–India Nuclear Deal', *Contemporary Security Policy*, 28:3, 464–93.

Carson, Rachel (1962 [1991]) *Silent Spring*, Harmondsworth: Penguin.

Carter, Ashton B. (2001/2) 'The Architecture of Government in the Face of Terrorism', *International Security*, 26:3, 5–23.

Carter, Ashton B., John Deutch and Philip Zelikow (1998) 'Catastrophic Terrorism', *Foreign Affairs*, 77:6, 80–94.

Carver, Terrell (ed.) (2003) 'The Forum: Gender and International Relations', *International Studies Review*, 5:2, 287–302.

Carver, Terrell, Molly Cochran and Judith Squires (1998) 'Gendering Jones', *Review of International Studies*, 24:2, 283–97.

CASE (2006) 'Critical Approaches to Security in Europe: A Networked Manifesto', *Security Dialogue*, 37:4, 443–87.

Casetti, Emilio (2003) 'Power Shifts and Economic Development: When Will China Overtake the USA?', *Journal of Peace Research*, 40:6, 661–76.

Cassidy, Robert M. (2006) *Counterinsurgency and the Global War on Terror: Military Culture and Irregular War*, Westport: Praeger.

Cavanaugh, Jeffrey M. (2007) 'From the "Red Juggernaut" to Iraqi WMD: Threat Inflation and How it Succeeds in the United States', *Political Science Quarterly*, 122:4, 555–84.

Caverley, Jonathan (2007) 'United States Hegemony and the New Economics of Defense', *Security Studies*, 16:4, 598–614.

Center for Nonproliferation Studies, (2001) 'Missile Proliferation and Defences: Problems and Prospects', *Occasional Paper no. 7*, Center for Nonproliferation Studies, and Mountbatten Centre for International Studies.

Cervenka, Zdenek and Barbara Rogers (1978) *The Nuclear Axis: Secret Collaboration between West Germany and South Africa*, London: Julian Friedmann.

Cha, Victor D. (2000a) 'Hate, Power and Identity in Japan–Korea Security', *Australian Journal of International Affairs*, 54:3, 309–23.

(2000b) 'Globalization and the Study of International Security', *Journal of Peace Research*, 37:3, 391–403.

(2001) 'The Second Nuclear Age: Proliferation Pessimism Versus Sober Optimism in South Asia and East Asia', *Journal of Strategic Studies*, 24:4, 79–120.

(2002) 'North Korea's Weapons of Mass Destruction: Badges, Shields, or Swords?', *Political Science Quarterly*, 117:2, 209–30.

Cha, Victor D. and David C. Kang (2005) 'The Debate over North Korea', *Political Science Quarterly*, 119:2, 229–54.

Chace, James (2003) 'Present at the Destruction: The Death of American Internationalism', *World Policy Journal*, 20:1, 1–5.

Chalmers, Malcolm (1993) 'Developing a Security Regime for Eastern Europe', *Journal of Peace Research*, 30:4, 427–44.

(1999) 'Bombs Away? Britain and Nuclear Weapons under New Labour', *Security Dialogue*, 30:1, 61–74.

Chan, Steve (2006) 'Is There a Power Transition Between the US and China? The Different Faces of National Power', *Asian Survey*, 45:5, 687–701.

Chapman, John, Reinhard Drifte and Ian M. Gow (1983) *Japan's Quest for Comprehensive Security*, London: Frances Pinter.

Chari, P. R. (1978) 'An Indian Reaction to US Nonproliferation Policy', *International Security*, 3:2, 57–61.

Chari, P. R. and Suba Chandran (eds.) (2005) *Bio-terrorism and Bio-defence*, New Delhi: Manohar.

Chatfield, Charles (1979) 'International Peace Research: The Field Defined by Dissemination', *Journal of Peace Research*, 16:2, 163–79.

Chatterjee, Partha (1974) 'The Equilibrium Theory of Arms Races', *Journal of Peace Research*, 11:3, 203–11; and see correspondence in 12:3, 1975, 235–41.

Chaudri, Mohammed A. (1968) 'Peace Research and the Developing Countries', *Journal of Peace Research*, 5:3, 365–74.

Chellaney, Brahma (1991) 'South Asia's Passage to Nuclear Power', *International Security*, 16:1, 43–72.

(1993) 'The Challenge of Nuclear Arms Control in South Asia', *Survival*, 35:3, 121–36.

(1998/9) 'After the Tests: India's Options', *Survival*, 40:4, 93–111.

(1999) 'India's Nuclear Planning, Force Structure, Doctrine and Arms Control Posture', *Australian Journal of International Affairs*, 53:1, 57–69.

Chiba, Akira and Lanxin Xiang (2005) 'Traumatic Legacies in China and Japan: An Exchange', *Survival*, 47:2, 215–32.

Chilton, Paul (1985) *Language and the Nuclear Arms Debate: Nukespeak Today*, London: Frances Pinter.

(1987) 'Metaphor, Euphemism and the Militarization of Language', *Current Research on Peace and Violence*, 24:1, 7–19.

Chojnacki, Sven (2006) 'Anything New or More of the Same? Wars and Military Interventions in the International System, 1946–2003', *Global Society*, 20:1, 25–46.

Chopra, Jarat and Thomas Weiss (1995) 'Prospects for Containing Conflict in the Former Second World', *Security Studies*, 4:3, 552–83.

Christensen, Thomas J. (1999) 'China, the US–Japan Alliance, and the Security Dilemma in East Asia', *International Security*, 23:4, 49–80.

(2006) 'Fostering Stability or Creating a Monster? The Rise of China and US Policy toward East Asia', *International Security*, 31:1, 81–126.

Christoferrersen, Gaye (2002) 'The Role of East Asia in Sino-American Relations', *Asian Survey*, 42:3, 369–96.

Chubin, Shahram (1992). 'Iran and Regional Security in the Persian Gulf', *Survival*, 34:3, 62–80.

(1995) 'Does Iran Want Nuclear Weapons?', *Survival*, 37:1, 86–104.

Chubin, Shahram and Charles Tripp (1996) 'Iran–Saudi Arabia Relations and Regional Order', *Adelphi* 304, London: IISS.

Chyba, Christopher F. (2004) 'Biotechnology and Bioterrorism: An Unprecedented World', *Survival*, 46:2, 143–61.

Cimbala, Stephen J. (1995) 'Deterrence Stability with Smaller Forces: Prospects and Problems', *Journal of Peace Research*, 32:1, 65–78.

(2002) 'Nuclear Proliferation and "Realistic Deterrence" in a New Century', *European Security*, 11:2, 33–47.

(2006) 'Parity in Peril? The Continuing Vitality of Russian–US Strategic Nuclear Deterrence', *Contemporary Security Policy*, 27:3, 417–34.

Cirincione, Joseph (2000) 'The Asian Nuclear Reaction Chain', *Foreign Policy*, 118, 120–36.

Clark, Ian (1982) *Limited Nuclear War*, Princeton: Princeton University Press.

Clark, J. C. D. (2004) 'Is There Still a West? The Trajectory of a Category', *Orbis*, 48:1, 577–91.

Clarke, Michael (2001) 'War in the New International Order', *International Affairs*, 77:3, 663–71.

(2004) 'Does my Bomb Look Big in This? Britain's Nuclear Choices after Trident', *International Affairs*, 80:1, 49–62.

Clarke, Richard A. (2004) *Against All Enemies: Inside America's War on Terror*, New York: Free Press.

Clunan, Anne L. (2006) 'The Fight against Terrorist Financing', *Political Science Quarterly*, 121:4, 569–96.

Clutterbuck, Richard L. (1976) *Living with Terrorism*, New Rochelle: Arlington House.

Coaffee, Jon and David Murakami Wood (2006) 'Security is Coming Home: Rethinking Scale and Constructing Resilience in the Global Urban Response to Terrorist Risk', *International Relations*, 20:4, 503–17.

Cochran, Edwin (1996) 'Deliberate Ambiguity: An Analysis of Israel's Nuclear Strategy', *Journal of Strategic Studies*, 19:3, 321–42.

Cohen, Avner (1998) *Israel and the Bomb*, New York: Columbia University Press.

Cohen, Avner and Jospeh F. Pilat (1998) 'Assessing Virtual Nuclear Arsenals', *Survival*, 40:1, 129–44.

Cohen, Eliot A. (1982/3) 'The Long-term Crisis of the Alliance', *Foreign Affairs*, 61:2, 325–43.

(1996) 'A Revolution in Warfare', *Foreign Affairs*, 75:2, 37–55.

(2004) 'Change and Transformation in Military Affairs', *Journal of Strategic Studies*, 27:3, 395–407.

Cohen, Eliot A., Michael J. Eisenstadt and Andrew J. Bacevich (1998) 'Israel's Revolution in Security Affairs', *Survival*, 40:1, 68–91.

Cohen, Lenard J. (1994) 'Russia and the Balkans: Pan-Slavism, Partnership and Power', *International Journal*, 49:4, 814–45.

Cohen, Raymond (1994) 'Pacific Unions: A Reappraisal of the Theory that "Democracies do not Go to War with Each Other"', *Review of International Studies*, 20:3, 207–23.

Cohen, Samy (1994) 'France, Civil–Military Relations, and Nuclear Weapons', *Security Studies*, 4:1, 163–79.

Cohn, Carol (1987) 'Sex and Death in the Rational World of Defense Intellectuals', *Signs*, 12:4, 687–718.

Cohn, Carol, Helen Kinsella and Sheri Gibbings (2004) 'Women, Peace and Security', *International Feminist Journal of Politics*, 6:1, 130–40.

Coker, Chrisopher (1992) 'Post-modernity and the End of the Cold War: Has War been Disinvented?', *Review of International Studies*, 18:3, 189–98.

(2002) 'Globalisation and Insecurity in the Twenty-first Century: NATO and the Management of Risk', *Adelphi* 345, London: IISS.

Colby, Elbridge (2007) 'Restoring Deterrence', *Orbis*, 51:3, 413–28.

Collins, Alan R. (1998) 'GRIT, Gorbachev and the End of the Cold War', *Review of International Studies*, 24:2, 201–19.

(ed.) (2007) *Contemporary Security Studies*, Oxford: Oxford University Press.

Committee on International Security and Arms Control, National Academy of
    Sciences (1985) *Nuclear Arms Control: Background and Issues*, Washington,
    DC: National Academy Press.
Conflict Resolution (1957) 'An Editorial', *Conflict Resolution*, 1:1, 1–2.
Connelly, Philip and Robert Perlman (1975) *The Politics of Scarcity: Resource Con-
    flict in International Relations*, London: Oxford University Press for the Royal
    Institute of International Affairs.
Connolly, William E. (1991) *Identity/Difference: Democratic Negotiations of Political
    Paradox*, Ithaca: Cornell University Press.
Constantinou, Costas (1995) 'NATO's Caps: European Security and the Future of
    the North Atlantic Alliance', *Alternatives*, 20:2, 147–64.
Contemporary Security Policy (2005) Special Issue, 'The Domestic Politics of Missile
    Defence', 26:3, 385–704.
Cooper, Chester L. (1970) *The Lost Crusade*, London: MacGibbon & Kee.
Cooper, Neil (2002) 'State Collapse as Business: The Role of Conflict Trade and the
    Emerging Control Agenda', *Development and Change*, 33:5, 935–55.
Cooper, Peter (1965) 'The Development of the Concept of War', *Journal of Peace
    Research*, 2:1, 1–17.
Cooper, Scott (2004) 'State-centric Balance-of-Threat Theory', *Security Studies*,
    13:2, 306–49.
Cordesman, Anthony H. (1982) 'Deterrence in the 1980s: American Strategic Forces
    and Extended Deterrence', *Adelphi* 175, London: IISS.
Cornish, Paul and Geoffrey Edwards (2005) 'The Strategic Culture of the European
    Union: A Progress Report', *International Affairs*, 81:4, 801–20.
Cossa, Ralph and Jane Khanna (1997) 'East Asia: Economic Interdependence and
    Regional Security', *International Affairs*, 73:2, 219–34.
Cottey, Andrew (2004) 'NATO: Globalization or Redundancy?', *Contemporary Secu-
    rity Policy*, 25:3, 391–408.
Cotton, James (1993) 'North Korea's Nuclear Ambitions', *Adelphi* 275, London:
    IISS.
    (2005) 'The Proliferation Security Initiative and North Korea: Legality and
    Limitations of a Coalition Strategy', *Security Dialogue*, 36:2, 193–211.
Cox, Michael (2003a) 'Martians and Venutians in the New World Order', *Interna-
    tional Affairs*, 79:3, 523–32.
    (2003b) 'The Empire's Back in Town: Or America's Imperial Temptation –
    Again', *Millennium*, 32:1, 1–27.
Coyle, Philip E. and John B. Rhinelander (2001) 'National Missile Defence and
    the ABM Treaty: No Need to Wreck the Accord', *World Policy Journal*, 18:3,
    15–22.
Crawford, Beverly and Ronnie D. Lipschutz (1997) 'Discourses of War: Security
    and the Case of Yugoslavia', in Keith Krause and Michael C. Williams (eds.)
    Critical Security Studies, Minneapolis: University of Minnesota Press, 149–85.

Crawford, Neta C. (2000) 'The Passion of World Politics: Propositions on Emotion and Emotional Relationships', *International Security*, 24:4, 116–56.

(2004) 'The Road to Global Empire: The Logic of US Foreign Policy After 9/11', *Orbis*, 48:1, 685–703.

Crenshaw, Martha (ed.) (1995) *Terrorism in Context*, Philadelphia: Pennsylvania State University Press.

Croft, Stuart (1994) 'Continuity and Change in British Thinking About Nuclear Weapons', *Political Studies*, 42:2, 228–42.

(1996) 'European Integration, Nuclear Deterrence and Franco-British Nuclear Cooperation', *International Affairs*, 72:4, 771–87.

(2006) *Culture, Crisis and America's War on Terror*, Cambridge: Cambridge University Press.

Cronin, Audrey K. (2002) 'Rethinking Sovereignty: American Strategy in the Age of Terror', *Survival*, 44:2, 119–39.

(2002/3) 'Behind the Curve: Globalization and International Terrorism', *International Security*, 27:3, 30–58.

(2006) 'How al-Qaida Ends: The Decline and Demise of Terrorist Groups', *International Security*, 31:1, 7–48.

Cushman, Thomas and Stjepan G. Mestrovic (eds.) (1996) *This Time we Knew: Western Responses to the Genocide in Bosnia*, New York: New York University Press.

Daalder, Ivo H. (1992) 'The Future of Arms Control', *Survival*, 34:1, 51–73.

(2000) *Getting to Dayton: The Making of America's Bosnia Policy*, Washington, DC: Brookings Institution Press.

(2001) 'Are the United States and Europe Heading for Divorce?', *International Affairs*, 77:3, 553–67.

Daalder, Ivo H., James M. Goldgeier and James M. Lindsay (2000) 'Deploying NMD: Not Whether, But How', *Survival*, 42:1, 6–28.

Daalder, Ivo H. and James M. Lindsay (2003) *America Unbound: The Bush Revolution in Foreign Policy*, Washington, DC: Brookings Institution Press.

Dahlitz, Julie (1984) *Nuclear Arms Control with Effective International Agreements*, New York: United Nations Institute for Disarmament Research.

Dalby, Simon (1988) 'Geopolitical Discourse: The Soviet Union as Other', *Alternatives*, 13:4, 415–42.

Dankbaar, Ben (1984) 'Alternative Defence Policies and the Peace Movement', *Journal of Peace Research*, 21:2, 141–55.

Dannreuther, Roland (2007a) *International Security: The Contemporary Agenda*, Cambridge: Polity.

(2007b) 'War and Insecurity: Legacies of Northern and Southern State Formation', *Review of International Studies*, 33:2, 307–26.

Dauphinée, Elizabeth (2007) 'Reading the Ethics of Imagery', *Security Dialogue*, 38:2, 139–56.

Dauvergne, Peter (1993) 'Nuclear Power Development in Japan', *Asian Survey*, 33:6, 576–91.

Davies, Sara E. (2008) 'Securitizing Infectious Disease', *International Affairs*, 84:2, 295–313.

Davies, Simon J. (2004) 'Community Versus Deterrence: Managing Security and Nuclear Proliferation in Latin America and South Asia', *International Relations*, 18:1, 55–72.

Davis, Lynn Etheridge (1975/6) 'Limited Nuclear Options: Deterrence and the New American Doctrine', *Adelphi* 121, London: IISS.

Davis, Zachary and Benjamin Frankel (eds.) (1993) *The Proliferation Puzzle: Why Nuclear Weapons Spread and What Results*, London: Frank Cass.

Dawisha, Adeed (2000) 'Arab Nationalism and Islamism: Competitive Past, Uncertain Future', *International Studies Review*, 2:1, 79–90.

Daxecker, Ursula E. (2007) 'Perilous Polities? An Assessment of the Democratization-Conflict Linkage', *European Journal of International Relations*, 13:4, 527–53.

De Goede, Marieke (2008) 'The Politics of Preemption and the War on Terror in Europe', *European Journal of International Relations*, 14:1, 161–85.

de Mesquita, Bruce B. and James D. Morrow (1999) 'Sorting Through the Wealth of Notions', *International Security*, 24:2, 56–73.

de Mesquita, Bruce B. and William H. Riker (1982) 'An Assessment of the Merits of Selective Nuclear Proliferation', *Journal of Conflict Resolution*, 26:2, 283–306.

De Nevers, Renée (2006) 'The Geneva Conventions and New Wars', *Political Science Quarterly*, 121:3, 369–95.

(2007a) 'NATO's International Security Role in the Terrorist Era', *International Security*, 31:4, 34–66.

(2007b) 'Imposing International Norms: Great Powers and Norm Enforcement', *International Studies Review*, 9:1, 53–80.

De Porte, A. W. (1979) *Europe Between the Superpowers: The Enduring Balance*, New Haven: Yale University Press.

de Wilde, Jaap (1991) *Saved from Oblivion: Interdependence Theory in the First Half of the 20th Century. A Study on the Causality Between War and Complex Interdependence*, Aldershot: Dartmouth.

Dean, Jonathan (1987/8) 'Alternative Defence: Answer to NATO's Central Front Problems?', *International Affairs*, 64:1, 61–82.

DeBlois, Bruce M., Richard L. Garwin, R. Scott Kemp and Jeremy C. Marwell (2004) 'Space Weapons: Crossing the US Rubicon', *International Security*, 29:2, 50–84.

Debrix, Francois (1999) *Re-envisioning Peacekeeping: The United Nations and the Mobilization of Ideology*, Minneapolis: University of Minnesota Press.

(2005) 'Discourses of War, Geographies of Abjection: Reading Contemporary American Ideologies of Terror', *Third World Quarterly*, 26:7, 1157–72.

(2006) 'The Sublime Spectatorship of War: The Erasure of the Event in America's Politics of Terror and Aesthetics of Violence', *Millennium*, 34:3, 767–91.

Deibel, Terry L. (2002) 'The Death of a Treaty', *Foreign Affairs*, 81:5, 142–61.

Deibert, Ronald J. (2000) 'International Plug 'n' Play? Citizen Activism, the Internet and Global Public Policy', *International Studies Perspectives*, 1:3, 255–72.

(2003) 'Black Code: Censorship, Surveillance and the Militarisation of Cyberspace', *Millennium*, 32:3, 501–30.

Delpech, Therese (1998/9) 'Nuclear Weapons and the "New World Order": Early Warning from Asia?', *Survival*, 40:4, 57–76.

Denov, Myriam S. (2006) 'Wartime Sexual Violence: Assessing a Human Security Response to War-affected Girls in Sierra Leone', *Security Dialogue*, 37:3, 319–42.

Der Derian, James (1987) *On Diplomacy: A Genealogy of Western Estrangement*, Oxford: Basil Blackwell.

(1990) 'The (S)Pace of International Relations: Simulation, Surveillance and Speed', *International Studies Quarterly*, 34:3, 295–310.

(1992) *Antidiplomacy: Spies, Terror, Speed and War*, Oxford: Basil Blackwell.

(1995) 'The Value of Security: Hobbes, Marx, Nietzsche and Baudrillard', in Ronnie D. Lipschutz (ed.) *On Security*, New York: Columbia University Press, 24–45.

(2001) *Virtuous War: Mapping the Military–Industrial–Media–Entertainment Network*, Boulder: Westview Press.

(2003) 'The Question of Information Technology in International Relations', *Millennium*, 32:3, 441–56.

(2004) '9/11 and its Consequences for the Discipline', *Zeitschrift für Internationale Beziehungen*, 1, 89–110.

(2005) 'Imaging Terror: Logos, Pathos and Ethos', *Third World Quarterly*, 26:1, 23–37.

Desch, Michael C. (1998) 'Culture Clash: Assessing the Importance of Ideas in Security Studies', *International Security*, 23:1, 141–70.

(2007/8) 'America's Liberal Illiberalism: The Ideological Origins of Overreaction in US Foreign Policy', *International Security*, 32:3, 7–43.

Desjardins, Marie-France (1996) 'Rethinking Confidence-building Measures', *Adelphi* 307, London: IISS.

Deudney, Daniel (1990) 'The Case Against Linking Environmental Degradation and National Security', *Millennium*, 19:3, 461–76.

(1995) 'The Philadelphian System: Sovereignty, Arms Control and Balance of Power in the American States-union, circa 1787–1861', *International Organization*, 49:2, 191–228.

(2007) *Bounding Power: Republican Security Theory from the Polis to the Global Village*, Princeton: Princeton University Press.

Deudney, Daniel and G. John Ikenberry (1991) 'Soviet Reform and the End of the Cold War', *Review of International Studies*, 17:3, 225–50.

(1991/2) 'The International Sources of Soviet Change', *International Security*, 16:3, 74–118.

Deutch, John (1992) 'The New Nuclear Threat', *Foreign Affairs*, 71:4, 120–34.

Deutch, John, Arnold Kanter, Ernest Moniz and Daniel Poneman (2004/5) 'Making the World Safe for Nuclear Energy', *Survival*, 46:4, 65–79.

Deutsch, Karl W. (1957) 'Mass Communications and the Loss of Freedom in National Decision-making: A Possible Research Approach to Interstate Conflicts', *Conflict Resolution*, 1:2, 200–11.

Deutsch, Karl W., Sidney A. Burrell, Robert A. Kann, Maurice Lee Jr., Martin Lichterman, Raymond E. Lindgren, Francis L. Loewenheim and Richard W. van Wagenen (1957) *Political Community and the North Atlantic Area: International Organization in the Light of Historical Experience*, Princeton: Princeton University Press.

Dewitt, David (ed.) (1987) *Nuclear Non-proliferation and Global Security*, London: Croom Helm.

(1994) 'Common, Comprehensive and Cooperative Security', *Pacific Review*, 7:1, 1–15.

Dewitt, David and Brian Bow (1996) 'Proliferation Management in South-east Asia', *Survival*, 38:3, 67–81.

Diamond, Matthew (2002) 'No Laughing Matter: Post-September 11 Political Cartoons in Arab/Muslim Newspapers', *Political Communication*, 19:2, 251–72.

Dibb, Paul (1995) 'Towards a New Balance of Power in Asia', *Adelphi* 295, London: IISS.

Dibb, Paul, David D. Hale and Peter Prince (1998) 'The Strategic Implications of Asia's Economic Crisis', *Survival*, 40:2, 5–26.

(1999) 'Asia's Insecurity', *Survival*, 41:3, 5–20.

Dick, C. J. (2002) 'Conflict in a Changing World: Looking Two Decades Forward', *European Security*, 11:3, 20–45.

Diehl, Paul F. (1983) 'Arms Races and Escalation, a Closer Look', *Journal of Peace Research*, 20:3, 205–12.

(1985) 'Armaments without War', *Journal of Peace Research*, 22:3, 249–59.

Diehl, Paul F. and Mark J. C. Crescenzi (1998) 'Reconfiguring the Arms Race–War Debate', *Journal of Peace Research*, 35:1, 111–18.

Dienstbien, Jire (1991) 'Central Europe's Security', *Foreign Policy*, 83, 119–27.

Dietz, Mary (2003) 'Current Controversies in Feminist Theory', *Annual Review of Political Science*, 6, 399–431.

Dillon, Michael (1990) 'The Alliance of Security and Subjectivity', *Current Research on Peace and Violence*, 13:3, 101–24.

(2003) 'Virtual Security: A Life Science of (Dis)Order', *Millennium*, 32:3, 531–58.

Dillon, Michael and Julian Reid (2001) 'Global Liberal Governance: Biopolitics, Security and War', *Millennium*, 30:1, 41–66.

Dinerstein, Herbert S. (1976) *The Making of the Missile Crisis, October 1962*, Baltimore: Johns Hopkins University Press.

Dittmer, Lowell (2002) 'East Asia in the "New Era" in World Politics', *World Politics*, 55:1, 38–65.

Dixit, Aabha (1995) 'India–Pakistan: Are Commonly Accepted Confidence-building Structures Relevant?', *Security Dialogue*, 26:2, 191–203.

Dobbins, James (2006) 'Preparing for Nation-building', *Survival*, 48:3, 27–40.

Dodds, Klaus (2007) 'Steve Bell's Eye: Cartoons, Geopolitics and the Visualization of the "War on Terror"', *Security Dialogue*, 38:2, 157–78.

Doder, Dusko (1993) 'Yugoslavia: New War, Old Hatreds', *Foreign Policy*, 91, 3–23.

Dodge, Toby (2005) 'Iraq's Future: The Aftermath of Regime Change', *Adelphi* 372, London: IISS.

(2007) 'The Causes of US Failure in Iraq', *Survival*, 49:1, 85–106.

Dodge, Toby and Steven Simon (2003) 'Iraq at the Crossroads: State and Society in the Shadow of Regime Change', *Adelphi* 354, London: IISS.

Dolan, Anthony (1992) *Undoing the Evil Empire: How Reagan Won the Cold War*, Washington DC: American Enterprise Institute.

Dombey, Norman, David Fischer and William Walker (1987) 'Becoming a Non-nuclear Weapon State: Britain, the NPT and Safeguards', *International Affairs*, 63:2, 191–204.

Dombrowski, Peter and Rodger A. Payne (2006) 'The Emerging Consensus for Preventive War', *Survival*, 48:2, 115–36.

Doran, Charles F. (1973) 'A Theory of Bounded Deterrence', *Journal of Conflict Resolution*, 17:2, 243–69.

Dorian, Thomas F. and Leonard S. Spector (1981) 'Covert Nuclear Trade and the International Nonproliferation Regime', *Journal of International Affairs*, 35:1, 29–68.

Doty, Roxanne Lynn (1996) *Imperial Encounters*, Minneapolis: University of Minnesota Press.

(2007) 'States of Exception on the Mexico–US Border: Security, "Decisions" and Civilian Border Patrols', *International Political Sociology*, 1:2, 113–37.

Douglas, Frank 'Scott' (2007) 'Waging the Inchoate War: Defining, Fighting and Second-guessing the "Long War"', *Journal of Strategic Studies*, 30:3, 391–420.

Downs, Erica S. (2004) 'The Chinese Energy Security Debate', *The China Quarterly*, 177, 21–41.

Doyle, Michael (1986) 'Liberalism and World Politics', *American Political Science Review*, 80:4, 1151–69.

Dreyer, June T. (2006) 'Sino-Japanese Rivalry and its Implications for Developing Nations', *Asian Survey*, 46:4, 538–57.

Drifte, Reinhard (1999) 'An Old Architecture for Peace? Reconfiguring Japan Among Unreconfigured Great Powers', *The Pacific Review*, 12:3, 479–89.

Dueck, Colin (2003/4) 'Hegemony on the Cheap, Liberal Internationalism from Wilson to Bush', *World Policy Journal*, 20:4, 1–11.

(2004a) 'New Perspectives on American Grand Strategy', *International Security*, 28:4, 197–216.

(2004b) 'Ideas and Alternatives in American Grand Strategy', *Review of International Studies*, 30:4, 511–35.

Dueck, Colin and Ray Takeyh (2007) 'Iran's Nuclear Challenge', *Political Science Quarterly*, 122:2, 189–205.

Duffield, John S. (1991) 'The Evolution of NATO's Strategy of Flexible Response: A Reinterpretation', *Security Studies*, 1:1, 132–56.

(1994/5) 'NATO's Functions After the Cold War', *Political Science Quarterly*, 109:5, 763–87.

(2001) 'Why is there no APTO? Why is there no OSCAP?: Asia–Pacific Security Institutions in Comparative Perspective', *Contemporary Security Policy*, 22:2, 69–95.

Duffield, Mark (2001) *Global Governance and the New Wars: The Merging of Development and Security*, London: Zed Books.

Dugard, John (1974) 'International Terrorism: Problems of Definition', *International Affairs*, 50:1, 67–81.

Dunlop, John (1993–4) 'Russia, Confronting a Loss of Empire', *Political Science Quarterly*, 108:4, 603–34.

Dunn, David H. (2005) 'Isolationism Revisited: Seven Persistent Myths in the Contemporary American Foreign Policy Debate', *Review of International Studies*, 31:2, 237–61.

(2007) 'Real Men Want to go to Tehran: Bush, Pre-emption and the Iranian Nuclear Challenge', *International Affairs*, 83:1, 19–38.

Dunn, Lewis A. (1991) 'Containing Nuclear Proliferation', *Adelphi* 263, London: IISS.

Dunn, Lewis A. and Victor Alessi (2000/1) 'Arms Control by other Means', *Survival*, 42:4, 129–40.

Dunne, Tim and Nicholas J. Wheeler (2004) '"We the Peoples": Contending Discourses of Security in Human Rights Theory and Practice', *International Relations*, 18:1, 9–23.

Dupont, Alan (2008) 'The Strategic Implications of Climate Change', *Survival*, 50:3, 29–54.

Dusch, William (1987) 'The Future of the ABM Treaty', *Adelphi* 223, London: IISS.

Eck, Kristine and Lisa Hultman (2007) 'One-sided Violence Against Civilians in War: Insights from New Fatality Data', *Journal of Peace Research*, 44:2, 233–46.

Edwardes, Michael (1967) 'India, Pakistan and Nuclear Weapons', *International Affairs*, 43:4, 655–63.

Edwards, Paul N. (1996) *The Closed World: Computers and the Politics of Discourse in Cold War America*, Cambridge, MA: MIT Press.

Egnell, Robert (2006) 'Explaining US and British Performance in Complex Expeditionary Operations: The Civil Military Dimension', *Journal of Strategic Studies*, 29:6, 1041–75.

Eichenberg, Richard C. (2003) 'Gender Differences in Public Attitudes Toward the Use of Force by the United States, 1990–2003', *International Security*, 28:1, 110–41.

Einhord, Robert J. and Gary Samore (2002) 'Ending Russian Assistance to Iran's Nuclear Bomb', *Survival*, 44:2, 51–70.

Eisenstadt, Michael (1999) 'Living with a Nuclear Iran', *Survival*, 41:3, 124–48.

Ekovich, Steven (2004) 'Iran and New Threats in the Persian Gulf and Middle East', *Orbis*, 48:1, 71–87.

El-Baradei, Mohamed (1996) 'On Compliance with Nuclear Nonproliferation Obligations', *Security Dialogue*, 27:1, 17–26.

Elbe, Stefan (2003) 'HIV/AIDS and the Changing Landscape of War in Africa', *International Security*, 24:2, 159–77.

(2006) 'Should HIV/AIDS be Securitized? The Ethical Dilemmas of Linking HIV/AIDS and Security', *International Studies Quarterly*, 50:1, 119–44.

Elden, Stuart (2007) 'Blair, Neo-Conservatism and the War on Territorial Integrity', *International Politics*, 44:1, 37–57.

Elshtain, Jean B. (1981) *Public Man, Private Woman: Women in Social and Political Thought*, Princeton: Princeton University Press.

(1987) *Women and War*, Chicago: University of Chicago Press.

Emmers, Ralf (2005) 'Regional Hegemonies and the Exercise of Power in Southeast Asia: A Study of Indonesia and Vietnam', *Asian Survey*, 45:4, 645–65.

Enders, Walter and Todd Sandler (2006) 'Distribution of Transnational Terrorism Among Countries by Income, Class and Geography After 9/11', *International Studies Quarterly*, 50:2, 367–93.

Enloe, Cynthia (1983) *Does Khaki Become You? The Militarisation of Women's Lives*, London: Pluto.

(1989) *Bananas, Beaches and Bases: Making Feminist Sense of International Politics*, Berkeley: University of California Press.

(2004a) *The Curious Feminist: Searching for Women in the New Age of Empire*, Berkeley: University of California Press.

(2004b) 'Wielding Masculinity Inside Abu Ghraib: Making Feminist Sense of an American Military Scandal', *Asian Journal of Women's Studies*, 10:3, 89–102.

Epstein, Charlotte (2007) 'Guilty Bodies, Productive Bodies, Destructive Bodies: Crossing the Biometric Borders', *International Political Sociology*, 1:2, 149–64.

Erickson, Andrew and Lyle Goldstein (2006) 'Hoping for the Best, Preparing for the Worst: China's Response to US Hegemony', *Journal of Strategic Studies*, 29:6, 955–86.

Erickson, Christian W. (2007) 'Counter-terror Culture: Ambiguity, Subversion, or Legitimization', *Security Dialogue*, 38:2, 197–214.

Erickson, John (1982) 'The Soviet View of Deterrence', *Survival*, 24:6, 242–51.

Ermarth, Fritz W. (1978) 'Contrasts in American and Soviet Strategic Thought', *International Security*, 3:2, 138–55.

Evangelista, Matthew (1984) 'Why the Soviets Buy the Weapons They Do', *World Politics*, 36:4, 357–618.

(1988) *Innovation and the Arms Race: How the United States and the Soviet Union Develop New Military Technologies*, Ithaca: Cornell University Press.

Evans, Glynne (1997) 'Responding to Crises in the African Great Lakes', *Adelphi* 311, London: IISS.

Everts, Philip P. (1972) 'Developments and Trends in Peace and Conflict Research, 1965–1971: A Survey of Institutions', *Journal of Conflict Resolution*, 16:4, 477–510.

Fahmy, Nabil (1998) 'Nuclear Proliferation: Is the Middle East Next?', *Asia-Pacific Review*, 5:3, 123–38.

Failey, Kathleen (1995) 'Responding to the Threat of Biological Weapons', *Security Dialogue*, 26:4, 383–98.

Falk, Richard A. and Richard J. Barnet (1965) *Security in Disarmament*, Princeton: Princeton University Press.

Falkenrath, Richard A. (1998) 'Confronting Nuclear, Biological and Chemical Terrorism', *Survival*, 40:3, 43–6.

(2001) 'Problems of Preparedness: US Readiness for a Domestic Terrorist Attack', *International Security*, 25:4, 147–86.

Farrell, Theo (2002) 'Constructivist Security Studies: Portrait of a Research Program', *International Studies Review*, 4:1, 49–72.

Farrell, Theo and Helene Lambert (2001) 'International Law, National Norms and American Nuclear Use', *Review of International Studies*, 27:3, 309–26.

Feaver, Peter D. (1992/3) 'Command and Control in Emerging Nuclear Nations', *International Security*, 17:3, 160–87.

(1997) 'Neooptimists and the Enduring Problem of Nuclear Proliferation', *Security Studies*, 6:4, 93–125.

Feaver, Peter D. and Emerson Niou (1996) 'Managing Nuclear Proliferation: Condemn, Strike or Assist?', *International Studies Quarterly*, 40:2, 209–34.

Fehl, Caroline (2008) 'Living with a Reluctant Hegemon: The Transatlantic Conflict Over Multilateral Arms Control', *European Journal of International Relations*, 14:2, 259–87.

Feldman, Shai (1981) 'A Nuclear Middle East', *Survival*, 23:3, 107–15.

Ferdinand, Peter (2007) 'Sunset, Sunrise: China and Russia Construct a New Relationship', *International Affairs*, 83:5, 841–67.

Ferguson, Michaele L. (2005) '"W" Stands for Women: Feminism and Security Rhetoric in the Post-9/11 Bush Administration', *Politics and Gender*, 1:1, 9–38.

Fierke, Karin M. (1996) 'Multiple Identities, Interfacing Games: The Social Construction of Western Action in Bosnia', *European Journal of International Relations*, 2:4, 467–97.

(1998) *Changing Games, Changing Strategies: Critical Investigations in Security*, Manchester: Manchester University Press.

(1999) 'Dialogues of Manoeuvre and Entanglement: NATO, Russia and the CEECs', *Millennium*, 28:1, 27–52.

(2000) 'Logics of Force and Dialogue: The Iraq/UNSCOM Crisis and Social Interaction', *European Journal of International Relations*, 6:3, 335–71.

(2007) *Critical Approaches to International Security*, Cambridge: Polity.

Finnemore, Martha (1996) 'Constructing Norms of Humanitarian Intervention', in Peter J. Katzenstein (ed.) *The Culture of National Security: Norms and Identity in World Politics*, New York: Columbia University Press, 153–85.

(2003) *The Purpose of Intervention: Changing Beliefs About the Use of Force*, Ithaca: Cornell University Press.

Fischer, David and Paul Szasz (1985) *Safeguarding the Atom: A Critical Appraisal*, Stockholm and London: SIPRI and Taylor & Francis.

Fischer, Dietrich (1982) 'Invulnerability without Threat: The Swiss Concept of General Defence', *Journal of Peace Research*, 19:3, 205–25.

Fishel, Wesley R. (1966) 'Vietnam: The Broadening War', *Asian Survey*, 6:1, 49–58.

Fisher, David (1992) *Stopping the Spread of Nuclear Weapons: The Past and Prospects*, London: Routledge.

Fisher, Georges (1971) *The Non-proliferation of Nuclear Weapons*, New York: St. Martin's Press.

Fitzpatrick, Mark (2006a) 'Iran and North Korea: The Proliferation Nexus', *Survival*, 48:1, 61–80.

(2006b) 'Assessing Iran's Nuclear Programme', *Survival*, 48:3, 5–26.

(2007) 'Can Iran's Nuclear Capability be Kept Latent?', *Survival*, 49:1, 33–58.

Fitzsimmons, Michael (2006) 'The Problem of Uncertainty in Strategic Planning', *Survival*, 48:4, 131–46.

Flibbert, Andrew (2006) 'The Road to Baghdad: Ideas and Intellectuals in Explanations of the Iraq War', *Security Studies*, 15:2, 310–52.

Floyd, Rita (2007) 'Towards a Consequentialist Evaluation of Security: Bringing Together the Copenhagen School of Security Studies and the Welsh School of Security Studies', *Review of International Studies*, 33:2, 327–50.

Foley, Gerald and Charlotte Nassim (1976) *The Energy Question*, Harmondsworth: Penguin Books.

Fontanel, Jacques (1986) 'An Underdeveloped Peace Movement: The Case of France', *Journal of Peace Research*, 23:2, 175–92.

Foot, Rosemary (2004) 'Human Rights and Counter-terrorism in America's Asia Policy', *Adelphi* 363, London: IISS.

(2006a) 'Chinese Strategies in a US-hegemonic Global Order: Accommodating and Hedging', *International Affairs*, 82:1, 77–94.

(2006b) 'Human Rights in Conflict', *Survival*, 48:3, 109–26.

Forsberg, Tuomas (1999) 'Power, Interests and Trust: Explaining Gorbachev's Choices at the End of the Cold War', *Review of International Studies*, 25:4, 603–21.

Fortmann, Michel (1992/3) 'The Other Side of Midnight: Opaque Proliferation Revisited', *International Journal*, 48:1, 151–75.

Foucault, Michel (1969) *The Archaeology of Knowledge*, London: Tavistock Publications.

(1970) *The Order of Things: An Archaeology of the Human Sciences*, New York: Random House.

Fowler, Michael C. (2005) *Amateur Soldiers, Global Wars: Insurgency and Modern Conflict*, Westport: Praeger.

Fox, Jonathan (2001) 'Religion as an Overlooked Element of International Relations', *International Studies Review*, 3:3, 53–73.

(2007) 'The Rise of Religion and the Fall of the Civilization Paradigm as Explanations for Intra-state Conflict', *Cambridge Review of International Affairs*, 20:3, 361–82.

Fox, Mary-Jane (2004) 'Girl Soldiers: Human Security and Gendered Insecurity', *Security Dialogue*, 35:4, 465–79.

Frank, Andre G. (1967) *Capitalism and Underdevelopment in Latin America*, New York: Monthly Review Press.

Fravel, M. Taylor (2005) 'Regime Insecurity and International Cooperation: Explaining China's Compromises in Territorial Disputes', *International Security*, 30:2, 46–83.

Freedman, Amy L. and Robert C. Gray (2004) 'The Implications of Missile Defense for Northeast Asia', *Orbis*, 48:2, 335–50.

Freedman, Lawrence (1975) 'Israel's Nuclear Policy', *Survival*, 17:3, 114–20.

(1981a) *The Evolution of Nuclear Strategy*, London: Macmillan. [Subsequent editions in 1989 and 2003.]

(1981b) 'Britain: The First Ex-nuclear Power?', *International Security*, 6:2, 80–104.

(1981/2) 'NATO Myths', *Foreign Policy*, 45, 48–68.

(1984a) 'Strategic Arms Control', in Josephine O'Connor Howe (ed.) *Armed Peace: The Search for World Security*, London: Macmillan, 31–47.

(1984b) 'Indignation, Influence and Strategic Studies', *International Affairs*, 60:2, 207–19.

(1988) 'I Exist; Therefore I Deter', *International Security*, 13:1, 177–95.

(1991) 'Whither Nuclear Strategy?', in Ken Booth (ed.) *New Thinking About Strategy and International Security*, London: HarperCollins, 75–89.

(1992) 'Order and Disorder in the New World', *Foreign Affairs*, 71:1, 20–37.

(1998) 'The Revolution in Strategic Affairs', *Adelphi* 318, London: IISS.

(1998/9) 'The Changing Forms of Military Conflict', *Survival*, 40:4, 39–56.

(2001) 'The Third World War?', *Survival*, 43:4, 61–87.

(2004) *Deterrence*, Cambridge: Polity.

(2005) 'Deterrence: A Reply', *Journal of Strategic Studies*, 28:5, 789–801.

(2006a) 'Iraq, Liberal Wars and Illiberal Containment', *Survival*, 48:4, 51–66.

(2006b) 'The Transformation of Strategic Affairs', *Adelphi* 378, London: IISS.

Freeman, Michael (2003) *Freedom or Security: The Consequences for Democracies Using Emergency Powers to Fight Terror*, New York: Praeger.

Frei, Daniel and Christian Catrina (1983) *Risks of Unintentional Nuclear War*, London: Croom Helm.

Friedberg, Aaron L. (1993) 'Ripe for Rivalry: Prospects for Peace in a Multipolar Asia', *International Security*, 18:3, 5–33.

(2000) 'Will Europe's Past be Asia's Future?', *Survival*, 42:3, 147–59.

(2002) '11 September and the Future of Sino-American Relations', *Survival*, 44:1, 33–49.

Frisch, Hillel (2006) 'Motivation or Capabilities? Israeli Counterterrorism Against Palestinian Suicide Bombings and Violence', *Journal of Strategic Studies*, 29:5, 843–69.

Fromkin, David (1975) 'The Strategy of Terrorism', *Foreign Affairs*, 53:4, 692–93.

Fromkin, David and James Chace (1984/5) 'What Are the Lessons of Vietnam?', *Foreign Affairs*, 63:4, 722–46.

Frost, Robin M. (2005) 'Nuclear Terrorism After 9/11', *Adelphi* 378, London: IISS.

Frye, Alton (1992) 'Zero Ballistic Missiles', *Foreign Policy*, 88, 3–20.

Fukuyama, Francis (1992) *The End of History and the Last Man*, London: Penguin.

Fuller, Graham E. (1993) 'The Fate of the Kurds', *Foreign Affairs*, 72:2, 108–21.

Funabashi, Yoichi (1991) 'Japan and the New World Order', *Foreign Affairs*, 70:5, 58–74.

Gaddis, John L. (1992/3) 'International Relations Theory and the End of the Cold War', *International Security*, 17:3, 5–58.

Gahlaut, Seema and Gary K. Bertsch (2004) 'The War on Terror and the Nonproliferation Regime', *Orbis*, 48:3, 489–504.

Gall, Norman (1976) 'Atoms for Brazil, Dangers for All', *Foreign Policy*, 23, 155–201.

Gallois, Pierre (1961) *The Balance of Terror: Strategy for the Nuclear Age*, Boston: Houghton Mifflin.

Galtung, Johan (1964) 'Foreign Policy Opinion as a Function of Social Position', *Journal of Peace Research*, 1:3/4, 206–31.

(1969) 'Violence, Peace and Peace Research', *Journal of Peace Research*, 6:3, 167–91.

(1971) 'A Structural Theory of Imperialism', *Journal of Peace Research*, 8:2, 81–117.

(1984) 'Transarmament: From Offensive to Defensive Defence', *Journal of Peace Research*, 21:2, 127–39.

Galtung, Johan and Mari H. Ruge (1965) 'The Structure of Foreign News', *Journal of Peace Research*, 2:1, 64–91.

Ganguly, Sumit (1993) 'Ethno-religious Conflict in South Asia', *Survival*, 35:2, 88–109.

(1999) 'India's Pathway to Pokhran II', *International Security*, 23:4, 148–78.

Ganguly, Sumit and Dinshaw Mistry (2006) 'The Case for the US/India Nuclear Agreement', *World Policy Journal*, 23:2, 11–9.

Ganguly, Sumit and R. Harrison Wagner (2004) 'India and Pakistan: Bargaining in the Shadow of Nuclear War', *Journal of Strategic Studies*, 27:3, 479–507.

Gantzel, Klaus J. (2002) 'Neue Kriege? Neue Kämpfer?', in Bruno Schoch, Corinna Hauswedell, Christoph Weller, Ulrich Ratsch and Reinhard Mutz (eds.) *Friedensgutachten 2002*, Hamburg: LIT, 80–8.

Gardner, Gary (1994) *Nuclear Nonproliferation Primer*, Boulder: Lynne Rienner.

Garnham, David (1988) *The Politics of European Defence Cooperation: Germany, France, Britain and America*, Cambridge: Ballinger.

Garrett, Banning N. and Bonnie S. Glaser (1995/6) 'Chinese Perspectives on Nuclear Arms Control', *International Security*, 20:3, 43–78.

Garthoff, Raymond (1988) 'Cuban Missile Crisis: The Soviet Story', *Foreign Policy*, 72, 61–80.

Garver, John W. (2001) 'The Restoration of Sino-Indian Comity Following India's Nuclear Tests', *China Quarterly*, 168, 865–89.

Gates, David (1987) 'Area Defence Concepts: The West German Debate', *Survival*, 29:4, 301–17.

Gates, Scott, Torbjørn Knutsen and Jonathon Moses (1996) 'Democracy and Peace: A More Skeptical View', *Journal of Peace Research*, 33:1, 1–10.

Gati, Charles (1992) 'From Sarajevo to Sarajevo', *Foreign Affairs*, 71:4, 64–78.

Gause, Gregory F. (2004) 'Balancing What? Threat Perception and Alliance Choice in the Gulf', *Security Studies*, 13:2, 273–305.

Gavin, Francis J. (2004) 'Blasts from the Past: Proliferation Lessons from the 1960s', *International Security*, 29:3, 100–13.

Gebhard, Paul (1994) 'The United States and European Security', *Adelphi* 286, London: IISS.

Gedza, Dimitrije S. (1976) 'Yugoslavia and Nuclear Weapons', *Survival*, 18:3, 116–18.

Gelber, Harry G. (1974) 'Technical Innovation and Arms Control', *World Politics*, 26:4, 509–41.

Gellner, Ernest (1983) *Nations and Nationalism*, Oxford: Basil Blackwell.

Gentry, John A. (2006) 'Norms and Military Power: NATO's War Against Yugoslavia', *Security Studies*, 15:2, 187–224.

George, Alexander L. (1984) 'Crisis Management: The Interaction of Political and Military Considerations', *Survival*, 25:5, 223–34.

Ghosh, Probal K. (2003) 'Layered Defence Concept: Some Architectural Options for an Expanding Ballistic Missile Shield', *Contemporary Security Policy*, 24:3, 67–90.

(2004) 'Deterrence Asymmetry and Other Challenges to Small Nuclear Forces', *Contemporary Security Policy*, 25:1, 37–53.

Gibler, Douglas M. (2007) 'Bordering on Peace: Democracy, Territorial Issues, and Conflict', *International Studies Quarterly*, 51:3, 509–32.

Giegerich, Bastian, Darya Pushkina and Adam Mount (2006) 'Towards a Strategic Partnership? The US and Russian Response to the European Security and Defence Policy', *Security Dialogue*, 37:3, 385–407.

Giegerich, Bastian and William Wallace (2004) 'Not Such a Soft Power: The External Deployment of European Forces', *Survival*, 46:2, 163–82.

Gill, Bates and Evan S. Medeiros (2000) 'Foreign and Domestic Influence on China's Arms Control and Nonproliferation Policies', *China Quarterly*, 161, 66–94.

Gilpin, Robert (1981) *War and Change in World Politics*, Cambridge: Cambridge University Press.

Gilson, Julie (2007) 'Strategic Regionalism in East Asia', *Review of International Studies*, 33:1, 145–63.

Girling, John L. S. (1980) *America and the Third World: Revolution and Intervention*, London: Routledge & Kegan Paul.

Gizweski, Peter (1999) 'Managed Proliferation in South Asia', *International Journal*, 54:2, 279–91.

Gjessing, Gutrom (1967) 'Ecology and Peace Research', *Journal of Peace Research*, 4:2, 125–39.

Glaser, Charles L. (1984) 'Why Even Good Defenses may be Bad', *International Security*, 9:2, 92–123.

(1985) 'Do we Want the Missile Defences we Can Build?', *International Security*, 10:1, 25–57.

(1993) 'Why NATO is Still Best: Future Security Arrangements for Europe', *International Security*, 18:1, 5–50.

(1998) 'The Flawed Case for Nuclear Disarmament', *Survival*, 40:1, 112–28.

(2004) 'When are Arms Races Dangerous? Rational versus Suboptimal Arming', *International Security*, 28:4, 44–84.

Glaser, Charles L. and Steve Fetter (2001) 'National Missile Defense and the Future of US Nuclear Weapons Policy', *International Security*, 26:1, 40–92.

Gleditsch, Nils P. (1967) 'Trends in World Airline Patterns', *Journal of Peace Research*, 4:4, 366–408.

(1977) 'Towards a Multilateral Aviation Treaty', *Journal of Peace Research*, 14:3, 239–59.

(1989) 'Focus On: Journal of Peace Research', *Journal of Peace Research*, 26:1, 1–5.

(1993) 'The Most-cited Articles in *JPS*', *Journal of Peace Research*, 30:4, 445–49.

　　　REFERENCES

(2004) 'Peace Research and International Relations in Scandinavia: From Endur-
ing Rivalry to Stable Peace?', in Stefano Guzzini and Dietrich Jung (eds.)
Contemporary Security Analysis and Copenhagen Peace Research, London:
Routledge, 15–26.

Gleditsch, Nils P. and Olav Njølstad (1990) *Arms Races: Technological and Political
Dynamics*, London: Sage and PRIO.

Glenny, Misha (1995) 'Heading Off War in the Southern Balkans', *Foreign Affairs*,
74:3, 98–108.

Global Society (2007) Special Issue, 'Risk and International Relations: A New
Research Agenda', 21:1, 1–132.

Goh, Evelyn (2007/8) 'Great Powers and Hierarchical Order in Southeast Asia:
Analyzing Regional Security Strategies', *International Security*, 32:3, 113–57.

Goldberg, Louis C. (1968) 'Ghetto Riots and Others: The Faces of Civil Disorder
in 1967', *Journal of Peace Research*, 5:2, 116–32.

Goldblat, Jozef (1978) *Arms Control: A Survey and Appraisal of Multilateral Agreement*, London: Taylor & Francis and SIPRI.

(2000) *Nuclear Disarmament: Obstacles to Banishing the Bomb*, London: I. B.
Tauris.

(2003) 'Efforts to Control Arms in Outer Space', *Security Dialogue*, 34:1, 103–8.

Goldfischer, David (1998) 'Rethinking the Unthinkable After the Cold War: Toward
Long-term Policy Planning', *Security Studies*, 7:4, 165–94.

Goldgeier, James M. and Michael McFaul (1992) 'A Tale of Two Worlds: Core
and Periphery in the Post-Cold War Era', *International Organization*, 46:2,
467–91.

Goldman, Emily O. and Richard B. Andres (1999) 'Systemic Effects of Military
Innovation and Diffusion', *Security Studies*, 8:4, 79–125.

Goldstein, Avery (2001) 'The Diplomatic Face of China's Grand Strategy: A Rising
Power's Emerging Choice', *China Quarterly*, 168, 835–64.

Goldstein, Lyle J. (2003) 'Do Nascent WMD Arsenals Deter? The Sino-Soviet Crisis
of 1969', *Political Science Quarterly*, 118:1, 53–79.

Gong, Ro-myung and Gerald Segal (1993) 'The Consequences of Arms Proliferation
in Asia', *Adelphi* 276, London: IISS.

Gonzalez-Perez, Margaret (2007) *Women and Terrorism: Female Activity in Domestic
and International Terror Groups*, London: Routledge.

Goodman, Allan E. (1972) 'South Vietnam and the New Security', *Asian Survey*,
12:2, 121–37.

Gordon, Michael R. (2006) 'Break Point? Iraq and America's Military Forces', *Survival*, 48:4, 67–81.

Gordon, Philip H. (1995) 'Charles de Gaulle and the Nuclear Revolution', *Security
Studies*, 5:1, 118–48.

(1998) 'The Transatlantic Allies and the Changing Middle East', *Adelphi* 322,
London: IISS.

(2001) 'Bush, Missile Defence and the Atlantic Alliance' *Survival*, 43:1, 17–36.

(2005) 'Trading Places: America and Europe in the Middle East', *Survival*, 47:2, 87–100.

Gordon, Sandy (1994) 'Capping South Asia's Nuclear Weapons Programs: A Window of Opportunity?', *Asian Survey*, 34:7, 662–73.

Gormley, Dennis M. (2001) 'Dealing with the Threat of Cruise Missiles', *Adelphi* 339, London: IISS.

(2002) 'Enriching Expectations: 11 September's Lessons for Missile Defence', *Survival*, 44:2, 19–35.

(2006) 'Securing Nuclear Obsolescence', *Survival*, 48:3, 127–48.

Gottemoeller, Rose (1996) 'Preventing a Nuclear Nightmare', *Survival*, 38:2, 170–4.

Gow, James (1997) *Triumph of the Lack of Will: International Diplomacy and the Yugoslav War*, London: Hurst.

Grant, Rebecca (1992) 'The Quagmire of Gender and International Security', in V. Spike Peterson (ed.) *Gendered States: Feminist (Re)Visions of International Relations Theory*, Boulder: Lynne Rienner, 83–97.

Gray, Chris H. (1997) *Postmodern War: The New Politics of Conflict*, London: Routledge.

Gray, Colin S. (1971) 'The Arms Race Phenomenon', *World Politics*, 24:1, 39–79.

(1974) 'The Urge to Compete: Rationales for Arms Racing', *World Politics*, 26:2, 207–33.

(1975) 'SALT II and the Strategic Balance', *British Journal of International Studies*, 1:3, 183–208.

(1977) 'Across the Nuclear Divide: Strategic Studies Past and Present', *International Security*, 2:1, 24–46.

(1980) 'Strategic Stability Reconsidered', *Daedalus*, 109:4, 135–54.

(1982a) *Strategic Studies and Public Policy: The American Experience*, Lexington: University Press of Kentucky.

(1982b) *Strategic Studies: A Critical Assessment*, London: Aldwych Press.

(1992) 'New Directions for Strategic Studies: How Can Theory Help Practice?', *Security Studies*, 1:4, 610–35.

(1996) 'Arms Races and Other Pathetic Fallacies: A Case for Deconstruction', *Review of International Studies*, 22:3, 323–35.

(1997) 'The American Revolution in Military Affairs: An Interim Assessment', *Occasional Paper 28*, Camberley: The Strategic and Combat Studies Institute.

(1999) 'Clausewitz Rules, OK? The Future is the Past – with GPS', *Review of International Studies*, 25: Special Issue, 161–82.

Gray, Victor (1999) 'The Albanian Diaspora and Security in the Balkans', *European Security*, 8:3, 133–48.

Green, Philip (1966) *Deadly Logic: The Theory of Nuclear Deterrence*, Columbus: Ohio State University Press.

Greenhill, Kelly M. (2001) 'Mission Impossible? Preventing Deadly Conflict in the African Great Lakes Region', *Security Studies*, 11:1, 77–124.

Greenwood, Ted, George W. Rathjens and Jack Ruina (1976) 'Nuclear Power and Weapons Proliferation', *Adelphi* 130, London: IISS.

Gresh, Alain (1998) 'Turkish–Israeli–Syrian Relations and Their Impact on the Middle East', *The Middle East Journal*, 52:2, 204–18.

Gries, Peter H. (2005a) 'China Eyes the Hegemon', *Orbis*, 49:3, 401–12.

(2005b) 'China's "New Thinking" on Japan', *China Quarterly*, 184, 831–50.

Griner, Shlomo (2002) 'Living in a World Risk Society: A Reply to Mikkel V. Rasmussen', *Millennium*, 31:1, 149–60.

Grinter, Laurence E. (1975) 'How They Lost: Doctrines, Strategies and Outcomes of the Vietnam War', *Asian Survey*, 15:12, 1114–32.

Gross, Michael L. (2005/6) 'Killing Civilians Intentionally: Double Effect, Reprisal, and Necessity in the Middle East', *Political Science Quarterly*, 120:4, 555–79.

Grosser, Alfred (1980) *The Western Alliance: Euro-American Relations Since 1945*, London: Macmillan.

Grovogui, Siba N. (2007) 'Postcolonialism', in Tim Dunne, Milja Kurki and Steve Smith (eds.) *International Relations Theory: Discipline and Diversity*, Oxford: Oxford University Press, 229–46.

GSC Newsletter (2001) Program on Global Security and Cooperation, Social Science Research Council, no. 1.

Guehenno, Jean-Marie (1998/9) 'The Impact of Globalization on Strategy', *Survival*, 40:4, 5–19.

Guertner, Gary L. (1988) 'Three Images of Soviet Arms Control Compliance', *Political Science Quarterly*, 103:2, 321–46.

Gugliamelli, Juan E. (1976) 'The Brazilian–German Nuclear Deal: A View from Argentina', *Survival*, 18:4, 162–65.

Guldimann, Tim (2007) 'The Iranian Nuclear Impasse', *Survival*, 49:3, 169–78.

Gummett, Philip (1981) 'From NPT to INFCE: Developments in Thinking about Nuclear Non-proliferation', *International Affairs*, 57:4, 549–67.

Gunnell, John G. (1993) *The Descent of Political Theory: The Genealogy of an American Vocation*, Chicago: University of Chicago Press.

Gupta, Amit (1999) 'Nuclear Forces in South Asia: Prospects for Arms Control', *Security Dialogue*, 30:3, 319–30.

Gurr, Ted R. (1970) *Why Men Rebel*, Princeton: Princeton University Press.

Guttman, Robert J. (ed.) (2001) *Europe in the New Century: Visions of an Emerging Superpower*, Boulder: Lynne Rienner.

Haas, Richard (1994) 'Military Force: A User's Guide', *Foreign Policy*, 96, 21–37.

Haftendorn, Helga (1991) 'The Security Puzzle: Theory-building and Discipline-building in International Security', *International Studies Quarterly*, 35:1, 3–17.

Hagerty, Devin T. (1995/6) 'Nuclear Deterrence in South Asia: The 1990 Indo-Pakistan Crisis', *International Security*, 20:3, 79–114.

(1999) 'South Asia's Big Bangs: Causes, Consequences and Prospects', *Australian Journal of International Affairs*, 53:1, 19–29.

Hagman, Hans C. (2002) 'European Crisis Management and Defence: The Search for Capabilities', *Adelphi* 353, London: IISS.

Hale, William (1992) 'Turkey, the Middle East and the Gulf Crisis', *International Affairs*, 68:4, 679–92.

Halperin, Morton H. (1966) *China and Nuclear Proliferation*, Chicago: Center for Policy Studies, University of Chicago.

Hamilton, Richard F. (1968) 'A Research Note on the Mass Support for "Tough" Military Initiatives', *American Sociological Review*, 33:3, 439–45.

Handrahan, Lori (2004) 'Conflict, Gender, Ethnicity and Post-conflict Reconstruction', *Security Dialogue*, 35:4, 429–45.

Hansen, Birthe (2000) *Unipolarity and the Middle East*, Richmond: Curzon Press.

Hansen, Lene (1996) 'Slovenian Identity: State Building on the Balkan Border', *Alternatives*, 21:4, 473–95.

(2000a) 'The Little Mermaid's Silent Security Dilemma and the Absence of Gender in the Copenhagen School', *Millennium*, 29:2: 285–306.

(2000b) 'Past as Preface: Civilization and the Politics of the "Third" Balkan War', *Journal of Peace Research*, 37:3: 345–62.

(2001) 'Gender, Nation, Rape: Bosnia and the Construction of Security', *International Feminist Journal of Politics*, 3:1, 55–75.

(2006) *Security as Practice: Discourse Analysis and the Bosnian War*, London: Routledge.

(forthcoming) 'The Clash of Cartoons? The Clash of Civilizations? Visual Securitization and the Muhammad Cartoon Crisis'.

Hansen, Lene and Helen Nissenbaum (forthcoming) 'Digital Disaster, Cyber Security and the Copenhagen School', *International Studies Quarterly*.

Hanson, Donald W. (1982/3) 'Is Soviet Strategic Doctrine Superior?', *International Security*, 7:3, 61–83.

Harkavy, Robert E. (1981) 'Pariah States and Nuclear Proliferation', *International Organization*, 35:1, 135–63.

Harris, Stuart (1993) 'The Economic Aspects of Pacific Security', *Adelphi* 275, London: IISS.

Harrison, Selig S. (1998) *Japan's Nuclear Future: The Plutonium Debate and East Asian Security*, Washington, DC: Carnegie Endowment for International Peace.

Hartung, William D. (2001) 'Eisenhower's Warning: The Military–Industrial Complex Forty Years Later', *World Policy Journal*, 18:1, 39–44.

(2002/3) 'Prevention, Not Intervention: Curbing the New Nuclear Threat', *World Policy Journal*, 19:4, 1–11.

Harvard Nuclear Study Group (1983) *Living with Nuclear Weapons*, Cambridge MA: Harvard University Press.

Harvey, Frank P. (1998) 'Rigor Mortis or Rigor, More Tests: Necessity, Sufficiency and Deterrence Logic', *International Studies Quarterly*, 42:4, 675–707.

(2000) 'The International Politics of National Missile Defence: A Response to the Critics', *International Journal*, 55:4, 545–66.

Harvey, John R. (1992) 'Regional Ballistic Missiles and Advanced Strike Aircraft: Comparing Military Effectiveness', *International Security*, 17:2, 41–83.

Hashmi, Sohail H. (1996) 'International Society and its Islamic Malcontents', *Fletcher Forum of World Affairs*, 20:2, 13–29.

Hassner, Pierre (1968) 'The Changing Context of European Security', *Journal of Common Market Studies*, 7:1, 1–21.

(2002) 'The United States: The Empire of Force or the Force of Empire?', *Chaillot Papers no. 54*, Paris: European Union Institute for Security Studies.

Hassner, Ron E. (2007) 'The Path to Intractability: Time and the Entrenchment of Territorial Disputes', *International Security*, 31:3, 107–38.

Haynes, Jeffrey (2008) 'Religion and Foreign Policy Making in the USA, India and Iran: Towards a Research Agenda', *Third World Quarterly*, 29:1, 143–65.

Heisbourg, François (1998/9) 'The Prospects for Nuclear Stability between India and Pakistan', *Survival*, 40:4, 77–92.

Heller, Mark A. (2000) 'Continuity and Change in Israeli Security Policy', *Adelphi* 335, London: IISS.

Hellmich, Christina (2005) 'Al-Qaeda – Terrorists, Hypocrites, Fundamentalists? The View from Within', *Third World Quarterly*, 26:1, 39–54.

Hemmer, Christopher and Peter Katzenstein (2002) 'Why is There No NATO in Asia? Collective Identity, Regionalism and the Origins of Multilateralism', *International Organization*, 56:3, 575–607.

Henderson, Jeannie (1999) 'Reassessing ASEAN', *Adelphi* 328, London: IISS.

Hendrickson, David C. (2002) 'The Dangerous Quest for Absolute Security', *World Policy Journal*, 19:3, 1–10.

Heng, Yee-Kuang (2002) 'Unravelling the War on Terrorism: A Risk-management Exercise in War Clothing?', *Security Dialogue*, 33:2, 227–42.

(2006) 'The "Transformation of War" Debate: Through the Looking Glass of Ulrich Beck's *World Risk Society*', *International Relations*, 20:1, 69–91.

Henriksen, Rune (2007) 'Warriors in Combat – What Makes People Actively Fight in Combat?', *Journal of Strategic Studies*, 30:2, 187–223.

Herbst, Jeffrey (1996/7) 'Responding to State Failure in Africa', *International Security*, 21:3, 120–44.

Herring, George C. (1991/2) 'America and Vietnam: The Unending War', *Foreign Affairs*, 70:5, 104–19.

Herz, John (1950) 'Idealist Internationalism and the Security Dilemma', *World Politics*, 2:2, 157–80.

Hettne, Björn (1991) 'Security and Peace in Post-Cold War Europe', *Journal of Peace Research*, 28:3, 279–94.

(2005) 'Beyond the "New" Regionalism', *New Political Economy*, 10:4, 543–71.

Heuser, Beatrice (1993) 'Containing Uncertainty: Options for British Nuclear Strategy', *Review of International Studies*, 19:3, 245–67.

Higashino, Atsuko (2004) 'For the Sake of "Peace and Security"? The Role of Security in the European Union Enlargement Eastwards', *Cooperation and Conflict*, 39:4, 347–68.

Higate, Paul and Marsha Henry (2004) 'Engendering (In)Security in Peace Support Operations', *Security Dialogue*, 35:4, 481–98.

Hildenbrand, Gunter (1978) 'A German Reaction to US Nonproliferation Policy', *International Security*, 3:2, 51–56.

Hills, Alice (2006) 'The Rationalities of European Border Security', *European Security*, 15:1, 67–88.

Hinton, Harold C. (1975) *Three and a Half Powers: The New Balance in Asia*, Bloomington: Indiana University Press.

Hodes, Cyrus and Mark Sedra (2007) 'The Search for Security in Post-Taliban Afghanistan', *Adelphi* 391, London: IISS.

Hodge, Carl C. (1998/9) 'Europe as a Great Power: A Work in Progress?', *International Journal*, 53:3, 487–504.

Hoffman, Bruce (1998) *Inside Terrorism*, New York: Columbia University Press.

Hoffman, Fred S. (1985) 'The SDI in US Nuclear Strategy', *International Security*, 10:1, 13–24.

Hoffmann, Stanley (1973) 'The Acceptability of Military Force' in 'Force in Modern Societies: Its Place in International Politics', *Adelphi* 102, London: IISS, 2–13.

(1981/2) 'NATO and Nuclear Weapons', *Foreign Affairs*, 60:2, 347–57.

Höivik, Tord (1971) 'Social Inequality. The Main Issues', *Journal of Peace Research*, 8:2, 119–42.

(1972) 'Three Approaches to Exploitation: Markets, Products and Communities', *Journal of Peace Research*, 9:3, 261–70.

Holbrooke, Richard (1991) 'Japan and the US: Ending the Unequal Partnership', *Foreign Affairs*, 70:5, 41–57.

Hollis, Rosemary (1997) 'Europe and the Middle East: Power by Stealth', *International Affairs*, 73:1, 15–29.

Hollist, W. Ladd (1977) 'An Analysis of Arms Processes in the United States and the Soviet Union', *International Studies Quarterly*, 21:3, 503–28.

Holloway, David (1980) 'Military Power and Political Purpose in Soviet Policy', *Daedalus*, 109:4, 13–30.

Holmes, Terence M. (2007) 'Planning versus Chaos in Clausewitz's *On War*', *Journal of Strategic Studies*, 30:1, 129–51.

Hoogensen, Gunhild and Svein V. Rottem (2004) 'Gender Identity and the Subject of Security', *Security Dialogue*, 35:2, 155–71.

Hoogensen, Gunhild and Kirsti Stuvøy (2006) 'Gender, Resistance and Human Security', *Security Dialogue*, 37:2, 207–28.

Hook, Glenn D. (1984) 'The Nuclearization of Language: Nuclear Allergy as Political Metaphor', *Journal of Peace Research*, 21:3, 259–75.

(1985) 'Making Nuclear Weapons Easier to Live With: The Political Role of Language in Nuclearization', *Bulletin of Peace Proposals*, 16:1, 67–77.

Hopf, Ted (1992) 'Managing Soviet Disintegration', *International Security*, 17:1, 44–75.

Hopple, Gerald W. (1982) 'Transnational Terrorism: Prospects for a Causal Modeling Approach', *Terrorism*, 6:1, 73–100.

Horelick, Arnold L. (1964) 'The Cuban Missile Crisis', *World Politics*, 16:3, 363–89.

Hoskins, Andrew (2006) 'Temporality, Proximity and Security: Terror in a Media-drenched Age', *International Relations*, 20:4, 453–66.

Hough, Peter (2004) *Understanding Global Security*, London: Routledge.

Howard, Michael (1964) 'Military Power and the International Order', *International Affairs*, 40:3, 397–408.

(1973) 'The Relevance of Traditional Strategy', *Foreign Affairs,* 51:2, 253–66.

(1976) 'The Strategic Approach to International Relations', *British Journal of International Studies*, 2:1, 67–75.

(1979) 'The Forgotten Dimensions of Strategy', *Foreign Affairs*, 57:5, 975–86.

(1981) *War and the Liberal Conscience*, Oxford: Oxford University Press.

(1999) 'When are Wars Decisive?', *Survival*, 41:1, 126–35.

(2006) 'A Long War?', *Survival*, 48:4, 7–14.

Howe, Herbert (1996/7) 'Lessons of Liberia: ECOMOG and Regional Peacekeeping', *International Security*, 21:3, 145–76.

Howlett, Darryl and John Simpson (1993) 'Nuclearisation and Denuclearisation in South Africa', *Survival*, 35:3, 154–73.

Howlett, Darryl, John Simpson, Emily Bailey and Ben Cole (1999) 'Surveying the Nuclear Future: Which Way from Here?', *Contemporary Security Policy*, 20:1, 5–41.

Hsieh, Alice Langley (1971) 'China's Nuclear-Missile Programme: Regional or Intercontinental?', *China Quarterly*, 45, 85–99.

Hsiung, James (ed.) (2007) *China and Japan at Odds*, Basingstoke: Palgrave.

Hudson, Heidi (2005) '"Doing" Security as Though Humans Matter: A Feminist Perspective on Gender and the Politics of Human Security', *Security Dialogue*, 36:2, 155–74.

Hughes, Christopher W. (1996) 'The North Korean Nuclear Crisis and Japanese Security', *Survival*, 38:2, 79–103.

(2004a) *Japan's Security Agenda: The Search for Regional Stability*, Boulder: Lynne Rienner.

(2004b) 'Japan's Re-emergence as a "Normal" Military Power', *Adelphi* 368/9, London: IISS.

(2004c) *Japan's Security Agenda: Military, Economic and Environmental Dimensions*, Boulder: Lynne Rienner.

(2006) 'Why Japan Could Revise its Constitution and What it Would Mean for Japanese Security Policy', *Orbis*, 50:4, 725–44.

Hughes, Christopher W. and Ellis S. Krauss (2007) 'Japan's New Security Agenda', *Survival*, 49:2, 157–76.

Hughes, Llewelyn (2007) 'Why Japan Will Not Go Nuclear (Yet): International and Domestic Constraints on the Nuclearization of Japan', *International Security*, 31:4, 67–96.

Hunt, Krista (2002) 'The Strategic Co-optation of Women's Rights: Discourse in the "War on Terrorism"', *International Feminist Journal of Politics*, 4:1, 116–21.

Hunter, Robert E. (2002) *The European Security and Defense Policy*, Washington, DC: RAND/Eurospan.

Hunter, Robert E. and Philip Windsor (1968) 'Vietnam and United States Policy in Asia', *International Affairs*, 44:1, 202–13.

Huntington, Samuel P. (1957) *The Soldier and the State: The Theory and Politics of Civil–Military Relations*, Cambridge, MA: Harvard University Press.

(1958) 'Arms Races: Prerequisites and Results', *Public Policy*, 8:1, 41–87.

(1993a) 'The Clash of Civilizations?', *Foreign Affairs*, 72:3, 22–49.

(1993b) 'Why International Primacy Matters', *International Security*, 17:4, 68–83.

(1996) *The Clash of Civilizations and the Remaking of World Order*, New York: Simon & Schuster.

(1999) 'The Lonely Superpower', *Foreign Affairs*, 78:2, 35–49.

Huntley, Wade L. (1999) 'Alternate Futures after the South Asian Nuclear Tests: Pokhran as Prologue', *Asian Survey*, 29:3, 504–24.

(2006) 'Rebels Without a Cause: North Korea, Iran and the NPT', *International Affairs*, 82:4, 723–42.

Hurrell, Andrew (1998) 'Security in Latin America', *International Affairs*, 74:3, 529–46.

(2002) '"There are no Rules" (George W. Bush): International Order after September 11', *International Relations*, 16:2, 185–204.

(2005) 'Pax Americana or the Empire of Insecurity?', *International Relations of the Asia-Pacific*, 5:2, 153–76.

Huth, Paul K. (1988) *Extended Deterrence and the Prevention of War*, New Haven: Yale University Press.

(1990) 'The Extended Deterrent Value of Nuclear Weapons', *Journal of Conflict Resolution*, 34:2, 270–90.

(1997) 'Reputations and Deterrence: A Theoretical and Empirical Assessment', *Security Studies*, 7:1, 72–99.

Huth, Paul K. and Bruce Russett (1984) 'What Makes Deterrence Work? Cases from 1900–1980', *World Politics*, 36:4, 496–526.

Huxley, Tim and Susan Willett (1999) 'Arming East Asia', *Adelphi* 329, London: IISS.

Huysmans, Jef (1994) 'Reading and Writing NOD: Closing the Debate?', *Cooperation and Conflict*, 29:2, 185–204.

    (1998a) 'Revisiting Copenhagen: Or, On the Creative Development of a Security Studies Agenda in Europe', *European Journal of International Relations*, 4:4, 479–506.

    (1998b) 'Security! What do You Mean? From Concept to Thick Signifier', *European Journal of International Relations*, 4:2, 226–55.

    (2006a) 'International Politics of Insecurity: Normativity, Inwardness and the Exception', *Security Dialogue*, 37:1, 11–30.

    (2006b) *The Politics of Insecurity: Security, Migration and Asylum in the EU*, London: Routledge.

Hveem, Helge (1973) 'The Global Dominance System: Notes on a Theory of Global Political Economy', *Journal of Peace Research*, 10:4, 319–40.

    (1979) 'Militarization of Nature: Conflict and Control over Strategic Resources and some Implications for Peace Politics', *Journal of Peace Research*, 16:1, 1–26.

Hymans, Jacques E. C. (2001) 'Of Gauchos and Gringos: Why Argentina Never Wanted the Bomb, and Why the United States Thought It Did', *Security Studies*, 10:3, 153–85.

IDS (1985) Issue on 'Disarmament and World Development', *IDS Bulletin*, 16:4.

IISS (1970) 'Survey of Strategic Studies', *Adelphi Papers* 64, London: IISS.

    (1975a) 'The Middle East and the International System I. The Impact of the 1973 War', *Adelphi* 114, London: IISS.

    (1975b) 'The Middle East and the International System II. Security and the Energy Crisis', *Adelphi* 115, London: IISS.

    (1981) 'Third World Conflict and International Security', *Adelphi* 166 and 167, London: IISS.

Ikenberry, G. John (2001a) *After Victory: Institutions, Strategic Restraint and the Rebuilding of Order After Major Wars*, Princeton: Princeton University Press.

    (2001b) 'American Grand Strategy in the Age of Terror', *Survival*, 43:4, 19–34.

    (ed.) (2002) *America Unrivaled: The Future of the Balance of Power*, Ithaca: Cornell University Press.

Ikenberry, G. John and Jitsuo Tsuchiyama (2002) 'Between Balance of Power and Community: The Future of Multilateral Security Co-operation in the Asia–Pacific', *International Relations of the Asia Pacific*, 2:1, 69–94.

Imai, Ryukichi (1974) 'A view from Japan', *Survival*, 16:5, 213–16.

    (1978) 'A Japanese Reaction to U.S. Nonproliferation Policy', *International Security*, 3:2, 62–66.

    (1993) 'Nuclear Proliferation in the Post-Cold War World', *Adelphi* 276, London: IISS.

Imber, Mark (1980) 'NPT Safeguards: The Limits of Credibility', *Arms Control*, 1:2, 177–98.

Inbar, Efraim and Shmuel Sandler (1993/4) 'Israel's Deterrence Strategy Revisited', *Security Studies*, 3:2, 330–58.

Independent Commission on Disarmament and Security Issues (1982) *Common Security: A Programme for Disarmament – The Report of the Independent Commission on Disarmament and Security Issues*, London: Pan Books.

Ingram, Barbara L. and Stephen E. Berger (1977) 'Sex-role Orientation, Defensiveness and Competitiveness in Women', *Journal of Conflict Resolution*, 21:3, 501–18.

Inoguchi, Takashi and Paul Bacon (2006) 'Japan's Emerging Role as a Global Ordinary Power', *International Relations of the Asia-Pacific*, 6:1, 1–21.

Institute for World Order (1981) *Peace and World Order Studies: A Curriculum Guide*, New York: Transnational Academic Program/Institute for World Order.

International Security (1976) 'Foreword', *International Security*, 1:1, 2.

Intrilligator, Michael and Dagobert L. Brito (1984) 'Can Arms Races Lead to the Outbreak of War?', *Journal of Conflict Resolution*, 28:1, 63–84.

Ish-Shalom, Piki (2008) '"The Civilization of Clashes": Misapplying the Democratic Peace in the Middle East', *Political Science Quarterly*, 122:4, 533–54.

Israeli, Ralph (2001) 'The Turkish–Israeli Odd Couple', *Orbis*, 45:1, 65–79.

Jabko, Nicolas and Steven Weber (1998) 'A Certain Idea of Nuclear Weapons: France's Nuclear Nonproliferation Policy in Theoretical Perspective', *Security Studies*, 8:1, 108–50.

Jabri, Vivienne (2006) 'War, Security and the Liberal State', *Security Dialogue*, 37:1, 47–64.

Jackson, Nicole (2006) 'International Organizations, Security Dichotomies and the Trafficking of Persons and Narcotics in Post-Soviet Central Asia: A Critique of the Securitization Framework', *Security Dialogue*, 37:3, 299–317.

Jackson, Paul (2007) 'Are Africa's Wars Part of a Fourth Generation of Warfare?', *Contemporary Security Policy*, 28:2, 267–85.

Jackson, Richard (2007) 'Language, Policy and the Construction of a Torture Culture in the War on Terrorism', *Review of International Studies*, 33:3, 353–72.

Jackson, Robert and Georg Sørensen (1999) *Introduction to International Relations*, Oxford: Oxford University Press.

Jahn, Egbert, Pierre Lemaitre and Ole Wæver (1987) *European Security: Problems of Research on Non-military Aspects*, Copenhagen Papers 1, Copenhagen: Center for Peace and Conflict Research.

Janis, Irving (1972) *Victims of Group-think*, Boston: Houghton Mifflin.

Jepperson, Ronald L., Alexander Wendt and Peter J. Katzenstein (1996) 'Norms, Identity, and Culture in National Security', in Peter J. Katzenstein (ed.) *The*

Culture of National Security: Norms and Identity in World Politics, New York: Columbia University Press, 33–75.

Jervis, Robert (1976) *Perception and Misperception in International Politics*, Princeton: Princeton University Press.

(1978) 'Cooperation Under the Security Dilemma', *World Politics*, 30:2, 167–214.

(1979) 'Deterrence Theory Revisited', *World Politics*, 31:2, 289–324.

(1979/80) 'Why Nuclear Superiority Doesn't Matter', *Political Science Quarterly*, 94:4, 617–33.

(1991/2) 'The Future of World Politics: Will it Resemble the Past?', *International Security*, 16:3, 39–73.

(1993) 'International Primacy: Is the Game Worth the Candle?', *International Security*, 17:4, 52–67.

(2002a) 'An Interim Assessment of September 11: What has Changed and What has Not', *Political Science Quarterly*, 117:1, 37–54.

(2002b) 'Theories of War in an Era of Leading Power Peace', *American Political Science Review*, 96:1, 1–14.

(2003a) 'The Confrontation Between Iraq and the US: Implications for the Theory and Practice of Deterrence', *European Journal of International Relations*, 9:2, 315–37.

(2003b) 'Understanding the Bush Doctrine', *Political Science Quarterly*, 118:3, 365–88.

(2005) 'Why the Bush Doctrine Cannot be Sustained', *Political Science Quarterly*, 120:3, 351–77.

(2006) 'Reports, Politics and Intelligence Failures: The Case of Iraq', *Journal of Strategic Studies*, 29:1, 3–52.

Jin, Xu (2006) 'The Strategic Implications of Changes in Military Technology', *Chinese Journal of International Politics*, 1:2, 163–93.

Joeck, Neil (1997) 'Maintaining Nuclear Stability in South Asia', *Adelphi* 312, London: IISS.

Joenniemi, Pertti (1990) 'Europe Changes – The Nordic System Remains', *Bulletin of Peace Proposals*, 21:2, 205–17.

Joffe, George (1993) 'Middle Eastern Views of the Gulf Conflict and its Aftermath', *Review of International Studies*, 19:2, 177–99.

Joffe, Josef (1981) 'European–American Relations: The Enduring Crisis', *Foreign Affairs*, 59:4, 835–51.

(1992/3) 'The New Europe: Yesterday's Ghosts', *Foreign Affairs*, 72:1, 29–43.

Johnson, A. Ross (1973) 'Yugoslavia's Total National Defence', *Survival*, 15:2, 54–8.

Johnson, Chalmers (1968a) 'Guerrilla Warfare in Asia', *Survival*, 10:10, 318–26.

(1968b) 'The Third Generation of Guerrilla Warfare', *Asian Survey*, 8:6, 435–47.

Johnson, Loch (ed.) (2007) *Handbook of Intelligence Studies*, London: Routledge.

Johnson, Thomas H. and M. Chris Mason (2007) 'Understanding the Taliban and Insurgency in Afghanistan', *Orbis*, 51:1, 71–89.

Johnston, Alastair Iain (1986) 'China and Arms Control: Emerging Issues and Interests in the 1980s', *Aurora Papers no. 3*, Ottawa: Center for Arms Control and Disarmament.

(1995) 'Thinking about Strategic Culture', *International Security*, 19:4, 32–64.

(2003) 'Is China a Status Quo Power?', *International Security*, 27:4, 5–56.

Jones, Adam (1994) 'Gender and Ethnic Conflict in Ex-Yugoslavia', *Ethnic and Racial Studies*, 17:1, 115–34.

(1996) 'Does "Gender" Make the World Go Round? Feminist Critiques of International Relations', *Review of International Studies*, 22:4, 405–29.

(1998) 'Engendering Debate', *Review of International Studies*, 24:2, 299–303.

Jones, Rodney W. and Mark G. McDonough (1998) *Tracking Nuclear Proliferation*, Washington DC: Carnegie Endowment for International Peace.

Jones, Seth G. (2003) 'The European Union and the Security Dilemma', *Security Studies*, 12:3, 114–56.

(2006) 'The Rise of a European Defense', *Political Science Quarterly*, 121:2, 241–67.

(2007) 'Pakistan's Dangerous Game', *Survival*, 49:1, 15–32.

Jørgensen, Knud Erik (2000) 'Continental IR Theory: The Best Kept Secret', *European Journal of International Relations*, 6:1, 9–42.

Joseph, Robert G. (1996) 'Proliferation, Counter-proliferation and NATO', *Survival*, 38:1, 111–30.

Joseph, Robert G. and John F. Reichart (1998) 'The Case for Nuclear Deterrence Today', *Orbis*, 42:1, 7–19.

Journal of Peace Research (1964) 'An Editorial', *Journal of Peace Research*, 1:1, 1–4.

(2002) Special Issue, 'Civil War in Developing Countries', *Journal of Peace Research*, 39:4.

Journal of Strategic Studies (1994) Special Issue, 'The Future of NATO', 17:4, 1–166.

(2000) Special Issue, 'NATO Enters the 21st Century', 23:3, 1–181.

(2001) Special Issue, 'Future Trends in East Asian International Relations', 24:4, 3–245.

Judah, Tim (2002) 'The Taliban Papers', *Survival*, 44:1, 69–80.

Jung, Dietrich and Wolfgang Piccoli (2000) 'The Turkish–Israeli Alignment: Paranoia or Pragmatism?', *Security Dialogue*, 31:1, 91–104.

Kagan, Robert (2002) 'Power and Weakness', *Policy Review*, 113, 1–29.

(2003) *Paradise and Power: America and Europe in the New World Order*, London: Atlantic Books.

Kahl, Colin H. (1998/9) 'Constructing a Separate Peace: Constructivism, Collective Liberal Identity, and Democratic Peace', *Security Studies*, 8:2/3, 94–144.

Kahn, Herman (1960) *On Thermonuclear War*, Princeton: Princeton University Press.

(1962) *Thinking About the Unthinkable*, New York: Horizon Press.

Kaiser, Karl (1989) 'Non-proliferation and Nuclear Deterrence', *Survival*, 31:2, 123–36.

Kalb, Marvin and Elie Abel (1971) *Roots of Involvement*, New York: W. W. Norton.

Kaldor, Mary (1982) *The Baroque Arsenal*, London: Andre Deutsch.

    (1990) *The Imaginary War: Understanding the East–West Conflict*, Oxford: Blackwell.

    (2001) *New and Old Wars: Organized Violence in a Global Era*, Cambridge: Polity Press.

Kaldor, Mary, Mary Martin and Sabine Selchow (2007) 'Human Security: A New Strategic Narrative for Europe', *International Affairs*, 83:2, 273–88.

Kalyvas, Stathis N. (2001) '"New" and "Old" Civil Wars: A Valid Distinction?', *World Politics*, 54:1, 99–118.

Kampani, Gaurav (2001) 'In Praise of Indifference Toward India's Bomb', *Orbis*, 45:2, 241–57.

Kang, David C. (1994) 'Preventive War and North Korea', *Security Studies*, 4:2, 330–64.

    (2003a) 'Getting Asia Wrong: The Need for New Analytical Frameworks', *International Security*, 27:4, 57–85.

    (2003b) 'Hierarchy, Balancing and Empirical Puzzles in Asian International Relations', *International Security*, 28:3, 165–81.

Kaplan, Fred M. (1983) *The Wizards of Armageddon*, New York: Simon & Schuster.

Kaplan, Morton A. (1966) 'The New Great Debate: Traditionalism vs. Science in International Relations', *World Politics*, 19:1, 1–20.

Kaplan, Seth (2007) 'The Wrong Prescription for the Congo', *Orbis*, 51:2, 299–311.

Kapstein, Ethan B. (1992) *The Political Economy of National Security: A Global Perspective*, New York: McGraw-Hill.

    (1999) 'Does Unipolarity Have a Future?', in Kapstein and Mastanduno (eds.) *Unipolar Politics*, 464–90.

Kapstein, Ethan B. and Michael Mastanduno (eds.) (1999) *Unipolar Politics: Realism and State Strategies After the Cold War*, New York: Columbia University Press.

Kapur, Ashok (1980a) 'The Nuclear Spread: A Third World View', *Third World Quarterly*, 2:1, 495–516.

    (1980b) 'A Nuclearizing Pakistan : Some Hypotheses', *Asian Survey*, 20:5, 495–516.

Kapur, S. Paul, (2003) 'Nuclear Proliferation, the Kargil Conflict, and South Asian Security', *Security Studies*, 13:1, 79–105.

    (2005) 'India and Pakistan's Unstable Peace: Why Nuclear South Asia is not like Cold War Europe', *International Security*, 30:2, 127–52.

Karawan, Ibrahim A. (1997) 'The Islamist Impasse', *Adelphi* 314, London: IISS.

Karl, David J. (1996/7) 'Proliferation, Pessimism and Emerging Nuclear Powers', *International Security*, 21:3, 87–119.

Karp, Aaron (1984/5) 'Ballistic Missiles in the Third World', *International Security*, 9:3, 166–95.

(1991) 'Controlling Ballistic Missile Proliferation', *Survival*, 33:6, 517–30.

(2004) 'The New Indeterminacy of Deterrence and Missile Defence', *Contemporary Security Policy*, 25:1, 71–87.

Karp, Regina C. (ed.) (1991) *Security With Nuclear Weapons?* Oxford: Oxford University Press.

Karsh, Efraim (1997) 'Cold War, Post-Cold War: Does it Make a Difference for the Middle East?', *Review of International Studies*, 23:3, 272–91.

Katzenstein, Peter J. (ed.) (1996a) *The Culture of National Security: Norms and Identity in World Politics*, New York: Columbia University Press.

(1996b) 'Introduction: Alternative Perspectives on National Security', in Katzenstein (1996a), 1–32.

(2003) 'Same War – Different Views: Germany, Japan and Counterterrorism', *International Organization*, 57:4, 731–60.

Katzenstein, Peter J., Robert O. Keohane and Steven Krasner (1998) '*International Organization* and the Study of World Politics', *International Organization*, 52:4, 645–85.

Katzenstein, Peter J. and Nobuo Okawara (1993) 'Japan's National Security: Structures, Norms, Policies', *International Security*, 17:4, 84–118.

Kaufmann, Chaim (1996) 'Possible and Impossible Solutions to Ethnic Civil Wars', *International Security*, 20:4, 136–75.

(2004) 'Threat Inflation and the Failure of the Marketplace of Ideas: The Selling of the Iraq War', *International Security*, 29:1, 5–48.

Kaufmann-Osborn, Timothy (2006) 'Gender Trouble at Abu Ghraib', *Politics and Gender*, 1:4, 597–619.

Kaye, Dalia Dassa and Frederic M. Wehrey (2007) 'A Nuclear Iran: The Reactions of Neighbours', *Survival*, 49:2, 111–28.

Keeley, James (1993/4) 'The IAEA and the Iraqi Challenge', *International Journal*, 49:1, 126–55.

Kegley, Charles W. and Gregory Raymond (1992) 'Must we Fear a Post-Cold War Multipolar System?', *Journal of Conflict Resolution*, 36:3, 573–85.

(1994) *A Multipolar Peace? Great Power Politics in the Twenty-first Century*, New York: St. Martins.

Keller, Edmond J. and Donald Rothchild (eds.) (1996) *Africa in the New International Order: Rethinking State Sovereignty and Regional Security*, Boulder: Lynne Rienner.

Kelly, Robert E. (1996) 'The Iraqi and South African Nuclear Projects', *Security Dialogue*, 27:1, 27–38.

(2007) 'Security Theory in the "New Regionalism"', *International Studies Review*, 9:2, 197–229.

Kelman, Herbert C. (ed.) (1965) *International Behavior*, New York: Holt, Rinehart & Winston.

Kemp, Anita (1985) 'Image of the Peace Field: An International Survey', *Journal of Peace Research*, 22:2, 129–40.

Kemp, Geoffrey (1998/9) 'The Persian Gulf Remains the Strategic Prize', *Survival*, 40:4, 132–49.

Kennan, George F. (1947) 'The Sources of Soviet Conduct', *Foreign Affairs*, 25:4, 566–82.

Kennedy, Andrew B. (2007) 'China's Perceptions of US Intentions toward Taiwan: How Hostile a Hegemon?', *Asian Survey*, 47:2, 268–87.

Kennedy, Robert F. (1969) *Thirteen Days: A Memoir of the Cuban Missile Crisis*, New York: W. W. Norton.

Kennedy-Pipe, Caroline (2007) 'Gender and Security', in Alan R. Collins (ed.) *Contemporary Security Studies*, Oxford: Oxford University Press, 75–90.

Kennedy-Pipe, Caroline and Andrew Mumford (2007) 'Torture, Rights, Rules and Wars: Ireland to Iraq', *International Relations*, 21:1, 119–26.

Kennedy-Pipe, Caroline and Nicholas Rengger (2006) 'Apocalypse Now? Continuities or Disjunctions in World Politics after 9/11', *International Affairs*, 82:3, 539–52.

Kenney, M. (2003) 'From Pablo to Osama: Counter-terrorism Lessons from the War on Drugs', *Survival*, 45:3, 187–206.

Kent, Alexandra (2006) 'Reconfiguring Security: Buddhism and Moral Legitimacy in Cambodia', *Security Dialogue*, 37:3, 343–61.

Kenyon, Ian, Mike Rance, John Simpson and Mark Smith (2001) 'Prospects for a European Ballistic Missile Defence System', *Southampton Papers in International Policy*, 4.

Keohane, Robert O. (1988) 'International Institutions: Two Approaches', *International Studies Quarterly*, 32:4, 379–96.

   (1989) 'International Relations Theory: Contributions of a Feminist Standpoint', *Millennium*, 18:2, 245–54.

Keohane, Robert O. and Joseph S. Nye (1977) *Power and Interdependence: World Politics in Transition*, Boston: Little, Brown & Co.

Kerr, David (2005) 'The Sino-Russian Partnership and US Policy Toward North Korea: From Hegemony to Concert in Northeast Asia', *International Studies Quarterly*, 49:3, 411–38.

Khalilzad, Zalmay (1995) 'The United States and the Persian Gulf: Preventing Regional Hegemony', *Survival*, 37:2, 95–120.

Khattak, Saba Gul (2003) 'In/Security: Afghan Refugees and Politics in Pakistan', *Critical Asian Studies*, 35:2, 195–208.

Khoo, Nicholas and Michael L. Smith (2002) 'The Future of American Hegemony in the Asia–Pacific: A Concert of Asia or a Clear Pecking Order?', *Australian Journal of International Affairs*, 56:1, 65–81.

Kier, Elizabeth (1995) 'Culture and Military Doctrine: France Between the Wars', *International Security*, 19:4, 65–93.

(1998) 'Homosexuals in the US Military: Open Integration and Combat', *International Security*, 23:2, 5–39.

Kihl, Young W. (2002) 'Security on the Korean Peninsula: Continuity and Change', *Security Dialogue*, 33:1, 59–72.

Kilcullen, David (2005) 'Countering Global Insurgency', *Journal of Strategic Studies*, 28:4, 597–617.

(2006) 'Counter-insurgency *Redux*', *Survival*, 48:4, 111–30.

Kim, Samuel S. (ed.) (2003) *The International Relations of Northeast Asia*, Lanham: Rowman & Littlefield.

Kim, Taehyun (1996) 'South Korean Perspectives on the North Korean Nuclear Question', *Mershon International Studies Review*, 40:2, 255–61.

King, Charles (2001) 'The New Near East', *Survival*, 43:2, 49–67.

King, Gary, Robert O. Keohane and Sidney Verba (1994) *Designing Social Inquiry: Scientific Inference in Qualitative Research*, Princeton: Princeton University Press.

King, Gary and Christopher J. L. Murray (2001/2) 'Rethinking Human Security', *Political Science Quarterly*, 116:4, 585–610.

Kinsella, David (2002) 'Rivalry, Reaction and Weapons Proliferation: A Time-series Analysis', *International Studies Quarterly*, 46:2, 209–30.

Kinsey, Christopher (2007) *Corporate Soldiers and International Security: The Rise of Private Military Companies*, London: Routledge.

Kissinger, Henry (1957) *Nuclear Weapons and Foreign Policy*, New York: Harper.

Kivimäki, Timo (2001) 'The Long Peace of ASEAN', *Journal of Peace Research*, 38:1, 5–25.

Klare, Michael (1993) 'The Next Great Arms Race', *Foreign Affairs*, 72:3, 136–52.

Klausen, Arne M. (1964) 'Technical Assistance and Social Conflict: A Case Study from the Indo-Norwegian Fishing Project in Kerala, South India', *Journal of Peace Research*, 1:1, 5–18.

Klein, Bradley S. (1990) 'How the West Was One: Representational Politics of NATO', *International Studies Quarterly*, 34:3, 311–25.

(1994) *Strategic Studies and World Order: The Global Politics of Deterrence*, Cambridge: Cambridge University Press.

Klick, Donna (1987) 'A Balkan Nuclear Weapon-free Zone: Viability of the Regime and Implications for Crisis Management', *Journal of Peace Research*, 24:2, 111–24.

Knopf, Jeffrey W. (2003) 'Recasting the Proliferation Optimism–Pessimism Debate', *Security Studies*, 12:1, 41–96.

Knorr, Klaus (1966) *On the Uses of Military Power in the Nuclear Age*, Princeton: Princeton University Press.

Knorr, Klaus and Frank N. Trager (1977) *Economic Issues and National Security*, Lawrence: Regents Press of Kansas for the National Security Education Program.

Koblentz, Gregory (2003/4) 'Pathogens as Weapons: The International Security Implications of Biological Warfare', *International Security*, 28:3, 84–122.

Kokoski, Richard (1996) *Technology and the Proliferation of Nuclear Weapons*, Oxford: Oxford University Press.

Kolcowicz, Roman (1971) 'Strategic Parity and Beyond: Soviet Perspectives', *World Politics*, 23:3, 431–51.

Kolodziej, Edward A. (1992) 'Renaissance in Security Studies? Caveat Lector!', *International Studies Quarterly*, 36:4, 421–38.

(2005) *Security and International Relations*, Cambridge: Cambridge University Press.

Kolodziej, Edward A. and Robert E. Harkavy (1982) *Security Policies of Developing Countries*, Lexington: Lexington Books.

Kötter, Wolfgang and Harald Müller (1991) *Germany, Europe and Nuclear Non-proliferation*, PPNN Study 1, Southampton: University of Southampton.

Koubi, Vally (1999) 'Military Technology Races', *International Organization*, 53:3, 537–65.

Krahmann, Elke (2003) 'Conceptualizing Security Governance', *Cooperation and Conflict*, 38:1, 5–26.

Krapels, Edward N. (1977) 'Oil and Security: Problems and Prospects of Importing Countries', *Adelphi* 136, London: IISS.

Krasner, Michael A. and Nikolaj Petersen (1986) 'Peace and Politics: The Danish Peace Movement and its Impact on National Security Policy', *Journal of Peace Research*, 23:2, 155–73.

Krause, Keith (1996) 'Insecurity and State Formation in the Global Military Order: The Middle Eastern Case', *European Journal of International Relations*, 2:3, 319–54.

Krause, Keith and Michael C. Williams (1996) 'Broadening the Agenda of Security Studies: Politics and Methods', *Mershon International Studies Review*, 40:2, 229–54.

(eds.) (1997) *Critical Security Studies*, Minneapolis: University of Minnesota Press.

Krebs, Ronald R. and Jennifer K. Lobasz (2007) 'Fixing the Meaning of 9/11: Hegemony, Coercion, and the Road to War in Iraq', *Security Studies*, 16:3, 409–51.

Krell, Gert (1981) 'Capitalism and Armaments: Business Cycles and Defence Spending in the US', *Journal of Peace Research*, 18:3, 221–40.

Krepon, Michael (2001) 'Moving Away from MAD', *Survival*, 43:2, 81–95.

Krishna, Sankaran (1993) 'The Importance of Being Ironic: A Postcolonial View on Critical International Relations Theory', *Alternatives*, 18:3, 385–417.

Kristensen, Hans and Joshua Handler (1996) 'The USA and Counter-proliferation: A New and Dubious Role for US Nuclear Weapons', *Security Dialogue*, 27:4, 387–99.

Kroenig, Matthew and Jay Stowsky (2006) 'War Makes the State, but not as it Pleases: Homeland Security and American Anti-Statism', *Security Studies*, 15:2, 225–70.

Kuhn, Thomas (1962) *The Structure of Scientific Revolutions*, Chicago: University of Chicago Press.

Kupchan, Charles A. (1998) 'After Pax Americana: Benign Power, Regional Integration and the Sources of Stable Multipolarity', *International Security*, 23:2, 40–79.

——— (2003) 'The Rise of Europe, America's Changing Internationalism and the End of US Primacy', *Political Science Quarterly*, 118:2, 205–31.

——— (2004) 'New Research Agenda? Yes. New Paradigm? No.', *Zeitschrift für Internationale Beziehungen*, 1, 101–10.

——— (2004/5) 'The Travails of Union: The American Experience and its Implications for Europe', *Survival*, 46:4, 103–19.

Kupchan, Charles and Peter Trubowitz (2007) 'Dead Center: The Demise of Liberal Internationalism in the United States', *International Security*, 32:2, 7–44.

Kurihara, Hiroyoshi (1998) 'The Future of the International Nonproliferation Regime', *Asia-Pacific Review*, 5:3, 151–66.

Kurki, Milja and Colin Wight (2007) 'International Relations and Social Science', in Tim Dunne, Milja Kurki and Steve Smith (eds.) *International Relations Theory: Discipline and Diversity*, Oxford: Oxford University Press, 13–33.

Kurth, James R. (1973) 'Why we Buy the Weapons we Do', *Foreign Policy*, 11, 33–56.

——— (2005) 'Ignoring History: US Democratization in the Muslim World', *Orbis*, 49:2, 305–22.

Kuusisto, Riikka (1998) 'Framing the Wars in the Gulf and in Bosnia: The Rhetorical Definitions of the Western Power Leaders in Action', *Journal of Peace Research*, 35:5, 603–20.

Kuzio, Taras (2000) 'Geopolitical Pluralism in the CIS: The Emergence of GUUAM', *European Security*, 9:2, 81–114.

Kydd, Andrew H. and Barbara F. Walter (2006) 'The Strategies of Terrorism', *International Security*, 31:1, 49–79.

Lacina, Bethany, Nils Petter Gleditsch and Bruce Russett (2006) 'The Declining Risk of Death in Battle', *International Studies Quarterly*, 50:3, 673–80.

Lafeber, Walter (2002) 'The Post-September 11 Debate over Empire, Globalization and Fragmentation', *Political Science Quarterly*, 117:1, 1–17.

Laffey, Mark and Jutta Weldes (1997) 'Beyond Belief: Ideas and Symbolic Technologies in the Study of International Relations', *European Journal of International Relations*, 3:2, 193–237.

Lake, David A. (1992) 'Powerful Pacifists: Democratic States and War', *American Political Science Review*, 86:1, 24–37.

(1999) 'Ulysses's Triumph: American Power and the New World Order', *Security Studies*, 8:4, 44–78.

Lake, David A. and Patrick M. Morgan (1997) *Regional Orders: Building Security in a New World*, Pennsylvania: Pennsylvania State University Press.

Lambelet, John C. (1975) 'Do Arms Races Lead to War?', *Journal of Peace Research*, 12:2, 123–8.

Lambeth, Benjamin S. (1997) 'The Technology Revolution in Air Warfare', *Survival*, 39:1, 65–83.

Landi, Dale, Bruno W. Augenstein, Cullen M. Crain, William R. Harris and Brian M. Jenkins (1984) 'Improving the Means for Intergovernmental Communications in Crisis', *Survival*, 26:5, 200–14.

Laqueur, Walter (1996) 'Postmodern Terrorism', *Foreign Affairs*, 75:5, 24–36.

(1998) 'The New Face of Terror', *Washington Quarterly*, 21:4, 169–78.

Larrabee, F. Stephen (1992) 'Instability and Change in the Balkans', *Survival*, 34:2, 31–49.

(1996) 'Ukraine's Balancing Act', *Survival*, 38:2, 143–65.

Larsen, Jeffrey A. (2002) *Arms Control: Cooperative Security in a Changing Environment*, Boulder: Lynne Rienner.

Lasswell, Harold D. (1941) 'The Garrison State', *American Journal of Sociology*, 46:4, 455–68.

(1950) *National Security and Individual Freedom*, New York, Toronto and London: McGraw-Hill.

Latham, Robert (ed.) (2003) *Bombs and Bandwith: The Emerging Relationship Between Information Technology and Security*, New York: The New Press.

Lausten, Carsten Bagge and Ole Wæver (2000) 'In Defence of Religion: Sacred Referent Objects for Securitization', *Millennium*, 29:3, 705–39.

Lawler, Peter (1995) *A Question of Values: Johan Galtung's Peace Research*, Boulder: Lynne Rienner.

Layne, Christopher (1993) 'The Unipolar Illusion: Why Other Great Powers will Rise', *International Security*, 17:4, 5–51.

(1997) 'From Preponderance to Offshore Balancing: America's Future Grand Strategy', *International Security*, 22:1, 86–124.

(2003) 'The "Poster Child for Offensive Realism": America as a Global Hegemon', *Security Studies*, 12:2, 120–64.

(2006) 'The Unipolar Illusion Revisited: The Coming End of the United States' Unipolar Moment', *International Security*, 31:2, 7–41.

Lebovic, James H. (2004) 'Unity in Action: Explaining Alignment Behavior in the Middle East', *Journal of Peace Research*, 41:2, 167–90.

Lebow, Richard N. (1983/4) 'The Cuban Missile Crisis: Reading the Lessons Correctly', *Political Science Quarterly*, 98:3, 431–58.

(1994) 'The Long Peace, the End of the Cold War and the Failure of Realism', *International Organization*, 48:2, 249–77.

(2005) 'Deterrence: Then and Now', *Journal of Strategic Studies*, 28:5, 765–73.

Lebow, Richard N. and Thomas Risse-Kappen (eds.) (1997) *International Relations Theory and the End of the Cold War*, New York: Columbia University Press.

Lee, Chung M. (2001) 'North Korean Missiles: Strategic Implications and Policy Responses', *The Pacific Review*, 14:1, 85–120.

Lee, Jung-Hoon and Chung-In Moon (2003) 'The North Korean Nuclear Crisis Revisited: The Case for a Negotiated Settlement', *Security Dialogue*, 34:2, 135–51.

Lee, Steven (1995) 'What's Wrong with Nuclear Proliferation?', *Security Studies*, 5:1, 164–70.

Leenders, Reinoud (2007) '"Regional Conflict Formations": Is the Middle East Next?', *Third World Quarterly*, 28:5, 959–82.

Legvold, Robert (1979) 'Strategic Doctrine and SALT: Soviet and American Views', *Survival*, 21:1, 8–13.

Leidy, Michael and Robert Staiger (1985) 'Economic Issues and Methodology in Arms Race Analysis', *Journal of Conflict Resolution*, 29:3, 503–30.

Leifer, Michael (1996) 'The ASEAN Regional Forum', *Adelphi* 302, London: IISS.

Lellouche, Pierre (1981) 'Breaking the Rules Without Stopping the Bomb', *International Organization*, 35:1, 39–58.

Lentner, Howard H. (1976) 'The Case of Canada and Nuclear Weapons', *World Politics*, 29:1, 29–66.

Lentz, Theodore F. (1955) *Towards a Science of Peace: Turning Point in Human Destiny*, New York: Bookman Associates.

Lesser, Ian O. (2006) 'Turkey, the United States and the Delusion of Geopolitics', *Survival*, 48:3, 83–96.

Levine, Herbert M. and David Carlton (eds.) (1986) *The Nuclear Arms Race Debated*, New York: McGraw-Hill.

Levine, Robert (2001) 'Deterrence and the ABM: Retreading the Old Calculus', *World Policy Journal*, 18:3, 23–31.

Levite, Ariel E. (2002/3) 'Never Say Never Again: Nuclear Reversal Revisited', *International Security*, 27:3, 59–88.

Levy, Jack S. (1984) 'The Offensive/Defensive Balance of Military Technology: A Theoretical and Historical Analysis', *International Studies Quarterly*, 28:2, 219–38.

Lewis, Julian (2006) 'Nuclear Disarmament versus Peace in the Twenty-first Century', *International Affairs*, 82:4, 667–73.

Lewis, Samuel W. (1999) 'The United States and Israel: Evolution of an Unwritten Alliance', *The Middle East Journal*, 53:3, 364–78.

Liberman, Peter (2000/1) 'Ties that Blind: Will Germany and Japan Rely Too Much on the United States?', *Security Studies*, 10:2, 98–138.

Liddell Hart, Basil (1946) *The Revolution in Warfare*, London: Faber & Faber.

Lieber, Keir A. (2000) 'Grasping the Technological Peace: The Offensive–Defensive Balance and International Security', *International Security*, 25:1, 71–104.

Lieber, Keir A. and Daryl G. Press (2006) 'The End of MAD? The Nuclear Dimension of US Primacy', *International Security*, 30:4, 7–44.

Lieber, Robert J. (1966) 'The French Nuclear Force: A Strategic and Political Evaluation', *International Affairs*, 42:3, 421–31.

Lieberman, Elli (1995) 'What Makes Deterrence Work? Lessons from the Egyptian–Israeli Enduring Rivalry', *Security Studies*, 4:4, 851–910.

Lind, Jennifer M. (2004) 'Pacifism or Passing the Buck? Testing Theories of Japanese Security Policy', *International Security*, 29:1, 92–121.

Lindley, Dan (2006) 'Cooperative Airborne Monitoring: Opening the Skies to Promote Peace, Protect the Environment and Cope with Natural Disasters', *Contemporary Security Policy*, 27:2, 325–43.

Lindley-French, Julian (2004) 'The Revolution in Security Affairs: Hard and Soft Security Dynamics in the 21st Century', *European Security*, 13:1/2, 1–15.

Linklater, Andrew (2007) 'Torture and Civilisation', *International Relations*, 21:1, 111–18.

Lisle, Debbie (2006) 'Local Symbols, Global Networks: Rereading the Murals of Belfast', *Alternatives*, 31:1, 27–52.

(2007) 'Benevolent Patriotism: Art, Dissent and *The American Effect*', *Security Dialogue*, 38:2, 233–50.

Litwak, Robert S. (2003) 'Non-proliferation and the Dilemmas of Regime Change', *Survival*, 45:4, 7–32.

(2008) 'Living with Ambiguity: Nuclear Deals with Iran and North Korea', *Survival*, 50:1, 91–118.

Litzinger, Ralph A. (1999) 'Reimagining the State in Post-Mao China', in Weldes *et al.* (eds.) *Cultures of Insecurity*, 293–318.

Lobell, Steven E. (2003) 'War is Politics: Offensive Realism, Domestic Politics and Security Strategies', *Security Studies*, 12:2, 165–95.

Locher, Birgit and Elisabeth Prügel (2001) 'Feminism and Constructivism: Worlds Apart or Sharing the Middle Ground?', *International Studies Quarterly*, 45:1, 111–29.

Lodal, Jan M. (1980) 'Deterrence and Nuclear Strategy', *Daedalus*, 109:4, 155–75.

Lodgaard, Sverre (1980) 'Prospects for Non-proliferation', *Survival*, 22:4, 161–66.

Lopez, George A. (1985) 'A University Peace Studies Curriculum for the 1990s', *Journal of Peace Research*, 22:2, 117–28.

Loustarinen, Heikki (1989) 'Finnish Russophobia: The Story of an Enemy Image', *Journal of Peace Research*, 26:2, 123–37.

Lovins, Amory B., L. Hunter Lovins and Leonard Ross (1980) 'Nuclear Power and Nuclear Bombs', *Foreign Affairs*, 58:5, 1137–77.

Lowrance, William W. (1976) 'Nuclear Futures for Sale: To Brazil from West Germany, 1975', *International Security*, 1:2, 47–166.

Luke, Timothy W. (1991) 'The Discipline of Security Studies and the Codes of Containment: Learning from Kuwait', *Alternatives*, 16:3, 315–44.

Lumpe, Lora (1999) 'Curbing the Proliferation of Small Arms and Light Weapons', *Security Dialogue*, 30:2, 151–64.

Lundestad, Geir (1986) 'Empire by Invitation? The United States and Western Europe 1945–1952', *Journal of Peace Research*, 23:3, 263–77.

Lustick, Ian S. (1997) 'The Absence of Middle Eastern Great Powers: Political "Backwardness" in Historical Perspective', *International Organization*, 51:4, 653–83.

Luttwak, Edward N. (1980a) 'The Problems of Extending Deterrence', *Adelphi* 160, London: IISS.

    (1980b) 'Why Arms Control has Failed', in Edward N. Luttwak, *Strategy and Politics: Collected Essays*, New Brunswick: Transaction Books, 121–39.

    (1995) 'Towards Post-heroic Warfare', *Foreign Affairs*, 74:3, 109–22.

    (1996) 'A Post-heroic Military Policy', *Foreign Affairs*, 75:4, 33–44.

    (1999) 'Give War a Chance', *Foreign Affairs*, 78:4, 36–44.

Lutzker, Daniel R. (1961) 'Sex Role, Cooperation and Competition in a Two-person, Non-zero Sum Game', *Journal of Conflict Resolution*, 5:4, 366–68.

MacFarlane, S. Neil (1993) 'Russia, the West and European Security', *Survival*, 35:3, 3–25.

    (2002) 'Intervention in Contemporary World Politics', *Adelphi* 350, London: IISS.

Mack, Andrew (1975) 'Why Big Nations Lose Small Wars: The Politics of Asymmetric Conflict', *World Politics*, 27:2, 175–200.

    (1991) 'North Korea and the Bomb', *Foreign Policy*, 83, 87–104.

    (1993) 'The Nuclear Crisis on the Korean Peninsula', *Asian Survey*, 33:4, 339–59.

    (1994) 'A Nuclear North Korea: The Choices are Narrowing', *World Policy Journal*, 11:2, 27–35.

Maddox, John (1975) 'Prospects for Nuclear Proliferation', *Adelphi* 113, London: IISS.

Mahapatra, Chintamani (2000) 'CTBT, the US and India', *International Studies*, 37:4, 339–49.

Mahmudul, Huque (1997) 'Nuclear Proliferation in South Asia and US Policy', *International Studies*, 34:1, 1–14.

Malik, J. Mohan (2000) 'China and the Nuclear Non-proliferation Regime', *Contemporary Southeast Asia*, 22:3, 445–78.

Malkasian, Carter (2006) 'Signaling Resolve, Democratization and the First Battle of Fallujah', *Journal of Strategic Studies*, 29:3, 423–52.

Malmvig, Helle (2001) 'The Reproduction of Sovereignties: Between Man and State During Practices of Intervention', *Cooperation and Conflict*, 36:3: 251–72.

(2006) *Sovereignty and Intervention: Constitutions of State Sovereignty During Interventionary and Non-interventionary Practices in Kosovo and Algeria*, London: Routledge.

Mandelbaum, Michael (1998/9) 'Is Major War Obsolete?', *Survival*, 40:4, 20–38.

Manosevitz, Jason U. (2004) 'Japan and South Korea: Security Relations Reach Adolescence', *Asian Survey*, 43:5, 801–25.

Maoz, Zeev (1997) 'Regional Security in the Middle East: Past Trends, Present Realities and Future Challenges', *Journal of Strategic Studies*, 20:1, 1–45.

(2003) 'The Mixed Blessing of Israel's Nuclear Policy', *International Security*, 28:2, 44–77.

Maoz, Zeev and Bruce Russett (1993) 'Normative and Structural Causes of Democratic Peace, 1946–1986', *American Political Science Review*, 87:3, 624–38.

Marcuse, Herbert (1964) *One Dimensional Man*, New York: John Wiley.

Mares, David R. (1996/7) 'Deterrence Bargaining in the Equador–Peru Enduring Rivalry', *Security Studies*, 6:2, 91–123.

Marten, Kimberly Z. (2007) 'Warlordism in Comparative Perspective', *International Security*, 31:3, 41–73.

Martin, Brian (1999) 'Social Defence Strategy: The Role of Technology', *Journal of Peace Research*, 36:5, 535–52.

Martin, Curtis H. (2002) 'Rewarding North Korea: Theoretical Perspectives on the 1994 Agreed Framework', *Journal of Peace Research*, 39:1, 51–68.

Martin, Lawrence (1973) 'The Utility of Military Force', in 'Force in Modern Societies: Its Place in International Politics', *Adelphi* 102, London: IISS, 14–21.

(1980) 'The Determinants of Change: Deterrence and Technology', in 'The Future of Strategic Deterrence: Part II Papers from the IISS 21st Annual Conference', *Adelphi* 161, London: IISS, 9–20.

Marwah, Onkar (1977) 'India's Nuclear and Space Programme: Intent and Policy', *International Security*, 2:2, 96–121.

(1981) 'India and Pakistan: Nuclear Rivals', *International Organization*, 35:1, 165–79.

Marwah, Onkar and Ann Schulz (eds.) (1975) *Nuclear Proliferation and the Near Nuclear Countries*, Cambridge, MA: Ballinger.

Masaki, Stuart (1994/5) 'The Korean Question: Assessing the Military Balance', *Security Studies*, 4:2, 365–425.

Masco, Joseph (1999) 'States of Insecurity: Plutonium and Post-Cold War Anxiety in New Mexico, 1992–96', in Weldes *et al.* (eds.) *Cultures of Insecurity*, 201–31.

Mastanduno, Michael (2005) 'Hegemonic Order, September 11 and the Consequences of the Bush Revolution', *International Relations of the Asia-Pacific*, 5:2, 177–96.

Mathews, Jessica T. (1989) 'Redefining Security', *Foreign Affairs*, 68:2, 162–77.

Mattern, Janice B. (2001) 'The Power Politics of Identity', *European Journal of International Relations*, 7:3, 349–97.

(2005) *Ordering International Politics: Identity, Crisis, and Representational Force*, New York: Routledge.

Matthies, Volker (2003) 'Was ist das neue an den neuen Kriegen? Einige Anmerkungen zu der Debatte über neuartige Aspekte gegenwärtiger Gewaltkonflikte', *edp-Entwicklungspolitik*, 8–9, 21–7.

Mattoo, Amitabh (1996) 'India's Nuclear Status Quo', *Survival*, 38:3, 41–57.

Maull, Hanns W. (1975) 'Oil and Influence: The Oil Weapon Examined', *Adelphi* 117, London: IISS.

(1995/6) 'Germany in the Yugoslav Crisis', *Survival*, 37:4, 99–130.

Mayall, James (1984) 'Reflections on the "New" Economic Nationalism', *Review of International Studies*, 10:4, 313–21.

(1990) *Nationalism and International Society*, Cambridge: Cambridge University Press.

Mazarr, Michael (1995a) 'Virtual Nuclear Arsenals', *Survival*, 37:3, 7–26.

(1995b) 'Going Just a Little Nuclear: Nuclear Proliferation Lessons from North Korea', *International Security*, 20:2, 92–122.

Mazrui, Ali (1980) 'Africa's Nuclear Future', *Survival*, 22:2, 76–81.

(1995) 'The Blood of Experience: The Failed State and Political Collapse in Africa', *World Policy Journal*, 12:1, 28–34.

Mazzitelli, Antonio L. (2007) 'Transnational Organized Crime in West Africa: The Additional Challenge', *International Affairs*, 83:6, 1071–90.

McCausland, Jeffrey D. (1996) 'Arms Control and European Security', *Adelphi* 301, London: IISS.

MccGwire, Michael (1998) 'NATO Expansion: "a Policy Error of Historic Importance"', *Review of International Studies*, 24:1, 23–42.

(2006) 'Comfort Blanket or Weapon of War: What is Trident for?', *International Affairs*, 82:4, 639–50.

McCormick, John (2006) *The European Superpower*, Basingstoke: Palgrave.

McDonald, Matt (2002) 'Human Security and the Construction of Security', *Global Society*, 16:3, 277–95.

(2008) 'Securitisation and the Construction of Security', *European Journal of International Relations*, 14:4, 563–87.

McDougall, Derek (2002) 'Asia–Pacific Security Regionalism: The Impact of Post-1977 Developments', *Contemporary Security Policy*, 23:2, 113–34.

McGann, James G. (2007) *Think Tanks and Policy Advice in the United States: Academics, Advisors and Advocates*, London: Routledge.

McInnes, Colin (1999) 'Spectator Sport Warfare', *Contemporary Security Policy*, 20:3, 142–65.

McInnes, Colin and Kelley Lee (2006) 'Health, Security and Foreign Policy', *Review of International Studies*, 32:1, 5–23.

McNaugher, Thomas (1987) 'Weapons Procurement: The Futility of Reform', *International Security*, 12:2, 63–104.

McSweeney, Bill (1996) 'Identity and Security: Buzan and the Copenhagen School', *Review of International Studies*, 22:1, 81–93.

(1998) 'Durkheim and the Copenhagen School: A Response to Buzan and Wæver', *Review of International Studies*, 24:1, 137–40.

(1999) *Security, Identity and Interests: A Sociology of International Relations*, Cambridge: Cambridge University Press.

Mearsheimer, John J. (1990) 'Back to the Future: Instability in Europe After the Cold War', *International Security*, 15:1, 5–56.

(2005) 'Hans Morgenthau and the Iraq War: Realism versus Neo-conservatism', at www.openDemocracy.net, posted: 21-04-2005.

Mearsheimer, John J. and Robert A. Pape (1993) 'The Answer: A Partition Plan for Bosnia', *The New Republic*, 208:24, 22–8.

Mearsheimer, John J. and Stephen Van Evera (1995) 'When Peace Means War: The Partition that Dare not Speak its Name', *The New Republic*, 213:25, 16–21.

Mearsheimer, John J. and Stephen M. Walt (2003) 'An Unnecessary War', *Foreign Policy*, 134: 50–60.

(2007) *The Israel Lobby and US Foreign Policy*, New York: Garrar, Straus & Giroux.

Mellor, Felicity (2007) 'Colliding Worlds: Asteroid Research and the Legitimization of War in Space', *Social Studies of Science*, 37:4, 499–531.

Mendle, Wolf (1965) 'The Background of French Nuclear Policy', *International Affairs*, 41:1, 22–36.

Menkhaus, Ken (2004) 'Somalia: State Collapse and the Threat of Terrorism', *Adelphi* 364, London: IISS.

Menon, Anand (2004) 'From Crisis to Catharsis: ESDP After Iraq', *International Affairs*, 80:4, 631–48.

Menon, Rajan and Henri Barkey (1992/3) 'The Transformation of Central Asia: Implications for Regional and International Security', *Survival*, 34:4, 68–89.

Mercer, Jonathan (1997) 'Reputation and Rational Deterrence Theory', *Security Studies*, 7:1, 100–13.

Merom, Gil (1999) 'Israel's National Security and the Myth of Exceptionalism', *Political Science Quarterly*, 114:3, 409–34.

Meyer, Berthold (1989) 'Common Security versus Western Security Cooperation? The Debate on European Security in the Federal Republic of Germany', in Ole Wæver, Pierre Lemaitre and Elzbieta Tromer (eds.) *European Polyphony: Perspectives Beyond East–West Confrontation*, Basingstoke: Macmillan, 168–85.

Mgbeoji, Ikechi (2006) 'The Civilized Self and the Barbaric Other: Imperial Delusions of Order and the Challenges of Human Security', *Third World Quarterly*, 25:5, 855–69.

Michishita, Narushige (2006) 'Coercing to Reconcile: North Korea's Response to US "Hegemony"', *Journal of Strategic Studies*, 29:6, 1015–40.

Michta, Andrew A. (2007) 'What Next for NATO?', *Orbis*, 51:1, 155–64.

Midford, Paul (2002) 'The Logic of Reassurance and Japan's Grand Strategy', *Security Studies*, 11:2, 1–43.

(2003) 'Japan's Response to Terror: Dispatching the SDF to the Arabian Sea', *Asian Survey*, 43:2, 329–51.

(2004) 'China Views the Revised US–Japan Defense Guidelines: Popping the Cork?', *International Relations of the Asia-Pacific*, 4:1, 113–45.

Miles, James (2002) 'Waiting Out North Korea', *Survival*, 44:2, 37–49.

Millennium (2000) Special Issue, 'Religion and International Relations', 29:3.

Miller, Benjamin (2006) 'Balance of Power or the State-to-Nation Balance: Explaining Middle East War-propensity', *Security Studies*, 15:4, 658–705.

Miller, Judith (1993) 'The Challenge of Radical Islam', *Foreign Affairs*, 72:2, 43–56.

Miller, Steven E. (1993) 'The Case Against a Ukranian Nuclear Deterrent', *Foreign Affairs*, 72:3, 52–80.

(2001a): 'International Security at Twenty-five: From One World to Another', *International Security*, 26:1, 5–39.

(2001b) 'The Flawed Case for Missile Defence', *Survival*, 43:3, 95–109

(2006) 'The Iraq Experiment and US National Security', *Survival*, 48:4, 17–50.

Milliken, Jennifer (1999) 'Intervention and Identity: Reconstructing the War in Korea', in Weldes *et al.* (eds.) *Cultures of Insecurity*, 91–117.

Mistry, Dinshaw (1999) 'Diplomacy, Sanctions, and the US Non-proliferation Dialogue with India and Pakistan', *Asian Survey*, 29:5, 753–71.

(2003a) 'Beyond the MTCR: Building a Comprehensive Regime to Contain Ballistic Missile Proliferation', *International Security*, 27:4, 119–49.

(2003b) 'The Unrealized Promise of International Institutions: The Test Ban Treaty and India's Nuclear Breakout', *Security Studies*, 12:4, 116–51.

Mitrany, David (1933) *The Progress of International Government*, New Haven: Yale University Press.

(1966) *A Working Peace System*, Chicago: Quadranglite Books.

Mitzen, Jennifer (2006) 'Ontological Security in World Politics: State Identity and the Security Dilemma', *European Journal of International Relations*, 12:3, 341–70.

Mochizuki, Michael M. (1994) 'The Past in Japan's Future: Will the Japanese Change?', *Foreign Affairs*, 73:5, 126–34.

(2007) 'Japan's Shifting Strategy Toward the Rise of China', *Journal of Strategic Studies*, 30:4/5, 739–76.

Modigliani, Andre (1972) 'Hawks and Doves, Isolationism and Political Distrust: An Analysis of Public Opinion on Military Policy', *The American Political Science Review*, 66:3, 960–78.

Mogami, Toshiki (1988) 'The South Pacific Nuclear Free Zone: A Fettered Leap Forward', *Journal of Peace Research*, 25:4, 411–30.

Møller, Bjørn (1987) 'The Need for an Alternative NATO Strategy', *Journal of Peace Research*, 24:1, 61–74.

    (1992) *Common Security and Nonoffensive Defense. A Neorealist Perspective*, Boulder and London: Lynne Rienner and UCL Press.

    (ed.) (1998) *Security, Arms Control and Defence Restructuring in East Asia*, Aldershot: Ashgate.

Møller, Bjørn and Håkan Wiberg (eds.) (1994) *Non-offensive Defence for the Twenty-first Century*, Boulder and London: Westview.

Möller, Frank (2007) 'Photographic Interventions in Post-9/11 Security Policy', *Security Dialogue*, 38:2, 179–96.

Moltz, James C. and Alexandre Y. Mansourov (eds.) (2000) *The North Korean Nuclear Program*, London: Routledge.

Moltz, James C., Vladimir A. Orlov and Adam N. Stulberg (eds.) (2004) *Preventing Nuclear Meltdown: Managing Decentralization of Russia's Nuclear Complex*, Aldershot: Ashgate.

Monaghan, Andrew (2006) '"Calmly Critical"': Evolving Russian Views of US Hegemony', *Journal of Strategic Studies*, 29:6, 987–1013.

Montgomery, Alexander H. (2005) 'Ringing in Proliferation: How to Dismantle an Atomic Bomb Network', *International Security*, 30:2, 153–87.

Monti, Daniel J. (1979) 'Patterns of Conflict Preceding the 1964 Riots', *Journal of Conflict Resolution*, 23:1, 41–69.

Moore, Gregory J. (2008) 'How North Korea Threatens China's Interests: Understanding Chinese "Duplicity" on the North Korean Nuclear Issue', *International Relations of the Asia-Pacific*, 8:1, 1–29.

Moore, J. D. L. (1987) *South Africa and Nuclear Proliferation*, London: Macmillan.

Moore, Rebecca (2002) 'NATO's Mission for the New Millennium: A Value-Based Approach to Building Security', *Contemporary Security Policy*, 23:1, 1–34.

Mor, Ben D. (1997) 'The Middle East Peace Process and Regional Security', *Journal of Strategic Studies*, 20:1, 172–202.

Moravscik, Andrew (2002) 'Why is US Human Rights Policy so Unilateralist?', in Stewart Patrick and Shepard Forman (eds.) *Multilateralism in US Foreign Policy*, Boulder: Lynne Rienner, 345–76.

Morgan, Patrick M. (2003) 'Information Warfare and Domestic Threats to American Security', *Contemporary Security Policy*, 24:1, 161–89.

    (1977) *Deterrence: A Conceptual Analysis*, London: SAGE.

    (1983) *Deterrence: A Conceptual Analysis,*, 2nd edn, London: SAGE.

    (2005) 'Taking the Long View of Deterrence', *Journal of Strategic Studies*, 28:5, 751–63.

Morgenthau, Hans J. (1946) *Scientific Man versus Power Politics*, Chicago: University of Chicago Press.

    (1951) *In Defense of the National Interest*, New York: Knopf.

(1978) *Politics Among Nations: The Struggle for Power and Peace*, 5th edn, New York: Knopf.

Mousavizadeh, Nader (ed.) (1996) *The Black Book of Bosnia: The Consequences of Appeasement, by the Writers and Editors of* The New Republic, New York: Basic Books.

Mousseau, Michael (2002/3) 'Market Civilization and its Clash with Terror', *International Security*, 27:3, 5–29.

Mousseau, Michael and Yubang Shi (1999) 'A Test for Reverse Causality in the Democratic Peace Relationship', *Journal of Peace Research*, 36:5, 639–63.

Mowle, Thomas S. (2006) 'Iraq's Militia Problem', *Survival*, 48:3, 41–58.

Mueller, John (1989) *Retreat from Doomsday: The Obsolescence of Major War*, New York: Basic Books.

Müftüler, Meltem (1998) 'Turkey and Israel: An Axis of Tension and Security', *Security Dialogue*, 29:1, 121–3.

Münkler, Herfried (2004) *The New Wars* Cambridge: Polity Press.

Muppidi, Himadeep (1999) 'Postcoloniality and the Production of International Insecurity: The Persistent Puzzle of US–Indian Relations', in Weldes *et al.* (eds.) *Cultures of Insecurity*, 119–46.

Murden, Simon (2002) *Islam, the Middle East, and the New Global Hegemony*, Boulder: Lynne Rienner.

Mutimer, David (1998) 'Reconstituting Security? The Practices of Proliferation Control', *European Journal of International Relations*, 4:1, 99–129.

(2000) 'Testing Times: Of Nuclear Tests, Test Bans and the Framing of Proliferation', *Contemporary Security Policy*, 21:1, 1–22.

(2007) 'Critical Security Studies: A Schismatic History', in Alan R. Collins (ed.) *Contemporary Security Studies*, Oxford: Oxford University Press, 53–74.

Nabers, Dirk (2002) 'The Social Construction of International Institutions: The Case of ASEAN + 3', *International Relations of the Asia Pacific*, 3:1, 113–36.

Nacos, Brigitte L. (2003) 'Terrorism as Breaking News: Attack on America', *Political Science Quarterly*, 118:1, 22–52.

Nalebuff, Barry (1988) 'Minimal Nuclear Deterrence', *Journal of Conflict Resolution*, 32:3, 411–25.

Nathanson, Charles (1988) 'The Social Construction of the Soviet Threat: A Study in the Politics of Representation', *Alternatives*, 13:4, 443–83.

Navias, Martin (1989) 'Ballistic Missile Proliferation in the Middle East', *Survival*, 31:3, 225–39.

Nayak, Meghana (2006) 'Orientalism and "Saving" US State Identity after 9/11', *International Feminist Journal of Politics*, 8:1, 42–61.

Neal, Andrew W. (2006) 'Foucault in Guantanamo: Towards an Archaeology of the Exception', *Security Dialogue*, 37:1, 31–46.

Neocleous, Mark (2006a) 'From Social to National Security', *Security Dialogue*, 37:3, 363–84.

(2006b) 'The Problem with Normality: Taking Exception to "Permanent Emergency"', *Alternatives*, 31:2, 191–213.

Nerlich, Uwe (1975/6) 'Nuclear Weapons and East–West Negotiations', *Adelphi* 120, London: IISS.

Ness, Cindy D. (ed.) (2007) *Female Terrorism and Militancy: Agency, Utility and Organization*, London: Routledge.

Neufeld, Mark (2004) 'Pitfalls of Emancipation and Discourses of Security: Reflections on Canada's "Security With a Human Face"', *International Relations*, 18:1, 109–23.

Neumann, Iver B. (1996a) 'Collective Identity Formation: Self and Other in International Relations', *European Journal of International Relations*, 2:2, 139–74.

(1996b) *Russia and the Idea of Europe: A Study in Identity and International Relations*, London: Routledge.

(1998) 'Identity and the Outbreak of War: Or Why the Copenhagen School of Security Studies should Include the Idea of "Violisation" in its Framework of Analysis', *International Journal of Peace Studies*, 3:2, 7–22.

(1999) *Uses of the Other: "The East" in European Identity Formation*, Minneapolis: University of Minnesota Press.

Neumann, Iver B. and Jennifer M. Welsh (1991) 'The Other in European Self-definition: An Addendum to the Literature on International Society', *Review of International Studies*, 17:4, 327–46.

Neumann, Peter R. and Michael L. R. Smith (2005) 'Strategic Terrorism: The Framework and its Fallacies', *Journal of Strategic Studies*, 28:4, 571–95.

Newhouse, John (1973) *Cold Dawn: The Story of SALT*, New York: Holt, Rinehart & Winston.

Newman, Andrew (2004) 'Arms Control, Proliferation and Terrorism: The Bush Administration's Post-September 11 Security Strategy', *Journal of Strategic Studies*, 27:1, 59–88.

Newman, Edward (2001) 'Human Security and Constructivism', *International Studies Perspectives*, 2:3, 239–51.

(2004) 'The "New Wars" Debate: A Historical Perspective is Needed', *Security Dialogue*, 35:2, 173–89.

Nichols, Thomas M. (2005) 'Anarchy and Order in the New Age of Prevention', *World Policy Journal*, 22:3, 1–23.

Nincic, Donna J. (2005) 'The Challenge of Maritime Terrorism: Threat Identification, WMD and Regime Response', *Journal of Strategic Studies*, 28:4, 619–44.

Niou, Emerson M. S. and Peter C. Ordeshook (1999) 'Return of the Luddites', *International Security*, 24:2, 84–96.

Nissenbaum, Helen (2005) 'Where Computer Security Meets National Security', *Ethics and Information Technology*, 7:2, 61–73.

Niva, Steve (1999) 'Contested Sovereignties and Postcolonial Insecurities in the Middle East', in Weldes *et al.* (eds.) *Cultures of Insecurity*, 147–72.

Nizamani, Haider K. (2001) 'South Asian Nuclear Weapons and Dilemmas of International Non-proliferation Regimes', *Contemporary Security Policy*, 22:2, 27–48.

Noel-Baker, Philip (1958) *The Arms Race: A Programme for World Disarmament*, London: John Calder.

Nye, Joseph S. Jr. (1974) 'Collective Economic Security', *International Affairs*, 50:4, 584–98.

 (1985) 'NPT: The Logic of Inequality', *Foreign Policy*, 59, 123–31.

 (1986) 'Nuclear Winter and Policy Choices', *Survival*, 28:2, 119–27.

 (1989) 'The Contribution of Strategic Studies: Future Challenges', *Adelphi* 235, London: IISS, 20–34.

 (1990) 'Soft Power', *Foreign Policy*, 80, 153–71.

 (1992) 'What New World Order?', *Foreign Affairs*, 71:2, 83–96.

 (1995) 'The Case for Deep Engagement', *Foreign Affairs*, 74:4, 90–103.

 (2002) *The Paradox of American Power: Why the World's Only Superpower can't go it Alone*, Oxford: Oxford University Press.

Nye, Joseph S. Jr. and Sean M. Lynn-Jones (1988) 'International Security Studies: A Report of a Conference on the State of the Field', *International Security*, 12:4, 5–27.

Ó Tuathail, Gearóid (1996) *Critical Geopolitics: The Politics of Writing Global Space*, London: Routledge.

O'Brennan, John (2006) 'Bringing Geopolitics Back In: Exploring the Security Dimension of the 2004 Eastern Enlargement of the European Union', *Cambridge Review of International Affairs*, 19:1, 155–69.

Odell, Peter, R. (1975) *Oil and World Power: Background to the Oil Crisis*, Harmondsworth: Penguin Books.

Ogilvie-White, Tanya (1996) 'Is There a Theory of Nuclear Proliferation? An Analysis of the Contemporary Debate', *The Nonproliferation Review*, 4:1, 43–60.

Ogunbadejo, Oye (1984) 'Africa's Nuclear Capability', *The Journal of Modern African Studies*, 22:1, 19–43.

Ogunbanwo, Sola (1996) 'The Treaty of Palindaba: Africa is Nuclear-Weapon Free', *Security Dialogue*, 27:2, 185–200.

O'Hanlon, Michael (1998) 'Can High Technology Bring US Troops Home?', *Foreign Policy*, 113, 72–86.

 (2008) 'Resurrecting the Test-Ban Treaty', *Survival*, 50:1, 119–32.

Ohtomo, Takafumi (2002) 'Bandwagoning to Dampen Suspicion: NATO and the US–Japan Alliance after the Cold War', *International Relations of the Asia Pacific*, 3:1, 29–55.

Oka, Takashi (2001) 'US–Japan Alliance: The Political Dimension', *Asia-Pacific Review*, 8:1, 10–20.

Olsen, Ole J. and Ib M. Jarvad (1970) 'The Vietnam Conference Papers: A Case Study of a Failure of Peace Research', *Peace Research Society (International) Papers*, 14, 155–70.

Oneal, John R. and Bruce Russett (1997) 'The Classical Liberals were Right: Democracy, Interdependence and Conflict, 1950–85', *International Studies Quarterly*, 41:2, 267–93.

(1999) 'The Kantian Peace: The Pacific Benefits of Democracy, Interdependence and International Organizations, 1885–1992', *World Politics*, 52:1, 1–37.

O'Neill, Robert (1995) 'Britain and the Future of Nuclear Weapons', *International Affairs*, 71:4, 747–61.

Onuf, Nicholas G. (1975) 'Peace Research Parochialism', *Journal of Peace Research*, 12:1, 71–8.

Orbis (1998) Special Issue, 'Religion in World Affairs', 43:2.

Oren, Ido (1994) 'The Indo-Pakistani Arms Competition: A Deductive and Statistical Analysis', *Journal of Conflict Resolution*, 38:2, 185–214.

(1995) 'The Subjectivity of the "Democratic Peace": Changing US Perceptions of Imperial Germany', *International Security*, 20:2, 147–84.

(2003) *Our Enemies and Us: America's Rivalries and the Making of Political Science*, Ithaca: Cornell University Press.

Orme, John (1997) 'The Utility of Force in a World of Scarcity', *International Security*, 22:3, 138–67.

Ortega, Martin (2001) 'Military Intervention and the European Union', *Chaillot Papers no. 45*, Paris: WEU.

Osgood, Charles E. (1953) *Method and Theory in Experimental Psychology*, Oxford: Oxford University Press.

(1959) 'Suggestions for Winning the Real War with Communism', *Journal of Conflict Resolution*, 3:4, 295–325.

(1962) *An Alternative to War or Surrender*, Urbana: University of Illinois Press.

Osgood, Robert (1957) *Limited War: The Challenge to American Strategy*, Chicago: University of Chicago Press.

Osiander, Andreas (2001) 'Sovereignty, International Relations, and the Westphalian Myth', *International Organization*, 55:2, 251–87.

Östgaard, Einar (1965) 'Factors Influencing the Flow of News', *Journal of Peace Research*, 2:1, 39–63.

Owens, Patricia (2003) 'Accidents Don't Just Happen: The Liberal Politics of High-technology "Humanitarian" War', *Millennium*, 32:3, 595–616.

(2007) 'Beyond Strauss, Lies and the War in Iraq: Hannah Arendt's Critique of Neoconservatism', *Review of International Studies*, 33:2, 265–84.

Oxenstierna, Maria T. (1999) 'Revisiting the Global Response to Nonproliferation Violations in Iraq: Tracing the Historical Political Roots', *Contemporary Security Policy*, 20:2, 77–108.

Paarlberg, Robert L. (2004) 'Knowledge as Power: Science, Military Dominance, and US Security', *International Security*, 29:1, 122–51.

Pace, Michelle (2006) *The Politics of Regional Identity: Meddling with the Mediterranean*, London: Routledge.

Pant, Harsh V. (2004) 'The Moscow–Beijing–Delhi "Strategic Triangle": An Idea Whose Time May Never Come', *Security Dialogue*, 35:3, 311–28.

(2007) 'The US–India Nuclear Deal: The Beginning of a Beautiful Relationship?', *Cambridge Review of International Affairs*, 20:3, 455–72.

Pape, Robert A. (1996) *Bombing to Win: Air Power and Coercion in War*, Ithaca: Cornell University Press.

Paris, Roland (2001) 'Human Security: Paradigm Shift or Hot Air?', *International Security*, 26:2, 87–102.

Parmar, Inderjeet (2005) 'Catalysing Events, Think Tanks and American Foreign Policy Shifts: A Comparative Analysis of the Impacts of Pearl Harbor 1941 and 11 September 2001', *Government and Opposition*, 40:1, 1–25.

Pastusiak, Longin (1977) 'Objective and Subjective Premises of Detente', *Journal of Peace Research*, 14:2, 185–93.

Pateman, Carol (1988) 'Feminist Critiques of the Public/Private Dichotomy', in Stanley I. Benn and G. F. Gaus (eds.) *Public and Private in Social Life*, London: St Martin's Press and Croom Helm, 118–40.

Patomäki, Heikki (2001) 'The Challenge of Critical Theories: Peace Research at the Start of the New Century', *Journal of Peace Research*, 38:6, 723–37.

Paul, T. V. (2003) 'Systemic Conditions and Security Cooperation: Explaining the Persistence of the Nuclear Non-proliferation Regime', *Cambridge Review of International Affairs*, 16:1, 135–54.

(2006) 'Why has the India–Pakistan Rivalry been so Enduring? Power Asymmetry and an Intractable Conflict', *Security Studies*, 15:4, 600–30.

Paul, T. V. and Mahesh Shankar (2007) 'Why the US–India Nuclear Accord is a Good Deal', *Survival*, 49:4, 111–22.

Payne, Keith B. (2000) 'The Case for National Missile Defense', *Orbis*, 44:2, 187–96.

Pedatzur, Reuven (1994) 'Evolving Ballistic Missile Capability and Theatre Missile Defence: The Israeli Predicament', *Security Studies*, 3:3, 521–70.

(2007) 'The Iranian Nuclear Threat and the Israeli Options', *Contemporary Security Policy*, 28:3, 513–41.

Peoples, Columba (2006) 'The Moral Obligation of Missile Defence? Preventive War Argumentation and Ballistic Missile Defence Advocacy', *Cambridge Review of International Affairs*, 19:3, 421–34.

Percy, Sarah (2006) 'Regulating the Private Security Industry', *Adelphi* 384, London: IISS.

Perkovich, George (1993a) 'The Plutonium Genie', *Foreign Affairs*, 72:3, 153–65.

(1993b) 'A Nuclear Third Way in South Asia', *Foreign Policy*, 91, 85–104.

Perle, Richard (1991) 'Military Power and the Passing Cold War', in Charles W. Kegley Jr. and Kenneth L. Schwab (eds.) *After the Cold War: Questioning the Morality of Nuclear Deterrence*, Boulder: Westview Press, 33–38.

Peters, Ingo (2004) 'ESDP as a Transatlantic Issue: Problems of Mutual Ambiguity', *The International Studies Review*, 6:3, 381–402.

Petersen, Karen Lund (2001) 'Trafficking in Women: The Danish Construction of Baltic Prostitution', *Cooperation and Conflict*, 36:2, 213–38.

Petersen, Philip (1995) 'Security Politics in Post-Soviet Central Asia', *European Security*, 4:1, 132–219.

Peterson, John E. (2002) 'Saudi Arabia and the Illusion of Security', *Adelphi* 348, London: IISS.

Peterson, Susan (2002/3) 'Epidemic Disease and National Security', *Security Studies*, 12:2, 43–81.

Pettifer, James (1992) 'The New Macedonian Question', *International Affairs*, 68:3, 475–85.

Pettman, Jan J. (2005) 'Gender issues', in John Baylis and Steve Smith (eds.) *The Globalization of World Politics: An Introduction to International Relations*, 3rd edn, Oxford: Oxford University Press, 669–88.

Philpott, Daniel (2002) 'The Challenge of September 11 to Secularism in International Relations', *World Politics*, 55:1, 66–95.

Pick, Otto (1982) 'Practice and Theory in Soviet Arms Control Policy', *The World Today*, 38:7–8, 257–63.

Pickup, Francine (1998) 'Deconstructing Trafficking in Women: The Example of Russia', *Millennium*, 94:4, 995–1021.

Pieragostini, Karl (1986) 'Arms Control Verification: Cooperating to Reduce Uncertainty', *Journal of Conflict Resolution*, 30:3, 420–44.

Pierre, Andrew J. (1970) *Nuclear Politics: The British Experience with an Independent Strategic Force, 1939–1970*, Oxford: Oxford University Press.

(1973) 'Can Europe's Security be Decoupled from America?', *Foreign Affairs*, 51:4, 761–77.

(1976) 'Coping with International Terrorism', *Survival*, 18:2, 60–67.

Pikayev, Alexander A., Leonard S. Spector, Elina V. Kirichenko and Ryan Gibson (1998) 'Russia, the US and the Missile Technology Control Regime', *Adelphi* 317, London: IISS.

Pin-Fat, Véronique and Maria Stern (2005) 'The Scripting of Private Jessica Lynch: Biopolitics, Gender and the "Feminization" of the US Military', *Alternatives*, 30:1, 25–53.

Pinkston, Daniel A. and Phillip C. Saunders (2003) 'Seeing North Korea Clearly', *Survival*, 45:3, 79–102.

Poleszynski, Dag (1977) 'Waste Production and Overdevelopment: An Approach to Ecological Indicators', *Journal of Peace Research*, 14:4, 285–98.

Pollack, Jonathan D. (1993) 'The United States in East Asia: Holding the Ring', *Adelphi* 275, London: IISS, 69–82.

(2003) 'China and the United States Post-9/11', *Orbis*, 47:4, 617–27.

Poneman, Daniel (1981) 'Nuclear Policies in Developing Countries', *International Affairs*, 57:4, 568–84.

Porter, Bruce (1995) 'Is the Zone of Peace Stable: Sources of Stress and Conflict in the Industrial Democracies of Post-Cold War Europe', *Security Studies*, 4:3, 520–51.

Porter, Gareth and Janet W. Brown (1991) *Global Environmental Politics*, Boulder: Westview Press.

Posen, Barry R. (1993) 'The Security Dilemma and Ethnic Conflict', *Survival*, 35:1, 27–47.

(1997) 'US Security Policy in a Nuclear-armed World', *Security Studies*, 6:3, 1–31.

(2000) 'The War for Kosovo', *International Security*, 24:4, 39–84.

(2001/2) 'The Struggle Against Terrorism: Grand Strategy, Strategy, and Tactics', *International Security*, 26:3, 39–55.

(2003) 'Command of the Commons: The Military Foundation of US Hegemony', *International Security*, 28:1, 5–46.

(2006) 'European Union Security and Defense Policy: Response to Unipolarity?', *Security Studies*, 15:2, 149–86.

(2007) 'Stability and Change in US Grand Strategy', *Orbis*, 51:4, 561–67.

Posen, Barry R. and Andrew L. Ross (1996/7) 'Competing Visions for US Grand Strategy', *International Security*, 21:3, 5–53.

Potter, William C. and Adam Stulberg (1990) 'The Soviet Union and the Spread of Ballistic Missiles', *Survival*, 32:6, 543–57.

Powell, Robert (1999) 'The Modeling Enterprise and Security Studies', *International Security*, 24:2, 97–106.

(2003) 'Nuclear Deterrence Theory, Nuclear Proliferation and National Missile Defense', *International Security*, 27:4, 86–118.

Power, Marcus (2007) 'Digitized Virtuosity: Video War Games and Post-9/11 Cyber-deterrence', *Security Dialogue*, 38:2, 271–88.

Power, Paul F. (1986) 'The South Pacific Nuclear Weapon-free Zone', *Pacific Affairs*, 59:3, 455–75.

Press-Barnathan, Galia (2001) 'The Lure of Regional Security Arrangements: The United States and Regional Security Cooperation in Asia and Europe', *Security Studies*, 10:2, 49–97.

(2006) 'Managing the Hegemon: NATO under Unipolarity', *Security Studies*, 15:2, 271–309.

Pressman, Jeremy (2001) 'September Statements, October Missiles, November Elections: Domestic Politics, Foreign-policy Making and the Cuban Missile Crisis', *Security Studies*, 10:3, 80–114.

Preston, Thomas (1997) 'From Lambs to Lions: Nuclear Proliferation's Grand Reshuffling of Interstate Security Relations', *Cooperation and Conflict*, 32:1, 79–117.

Prestowitz, Clyde P. (2003) *Rogue Nation: American Unilateralism and the Failure of Good Intentions*, New York: Basic Books.

Price, Richard (1995) 'A Genealogy of the Chemical Weapons Taboo', *International Organization*, 49:1, 73–103.

(1997) *The Chemical Weapons Taboo*, Ithaca: Cornell University Press.

Price, Richard and Nina Tannenwald (1996) 'Norms and Deterrence: The Nuclear and Chemical Weapons Taboos', in Peter J. Katzenstein (ed.) *The Culture of National Security: Norms and Identity in World Politics*, New York: Columbia University Press, 114–52.

Prozorov, Sergei (2006) 'Liberal Enmity: The Figure of the Foe in the Political Ontology of Liberalism', *Millennium*, 35:1, 75–99.

Pry, Peter (1984) *Israel's Nuclear Arsenal*, Boulder: Westview.

Qin, Yaqing (2007) 'Why is there no Chinese International Relations Theory?', *International Relations of the Asia-Pacific*, 7:3, 313–40.

Quester, George H. (1970) 'The Nuclear Nonproliferation Treaty and the International Atomic Energy Agency', *International Organization*, 24:2, 163–82.

(1973) *The Politics of Nuclear Proliferation*, Baltimore: Johns Hopkins Press.

(1977) *Offense and Defense in the International System*, New York: John Wiley.

Quinlan, Michael (1993) 'The Future of Nuclear Weapons: Policy for Western Possessors', *International Affairs*, 69:3, 485–96.

(2000/1) 'How Robust is India–Pakistan Deterrence?', *Survival*, 42:4, 141–54.

(2005) 'India–Pakistan Deterrence Revisited', *Survival*, 47:3, 103–16.

(2006) 'The Future of United Kingdom Nuclear Weapons: Shaping the Debate', *International Affairs*, 82:4, 627–37.

(2007) 'Abolishing Nuclear Armouries: Policy or Pipedream?', *Survival*, 49:4, 7–15.

Raas, Whitney and Austin Long (2007) 'Osirak Redux? Assessing Israeli Capabilities to Destroy Iranian Nuclear Facilities', *International Security*, 31:4, 7–33.

Rabasa, Angel M. (2003) 'Political Islam in Southeast Asia: Moderates, Radicals and Terrorists', *Adelphi* 358, London: IISS.

Rangsimaporn, Paradorn (2006) 'Russia's Debate on Military–Technological Cooperation with China: From Yeltsin to Putin', *Asian Survey*, 46:3, 477–95.

Rao, R. V. R. Chandrasekhara (1974) 'A View from India', *Survival*, 16:5, 210–13.

Rapoport, Anatol (1957) 'Lewis F. Richardson's Mathematical Theory of War', *Conflict Resolution*, 1:3, 249–99.

(1960) *Fights, Games and Debates*, Ann Arbor: University of Michigan Press.

(1964) *Strategy and Conscience*, New York: Harper & Row.

Rasmussen, Mikkel Vedby (2001) 'Reflexive Security: NATO and International Risk Society', *Millennium*, 30:2, 285–309.

(2002) '"A Parallel Globalization of Terror": 9–11, Security and Globalization', *Cooperation and Conflict*, 37:1, 323–49.

(2004) 'It Sounds Like a Riddle: Security Studies, the War on Terror and Risk', *Millennium*, 33:2, 381–95.

Rattinger, Hans (1976) 'From War to War : Arms Races in the Middle East', *International Studies Quarterly*, 20:4, 501–31.

Ravenal, Earl C. (1974) 'Was Vietnam a "Mistake"?', *Asian Survey*, 14:7, 589–607.

(1974/5) 'Consequences of the End Game in Vietnam', *Foreign Affairs*, 53:4, 651–67.

Redick, John R. (1975) 'Regional Nuclear Arms Control in Latin America', *International Organization*, 29:4, 415–45.

(1981) 'The Tlatelolco Regime and Nonproliferation in Latin America', *International Organization*, 35:1, 103–34.

Rees, Martin (2003) *Our Final Century*, London: Heinemann.

Rees, Wyn (2007) 'European and Asian Responses to the US-led "War on Terror"', *Cambridge Review of International Affairs*, 20:2, 215–31.

Rees, Wyn and Richard J. Aldrich (2005) 'Contending Cultures of Counterterrorism: Transatlantic Divergence or Convergence?', *International Affairs*, 81:5, 905–23.

Regan, Patrick M. and Aida Paskeviciute (2003) 'Women's Access to Politics and Peaceful States', *Journal of Peace Research*, 40:3, 287–302.

Reid, Herbert G. and Ernest J. Yanarella (1976) 'Toward a Critical Theory of Peace Research in the United States: The Search for an "Intelligible Core"', *Journal of Peace Research*, 13:4, 315–41.

Reilly, James (2004) 'China's History Activists and the War of Resistance Against Japan: History in the Making', *Asian Survey*, 44:3, 276–94.

Reiss, Mitchell B. (1993) 'Safeguarding the Nuclear Peace in South Asia', *Asian Survey*, 33:12, 1107–21.

(2006) 'A Nuclear-armed North Korea: Accepting the "Unacceptable"?', *Survival*, 48:4, 97–109.

Rendall, Matthew (2007) 'Nuclear Weapons and Intergenerational Exploitation', *Security Studies*, 16:4, 525–54.

Rhode, David (2007) 'Army Enlists Anthropology in War Zones', *The New York Times*, October 5, Section A, p. 1.

Richardson, Lewis F. (1960a) *Arms and Insecurity*, Pittsburgh: Boxwood Press.

(1960b) *Statistics of Deadly Quarrels*, Chicago: Quadrangle Books.

Richardson, Stephen A. (1957) 'Lewis Fry Richardson (1881–1953): A Personal Biography', *Conflict Resolution*, 1:3, 300–4.

Richmond, Oliver P. (2000) 'Emerging Concepts of Security in the European Order: Implications for the "Zone of Conflict" at the Fringes of the EU', *European Security*, 9:1, 41–67.

Riedel, Bruce (2008) 'South Asia's Nuclear Decade', *Survival*, 50:2, 107–26.

Rieff, David (1996) *Slaughterhouse: Bosnia and the Failure of the West*, New York: Touchstone. 1st Touchstone edn with new afterword by the author.

Risse-Kappen, Thomas (1991) 'Did "Peace Through Strength" End the Cold War? – Lessons from INF', *International Security*, 16:1, 162–88.

(1996) 'Collective Identity in a Democratic Community: The Case of NATO', in Katzenstein (ed.) *The Culture of National Security*, 357–99.

Rivkin, David (1987) 'The Soviet Approach to Nuclear Arms Control', *Survival*, 29:6, 483–510.

Roberts, Adam (1967) *The Strategy of Civilian Defence: Non-violent Resistance to Aggression*, London: Faber & Faber.

(1976) *Nations in Arms: The Theory and Practice of Territorial Defence*, London: Chatto & Windus.

(1995) 'Communal Conflict as a Challenge to International Organization: The Case of Former Yugoslavia', *Review of International Studies*, 21:4, 389–410.

(1996) 'Humanitarian Action in War', *Adelphi* 305, London: IISS.

(2002) 'Counter-terrorism, Armed Force and the Laws of War', *Survival*, 44:1, 7–32.

(2005) 'The "War on Terror" in Historical Perspective', *Survival*, 47:2, 101–30.

Roberts, Brad (1993) 'From Non-proliferation to Anti-proliferation', *International Security*, 18:1, 139–71.

Roberts, Brad, Robert A. Manning and Ronald N. Montaperto (2000) 'China: The Forgotten Nuclear Power', *Foreign Affairs*, 79:4, 53–63.

Robinson, J. P. Perry (1984) 'Approaches to Chemical Arms Control', in Josephine O'Connor Howe (ed.) *Armed Peace: The Search for World Security*, London: Macmillan, 44–68.

(1996) 'Implementing the Chemical Weapons Convention', *International Affairs*, 72:1, 73–89.

(2008) 'Difficulties Facing the Chemical Weapons Convention', *International Affairs*, 84:2, 223–39.

Rodgers, Jane (1998) 'Bosnia, Gender and the Ethics of Intervention in Civil Wars', *Civil Wars*, 1:1, 103–16.

Roe, Paul (2005) *Ethnic Violence and the Societal Security Dilemma*, London: Routledge.

Rogers, Bernard W. (1982) 'The Atlantic Alliance: Prescriptions for a Difficult Decade', *Foreign Affairs*, 60:5, 1145–56.

Rogers, Paul (2007) 'Peace Studies', in Alan R. Collins (ed.) *Contemporary Security Studies*, Oxford: Oxford University Press, 35–52.

Roman, Peter J. (2002) 'The Dark Winter of Biological Terrorism', *Orbis*, 46:3, 469–82.

Rosecrance, Richard (1975) 'Strategic Deterrence Reconsidered', *Adelphi* 116, London: IISS.

Rosén, Frederik (2008) 'Commercial Security: Conditions of Growth', *Security Dialogue*, 39:1, 77–97.

Rosen, Steven (ed.) (1973) *Testing the Theory of the Military–Industrial Complex*, Lexington: Lexington Books.

(1977) 'A Stable System of Mutual Nuclear Deterrence in the Arab–Israeli Conflict', *American Political Science Review*, 71:4, 1367–83.

Rosenbaum, H. Jon and Glenn M. Cooper (1970) 'Brazil and the Nuclear Nonproliferation Treaty', *International Affairs*, 46:1, 74–90.

Ross, Robert S. (1999) 'The Geography of Peace: East Asia in the Twenty-first Century', *International Security*, 23:4, 81–118.

(2002) 'Navigating the Taiwan Strait: Deterrence, Escalation Dominance and US–China Relations', *International Security*, 27:2, 48–85.

(2006) 'Balance of Power Politics and the Rise of China: Accommodation and Balancing in East Asia', *Security Studies*, 15:3, 355–95.

Rotfeld, Adam D. (2001) 'Europe: An Emerging Power', *SIPRI Yearbook 2001*, Oxford: Oxford University Press, 175–207.

Roth, Ariel I. (2007) 'Nuclear Weapons in Neo-realist Theory', *International Studies Review*, 9:3, 369–84.

Rothschild, Emma (1995) 'What is Security?', *Daedalus*, 124:3, 53–98.

Rowan, Joshua P. (2005) 'The US–Japan Security Alliance, ASEAN and the South China Sea Dispute', *Asian Survey*, 45:3, 414–36.

Roy, Denny (1994) 'Hegemon on the Horizon? China's Threat to East Asian Security', *International Security*, 19:1, 149–68.

(1996) 'China's Threat Environment', *Security Dialogue*, 27:4, 437–48.

(2002) 'China and the War on Terrorism', *Orbis*, 46:3, 511–21.

(2003) 'Rising China and US Interests: Inevitable vs. Contingent Hazards', *Orbis*, 47:1, 125–37.

(2005) 'The Sources and Limits of Sino-Japanese Tensions', *Survival*, 47:2, 191–214.

Roy, Olivier, Reuven Paz, Bruce Hoffman, Steven Simon and Daniel Benjamin (2000) 'America and the New Terrorism: An Exchange', *Survival*, 42:2, 156–72.

Rozman, Gilbert (1999) 'China's Quest for Great Power Identity', *Orbis*, 43:3, 383–404.

(2002a) 'Japan's Quest for Great Power Identity', *Orbis*, 46:1, 73–91.

(2002b) 'China's Changing Images of Japan 1989–2001: The Struggle to Balance Partnership and Rivalry', *International Relations of the Asia Pacific*, 2:1, 95–129.

(2003) 'Japan's North Korea Initiative and US–Japanese Relations', *Orbis*, 47:3, 527–39.

(2004) 'The Northeast Asian Regionalism Context', *Orbis*, 48:2, 217–31.

(2007) 'The North Korean Nuclear Crisis and US Strategy in Northeast Asia', *Asian Survey*, 47:4, 601–21.

Rubin, Barry and Kemal Kirisci (eds.) (2001) *Turkey in World Politics: An Emerging Multiregional Power*, Boulder: Lynne Rienner.

Rubinstein, Alvin Z. (1991) 'New World Order or Hollow Victory?', *Foreign Affairs*, 70:4, 53–65.

Ruddick, Sara (1989) *Maternal Thinking: Toward a Politics of Peace*, Boston: Beacon Press.

Ruggie, John G. (1983) 'Continuity and Transformation in the World Polity: Towards a Neo-realist Synthesis', *World Politics*, 35:2, 261–85.

(1993) 'Territoriality and Beyond: Problematizing Modernity in International Relations', *International Organization*, 47:1, 139–74.

Rumelili, Bahar (2004) 'Constructing Identity and Relating to Difference: Understanding the EU's Mode of Differentiation', *Review of International Studies*, 30:1, 27–47.

Russell, James A. and James J. Wirtz (2004) 'United States Nuclear Strategy in the Twenty-first Century', *Contemporary Security Policy*, 25:1, 91–108.

Russell, Richard L. (2001) 'A Saudi Nuclear Option?', *Survival*, 43:2, 69–79.

(2002) 'Swords and Shields: Ballistic Missiles and Defenses in the Middle East and South Asia', *Orbis*, 46:3, 483–98.

Russett, Bruce (1975) 'The Americans' Retreat from World Power', *Political Science Quarterly*, 90:1, 1–21.

(1983) *The Prisoners of Insecurity*, San Francisco: Freeman.

(1993) *Grasping the Democratic Peace: Principles for a Post-Cold War World*, Princeton: Princeton University Press.

Russett, Bruce and Marguerite Kramer (1973) 'New Editors for an "Old" Journal', *Journal of Conflict Resolution*, 17:1, 3–6.

Russett, Bruce and Miroslav Nincic (1976) 'American Opinion on the Use of Military Force Abroad', *Political Science Quarterly*, 91:3, 411–31.

Sagan, Carl (1983/4) 'Nuclear War and Climatic Catastrophe', *Foreign Affairs*, 62:2, 257–92.

Sagan, Scott D. (1994) 'The Perils of Proliferation: Organization Theory, Deterrence Theory and the Spread of Nuclear Weapons', *International Security*, 18:4, 66–107.

(1996/7) 'Why do States Build Nuclear Weapons? Three Models in Search of a Bomb', *International Security*, 21:3, 54–86.

(2000) 'The Commitment Trap: Why the United States should not use Nuclear Threats to Deter Biological and Chemical Weapons Attacks', *International Security*, 24:4, 85–115.

Sagan, Scott D. and Kenneth Waltz (1995) *The Spread of Nuclear Weapons: A Debate*, New York: W. W. Norton.

Said, Edward W. (1978) *Orientalism*, New York: Pantheon Books.

Sakwa, Richard (2008) '"New Cold War" or Twenty Years' Crisis? Russia and International Politics', *International Affairs*, 84:2, 241–67.

Salame, Ghassan (1993) 'Islam and the West', *Foreign Policy*, 90, 22–37.

Salik, Naeem A. (2004) 'Regional Dynamics and Deterrence: South Asia (2)', *Contemporary Security Policy*, 25:1, 179–201.

Salmon, Trevor (2006) 'The European Union: Just an Alliance or a Military Alliance?', *Journal of Strategic Studies*, 29:5, 813–42.

Salmon, Trevor and Alistair J. K. Shepherd (2003) *Toward a European Army: A Military Power in the Making?* Boulder: Lynne Rienner.

Salter, Mark B. (2006) 'The Global visa Regime and the Political Technologies of the International Self: Borders, Bodies, Biopolitics', *Alternatives*, 31:2, 167–89.

Samore, Gary (2003) 'The Korean Nuclear Crisis', *Survival*, 45:1, 7–24.

Sample, Susan G. (1997) 'Arms Races and Dispute Escalation: Resolving the Debate?', *Journal of Peace Research*, 34:1, 7–22.

Samson, Victoria (2007) 'Prospects for Russian–American Missile Defence Cooperation: Lessons from RAMOS and JDEC', *Contemporary Security Policy*, 28:3, 494–512.

Samuels, Richard J. (2007/8) '"New Fighting Power!" Japan's Growing Maritime Capabilities and East Asian Security', *International Security*, 32:3, 84–112.

Sandole, Dennis J. D., Sean Byrne, Ingrid Sandole-Staroste and Jessica Senehi (eds.) (2008) *Handbook of Conflict Analysis and Resolution*, London: Routledge.

Saperstein, Alvin (1987) 'An Enhanced Non-provocative Defence in Europe', *Journal of Peace Research*, 24:1, 47–60.

Sartori, Leo (1985/6) 'Will SALT II Survive?', *International Security*, 10:3, 147–74.

Saunders, Phillip C. (2007) 'The United States and East Asia after Iraq', *Survival*, 49:1, 141–52.

Sauvant, Karl P. (1976) 'Multinational Enterprises and the Transmission of Culture: The International Supply of Advertising Services and Business Education', *Journal of Peace Research*, 13:1, 49–65.

Sayed, Abdulhay (1993) 'The Future of the Israeli Nuclear Force and the Middle East Peace Process', *Security Dialogue*, 24:3, 31–48.

Schear, James (1985) 'Arms Control Treaty Compliance', *International Security*, 10:2, 141–82.

Scheinmann, Lawrence (1992) 'Nuclear Safeguards and Nonproliferation in a Changing World Order', *Security Dialogue*, 23:4, 37–50.

Schelling, Thomas C. (1960) *The Strategy of Conflict*, Cambridge: Harvard University Press.

  (1966) *Arms and Influence*, New Haven: Yale University Press.

(1976) 'Who Will Have the Bomb?', *International Security*, 1:1, 77–91.

(1985/6) 'What Went Wrong with Arms Control?', *Foreign Affairs*, 64:2, 219–33.

Schelling, Thomas C. and Morton H. Halperin (1961) *Strategy and Arms Control*, New York: The Twentieth Century Fund.

Schiff, Benjamin (1984) *International Nuclear Technology Transfer: Dilemmas of Dissemination and Control*, London: Croom Helm.

Schimmelfennig, Frank (1994) 'Arms Control Regimes and the Dissolution of the Soviet Union', *Cooperation and Conflict*, 29:2, 115–48.

Schlotter, Peter (1983) 'Détente: Models and Strategies', *Journal of Peace Research*, 20:3, 213–20.

Schmid, Alex P. and Ronald D. Crelinsten (eds.) (1993) *Western Responses to Terrorism*, London: Frank Cass.

Schmid, Herman (1968) 'Peace Research and Politics', *Journal of Peace Research*, 5:3, 217–32.

Schmidt, Brian (1998) *The Political Discourse of Anarchy: A Disciplinary History of International Relations*, Albany, NY: SUNY Press.

Schmitt, Burkhard (ed.) (2001) 'Nuclear Weapons: A Great New Debate', *Chaillot Papers no. 48*, WEU.

Schneider, Barry (1994) 'Nuclear Proliferation and Counter-proliferation: Policy Issues and Debates', *Mershon International Studies Review*, 38:2, 209–34.

Schwartz, Benjamin E. (2007) 'America's Struggle Against the Wahhabi/Neo-Salafi Movement', *Orbis*, 51:1, 107–28.

Schweller, Randall (1992) 'Domestic Structure and Preventative War: Are Democracies More Pacific?', *World Politics*, 44:2, 235–69.

Scott, David (2008) 'The Great Power "Great Game" Between India and China: "The Logic of Geography"', *Geopolitics*, 13:1, 1–26.

Scott, Joan W. (1992) '"Experience"', in Judith Butler and Joan W. Scott, *Feminists Theorize the Political*, London: Routledge, 22–40. [Shorter version of 'The Evidence of Experience', *Critical Inquiry*, 17:4, 773–97, 1991.]

Scott, Lenn and Steve Smith (1994) 'Lessons of October: Historians, Political Scientists, Policy-makers and the Cuban Missile Crisis', *International Affairs*, 70:4, 659–84.

Searle, John R. (1969) *Speech Acts: An Essay in the Philosophy of Language*, Cambridge: Cambridge University Press.

Security Dialogue (2004) 'Special Section: What is "Human Security"?', 35:3, 345–87.

(2008) 'Special Issue on Security, Technologies of Risk, and the Political', 39:2–3, 147–357.

Segal, Gerald (1981) 'China's Nuclear Posture for the 1980s', *Survival*, 23:1, 11–18.

(1982) *The Great Power Triangle*, London: Macmillan.

(1985) 'China and Arms Control', *The World Today*, 41: 8–9, 162–6.

(1987) *Arms Control in Asia*, London: Macmillan.

(1997) 'How Insecure is Pacific Asia?', *International Affairs*, 73:2, 235–49.

Seignious, George M. and Jonathan P. Yates (1984) 'Europe's Nuclear Superpowers', *Foreign Policy*, 55, 40–53.

Selby, Jan (2005) 'The Geopolitics of Water in the Middle East: Fantasies and Realities', *Third World Quarterly*, 26:2, 329–49.

Senghaas, Dieter (1975) 'Introduction', *Journal of Peace Research*, 12:4, 249–56.

Serfaty, Simon (1998) 'Bridging the Gulf Across the Atlantic: Europe and the United States in the Persian Gulf', *The Middle East Journal*, 52:3, 337–50.

Sesay, Max Ahmadu (1995) 'Collective Security or Collective Disaster? Regional Peacekeeping in West Africa', *Security Dialogue*, 26:2, 205–22.

Seul, Jeffrey R. (1999) 'Ours is the Way of God: Religion, Identity and Intergroup Conflict', *Journal of Peace Research*, 36:5, 553–69.

Shaikh, Farzana (2002) 'Pakistan's Nuclear Bomb: Beyond the Non-proliferation Regime', *International Affairs*, 78:1, 29–48.

Shambaugh, David (1996) 'Containment or Engagement of China? Calculating Beijing's Responses', *International Security*, 21:2, 180–209.

(2004) 'China Engages Asia: Reshaping the Regional Order', *International Security*, 29:3, 64–99.

Shan, Jun (1994) 'China Goes to the Blue Waters', *Journal of Strategic Studies*, 17:3, 180–208.

Shapiro, Michael J. (1981) *Language and Political Understanding: The Politics of Discursive Practice*, Madison: The University of Wisconsin Press.

(1988) *The Politics of Representation: Writing Practices in Biography, Photography and Policy Analysis*, Madison: The University of Wisconsin Press.

(1990) 'Strategic Discourse/Discursive Strategy: The Representation of "Security Policy" in the Video Age', *International Studies Quarterly*, 34:3, 327–40.

(1992) 'That Obscure Object of Violence: Logistics, Desire, War', *Alternatives*, 17:4: 453–77.

(1997) *Violent Cartographies: Mapping Cultures of War*, Minneapolis: University of Minnesota Press.

Sharp, Gene (1973) *The Politics of Non-violent Action*, Boston: Porter Sargent.

(1985) *Making Europe Unconquerable: The Potential of Civilian-based Deterrence and Defence*, London: Taylor & Francis.

Sharp, Jane M. O. (1981/2) 'Restructuring the SALT Dialogue', *International Security*, 6:3, 144–76.

Shaun, Narine (1997) 'ASEAN and the ARF: The Limits of the "ASEAN Way"', *Asian Survey*, 37:10, 961–78.

Shearer, David (1999) 'Africa's Great War', *Survival*, 41:2, 89–105.

Sheehan, Michael (2005) *International Security: An Analytical Survey*, Boulder: Lynne Rienner.

Shepherd, Laura J. (2006) 'Veiled References: Constructions of Gender in the Bush Administration Discourse on the Attacks on Afghanistan Post-9/11', *International Feminist Journal of Politics*, 8:1, 19–41.

Sherr, James (1997) 'Russia–Ukraine Rapprochement? The Black Sea Fleet Accords',
    Survival, 39:3, 33–50.

Shoham, Dany (2007) 'How Will Iran Retaliate to a Strike on its Nuclear Facilities?',
    Contemporary Security Policy, 28:3, 542–58.

Shultz, Richard H. Jr. and Andrea J. Dew (2006) *Insurgents, Terrorists and
    Militias – The Warriors of Contemporary Combat*, New York: Columbia Uni-
    versity Press.

Sick, Gary (1998) 'Rethinking Dual Containment', *Survival*, 40:1, 5–32.

Sidhu, Waheguru P. S. (2004) 'Regional Dynamics and Deterrence: South Asia (1)',
    Contemporary Security Policy, 25:1, 166–78.

Sidhu, Waheguru P. S. and Jing-dong Yuan (2003) *China and India: Cooperation or
    Conflict?* Boulder: Lynne Rienner.

Sienkiewicz, Stanley (1978) 'SALT and Soviet Nuclear Doctrine', *International Secu-
    rity*, 2:4, 84–100.

Simms, Brendan (2001) *Unfinest Hour: Britain and the Destruction of Bosnia*, Lon-
    don: Penguin Books.

Simon, Sheldon W. (1994) 'East Asian Security: The Playing Field has Changed',
    Asian Survey, 34:12, 1047–76.

Simon, Steven (2007) 'America and Iraq: The Case for Disengagement', *Survival*,
    49:1, 61–84.

Simon, Steven and Daniel Benjamin (2001) 'The Terror', *Survival*, 43:4, 5–17.

Simpson, John (1982) 'Global Non-proliferation Policies: Retrospect and Prospect',
    Review of International Studies, 8:2, 69–88.

    (ed.) (1987) *Nuclear Non-proliferation: An Agenda for the 1990s*, Cambridge:
    Cambridge University Press.

    (1994) 'Nuclear Non-proliferation in the Post-Cold War Era', *International
    Affairs*, 70:1, 17–39.

    (2004) 'France, the United Kingdom and Deterrence in the Twenty-first Century',
    Contemporary Security Policy, 25:1, 136–51.

Simpson, John and Darryl Howlett (1994) 'The NPT Renewal Conference: Stum-
    bling Towards 1995', *International Security*, 19:1, 41–71.

Singer, Clifford E., Jyotika Saksena and Milan Thakar (1998) 'Feasible Deals with
    India and Pakistan After the Nuclear Tests: The Glenn Sanctions and US
    Negotiations', *Asian Survey*, 38:12, 1161–78.

Singer, J. David (1962) *Deterrence, Arms Control and Disarmament*, Columbus:
    Ohio State University Press.

    (1970) 'Tensions, Political Settlement and Disarmament', in John Garnett (ed.)
    Theories of Peace and Security: A Reader in Contemporary Strategic Thought,
    London: Macmillan, 148–59.

    (1979) *The Correlates of War I: Research Origins and Rationale*, New York: Free
    Press.

(1980) *The Correlates of War II: Testing Some Realpolitik Models*, New York: Free Press.

(2007) 'Nuclear Proliferation and the Geocultural Divide: The March of Folly', *International Studies Review*, 9:4, 663–72.

Singer, Max and Aaron Wildavsky (1993) *The Real World Order: Zones of Peace/Zones of Turmoil*, Chatham: Chatham House Publishers.

Singer, P. W. (2001/2) 'Corporate Warriors: The Rise of the Privatized Military Industry and Its Ramifications for International Security', *International Security*, 26:3, 186–220.

(2002) 'AIDS and International Security', *Survival*, 44:1, 145–58.

Singh, Jaswant (1998) 'Against Nuclear Apartheid', *Foreign Affairs*, 77:5, 41–52.

Sjoberg, Laura (2006) 'Gendered Realities of the Immunity Principle: Why Gender Analysis Needs Feminism', *International Studies Quarterly*, 50:4, 889–910.

Sjoberg, Laura and Caron E. Gentry (2007) *Mothers, Monsters, Whores: Women's Violence in Global Politics*, London: Zed Books.

Sjöstedt, Roxanna (2008) 'Exploring the Construction of Threats: The Securitization of HIV/AIDS in Russia', *Security Dialogue*, 39:1, 7–29.

Skjelsbæk, Inger (2001) 'Sexual Violence and War: Mapping Out a Complex Relationship', *European Journal of International Relations*, 7:2, 211–37.

Slater, Jerome (2003) 'Ideology vs. the National Interest: Bush, Sharon and US Policy in the Israeli–Palestinian Conflict', *Security Studies*, 12:1, 164–206.

(2006) 'Tragic Choices in the War on Terrorism: Should We Try to Regulate and Control Torture?', *Political Science Quarterly*, 121:2, 191–215.

Slaughter, Anne-Marie (1997) 'The Real New World Order', *Foreign Affairs*, 76:5, 183–97.

Sloan, Stanley (1995) 'US Perspectives on NATO's Future', *International Affairs*, 71:2, 217–31.

Slocombe, Walter B. (2008) 'Europe, Russia and American Missile Defence', *Survival*, 50:2, 19–24.

Smith, Derek D. (2006) *Deterring America: Rogue States and the Proliferation of Weapons of Mass Destruction*, Cambridge: Cambridge University Press.

Smith, Hazel (2005) 'Crime and Economic Instability: The Real Security Threat from North Korea and What to do About it', *International Relations of the Asia-Pacific*, 5:2, 235–49.

Smith, Mark (2006) 'Pragmatic Micawberism? Norm Construction on Ballistic Missiles', *Contemporary Security Policy*, 27:3, 526–42.

Smith, Martin, Graham Timmins and James Sperling (2005) *European Security: An Introduction to Theory and Practice*, London: Routledge.

Smith, Raymond (1969) 'On the Structure of Foreign News: A Comparison of *The New York Times* and the Indian *White Papers*', *Journal of Peace Research*, 6:1, 23–36.

Smith, Roger K. (1987) 'Explaining the Non-proliferation Regime: Anomalies for Contemporary International Relations Theory', *International Organization*, 41:2, 253–81.

Smith, Steve (1999) 'The Increasing Insecurity of Security Studies: Conceptualizing Security in the Last Twenty Years', *Contemporary Security Policy*, 20:3, 72–101.

(2005) 'The Contested Concept of Security', in Ken Booth (ed.), *Critical Security Studies and World Politics*, Boulder: Lynne Rienner, 27–62.

Smoke, Richard (1975) 'National Security Affairs', in Fred Greenstein and Nelson W. Polsby (eds.) *Handbook of Political Science*, vol. 8, Reading, MA: Addison-Wesley, 247–361.

Smoker, Paul (1964) 'Fear in the Arms Race: A Mathematical Study', *Journal of Peace Research*, 1:1, 55–64.

Snider, Don M. (1992/3) 'US Military Forces in Europe: How Low Can We Go?', *Survival*, 34:4, 24–39.

Snow, Donald M. (1979) 'Current Nuclear Deterrence Thinking', *International Studies Quarterly*, 23:3, 445–86.

(1996) *Uncivil Wars: International Security and the New Internal Conflicts*, Boulder: Lynne Rienner.

Snyder, Glenn H. (1961) *Deterrence and Defence*, Princeton: Princeton University Press.

(1971) '"Prisoner's Dilemma" and "Chicken" Models in International Politics', *International Studies Quarterly*, 15:1, 66–103.

Snyder, Jack L. (1978) 'Rationality at the Brink: The Role of Cognitive Processes in Failures of Deterrence', *World Politics*, 30:3, 345–65.

Soderlund, Walter C. (1970) 'An Analysis of the Guerrilla Insurgency and Coup D'Etat as Techniques of Indirect Aggression', *International Studies Quarterly*, 14:4, 335–60.

Soeya, Yoshihide (2001) 'Taiwan in Japan's Security Considerations', *China Quarterly*, 165, 130–46.

Sokolsky, Richard (2001) 'Imagining European Missile Defence', *Survival*, 43:3, 111–28.

Solana, Javier (2003) *A Secure Europe in a Better World: European Security Strategy*, Paris: The European Union Institute for Security Studies.

Solingen, Etel (2001) 'Middle East Denuclearisation? Lessons from Latin America's Southern Cone', *Review of International Studies*, 27:3, 375–94.

(2007) 'Pax Asiatica versus Bella Levantina: The Foundations of War and Peace in East Asia and the Middle East', *American Political Science Review*, 101:4, 757–80.

Sontag, Susan (2004) 'Regarding the Torture of Others', *The New York Times*, May 23, Section 6, p. 25.

Sørensen, Georg (2001) 'War and State-making: Why Doesn't it Work in the Third World?', *Security Dialogue*, 32:3, 341–54.

Sorokin, Pitirim A. (1937) *Social and Cultural Dynamics*, 3 vols, New York: American Books.

Sovacool, Benjamin and Saul Halfon (2007) 'Reconstructing Iraq: Merging Discourse of Security and Development', *Review of International Studies*, 33:2, 223–44.

Spector, Leonard S. (1992) 'Repentant Nuclear Proliferants', *Foreign Policy*, 88, 21–37.

Sperandei, Maria (2006) 'Bridging Deterrence and Compellence: An Alternative Approach to the Study of Coercive Diplomacy', *International Studies Review*, 8:2, 253–80.

Spivak, Gayatri C. (1999) *A Critique of Postcolonial Reason: Toward a History of the Vanishing Present*, Cambridge MA: Harvard University Press.

Sprinzak, Ehud (1998) 'The Great Superterrorism Scare', *Foreign Policy*, 112, 110–24.

Spruyt, Hendrik (1998) 'A New Architecture for Peace: Reconfiguring Japan Among the Great Powers', *Pacific Review*, 11:3, 364–88.

St. John, Peter (1991) *Air Piracy, Airport Security and International Terrorism: Winning the War against Hijackers*, New York: Quorum Books.

Stanley, Penny (1999) 'Reporting of Mass Rape in the Balkans: *Plus Ça Change, Plus C'est Même Chose?* From Bosnia to Kosovo', *Civil Wars*, 2:2, 74–110.

Starr, Harvey (1997) 'Democracy and Integration: Why Democracies Don't Fight Each Other', *Journal of Peace Research*, 34:2, 153–62.

Steel, Ronald (2007) 'An Iraq Syndrome?', *Survival*, 49:1, 153–62.

Stein, Janice G. (1992) 'Deterrence and Compellence in the Gulf 1990–1: A Failed or Impossible Task?', *International Security*, 17:2, 147–79.

—— (1996) 'Deterrence and Learning in an Enduring Rivalry: Egypt and Israel, 1948–73', *Security Studies*, 6:1, 104–52.

Steinberg, Gerald M. (1985) 'The Role of Process in Arms Control Negotiations', *Journal of Peace Research*, 22:3, 261–72.

—— (1997) 'Deterrence and Middle East Stability – An Israeli Perspective: A Rejoinder', *Security Studies*, 28:1, 49–56.

Steinbruner, John D. (1976) 'Beyond Rational Deterrence', *World Politics*, 28:2, 223–45.

—— (1985) 'Arms Control: Crisis or Compromise', *Foreign Affairs*, 63:5, 1036–49.

—— (1997/8) 'Biological Weapons: A Plague on All Houses', *Foreign Policy*, 109, 85–112.

Stephens, Angharad Closs (2007) '"Seven Million Londoners, One London": National and Urban Ideas of Community in the Aftermath of the 7 July 2005 Bombings in London', *Alternatives*, 32:2, 155–76.

Stern, Geoffrey (1975/6) 'The Use of Terror as a Political Weapon', *Millennium*, 4:3, 263–69.

Stern, Maria (2006) '"We" the Subject: The Power and Failure of (In)Security', *Security Dialogue*, 37:2, 187–205.

Stevenson, Jonathan (2001) 'Pragmatic Counter-terrorism', *Survival*, 43:4, 35–48.

    (2004) 'Counter-terrorism: Containment and Beyond', *Adelphi* 367, London: IISS.

    (2006) 'Demilitarising the "War on Terror"', *Survival*, 48:2, 37–54.

Stiglmayer, Alexandra (ed.) (1994) *Mass Rape: The War Against Women in Bosnia-Herzegovina*, Lincoln: University of Nebraska Press.

Stinson, Hugh B. and James D. Cochrane (1971) 'The Movement for Regional Arms Control in Latin America', *Journal of Interamerican Studies and World Affairs*, 13:1, 1–17.

Stocker, Jeremy (2007) 'The United Kingdom and Nuclear Deterrence', *Adelphi* 386, London: IISS.

Stokes, Bruce (1996) 'Divergent Paths: US–Japan Relations Towards the Twenty-first Century', *International Affairs*, 72:2, 281–91.

Stokes, Doug (2007) 'Blood for Oil? Global Capital Counter-insurgency and the Dual Logic of American Energy Security', *Review of International Studies*, 33:2, 245–64.

Stone, Jeremy J. (1968) 'The Case Against Missile Defences', *Adelphi* 47, London: IISS.

Stone, John (2004) 'Politics, Technology and the Revolution in Military Affairs', *Journal of Strategic Studies*, 27:3, 408–27.

Strachan, Hew (2006) 'Making Strategy: Civil–Military Relations After Iraq', *Survival*, 48:3, 59–82.

Stritzel, Holger (2007) 'Towards a Theory of Securitization: Copenhagen and Beyond', *European Journal of International Relations*, 13:3, 357–84.

Stubbs, Richard (1993) 'Subregional Security Cooperation in ASEAN', *Asian Survey*, 32:5, 397–410.

    (2002) 'ASEAN Plus Three: Emerging East Asian Regionalism', *Asian Survey*, 42:3, 440–55.

Suhrke, Astri (1999) 'Human Security and the Interests of the State', *Security Dialogue*, 30:3, 265–76.

Sullivan, Daniel P. (2007) 'Tinder, Spark, Oxygen and Fuel: The Mysterious Rise of the Taliban', *Journal of Peace Research*, 44:1, 93–108.

Sullivan, Patricia (2007) 'War Aims and War Outcomes: Why Powerful States Lose Limited Wars', *Journal of Conflict Resolution*, 51:3, 496–524.

Survival (1998/9) 'WMD Terrorism: An Exchange', *Survival*, 40:4, 168–83.

    (1999) 'Is Major War Obsolete: An Exchange' *Survival*, 41:2, 139–48.

    (2001) 'A Consensus on Missile Defence?', *Survival*, 43:3, 61–94.

Sylvester, Christine (1980) 'UN Elites: Perspectives on Peace', *Journal of Peace Research*, 17:4, 305–23.

(1987) 'Some Dangers in Merging Feminist and Peace Projects', *Alternatives*, 12:4, 493–509.

(1994) *Feminist Theory and International Relations in a Postmodern Era*, Cambridge: Cambridge University Press.

(2005) 'The Art of War/The War Question in (Feminist) IR', *Millennium*, 33:3, 855–78.

(2007a) 'Anatomy of a Footnote', *Security Dialogue*, 38:4, 547–58.

(2007b) 'Whither the International at the End of IR', *Millennium*, 35:3, 551–73.

Synnott, Hilary (1999) 'The Causes and Consequences of South Asia's Nuclear Tests', *Adelphi* 332, London: IISS.

Takeyh, Ray (2003) 'Iran's Nuclear Calculations', *World Policy Journal*, 20:2, 21–8.

(2004/5) 'Iran Builds the Bomb', *Survival*, 46:4, 51–63.

(2006) 'Iran, Israel and the Politics of Terrorism', *Survival*, 48:4, 83–96.

Talbott, Strobe (1999) 'Dealing with the Bomb in South Asia', *Foreign Affairs*, 78:2, 110–22.

Talentino, Andrea K. (2004) 'US Intervention in Iraq and the Future of the Normative Order', *Contemporary Security Policy*, 25:2, 312–38.

Taliaferro, Jeffrey W. (2006) 'State Building for Future Wars: Neoclassical Realism and the Resource-extractive State', *Security Studies*, 15:3, 464–95.

Tamamoto, Masaru (2005) 'How Japan Imagines China and Sees Itself', *World Policy Journal*, 22:4, 55–62.

Tammen, Ronald L. and Jacek Kugler (2006) 'Power Transition and China–US Conflicts', *Chinese Journal of International Politics*, 1:1, 35–55.

Tan, Qingshan (1989) 'US–China Nuclear Cooperation Agreement: China's Non-proliferation Policy', *Asian Survey*, 29:9, 870–82.

Taniguchi, Tomohiko (2005) 'A Cold Peace: The Changing Security Equation in Northeast Asia', *Orbis*, 49:3, 445–57.

Tannenwald, Nina (1999) 'The Nuclear Taboo: The United States and the Normative Basis of Nuclear Non-use', *International Organization*, 53:3, 433–68.

(2005) 'Stigmatizing the Bomb: Origins of the Nuclear Taboo, *International Security*, 29:4, 5–49.

Taremi, Kamran (2005) 'Beyond the Axis of Evil: Ballistic Missiles in Iran's Military Thinking', *Security Dialogue*, 36:1, 93–108.

Tarock, Adam (2006) 'Iran's Nuclear Programme and the West', *Third World Quarterly*, 27:4, 645–64.

Tate, Trevor McMorris (1990) 'Regime-building in the Non-proliferation System', *Journal of Peace Research*, 27:4, 399–414.

Taureck, Rita (2006) 'Securitization Theory and Securitization Studies', *Journal of International Relations and Development*, 9:1, 53–61.

Taylor, Brian D. and Roxana Botea (2008) 'Tilly Tally: War-making and State-making in the Contemporary Third World', *International Studies Review*, 10:1, 27–56.

Taylor, Trevor (1994) 'Western European Security and Defence Cooperation', *International Affairs*, 70:1, 1–16.

Telhami, Shible (2007) 'America in Arab Eyes', *Survival*, 49:1, 107–22.

Tellis, Ashely J. (2002) 'The Strategic Implications of a Nuclear India', *Orbis*, 46:1, 13–45.

(2006) 'The Evolution of US–Indian Ties: Missile Defense in an Emerging Strategic Relationship', *International Security*, 30:4, 113–51.

Terchek, Ronald J. (1970) *The Making of the Test-Ban Treaty*, The Hague: Martinus Nijhoff.

Terrorism and Political Violence (1999) Special Issue, 'The Future of Terrorism', *Terrorism and Political Violence*, 11:4.

Tertrais, Bruno (1999) 'Nuclear Policies in Europe', *Adelphi* 327, London: IISS.

Thakur, Ramesh (1999) 'South Asia and the Politics of Non-proliferation', *International Journal*, 54:3, 404–17.

(2000) 'Envisioning Nuclear Futures', *Security Dialogue*, 31:1, 25–40.

Thayer, Bradley A. (1995a) 'The Causes of Nuclear Proliferation and the Utility of the Non-proliferation Regime', *Security Studies*, 4:3, 463–519.

(1995b) 'Nuclear Weapons as a Faustian Bargain', *Security Studies*, 5:1, 149–63.

Thies, Wallace and Patrick Bratton (2004) 'When Governments Collide in the Taiwan Strait', *Journal of Strategic Studies*, 27:4, 556–84.

Thomas, Caroline (1987) *In Search of Security: The Third World in International Relations*, Brighton: Wheatsheaf.

(2001) 'Global Governance Development and Human Security: Exploring the Links', *Third World Quarterly*, 22:2, 159–75.

Thomas, Nicholas and William T. Tow (2002a) 'The Utility of Human Security: Sovereignty and Humanitarian Intervention', *Security Dialogue*, 33:2, 177–92.

(2002b) 'Gaining Security by Trashing the State? A Reply to Bellamy & McDonald', *Security Dialogue*, 33:3, 379–82.

Thomas, Raju (1986) 'India's Nuclear and Space Programmes: Defence or Development?', *World Politics*, 38:2, 315–42.

(1993) 'South Asian Security in the 1990s', *Adelphi* 278, London: IISS.

Thomas, Scott M. (2000) 'Taking Religious and Cultural Pluralism Seriously: The Global Resurgence of Religion and the Transformation of International Society', *Millennium*, 29:3, 815–41.

(2005) *The Global Resurgence of Religion and the Transformation of International Relations: The Struggle for the Soul of the Twenty-first Century*, Basingstoke: Palgrave.

Thomas, Timothy L. (2006) 'Cyber Mobilization: A Growing Counterinsurgency Campaign', *IO Sphere*, Summer, 23–28.

Thomas, Ward (2000) 'Norms and Security: The Case of International Assassination', *International Security*, 25:1, 105–33.

(2006) 'Victory by Duress: Civilian Infrastructure as a Target in Air Campaigns', *Security Studies*, 15:1, 1–33.

Thompson, Robert (1969) 'Vietnam: Which Way Out?', *Survival*, 11:5, 142–5.

Thrall, A. Trevor (2007) 'A Bear in the Woods? Threat Framing and the Marketplace of Values', *Security Studies*, 16:3, 452–88.

Thyagaraj, Manohar and Raju G. C. Thomas (2006) 'The US–Indian Nuclear Agreement: Balancing Energy Needs and Nonproliferation Goals', *Orbis*, 50:2, 355–69.

Tickner, J. Ann (1992) *Gender in International Relations: Feminist Perspectives on Achieving Global Security*, New York: Columbia University Press.

(1997) 'You Just Don't Understand: Troubled Engagements Between Feminists and IR Theorists', *International Studies Quarterly*, 41:4, 611–32.

(2001) *Gendering World Politics: Issues and Approaches in the Post-Cold War Era*, New York: Columbia University Press.

(2002) 'Feminist Perspectives on 9/11', *International Studies Perspectives*, 3:4, 333–50.

(2004) 'Feminist Responses to International Security Studies', *Peace Review*, 16:1, 43–48.

(2005) 'What Is Your Research Program? Some Feminist Answers to International Relations Methodological Questions', *International Studies Quarterly*, 49:1, 1–22.

Tickner, J. Ann and Laura Sjoberg (2007) 'Feminism', in Tim Dunne, Milja Kurki and Steve Smith (eds.) *International Relations Theories: Discipline and Diversity*, Oxford: Oxford University Press, 185–202.

To, Lee L. (1997) 'East Asian Assessments of China's Security Policy', *International Affairs*, 73:2, 251–62.

Toft, Monica D. (2006) 'Issue Indivisibility and Time Horizons as Rationalist Explanations for War', *Security Studies*, 15:1, 34–69.

Togeby, Lise (1994) 'The Gender Gap in Foreign Policy Attitudes', *Journal of Peace Research*, 31:4, 375–92.

Toje, Asle (2003) 'The First Casualty in the War Against Terror: The Fall of NATO and Europe's Reluctant Coming of Age', *European Security*, 12:2, 63–76.

Toulmin, Stephen (1990) *Cosmopolis: The Hidden Agenda of Modernity*, New York: Free Press.

Trachtenberg, Marc (1985) 'The Influence of Nuclear Weapons in the Cuban Missile Crisis', *International Security*, 10:1, 137–63.

Trager, Robert F. and Dessislava P. Zagorcheva (2005/6) 'Deterring Terrorism: It can be Done', *International Security*, 30:3, 87–123.

Treverton, Gregory F. (1983) 'Managing NATO's Nuclear Dilemma', *International Security*, 7:4, 93–115.

(1992) 'America's Stakes and Choices in Europe', *Survival*, 34:3, 119–35.

Tuchman, Barbara (1984) 'The Alternative to Arms Control', in Roman Kolkow-icz and Neil Joeck (eds.) *Arms Control and International Security*, Boulder: Westview Press, 129–41.

Tucker, Jonathan B. (1996) 'Chemical/Biological Terrorism: Coping with a New Threat', *Politics and the Life Sciences*, 15:2, 167–83.

(1999) 'Historical Trends Related to Bioterrorism: An Empirical Analysis', *Emerging Infectious Diseases*, 5:4, 498–504.

(2000) 'Chemical and Biological Terrorism: How Real a Threat?', *Current History*, 99:636, 147–53.

(2006) 'Preventing the Misuse of Biology: Lessons from the Oversight of Small-pox Virus Research', *International Security*, 31:2, 116–50.

Tunander, Ola (1989) 'The Logic of Deterrence', *Journal of Peace Research*, 26:4, 353–65.

(1995) 'A New Ottoman Empire: The Choice for Turkey', *Security Dialogue*, 26:4, 413–26.

Twomey, Christopher (2000) 'Japan, a Circumscribed Balancer: Building on Defensive Realism to Make Productions About East Asian Security', *Security Studies*, 9:4, 167–205.

Ulfstein, Geir (2003) 'Terrorism and the Use of Force', *Security Dialogue*, 34:2, 153–67.

Ullman, Richard (1983) 'Redefining Security', *International Security*, 8:1, 129–53.

UNDP (1994) *Human Development Report 1994*, Oxford: Oxford University Press.

Urayama, Kori J. (2000) 'Chinese Perspectives on Theatre Missile Defence: Policy Implications for Japan', *Asian Survey*, 40:4, 599–621.

Utgoff, Victor A. (2002) 'Proliferation, Missile Defence and American Ambitions', *Survival*, 44:2, 85–102.

Vale, Peter (1996) 'Regional Security in Southern Africa', *Alternatives*, 21:3, 363–91.

Valencia, Mark J. (2005) 'The Proliferation Security Initiative: Making Waves in Asia', *Adelphi* 376, London: IISS.

Valentino, Benjamin (1997/8) 'Allies no More: Small Nuclear Powers and Opponents of BMD in the PCW Era', *Security Studies*, 7:2, 215–34.

van Creveld, Martin (1991) *The Transformation of War*, New York: Free Press.

(1993) *Nuclear Proliferation and the Future of Conflict*, New York: Free Press.

Van Evera, Stephen (1984) 'The Cult of the Offensive and the Origins of the First World War', *International Security*, 9:1, 58–107.

(1994) 'Hypotheses on Nationalism and War', *International Security*, 18:4, 5–39.

(1997) 'Offense, Defense, and the Causes of War', *International Security*, 22:4, 5–43.

van Ham, Peter (1993) *Managing Non-proliferation Regimes in the 1990s*, London: Pinter.

Van Munster, Rens (2007) 'Review Essay: Security on a Shoestring: A Hitchhiker's Guide to Critical Schools of Security in Europe', *Cooperation and Conflict*, 42:2, 235–43.

Van Ness, Peter (1999) 'Globalization and Security in East Asia', *Asian Perspective*, 23:4, 315–42.

(2002) 'Hegemony not Anarchy: Why China and Japan are not Balancing US Unipolar Power', *International Relations of the Asia Pacific*, 2:1, 131–50.

(2004/5) 'China's Response to the Bush Doctrine', *World Policy Journal*, 21:4, 38–48.

van Oudenaren, John (2005) 'Transatlantic Bipolarity and the End of Multilateralism', *Political Science Quarterly*, 120:1, 1–32.

Varshney, Ashutosh (1991) 'India, Pakistan and Kashmir', *Asian Survey*, 31:11, 997–1019.

Vasquez, John A. (1976) 'Toward a Unified Strategy for Peace Education: Resolving the Two Cultures Problem in the Classroom', *The Journal of Conflict Resolution*, 20:4, 707–28.

Vaughan-Williams, Nick (2007) 'The Shooting of Jean Charles de Menezes: New Border Politics', *Alternatives*, 32:2, 177–95.

Väyrynen, Raimo (1984) 'Regional Conflict Formations', *Journal of Peace Research*, 21:4, 337–59.

(ed.) (1985) *Policies for Common Security*, London: Taylor & Francis and SIPRI.

(2004) 'Peace Research Between Idealism and Realism: Fragments of a Finnish Debate', in Stefano Guzzini and Dietrich Jung (eds.) *Contemporary Security Analysis and Copenhagen Peace Research*, London: Routledge, 27–39.

Verba, Sidney, Richard A. Brody, Edwin B. Parker, Norman H. Nie, Nelson W. Polsby, Paul Ekman and Gordon S. Black (1967) 'Public Opinion and the War in Vietnam', *The American Political Science Review*, 61:2: 317–33.

Vinci, Anthony (2008) 'Becoming the Enemy: Convergence in the American and Al Qaeda Ways of Warfare', *Journal of Strategic Studies*, 31:1, 69–88.

Vivekanandan, B. (1981) 'The Indian Ocean as a Zone of Peace: Problems and Prospects', *Asian Survey*, 21:12, 1237–49.

(1999) 'CTBT and India's Future', *International Studies*, 36:4, 355–73.

Voas, Jeanette (1986) 'The Arms Control Compliance Debate', *Survival*, 28:1, 8–31.

von Eschen, Donald, Jerome Kirk and Maurice Pinard (1969) 'The Disintegration of the Negro Non-violent Movement', *Journal of Peace Research*, 6:3, 215–34.

Vuori, Juha A. (2008) 'Illocutionary Logic and Strands of Securitization: Applying the Theory of Securitization to the Study of Non-democratic Political Orders', *European Journal of International Relations*, 14:1, 65–99.

Wæver, Ole (1989a) 'Moments of the Move: Politico-linguistic Strategies of Western Peace Movements', *Working Paper no. 1989/13*, Copenhagen: Center for Peace and Conflict Research.

(1989b) 'Conceptions of Détente and Change: Some Non-military Aspects of Security Thinking in the FRG', in Ole Wæver, Pierre Lemaitre and Elzbieta Tromer (eds.) *European Polyphony: Perspectives Beyond East–West Confrontation*, Basingstoke and London: Macmillan, 186–224.

(1995) 'Securitization and Desecuritization', in Ronnie D. Lipschutz (ed.) *On Security*, New York: Columbia University Press, 46–86.

(1996) 'European Security Identities', *Journal of Common Market Studies*, 34:1, 103–32.

(1997) 'The Baltic Sea: A Region after Post-modernity?', in Pertti Joenniemi (ed.) *Neo-nationalism or Regionality: The Restructuring of Political Space Around the Baltic Rim*, Stockholm: NordREFO, 293–342.

(1998) 'The Sociology of a not so International Discipline: American and European Developments in International Relations', *International Organization*, 52:4, 687–727.

(2004a) 'Aberystwyth, Paris, Copenhagen: New "Schools" in Security Theory and their Origins between Core and Periphery', paper for ISA Montreal, March 2004. http://zope.polforsk1.dk/securitytheory/waevermontreal/

(2004b) 'Peace and Security: Two Concepts and their Relationship', in Stefano Guzzini and Dietrich Jung (eds.) *Contemporary Security Analysis and Copenhagen Peace Research*, London: Routledge, 53–65.

(2006) 'Security: A Conceptual History for International Relations', manuscript in preparation – March 2006 version posted on www.libertysecurity.org

(2007) 'Still a Discipline After all these Debates?', in Tim Dunne, Milja Kurki and Steve Smith (eds.) *International Relations Theories: Discipline and Diversity*, Oxford: Oxford University Press, 288–308.

(2008) 'Peace and Security: Two Evolving Concepts and their Changing Relationship', in Hans Günter Brauch, Úrsula Oswald Spring, Czeslaw Mesjasz, John Grin, Pál Dunay, Navnita Chadha Behera, Béchir Chourou, Patricia Kameri-Mbote and P. H. Liotta (eds.) *Globalization and Environmental Challenges: Reconceptualizing Security in the 21st Century*, Hexagon Series on Human and Environmental Security and Peace, vol. 3, Heidelberg/Berlin/New York: Springer, 99–112.

Wæver, Ole and Barry Buzan (2007) 'After the Return to Theory: The Past, Present and Future of Security Studies', in Alan R. Collins (ed.) *Contemporary Security Studies*, Oxford: Oxford University Press, 383–402.

Wæver, Ole, Barry Buzan, Morten Kelstrup and Pierre Lemaitre (1993) *Identity, Migration and the New Security Agenda in Europe*, London: Pinter.

Walker, R. B. J. (1987) 'Realism, Change and International Political Theory', *International Studies Quarterly*, 31:1, 65–86.

(1988) *One World, Many Worlds: Struggles for a Just World Peace*, London: Zed Books.

(1990) 'Security, Sovereignty. and the Challenge of World Politics', *Alternatives*, 15:1, 3–27.

(1993) *Inside/Outside: International Relations as Political Theory*, Cambridge: Cambridge University Press.

(1997) 'The Subject of Security', in Keith Krause and Michael C. Williams (eds.) *Critical Security Studies*, Minneapolis: University of Minnesota Press, 61–81.

(2006) 'Lines of Insecurity: International, Imperial, Exceptional', *Security Dialogue*, 37:1, 65–82.

Walker, William (1975) 'Weapons of Mass Destruction and International Order', *Adelphi* 370, London: IISS.

(1992) 'Nuclear Weapons and the Former Soviet Republics', *International Affairs*, 68:2, 255–77.

(2000) 'Nuclear Order and Disorder', *International Affairs*, 76:4, 725–39.

(2006) 'Destination Unknown: Rokkasho and the International Future of Nuclear Reprocessing', *International Affairs*, 82:4, 743–61.

Wallace, Michael, Brian Crissey and Linn Sennott (1986) 'Accidental Nuclear War: A Risk Assessment', *Journal of Peace Research*, 23:1, 9–27.

Wallander, Celeste A. (2000) 'Institutional Assets and Adaptability: NATO After the Cold War', *International Organization*, 54:4, 705–35.

Wallensteen, Peter and Margareta Solenberg (1996) 'The End of International War? Armed Conflict 1989–95', *Journal of Peace Research*, 33:3, 353–70.

Wallerstein, Mitchel B. (1996) 'China and Proliferation: A Path not Taken?', *Survival*, 38:3, 58–66.

(2002) 'Whither the Role of Private Foundations in Support of International Security Policy?', *The Nonproliferation Review*, 9:1, 83–91.

Walt, Stephen M. (1987) *The Origins of Alliances*, Ithaca: Cornell University Press.

(1991) 'The Renaissance of Security Studies', *International Studies Quarterly*, 35:2, 211–39.

(1999a) 'Rigor or Rigor Mortis? Rational Choice and Security Studies', *International Security*, 23:4, 5–48.

(1999b) 'A Model Disagreement', *International Security*, 24:2, 115–30.

(2001/2) 'Beyond bin Laden: Reshaping US Foreign Policy', *International Security*, 26:3, 56–78.

Walton, C. Dale (1997) 'Europa United: The Rise of a Second Superpower and its Effect on World Order', *European Security*, 6:4, 44–54.

Waltz, Kenneth N. (1964) 'The Stability of a Bipolar World', *Daedalus*, 93:3, 881–909.

(1979) *Theory of International Politics*, Reading MA: Addison-Wesley.

(1981) 'The Spread of Nuclear Weapons: More may be Better', *Adelphi* 171, London: IISS.

(1988) 'The Origins of War in Neorealist Theory', *Journal of Interdisciplinary History*, 18:4, 615–28.

(1993) 'The Emerging Structure of International Politics', *International Security*, 18:2, 44–79.

(2000a) 'NATO Expansion: A Realist's View', *Contemporary Security Policy*, 21:2, 23–38.

(2000b) 'Structural Realism after the Cold War', *International Security*, 25:1, 5–41.

Wan, Ming (2004) 'Tensions in Recent Sino-Japanese Relations: The May 2002 Shenyang Incident', *Asian Survey*, 43:5, 826–44.

Wanandi, Jusuf (1996) 'ASEAN's China Strategy: Towards Deeper Engagement', *Survival*, 38:3, 117–28.

Wang, Qingxin Ken (2003) 'Hegemony and Socialisation of the Mass Public: The Case of Postwar Japan's Cooperation with the United States on China Policy', *Review of International Studies*, 29:1, 99–119.

Ward, Adam (2003) 'China and America: Trouble Ahead?', *Survival*, 45:3, 35–56.

Watkins, Eric (1997) 'The Unfolding US Policy in the Middle East', *International Affairs*, 73:1, 1–14.

Webber, Douglas (2001) 'Two Funerals and a Wedding? The Ups and Downs of Regionalism in East Asia and Asia–Pacific After the Asian Crisis', *The Pacific Review*, 14:3, 339–72.

Webber, Mark, Terry Terriff, Jolyon Howorth and Stuart Croft (2002) 'The Common European Security and Defence Policy and the "Third Country" Issue', *European Security*, 11:2, 75–100.

Weber, Cynthia (1995) *Simulating Sovereignty: Intervention, the State and Symbolic Exchange*, Cambridge: Cambridge University Press.

(1998) 'Performative States', *Millennium*, 27:1, 77–95.

(2006a) 'An Aesthetics of Fear: The 7/7 London Bombings, the Sublime and Werenotafraid.com', *Millennium*, 34:3, 683–710.

(2006b) *Imagining America at War: Morality, Politics and Film*, London: Routledge.

Weede, Erich (1983) 'Extended Deterrence by Superpower Alliance', *Journal of Conflict Resolution*, 27:2, 231–53.

(2005) 'Living with the Transatlantic Drift', *Orbis*, 49:2, 323–35.

Wehr, Paul and Michael Washburn (1976) *Peace and World Order Studies: Teaching and Research*, Beverly Hills: SAGE.

Weiner, Sharon K. (2002) 'Preventing Nuclear Entrepreneurship in Russia's Nuclear Cities', *International Security*, 27:2, 126–58.

Weinstein, Jeremy M. (2000) 'Africa's "Scramble for Africa": Lessons of a Continental War', *World Policy Journal*, 27:2, 11–20.

Weldes, Jutta (1996) 'Constructing National Interests', *European Journal of International Relations*, 2:3, 275–318.

(1999) *Constructing National Interests: The United States and the Cuban Missile Crisis*, Minneapolis: University of Minnesota Press.

Weldes, Jutta, Mark Laffey, Hugh Gusterson and Raymond Duvall (eds.) (1999) *Cultures of Insecurity: States, Communities, and the Production of Danger*, Minneapolis: University of Minnesota Press.

Weltman, John J. (1981/2) 'Managing Nuclear Multipolarity', *International Security*, 6:3, 182–94.

Wendt, Alexander (1999) *Social Theory of International Relations*, Cambridge: Cambridge University Press.

(2003) 'Why a World State is Inevitable', *European Journal of International Relations*, 9:4, 491–542.

Westing, Arthur H. (1988) 'The Military Sector vis-à-vis the Environment', *Journal of Peace Research*, 25:3, 257–64.

White, Stephen, Julia Korosteleva and Roy Allison (2006) 'NATO: The View from the East', *European Security*, 15:2, 165–90.

Whitman, Richard G. (2004) 'NATO, the EU and ESDP: An Emerging Division of Labour?', *Contemporary Security Policy*, 25:3, 430–51.

Wiberg, Håkan (1976) *Konfliktteori och fredsforskning*, Stockholm: Scandinavian University Books.

(1981) 'JPR 1964–1980 – What have we Learnt about Peace?', *Journal of Peace Research*, 18:2, 111–48.

(1988) 'The Peace Research Movement', in Peter Wallensteen (ed.) *Peace Research: Achievements and Challenges*, Boulder and London: Westview Press, 30–53.

Wight, Martin (1966) 'Why is there no International Theory?', in Herbert Butterfield and Martin Wight (eds.) *Diplomatic Investigations: Essays in the Theory of International Politics*, London: Allen & Unwin, 7–34.

Wilkening, Dean A. (2000a) 'Amending the ABM Treaty', *Survival*, 42:1, 29–45.

(2000b) 'Ballistic Missile Defence and Strategic Stability', *Adelphi* 334, London: IISS.

Wilkinson, Claire (2007) 'The Copenhagen School on Tour in Kyrgyzstan: Is Securitization Theory Useable Outside Europe?', *Security Dialogue*, 38:1, 5–25.

Wilkinson, Paul (1986) *Terrorism and the Liberal State*, 2nd edn, New York: New York University Press.

Wilkinson, Paul and Alasdair M. Stewart (eds.) (1987) *Contemporary Research on Terrorism*, Aberdeen: Aberdeen University Press.

Willett, Susan (2001) 'Globalisation and Insecurity', *IDS Bulletin*, 32:2, 1–12.

Williams, Frederick (1978) 'The United States Congress and Nonproliferation', *International Security*, 3:2, 45–50.

Williams, M. J. (2008) '(In)Security Studies, Reflexive Modernization and the Risk Society', *Cooperation and Conflict*, 43:1, 57–79.

Williams, Michael C. (1997) 'The Institutions of Security: Elements of a Theory of Security Organizations', *Cooperation and Conflict*, 32:3, 287–307.

(1998) 'Identity and the Politics of Security', *European Journal of International Relations*, 4:2, 204–25.

(2003) 'Words, Images, Enemies: Securitization and International Politics', *International Studies Quarterly*, 47:4, 511–31.

(2005) 'What is the National Interest? The Neoconservative Challenge in IR Theory', *European Journal of International Relations*, 11:3, 307–37.

(2007) *Culture and Security: Symbolic Power and the Politics of International Security*, London: Routledge.

Williams, Michael C. and Iver B. Neumann (2000) 'From Alliance to Security Community: NATO, Russia, and the Power of Identity', *Millennium*, 29:2, 357–88.

Williams, Paul D. (2007) 'Thinking about Security in Africa', *International Affairs*, 83:6, 1021–38.

(ed.) (2008) *Security Studies: An Introduction*, Abingdon: Routledge.

Williams, Phil (1994) 'Transnational Criminal Organisations and International Security', *Survival*, 36:1, 96–113.

Williams, Phil and Doug Brooks (1999) 'Captured, Criminal and Contested States: Organised Crime in Africa', *South African Journal of International Affairs*, 6:2, 81–99.

Williams, Phil, Paul Hammond and Michael Brenner (1993) 'The US and Western Europe after the Cold War', *International Affairs*, 69:1, 1–17.

Wilson, Laurie J. and Ibrahim Al-Muhanna (1985) 'The Political Economy of Information: The Impact of Transborder Data Flows', *Journal of Peace Research*, 22:4, 289–301.

Windass, Stan (ed.) (1985) *Avoiding Nuclear War: Common Security as a Strategy for the Defence of the West*, London: Brassy's.

Windsor, Philip (1982) 'On the Logic of Security and Arms Control in the NATO Alliance', in Lawrence S. Hagen (ed.) *The Crisis in Western Security*, London: Croom Helm, 27–40.

Winer, Jonathan M. and Trifin J. Roule (2002) 'Fighting Terrorist Finance', *Survival*, 44:3, 87–103.

Winner, Andrew C. and Toshi Yoshihara (2002) 'India and Pakistan at the Edge', *Survival*, 44:3, 69–86.

Winters, Francis X. (1986) 'Ethics and Deterrence', *Survival*, 28:4, 338–49.

Wohlforth, William C. (1999) 'The Stability of a Unipolar World', *International Security*, 24:1, 5–41.

Wohlstetter, Albert J. (1959) 'The Delicate Balance of Terror', *Foreign Affairs*, 37:2, 211–34.

(1974) 'Is there a Strategic Arms Race?', *Survival*, 16:2, 277–92.

Wohlstetter, Albert J., Thomas A. Brown, Gregory Jones, David C. McGarvey, Henry S. Rowen, Vince Taylor and Roberta Wohlstetter (1979) *Swords from*

Plowshares: The Military Potential of Civilian Nuclear Energy, Chicago: University of Chicago Press.

Wohlstetter, Albert J., Fred S. Hoffman, Robert J. Lutz and Henry S. Rowen (1954) *Selection and Use of Strategic Air Bases*, R-266, Santa Monica: The RAND Corporation.

Wohlstetter, Roberta (1976) 'Terror on a Grand Scale', *Survival*, 18:3, 98–104.

Wolf, Klaus Dieter, Nicole Deitelhoff and Stefan Engert (2007) 'Corporate Security Responsibility: Towards a Conceptual Framework for a Comparative Research Agenda', *Cooperation and Conflict*, 42:3, 294–320.

Wolfers, Arnold (1952) 'National Security as an Ambiguous Symbol', *Political Science Quarterly*, 67:4, 481–502.

Wolfsthal, Jon B. and Tom Z. Collina (2002) 'Nuclear Terrorism and Warhead Control in Russia', *Survival*, 44:2, 71–83.

Wood, Pia C. (1994) 'France and the Post-Cold War Order: The Case of Yugoslavia', *European Security*, 3:1, 129–52.

Woods, Matthew (2002) 'Reflections on Nuclear Optimism: Waltz, Burke and Proliferation', *Review of International Studies*, 28:1, 163–89.

Wooster, Martin M. (2006) *Freedom's Champion: How the John M. Olin Foundation Achieved Greatness.* http://www.philanthropyroundtable.org/printarticle.asp?article=1093.

Wright, Quincy (1942) *A Study of War*, Chicago: University of Chicago Press.

Wrobel, Paulo (1996) 'Brazil and the NPT: Resistance to Change', *Security Dialogue*, 27:3, 337–47.

Wyn Jones, Richard (1995) '"Message in a Bottle"? Theory and Praxis in Critical Security Studies', *Contemporary Security Policy*, 16:3, 299–319.

— (1999) *Security, Strategy and Critical Theory*, Boulder: Lynne Rienner.

— (2005) 'On Emancipation: Necessity, Capacity and Concrete Utopias', in Ken Booth (ed.) *Critical Security Studies and World Politics*, Boulder: Lynne Rienner, 215–36.

Xiang, Lanxin (2001) 'Washington's Misguided China Policy', *Survival*, 43:3, 7–30.

— (2004) 'China's Eurasian Experiment', *Survival*, 46:2, 109–21.

Xinghao, Ding (1991) 'Managing Sino-American Relations in a Changing World', *Asian Survey*, 31:12, 1155–69.

Xuetong, Yan (2006) 'The Rise of China and its Power Status', *Chinese Journal of International Politics*, 1:1, 5–33.

Yager, Joseph A. (ed.) (1980) *Non-proliferation and US Foreign Policy*, Washington, DC: Brookings.

Yamanouchi, Yasuhide (1997) 'Nuclear Energy and Japan's Security Policy', *Japan Review of International Affairs*, 11:3, 204–18.

Yang, Philip (2006) 'Doubly Dualistic Dilemma: US Strategies towards China and Taiwan', *International Relations of the Asia-Pacific*, 6:2, 209–25.

Yasmeen, Samina (1999) 'Pakistan's Nuclear Tests: Domestic Debate and International Determinants', *Australian Journal of International Affairs*, 53:1, 43–56.

Yeilada, Birol, Brian Efird and Peter Noordijk (2006) 'Competition among Giants: A Look at how Future Enlargement of the European Union Could Affect Global Power Transition', *International Studies Review*, 8:4, 607–22.

Yergin, Daniel (1978) *Shattered Peace: The Origins of the Cold War and the National Security State*, Boston: Houghton Mifflin.

Yoda, Tatsuro (2006) 'Japan's Host Nation Support Program for the US–Japan Security Alliance: Past and Prospects' *Asian Survey*, 46:6, 937–61.

York, Herbert (1983) 'Beginning Nuclear Disarmament at the Bottom', *Survival*, 25:5, 227–31.

Yost, David S. (1996) 'France's Nuclear Dilemmas', *Foreign Affairs*, 75:1, 108–18.
    (1999) 'The US and Nuclear Deterrence', *Adelphi* 326, London: IISS.
    (2005a) 'New Approaches to Deterrence in Britain, France, and the United States', *International Affairs*, 81:1, 83–114.
    (2005b) 'France's Evolving Nuclear Strategy', *Survival*, 47:3, 117–46.

Young, Elizabeth (1972) *A Farewell to Arms Control*, Harmondsworth: Penguin.

Youngs, Richard (2002) 'The European Security and Defence Policy: What Impact on the EU's Approach to Security Challenges?', *European Security*, 11:2, 101–24.

Zagare, Frank C. (1999) 'All Mortis, No Rigor', *International Security*, 24:2, 107–14.

Zagare, Frank C. and D. Marc Kilgour (1995) 'Assessing Competing Defence Postures: The Strategic Implications of Flexible Response', *World Politics*, 47:3, 373–417.
    (2006) 'The Deterrence–Versus–Restraint Dilemma in Extended Deterrence: Explaining British Policy in 1914', *International Studies Review*, 8:4, 623–42.

Zagorski, Andrei (1992) 'Post-Soviet Nuclear Proliferation Risks', *Security Dialogue*, 23:3, 27–40.

Zametica, John (1992) 'The Yugoslav Conflict', *Adelphi* 270, London: IISS.

Zehfuss, Maja (2001) 'Constructivism and Identity: A Dangerous Liaison', *European Journal of International Relations*, 7:3, 315–48.
    (2007) 'Subjectivity and Vulnerability: On the War in Iraq', *International Politics*, 44:1, 58–71.

Zielonka, Jan (1992) 'Security in Central Europe', *Adelphi* 272, London: IISS.

Zongyou, Wei (2006) 'In the Shadow of Hegemony: Strategic Choices', *Chinese Journal of International Politics*, 1:2, 195–229.

Zook, Darren C. (2000) 'A Culture of Deterrence: Nuclear Myths and Cultural Chauvinism in South Asia', *World Policy Journal*, 17:1, 39–46.

AUTHOR INDEX

Abelson, Donald E. 95
Adler, Emanuel 197–8, 222
Adorno, Theodor 127, 207–8
Agamben, Giorgio 248–9
Alker, Hayward R. 223
Amin, Samir 125
Anderson, Benedict 26
Angell, Norman 132
Art, Robert 251
Ashley, Richard K. 142, 144, 223
Austin, John L. 141
Ayoob, Mohammed 51, 200

Baldwin, David A. 67
Barkawi, Tarak 223
Barnett, Michael 198, 222
Baudrillard, Jean 221
Beck, Ulrich 250
Bellamy, Alex J. 204
Benedict, Kennette 151
Betts, Richard K. 66–7, 251
Biersteker, Thomas 223
Bigo, Didier 217, 250
Booth, Ken 20, 205–7, 215
Boulding, Elise 139, 150
Boulding, Kenneth E. 122, 127,
    129–30, 131, 133, 134, 149, 150, 163
Bourdieu, Pierre 217
Bremer, Stuart 150
Brown, Neville 74
Bull, Hedley 90, 92, 112, 136
Buzan, Barry 9, 102, 135, 136, 212–13

Calleo, David P. 166–7
Campbell, David 144, 218–19, 220
Caprioli, Mary 210–11
Cardoso, Fernando H. 125

Carpenter, R. Charli 210–11
Carr, E. H. 31
Carson, Rachel 128
Carter, Aston B. 229
Chatfield, Charles 130, 132, 150
Chilton, Paul 141
Clausewitz, Carl von 1, 9, 232
Cohn, Carol 141–2
Collins, Alan R. 3, 189
Crawford, Neta 222

Dalby, Simon 144
Dannreuther, Roland 3
Dencik, Lars 124
Der Derian, James 144, 221, 245, 246
Derrida, Jacques 142, 220
Desch, Michael C. 251
Deudney, Daniel 128
Deutsch, Karl W. 20, 119, 120, 198,
    259
Duvall, Raymond 223

Eide, Asbjørn 124
Einstein, Albert 147
Elshtain, Jean B. 139
Enloe, Cynthia 140, 208, 210
Everts, Philip P. 130, 138

Faletto, Enzo 125
Falk, Richard 132
Fierke, Karin M. 189, 198–9
Finnemore, Martha 197, 222
Foucault, Michel 8, 142, 143, 217,
    248–9, 262
Frank, Andre G. 125
Freedman, Lawrence 68
Fukuyama, Francis 62

SUBJECT INDEX

9/11 attacks 7, 31, 40, 48–9, 51–2,
54–5, 166, 177, 181, 191, 221, 225
impact on ISS 226, 227–35, 237–9,
241, 243–50, 253–5, 260
institutional impact 252–3, 271–2
international response 238
political/media representations 244

Abu Ghraib 245–6, 247–8
academic associations, ISS sections in
91–2, 147
Adelphi Papers (journal) 94
Afghanistan 25, 252
2002 invasion of 228–9, 234–5, 238,
243, 246–7
Africa 44, 87, 216, 266
nuclear developments 117, 174
regional security 179, 235
superpower engagement in 86
AIDS *see* HIV/AIDS
aircraft/travel, developments in 65, 74
al-Qaeda 230, 238, 246, 251
Alternatives (journal) 132, 141, 145,
150, 212, 224
American Academy of Arts and
Sciences, Committee on
International Security Studies 93
American Anthropological Association
252
American Civil War 27
American Enterprise Institute 61, 93,
94–5, 252
American Political Science Review 97
American Revolution 26, 29
amity/enmity, constructions of 51–3,
67, 70, 73, 120–1, 218–19, 231
Andrew W. Mellon Foundation 152

Anthropology 131, 201–2, 209, 225,
252
Anti-Ballistic Missile (ABM) *see*
Ballistic Missile Defence (BMD)
systems
Arbeitsgemeinschaft für Friedens- und
Konfliktforschung (AFK), Bonn
148
Argentina 80, 173
arms control 16, 38–9, 69, 106, 110,
112–14, 175–6, 197, 231–2,
239–40, 265
adjacent concept 13, 102
Cuba Missile Crisis 85
Hedley Bull on 90, 112
institutions 147, 149, 151, 183
JSS textbooks 112
negotiations 75, 112–14, 171
nuclear proliferation 113, 172
Palme Commission 102, 137
peace movements 121
Soviet Union 71–2
Arms Control 3–9, 90, 101–3, 104–7,
118, 132, 153, 157, 165, 176, 190,
239–40, 258, 265
critical approaches 96
(diversity of) objectives 112–17
driving forces, framework of 106–9,
154
genesis/development 11–13, 222
literature on technology 109–10
participants 112
position on ideological spectrum
111–12
problems 113
university courses/institutions 93,
145, 149–52, 183